British Society, 1680–1880
Dynamism, Containment and

Richard Price here offers a sweeping new interpretation of modern British history. He challenges the dominant assumption that the nineteenth century marked the beginning of modern Britain. *British Society* argues, on the contrary, that nineteenth-century British society was the extension of an earlier era of which the main themes first appeared in the late seventeenth century and which continued to shape the social, economic and political history of the country until the end of the nineteenth century. It is a book which casts a new light on economic, political and social history; it offers new interpretations on questions and issues that are central to the history of modern Britain. It follows in the great tradition of works such as Briggs's *Age of Improvement*, and Perkin's *Origins of Modern English Society*, and will be of enormous interest to all students and scholars of the period.

RICHARD PRICE is Professor of History at the University of Maryland, College Park. He has written widely on British history; his books include *An Imperial War and the British Working Class* (1972), *Masters, Unions and Men* (Cambridge University Press, 1980) and *Labour and British Society* (1986).

British Society, 1680–1880

Dynamism, Containment and Change

Richard Price

CAMBRIDGE
UNIVERSITY PRESS

CAMBRIDGE UNIVERSITY PRESS
Cambridge, New York, Melbourne, Madrid, Cape Town, Singapore, São Paulo

Cambridge University Press
The Edinburgh Building, Cambridge CB2 2RU, UK

Published in the United States of America by Cambridge University Press, New York

www.cambridge.org
Information on this title: www.cambridge.org/9780521651721

First published 1999

A catalogue record for this publication is available from the British Library

Library of Congress Cataloguing in Publication data

Price, Richard, 1944–
    British society, 1680–1880: dynamism, containment and change /
Richard Price.
    p.   cm.
ISBN 0 521 65172 7
1. Great Britain – Economic conditions – 18th century.   2. Great Britain –
Economic conditions – 19th century.   3. Great Britain – Social conditions –
18th century.   4. Great Britain – Social conditions
– 19th century.   I. Title.
HC254.5.P92   1999
306'.0942 – dc21   99-11993 CIP

ISBN-13 978-0-521-65172-1 hardback
ISBN-10 0-521-65172-7 hardback

ISBN-13 978-0-521-65701-3 paperback
ISBN-10 0-521-65701-6 paperback

Transferred to digital printing 2006

For Adele

Contents

Preface

When I have been asked to describe this book I have found myself saying "it is a general history, but it is not a textbook." By "a general history" I mean a book that makes an argument about a particular phase of a society's history, but (unlike a textbook) a book that contains no ambition to offer a survey of social experience. I also mean that I have endeavored to produce a work that could be read with profit by persons with differing degrees of knowledge about the period the book covered. This is a book that I hope will interest experts in the many subspecialties of modern British history. Yet the book has not been written only for them. I have tried to make it accessible to less specialized audiences of students and others who might have the inclination to read what is undeniably an "academic" history.

The "general" character of the book was determined by the argument that developed in the course of its writing. The book presents the argument that the years from the end of the seventeenth century to the end of the nineteenth century composed a distinct stage in the history of modern Britain. This perspective presents the eighteenth and nineteenth centuries in a very different light than most of the historical writing about those centuries. Yet it is a perspective, I would maintain, that provides a fuller understanding of both centuries than most conventional accounts; it illuminates more historical fact.

In order to make this argument I have engaged with much of the historiography of modern Britain. In addition, I have offered my own reckoning about large swathes of that history. I have done so through themes that are common to much of the historical writing of the period. Thus, I have endeavored to make coherent arguments about the structure of the imperial and domestic economies, about the organization of civil society, about the spatial distribution of administrative power between region and nation, about the stabilities and instabilities of gender relations, about the animating forces of the political order and about the dynamics of class and social relations. In doing this I have ventured across a historical landscape well traveled by those who have preceded me. My aim has been to shift the contours of that terrain a bit.

Acknowledgments

I have acquired many debts in the writing of this book. The University of Maryland, College Park, has been most generous with research leave and support without which the book could not have been started, let alone completed. I received a sabbatical term from my College in 1992 and Dean Robert Griffith generously awarded me a semester research leave in 1993. The Graduate School General Research Board awarded me a semester leave in 1996 which Acting Dean Ira Berlin generously complemented with an additional semester research award. These awards came at a critical time; they made it possible for me to complete a working draft of the whole manuscript. The semester research award was made in connection with my service as acting director of the School of Music and, although it would be hard to tie directly anything in this book to that year, I like to think that the delay it imposed on the completion of the manuscript allowed a more mature work to emerge. In other respects, too, that was an important year for me and it is a pleasure here to thank Ira Berlin and the talented faculty of the School of Music for the opportunity to work with them during the academic year 1995–96.

I was very honored to hold a Visiting Fellowship at the International Institute for Social History, Amsterdam, in 1992–93. I want to pay a special thanks to the staff of the Institute for their generous provision of research facilities. Dr. Erich Fischer, who was then the director of the Institute, and the person most responsible for projecting the Institute into its current centrality to European social history, was kind enough to issue me the invitation to be a visiting fellow. I was extremely fortunate to work closely with two excellent Dutch scholars: Dr. Marcel van der Linden, then head of the publications division, and Dr. Jan Lucassen, head of the research division. Both Dr. van der Linden and Dr. Lucassen did more than offer a professional welcome. They smoothed my way into Dutch society, provided personal support, included me in scholarly conferences and seminars at The Hague and in Paris, and integrated me into the Institute's community of scholars, archivists and researchers for the year. Other members of the Institute staff also extended themselves in many ways. Meike Izjermans generously provided personal and professional help. Willem Korthals Altes shared with me his enthusiasms for economic history, and much else besides. The staff of the Secretariat must also be recognized. They provided me with valuable and willing secretarial assistance during my stay at the Institute.

In addition to its remarkable holdings across a wide range of historical fields, the International Institute for Social History houses the Kashnor Collection, a little-known collection of British books, pamphlets and periodicals. I used it extensively in researching this book and it is a collection that deserves to be more widely appreciated. In range and coverage, the Kashnor Collection is second only to the combined resources of the Goldsmith and Kress Libraries for original printed sources in British social and economic history of the early modern and modern periods.

The furthest public origins of this book lay in a paper I gave at the Western Canada Victorian Studies Association in Vancouver, BC, in 1988. I delivered subsequent versions at conferences or seminars at the University of Southern California in 1989, Bielefeld University in 1993, Gothenburg University in 1993, Erasmus University, Rotterdam, also in 1993, Trinity and All Saints' College, Leeds University, 1997, and at Wayne State University, Detroit, 1998. I would like to thank Klaus Tenfelde, Birger Simonson, Burt Alteena and Martin Hewitt in particular for their invitations and generous hospitality and the participants at those meetings for the helpful criticisms and comments they made.

Over the years I have received considerable help from my various summer research assistants. In particular I would like to thank Yong Ook Jo, now of Seoul, Korea, and John Loukedelis, now of Toronto, for their work in identifying bibliographical and other tasks central to the research for this book.

I would also like to acknowledge my editor Richard Fisher of Cambridge University Press: he was an attentive, intelligent and very helpful editor and it has been a pleasure to work with him. Richard Fisher was not responsible for the opinions of the three anonymous readers he secured. But he was responsible for choosing them, for which I was very grateful. Their comments were generally approving of the book; more important was the intelligence of their critical responses.

Criticism and commentary are absolutely essential to any academic enterprise and I owe a special debt to the many friends and colleagues who over the years have commented upon early versions and various pieces of this work. Without exception, the following colleagues gave generously of their time to read and critically respond to the material I sent them: Ted Koditschek, Peter Mandler, Terry Parsinnen, Laura

Tabili, Peter Weiler, Jim Cronin, Ira Berlin, Peter Marsh and Frank Trentmann, whose comments on free trade I found especially useful.

Particular notice must be made of the following friends whose work went beyond the demands even of friendship. They read the completed work at least once, and their comments were essential to its current shape. The responses of James Cockburn, James Epstein and John Belchem to my efforts were the best one could hope for: constructive, critical, supportive and encouraging. My good friend Robert Cohen also read the manuscript. As a historian of nineteenth-century French music, Robert Cohen brought to the manuscript the reading of the well-informed non-specialist. His recommendations were all the more important for that. I owe all of these friends and colleagues a considerable debt. Naturally, I remain entirely responsible for the final product.

Finally, and most important of all, this book is dedicated to Adele Seeff. Her contributions to this book are too many to detail. Yet one must be recognized. She read the manuscript not once but twice, and her editorial assistance and commentary were absolutely fundamental to its final shape. She prodded me to clarify my arguments and to render lucid my prose. Her assistance has strengthened enormously any virtues the book may possess; for that and for much else besides, this book is dedicated to her.

Introduction: beginnings, periods and problems

Beginnings possess an implicit power to produce meaning. The beginning of an argument declares more than just a point of departure. It is less an innocent first place, and more the disclosure of an attitude of mind, a consciousness of understanding. A beginning anticipates the ensuing argument to a terminus that is in some sense inferred at the very outset. Sometimes this is unproblematic and uninteresting. If we are writing the military history of the First World War, the end of the book is predetermined. At other times, a beginning raises more intriguing questions. A book on the origins of the First World War, conversely, does not possess a self-declared beginning. No precise event announced the opening of a route to war and it is impossible to say without contention that this or that episode lit the long fuse to August 1914. The author has, therefore, to construct a moment to appoint as the first step to war. Similarly, to nominate a certain set of years as designating, say, the Renaissance is to declare a historical problem by a process of naming. Where we begin, therefore, may serve to define the problem we address.[1]

To establish boundaries of beginnings and endings around historical periods may be regarded as a policing strategy. The practice of boundary setting involves the installation of a series of premises and assumptions which determine what follows. Where we start and where we end and how we get there do not lie implicit and latent in the matter of history itself, waiting only to be teased out by the skilled historian. Such matters are constructed by historians themselves as they order the material within certain categories and declare certain chronologies "periods." In this process, some things are suppressed, while others are privileged. It is sometimes thought that this allows historical statements only the status of fiction. Yet it is equally arguable that such artifices are enabling and empowering, for they do allow us to make historical statements that

---

[1] For a discussion of beginnings upon which I have drawn, see Edward Said, *Beginnings: Intention and Method* (New York, 1975), pp. xi, xii, 7–13, 32.

1

illuminate a problem or a period. And since it is this latter claim that I would like to make for this book, it is as well for me to explain its beginnings and how they have conditioned the arguments it contains and the ending it declares.[2]

The idea of this book first took shape in the late 1980s when I was afforded the opportunity to read widely and eclectically out of my appointed "period" of nineteenth-century social and labor history. It is not very surprising, perhaps, that such a distancing led me to appreciate more acutely the difficulties that are presented by the assumptions that underpin nineteenth-century historiography. I had lived with nineteenth-century history for a very long time, of course, and I was mindful of its implicit posture as recording the moment when modern Britain was born. Yet for quite some time I had been equally aware of the sophisms necessary to sustain that position, of the qualifications that were required to bolster that framework. Ultimately, it seemed time to confront those issues if only for my own satisfaction. This book is the result.

It is a book which I would describe as both an engagement with the historiography of its chosen period and an argument about that period. The one led to the other. The book began as an encounter with the historiography of the nineteenth century and it ended with the persuasion that modern British history needed to be reperiodized. In contrast to the way in which British history is commonly conceived, I am concerned to collapse the nineteenth century into a wider period that stretches from the late seventeenth century to the late nineteenth century. The essential argument of this book is that more is to be understood about both the eighteenth and the nineteenth centuries once the chronologies are flattened out. The substance of the book traces the common themes and content that frame the unity of the two centuries from the late 1600s.

The historiography of the nineteenth century has tended to assume a fundamentally unreflective stance toward the subject of its study: the nineteenth century itself. This is true of the foundational scholarship of the field which laid down its paradigmatic boundaries in the 1950s and 1960s.[3] It is equally true of revisionist attempts to disrupt those paradigms. It is, of course, undeniable that an extremely rich and varied scholarship exists about the Victorian age. The nineteenth century has never been short of talented historians to explore its many regions and

---

[2] See Hans Kellner, *Language and Historical Representation: Getting the Story Crooked* (Madison, WI, 1989), pp. 7, 60–63; Lloyd S. Kramer, "Literature, Criticism and the Historical Imagination: The Literary Challenge of Hayden White and Dominick LaCapra," in Lynn Hunt (ed.), *The New Cultural History* (Berkeley, 1989), pp. 97–128.

[3] For a survey and an argument about the conservative roots of a main division of that scholarship – social history – see Miles Taylor, "The Beginnings of Modern British Social History?," *History Workshop Journal*, 43 (Spring 1997), pp. 155–76.

domains. Yet there has been relatively little interest in "problematizing" the nineteenth century. This is all the more surprising because it requires only a limited probing to challenge in quite serious ways the foundations of nineteenth-century historiography.

A convenient place to begin is to note the frequent disjuncture between the broad assumptions and premises that guide the historiography and the narrative stories that are told of the component elements of the century. The explosion of subfields and their research over the past forty years, particularly in social history and its related areas, has widened and accentuated this gap.[4] The findings, arguments and direction of the specific monographic studies and the broad assumptions that continue to shape our thinking about the period are seldom brought together. Indeed, local research is commonly conducted within a global framework that is clearly at odds with its findings. It is generally true to say that the field of modern British history turns on the notion of an economic, political and social caesura at some time in the late eighteenth century. Yet this vision is dependent on the conception of the disjuncture of an "industrial revolution" that is itself increasingly discounted by specialists. Nevertheless, the way those outside economic history conceptualize the field remains unchanged.[5]

A tension between local and global ways of thinking about the nineteenth century is not confined to economic history alone. The origins of this tension flow, I believe, from another impulse of the historiography: the idea of the nineteenth century as the moment of modernity. The notion that the nineteenth century was the pivot of modern times pervades the scholarship. It is a fancy that inspires a tendency to focus the

---

[4] See Richard Price, "The Future of British Labour History," *International Review of Social History*, 36, 2 (1991), pp. 37–50.

[5] No other segment of British history contains such a bewildering variety of demarcations, perhaps reflecting this underlying conceptual confusion. Trevelyan opened his *British History in the Nineteenth Century* in 1782 and in the first edition ended in 1901. In later additions the story ran to 1919. Most politically oriented textbooks begin in 1815 and end in 1914. Eric Evans's *Forging of the Modern State: Early Industrial Britain 1783–1870* (London, 1983) opens in 1783 and ends in 1870 – though the very first sentence of the book is a quote from the 1760s. Philip Corrigan and Derek Sayer in *The Great Arch: English State Formation as Cultural Revolution* (Oxford, 1985), on the other hand, see the modern state as essentially created by the year 1870. Asa Briggs's *The Age of Improvement 1783–1867* (London, 1959) opens in 1780 and ends in 1867; Harold Perkin's *Origins of Modern English Society 1780–1880* (London, 1969), too, begins in 1780 but closes in 1880. G. M. Young's nineteenth century in *Portrait of an Age* (2nd edn., London, 1953) extended from 1810 to c. 1880, although it was different elsewhere, most notably in his *Early Victorian England 1830–1865* (2 vols., London, 1934). Recent publications such as the Penguin Social History also follow this variegated pattern. Roy Porter's *English Society in the Eighteenth Century* opens in 1688 (everyone seems to be agreed on this for the eighteenth century) and ends with the Peace of Amiens in 1802 and, when it appears, Gatrell's volume will extend to 1870.

history of the nineteenth century through the lens of the twentieth century. A notorious example would be the history of social policy, which has often been written as the origins of the welfare state. Likewise, for a long time the political history of the nineteenth century was framed as an ineluctable move toward the democratic state of the twentieth century once the concession of reform was granted in 1832. Historical study, of course, has always tended to drift between, on the one hand, allowing contemporary concerns to drive its agenda and, on the other hand, faithfully recapturing the animating forces of past time. The line between anachronism and antiquarianism is a thin one, and the historiography of the nineteenth century has frequently teetered along its path.

The habit of treating the nineteenth century as if it were prefigurative of the twentieth century is a proclivity that has its origins in Victorian times. The idea that the early nineteenth century was the moment of modernity, the turning point from the "old" world to the "new" is not an invention of historians.[6] It was an invention of the early Victorian intelligentsia. The notion of transition was a commonplace among the early and mid-Victorian intellectual elite. Thomas Arnold spoke of the first train passing Rugby as meaning the end of feudality; William Cobbett spoke of the chains of connection in society as being ruptured by such forces as the enclosure movement; and John Stuart Mill defined the character of the age as the struggle between the forces of change and the resistance of the "old" institutional arrangements. Such reflections constructed a view of society that was integrated into the interpretations of twentieth-century historians.[7]

Historians have too readily accepted the governing notions of the Victorians themselves as describing the appropriate historical categories of the period. The principles and assumptions of Victorian liberalism have tended to find confirmation and replication in twentieth-century historiography. The most important shared value in the writing of Victorian history, therefore, has been its subordination to the assumptions of the Victorians themselves. This was particularly true of literature that established the main lines of interpretation of the period. G. M. Young's

[6] This was always closely connected with the idea of an "industrial revolution," the descriptive purpose of which originally was to draw the parallel between political revolutions on the Continent with technical innovation in sectors like cotton spinning: D. C. Coleman, *Myth, History and the Industrial Revolution* (London, 1992), pp. 3–8.

[7] Walter Houghton, *The Victorian Frame of Mind* (New Haven, 1957), pp. 1–4; Richard Price, "Historiography, Narrative and the Nineteenth Century," *Journal of British Studies*, 35 (April 1996), pp. 224–26; John Stuart Mill, "The Spirit of the Age," in *The Collected Works of John Stuart Mill*, ed. Ann P. Robson and John M. Robson (Toronto and London, 1986), vol. XXIII, pp. 228–31, 238–53.

elegantly drawn portrait of the mid-Victorian age was mounted on the two very Victorian stays of Evangelicalism and Benthamism. Victorian keywords frequently established the organizing categories for historians' accounts. Asa Briggs's masterly study, *The Age of Improvement*, for example, took as its starting point the Victorian conceit that their age *was* one of improvement. The dangers of borrowing organizing concepts from Victorian sources are not unknown. Yet, to my knowledge, there has been no sustained discussion of the implications of these dangers or how they can be avoided.[8]

Writing the history of the nineteenth century within the framework of the transition to modernity was the mission of the Whig interpretation of history. Before the late nineteenth century, Whig history was just another version of British history. It became the national history only in the late nineteenth century. At that particular moment, when mass democracy threatened to disrupt the boundaries of political convention, and mass education, among other things, promised to undermine the bases of social authority, the Whig interpretation of historical change offered a comforting context for the transition to a democratic state. The bias of the Whig interpretation of the past had always been to emphasize the successful balance between past, present and future in British political culture. Well into the middle of the nineteenth century the accent in Whig historiography was the continuity between the traditions of civic humanism and the ancient constitution. By the late nineteenth century, however, this balance had shifted to emphasize change as the key theme of British history. It was, perhaps, J. R. Seeley who first contextualized the themes of the nineteenth century through a positivist conception of progress and development. Seeley saw movement in history lying in the growth and expansion of the material forces of the state and empire.[9]

---

[8] Young, *Portrait of an Age*, p. 77. A revival of interest in Young's view of history can be detected among revisionist historians. As the title suggests, F. M. L. Thompson's *Rise of Respectable Society* (London, 1988) takes the Victorian notion of "respectability" as its very own organizing principle. For similar borrowings in intellectual history, see Frank M. Turner, *Contesting Cultural Authority* (Cambridge, 1993), p. xi. Asa Briggs, for example, in *Age of Improvement*, pp. 3–4, warned against historical borrowing, but the book ends up emphasizing the "commanding themes" recommended by the Victorians. At a different level, Keith Robbins's *Nineteenth-Century Britain: England, Scotland and Wales. The Making of a Nation* (Oxford, 1989) is unpersuasive because its title implies that the "nation" was made for the first time then, but fails to ask what was peculiar about British identity in the nineteenth century as compared to that before or (for that matter) afterwards.

[9] See Richard Price, "Historiography, Narrative and the Nineteenth Century," pp. 221–27; J. W. Burrow, *A Liberal Descent: Victorian Historians and the English Past* (Cambridge, 1981), pp. 286–98; J. R. Seeley, *The Expansion of England* (2nd edn., London, 1895), pp. 1–19.

Seeley's interpretation of history projected a modernist conception of change, a conception that imagined historical development as a species of organic growth. This has been the way twentieth-century historians have tended to read the nineteenth century. It is for this reason that accounts of the nineteenth century tend to take for granted the motif of change as the key descriptor. Later historians had to face a truth that Seeley could safely ignore, however: that any model of change also had to allow for the encumbrances of the past that littered the landscape of Victorian Britain. It was always clear, for example, that in spite of modernizing forces, or the struggles of transition, the conventions of the past retained a prominent presence over wide swathes of society and remained powerfully resistant to the forces of the present. A historical framework that privileged change, that saw change as a movement from lower to higher forms, or even as a passage from "then" to "now," needed to account for the persistence of features, institutions, even social groups that hardly fit a steady move toward the modern world of the twentieth century.

Urbanization and the growth of manufacturing, for example, did not mean that the local power of the Northern bourgeoisie was projected into a national presence. However successful they may have been locally in displacing the earlier, county-based elites, the commanding heights of economic, social and political power continued to be occupied with an obstinate tenacity by traditional social groups. The enduring power and influence of the landed elite stood against the main direction of assumed change over the period. Likewise, the continued importance of small-scale manufacture in the economy needed to be reconciled with the accepted trend to industrial bigness. Similarly, it was necessary to account for the resilience of older forms of popular culture in the face of the civilizing pressures of rational recreation.

Such well-known aspects of Victorian Britain contradict what was perceived as the main current of the history of Britain since the industrial revolution. Explaining them became, therefore, a major preoccupation of the historiography. Thus, an interpretive instability was installed in the field as, on the one hand, historians wrote about the nineteenth century as if it prefigured the twentieth and as, on the other hand, they struggled to account for those aspects that clearly did not fit this model. The device commonly used to reconcile this contradiction was the concept of "survivals."[10]

The notion of "survivals" was first developed by ethnographers in the late nineteenth century. It was used to explain the remnants of earlier

---

[10] Thus, see for example George Kitson Clark, *The Making of Victorian England* (Oxford, 1962); Perkin, *Origins of Modern English Society*.

social formations left behind in the course of evolutionary social development.[11] It is a notion that proceeds from a positivist view of social formations as progressing along various scales of growth and improvement. In the conventional historical literature on the nineteenth century, historians tended to find "survivals" particularly among the top and the bottom social strata of society. It was easy, therefore, to conceptualize them as the remains of an "old society" which the nineteenth century struggled generally successfully to transcend. Harold Perkin's *Origins of Modern English Society*, published in 1969, was a book that illustrated the power of this kind of framework.

Perkin's work was a serious attempt to reconcile the presence of sociopolitical continuities within the paradigmatic framework of transformation and change. His account revolved around the process of class accommodation and stabilization. Between 1815 and the 1840s, various "ideals" competed to be the defining ideology of the nation, a process Perkin termed the battle for the mind. The mainstream of historical evolution in Perkin's narrative was represented by the "entrepreneurial" ideal of the middle classes which drew support from renegade members of the lower and upper classes and was interpreted and humanized by the floating class of intellectuals. Only the "aristocratic" ideal which represented a revitalized paternalism really put up much of a contest against the ascendant "entrepreneurial" ideal. Ultimately, of course, paternalism had no future and by the early nineteenth century it had succumbed to the superior arguments of the entrepreneurial idea. This victory was a particularly neat solution to the difficulty of nineteenth-century "survivals." It removed the "problem" of a continued aristocratic presence in government, for example, because the aristocrats could be seen to speak the language and follow the policies of the entrepreneurial middle class.

In imagining Victorian England as a site of battle between the forces of civilized progress represented by the middle class and the uncivilized past represented by sections of the plebeians and patricians, Perkin was well within conventional historiographical boundaries. Perkin's account was serious and scholarly. Not all accounts had the qualities that Perkin brought to bear, however. More commonly, the weakness of the conceptual framework lay just beneath the surface of the historical accounts. Thus, "survivals" could be treated as the scars that marked Victorian society's recent emergence "from the animalism and brutality of primitive society." The past was an "unlawful" time of dog fights, public

---

[11] On the concept of survivals, see Robert Nisbet, "Ethnocentrism and the Comparative Method," in A. R. Desai, *Essays on the Modernization of Underdeveloped Societies* (Bombay, 1971), pp. 109–11.

hangings, pillories and the like. Victorian society was distinguished by the coming of "order."[12]

Yet "survivals" do not necessarily betoken deviation from a progressive norm. They might disclose a counternarrative that also provides an authentic description of the society. After all, evidence of survivals littered the landscape of Victorian society. The last public hanging took place in 1868, and skimmingtons,[13] dog fights and other rude practices were far from unknown in early and mid-Victorian England. What is truly interesting about this conception of the nineteenth century as having finally escaped from the "old" society, however, is the commentary it contains about the eighteenth century.

Two competing views of the eighteenth century are on offer from historians of the eighteenth century. One view presents the eighteenth century as an *ancien régime* where the themes of tradition were dominant; another view argues for the leading role of bourgeois culture of the middling classes. The former perspective proposes a "long eighteenth century" in which an Anglican aristocracy retained its grip on politics and society until 1832. The alternative perspective on the eighteenth century is that of a period of vibrant growth and expansion where urban centers provided the sites for middle-class identity and consciousness to be "made" and its political, social and cultural programs projected into society.[14]

Each of these views of the eighteenth century challenges the typical assumptions that underlie nineteenth-century historiography. Neither view is compatible with the conception of the nineteenth century as the

---

[12] For representative examples of both the recognition of continuities and their treatment as anachronistic survivals, see G. Kitson Clark, *Making of Victorian England*, pp. 59–63, 206–10, 277, from whom these quotes are taken; G. Kitson Clark, *An Expanding Society: Britain 1830–1900* (Cambridge, 1967), pp. 10, 12–13, 18, 20, 28. The notion of an "old society" is central to the analytical schema of Perkin's *Origins of Modern English Society.*

[13] Skimmingtons were demonstrations of popular disapproval of individual moral behavior usually associated with cases of adultery. The offender(s) would be subject to raucous clamor – loud music, it was called – by a crowd gathered specifically for the purpose.

[14] For the *ancien régime* interpretation of the period, see, of course, J. C. D. Clark, *English Society 1688–1832: Ideology, Social Structure and Political Practice During the Ancien Régime* (Cambridge, 1985), and J. C. D. Clark, *Revolution and Rebellion: State and Society in England in the Seventeenth and Eighteenth Centuries* (Cambridge, 1986). For the more widely accepted interpretation of the eighteenth century as a middle-class century, see Paul Langford, *A Polite and Commercial People: England 1727–1783* (Oxford, 1989), and Langford, *Public Life and the Propertied Englishman 1689–1798: The Ford Lectures Delivered in the University of Oxford* (Oxford, 1991); Neil McKendrick, John Brewer and J. H. Plumb, *The Birth of a Consumer Society: The Commercialization of Eighteenth-Century England* (Bloomington, 1982); Roy Porter and John Brewer (eds.), *Consumption and the World of Goods* (London, 1993); Linda Colley, *Britons: Forging the Nation 1707–1832* (New Haven, 1992). Eighteenth-century historians have not given much thought to this issue, either, although some, like J. C. D. Clark, have been more willing to confront the conceptual assumptions of their historiography than most nineteenth-century historians.

hinge of modernity. Equally, neither supports more recent tendencies in nineteenth-century scholarship to treat the century as merely another variant of a "traditional" society. A long eighteenth century casts doubt on the transformations of the early nineteenth century, and a modernized eighteenth century diminishes both the modernity and the traditionalism of the nineteenth century. Yet why do we need to plump for either an aristocratic or a bourgeois eighteenth century? Is it necessary to favor a nineteenth century of continuity or an eighteenth century of change? The answer to those questions according to the argument of this book is that we do not, and, furthermore, that a more encompassing interpretation of both centuries is possible.

Although the dominant tone of nineteenth-century historiography has been to privilege the paradigm of change, undercurrents of doubt have always existed. The centrality of gradualism to economic change was the main narrative line of the best economic history of the pre-Second World War period.[15] One of the most sophisticated presentations of an alternative conception of British history that rested on the great arch of continuity was made by Perry Anderson in the 1960s during the celebrated "peculiarities of the English" debate between Anderson, Tom Nairn and Edward Thompson.[16] The brilliant forensic and intellectual talents of Edward Thompson effectively closed off the openings suggested by Anderson and Nairn, yet it is not clear that this scored a gain for historical knowledge. More recently, the alternative paradigm of continuity has attained a prominent influence in economic history where ingenious reworkings of existing statistical series seemed to provide it with a solid empirical footing. At the same time, a revitalized version of continuity as the central organizing principle of the historical material flowed into political and social history on the tide of post-structuralist philosophy.

Post-structuralism confronted British social history in the guise of a theory of representation that placed language at the center of our understanding of social processes. As such, post-structuralism posed a direct challenge to the positivist foundations of most of the traditional historiography. In brief, the main consequence of post-modernist thinking has been to provide theoretical support for the revisionist emphasis on continuity as the consistent theme to nineteenth-century history. Traditional

---

[15] J. H. Clapham's three-volume *Economic History of Modern Britain* (Cambridge, 1926–37) projected a nuanced view of economic change in this period. The same was also true of the works of E. Lipson, such as *The Economic History of England* (1st edn., London, 1931), vol. III.

[16] Perry Anderson, "The Origins of the Present Crisis," in Perry Anderson and Robin Blackburn, *Towards Socialism* (Ithaca, 1966), pp. 11–52; E. P. Thompson, "The Peculiarities of the English," in Ralph Miliband and John Saville (eds.), *The Socialist Register* (London, 1965), pp. 311–62.

historiography treated the popular radicalism of the late nineteenth century, for example, as fundamentally different from the radicalism of the early nineteenth century. Revisionist scholarship (not all of which was theoretically self-conscious) began to emphasize the continuities that ran through popular political movements during the century. Similarly, whereas the older historiography treated social relations as inherently conflictual, revisionism highlighted the unproblematic nature of elite authority, particularly over the "long" eighteenth century to 1832. One way of understanding the drift of revisionist history in this field is to say that it has inverted the main themes of positivist-based history of the nineteenth century. Revisionism has tended to turn the "survivals" of the past into the defining elements of nineteenth-century history. The logic of revisionism, for example, is to treat middle-class power as the anomaly in the nineteenth century, and landowning power as the norm; class as the deviation, crossclass solidarity as the standard.[17]

My own beginning for this book, then, lay in a contemplation of these various and contradictory themes in the historiography. The problem they presented, of course, could be resolved by selecting one or other as capturing a meaningful narrative of the nineteenth century. Yet I was not inclined to choose between the broad alternative conceptual approaches and emphases that were on offer. Nor was I inclined to try and reconcile their different approaches. I no more wanted to dismiss class conflict than I did the tendencies that made for class cooperation, for example. Although the notion of an "industrial revolution" in the late eighteenth century was increasingly problematic, the fact of economic change and growth still required explanation. I did not want to opt for an eighteenth century that was either an age of aristocracy *or* populated by the "commercial and polite" middle classes any more than I wanted to privilege the landowning elite *or* the urban bourgeoisie in the nineteenth century. Binary opposites belong in mother boards, not in history.

The difficulty, it appeared to me, originated in the place the nineteenth century was imagined to occupy in the chronology of British history. It

---

[17] J. C. D. Clark, *English Society*, reduces radicalism to the disaffected, very minor sects of Protestant dissent. For an emphasis upon continuities in popular politics and social relations, see, for example, Eugenio Biagini and Alastair Reid (eds.), *Currents of Radicalism: Popular Radicalism, Organized Labour and Party Politics in Britain 1850–1914* (Cambridge, 1991); Eugenio Biagini, *Liberty, Retrenchment and Reform: Popular Liberalism in the Age of Gladstone 1860–1880* (Cambridge, 1992); Patrick Joyce, *Democratic Subjects: The Self and the Social in Nineteenth-Century England* (Cambridge, 1994). For a critique of these trends, see Richard Price, "Languages of Revisionism: Historians and Popular Politics in Nineteenth-Century Britain," *Journal of Social History*, 30, 1 (Fall 1996), pp. 229–51. For the conservative implications of this revisionism, see David Mayfield and Susan Thorne, "Social History and Its Discontents: Gareth Stedman Jones and the Politics of Language," *Social History*, 17, 2 (May 1992), pp. 165–88.

was for this reason that I was driven to the matter of periodization. Although I was aware of Lord Acton's dictum to study problems, not periods,[18] I had felt for some time that historians interrogated their chronologies too infrequently. In this case, I felt there was no partition between the problem and the period. Beginning with a problem how to understand the absences and contradictions in nineteenth-century historiography led to a consideration of how the nineteenth century could be located both in time and in conceptual interpretation. I came to the conclusion that making sense of the nineteenth century was as much a matter of reorienting our conception of the period itself as it was of selecting which descriptor – change or continuity, aristocratic or bourgeois, industrial or commercial, class conflict or class cooperation, for example – best depicted the essential character of the society. I was thus led to dissolve the common conception of the nineteenth century. Instead of seeing it as prologue to the twentieth century, I see it as linked more closely to the eighteenth century. Instead of seeing the Victorian age until the late nineteenth century as the moment of modernity – as the time when the blueprints of the modern world were sketched – I came to see it as the tail end of a longer period that stretched from the late seventeenth century to the late nineteenth century.

I would not want to insist on rigid markers at either point. I begin in the late seventeenth century because I am reasonably well convinced that at that moment an architecture of society became visible that was to define the major themes of British society for the next two centuries. And I end two centuries later because I am also persuaded that this was the moment when those formations shifted paradigmatically. I see my conception as one way of organizing the oftimes conflicting and contradictory themes that run through the period. I am persuaded that such an ordering is a meaningful way of understanding this period. Equally, I am sensitive to the dangers of "straightening out" issues that should remain crooked and incongruous. Thus, I would not wish this period to be read as a closed system that "rose" and "fell" in response to some metahistorical process. For this reason I have refrained from giving this period a name. On the other hand, I would argue that the historical formations and processes that I discuss here endowed the period with its peculiar qualities to greater and lesser degrees. I do envisage these two centuries as constituting a distinct stage and system within the sweep of British history.

I am concerned, therefore, to present more than just an argument about reperiodization. I wish to propose a framework of interpretation about the period. In the course of my researching and writing this book

[18] Lord Acton, "Inaugural Lecture on the Study of History," in Acton, *Lectures on Modern History*, intro. by Hugh Trevor-Roper (Cleveland and New York, 1967), p. 37.

three recurrent motifs seemed to me to capture the defining historical rhythm of the period: dynamism, containment and change. It is for this reason that those words are to be found in the subtitle. This was a period driven by creative energies which pulsated through all spheres of society. The shape and structuring of those energies were distinctive to this period; they provided the occasions and opportunities for change as well as for friction and disputation between different interests, policies and groups. Equally, dynamism was met by measures of constraint. The dynamic forces were fashioned and contained by the limitations of the forms available for their expression and representation. Ultimately, therefore, the pressures for change were enclosed within established and familiar boundaries and did not disrupt the fields of engagement in society.

It might be helpful to explain that I have come to imagine this period in pictorial terms, as a terrain demarcated by clear boundaries within which multiple arenas or stages formed the sites for social action. Tensions between different structural forms, contestation and negotiation within social relations occurred within and between these sites using codes, vocabularies and procedures that were (or became) generally well understood. Such events were common – indeed, normal – features of the historical process of this era. On occasion the boundaries that enclosed these processes were challenged, or bumped up against – they were flexible and translucent boundaries, not rigid and opaque, and they were mapped differently for different spheres of society. Yet the boundaries were not breached or overturned. It is this that composes the stability – the continuities – that may be detected running through the period.

On the other hand, the particular systems of politics, economics and social relations that developed and thrived in this period were charged with energy. Within each sector change could quite decisively alter the complexion of the case. The definition of trade policy over the period alters quite sharply, for example, even if there is much that remains the same. In addition, of course, certain chronologies can be attached to different phenomena, some of which I shall explain more fully in the relevant chapters. Within this broad period it is possible, therefore, to distinguish stages both at the global and at the particular levels. Yet these stages did not represent the kinds of disjunctive transformations that are typically superimposed upon the period, especially around the end of the eighteenth century.

The power of the traditional argument for disruptive change around the late eighteenth century is not without force, for example. These years were, indeed, a time of both quickened economic change and of political and social instability. Yet in the final analysis it is not helpful to treat these instabilities as caesuras. In Britain – and I would not extend the argument – beyond its shores political, economic and social volatilities moved along tracks that had been laid down earlier. The inflated pace of economic growth was achieved through the methods and techniques of the past: its scale was new; its mechanisms were not. Politics were disrupted by the French revolution; yet from a historical perspective the critical interventions had been made by Wilkes and the American war of independence. Reform, when it came in the 1830s, hardly represented a giant step toward a modern polity and state; it was more an attempt to repair and restore the systems of the past. The transition to a mid-Victorian "equipoise" after 1848 was one indication of the success of these efforts. Such historical stages as these, however, can best be seen as shifts of direction rather than the introduction of new paradigms.

If beginnings are almost always unavoidably arbitrary, endings tend to follow from beginnings in a less haphazard way. By the end of the nineteenth century, the configurations and dynamics that had shaped society from the late seventeenth century were eroded and displaced. To return to the metaphor I used above, the terrain across which societal relations had played and roamed during these two centuries was replaced by new topographies. This amounted, it is plain, to a virtual remaking of society. The transition at the end of the nineteenth century moved the world described in this book to the world that eventually was to shape the twentieth century. This transition was particularly sharp and the specific dynamics varied widely across the spectrum of society's constituent parts. No single explanation will suffice for why this happened when it did, nor for how the transition to a different social dynamic happened as it did. In the afterword to this volume, however, I suggest a framework for understanding the nature of this shift at the end of the nineteenth century.

I have written this book as an interpretive study. I conceive it as a work of synthesis which engages existing scholarship in order to make a series of arguments about the period. As a work of synthesis, it also intends to make a general argument. I would want to eschew the notion that the book puts forward a metanarrative. I have not reduced the history of the period to one governing theme; one big narrative does not capture the historical meaning of the period. On the other hand, I do believe that the argument presented here affords a more capacious explanation about the period it covers than narratives that are in the traditions I mentioned earlier. To be more precise: it makes better sense of those parts of the period that have long engaged and puzzled me.

Yet the synthetic approach did not only follow from a personal preoccupation about the history of Victorian Britain. It was a deliberate response to the recent tendency of historical studies to move away from general statement and toward a large number of fragmented, specific statements. A variety of intellectual, social and even political circumstances have combined to effect this shift. Indeed, this current fashion in history writing is more than just a mode; it is also an epistemology. Linking the specific to the general is regarded as a highly problematic enterprise reflective of the discredited knowledge system of positivism.[19] This is a trend which contains very vibrant and healthy currents. Yet, precisely because of this predominance, I am persuaded that the kind of general statement offered in this book needs to be made.

One good reason for resisting the general statement, which I have touched on before, is that it embodies practices of selection, prioritizing and privileging. This is no different, of course, from any exercise of historical writing. Yet, with synthetic works, selectivity must operate on a larger and more ruthless scale. I would not wish to disclaim the choices and inclinations disclosed in this book. I would not deny the biases that I bring to the study of history. One choice I made in writing this book was not to try to provide equal coverage for all the various tendencies or schools of thought on particular issues. I have tried to be attentive to the latest scholarship in the areas I address. But I have not felt obliged to give equal consideration to a trend of thinking just because it is there. Ultimately I have been guided by what I take to be the most helpful reflection on the particular issues that I propose to highlight. This has often meant going back to an older generation of scholarship, which I have found to be a most instructive and useful exercise.

I am, however, very conscious of the absences in this account and of much that has been given short shrift. I think this is particularly serious in the area of cultural regionalism. In writing this book I have become especially aware of how Anglocentric it is and how this reflects most history that passes for British history. I see no easy way around this problem, although various attempts have been made to foreground the reality that Britain was an association of four cultures, each of which was distinct to one degree or another, and each of which also stood at varying distances from the other. Once we accept the significance of regional variation, it is easy to fall into a choice between a national history that subordinates regions and a microhistory that allows only the history of a town, village or person. Neither is particularly satisfactory. Yet it would

---

[19] F. R. Ankersmit, one of the most impressive post-structuralist philosophers of history, has argued that the possibility of studying history as a totality has been undermined by the post-modernist rejection of context. What remains for the historical project is merely to study the leaves that have fallen from the tree of a (previously) unitary conception of knowledge; the actual place that the leaves once held on the tree do not matter. See Ankersmit, *History and Tropology: The Rise and Fall of Metaphor* (Berkeley, 1994), pp. 176–78.

be a mistake to ignore the degree of integration between those cultural and political regions that did exist. Scots were not only the subjects of English imperialism, for example; they were also often the agents of British imperialism as the economic history of early America bears ample witness. One of the future tasks for the historiography of this period will be to write from the perspective of the interrelationships between the regional and the national levels.[20]

Finally, on this matter of bias and choices. One of the anonymous readers of this manuscript noted that its author remained stolidly within his own generation and its paradigms rather than considering contemporary changes in the conceptions underlying social analysis. There is some truth to this point which I would not wish to deny.[21] I have always thought of historical learning as cumulative and accretive rather than as a series of ruptured lurches into new concepts or methodologies. It is not a wise intellectual procedure to abandon one epistemology in the manner of exchanging this year's clothing fashion. It is equally ill advised to remain resolutely resistant to the new. It is not for me to say how far I have realized that ideal balance. I would freely admit that I have not yet taken my leave of the lessons of the social history of the 1960s, although I have certainly departed from some of its tendencies.

In particular, I retain a conception of social history that emphasizes the importance of *interconnections* between the various spheres of experience in society. This has been one of the principal strengths of the British Marxist tradition of social history. I have found this predilection of great value in this attempt to think generally about a long period of British history. Yet approaches and epistemologies should not become dogmas; historians need to mix and match as they see fit according to the particular problem they are addressing. Naturally, the period and processes I have chosen to emphasize could be explored in many other ways. My own preference has been to give priority to the material categories of economics, politics, social relations and the state. This is because they are the

---

[20] Michael Hechter, *Internal Colonialism: The Celtic Fringe in British National Development, 1536–1966* (Berkeley, 1975); Raphael Samuel, "British Dimensions: Four Nations History," *History Workshop Journal*, 40 (Autumn 1995), pp. 3–22; Robbins, *Nineteenth-Century Britain*. Hugh Kearney's *The British Isles: A History of Four Nations* (Cambridge, 1989) is a brave attempt to write the history of Britain as the history of the interrelationship between its four cultures of Scotland, Ireland, Wales and England. I have not tried to incorporate the local histories of Scotland, Wales and Ireland. And although their histories *can* be subsumed under the themes I have discussed here, I would not claim that this is a superior way to understand them, let alone the only way.

[21] On the other hand, I would claim to have critically engaged with alternative conceptions of history and to have integrated what I find most useful from all the most recent work. See my "Postmodernism as Theory and History," in Neville Kirk and John Belchem (eds.), *Languages of Labour* (Aldershot, 1997), pp. 11–43.

categories that occupy much of the historiography I have been engaged with these past years. It also reflects my inclination to regard those sites as containing some of the supremely important dynamics and events in the history of society. I am not prepared to claim a sovereignty for those categories over others that could be used to write the history of this period. I am prepared to admit them as categories that I have found useful in thinking about the problem that led to my beginning this particular enterprise.

1 The economy of manufacture

Narratives of economic change

The production system of the period covered by this book was an economy of manufacture. It was not an industrial economy as we came to understand that term in the twentieth century. The application of machine technology and science to production, the factory as the typical worksite of the productive process, and managerial bureaucratization and hierarchy are the key elements to an industrial economy. Yet this manner of organizing the production of goods did not emerge in Britain until the end of the nineteenth century, after which it came to dominate the economy for the next hundred years. By contrast, the economy of the period 1680 to 1880 was an economy directed by customary methods rather than one driven by "modern" forms. The enormous and growing productive capacity of the economy was achieved through small-scale units of production – the workshop and the home preponderantly. It was an economy where technology continued to move at the speed determined by the hand rather than the reverse.

The economy of manufacture was, therefore, a distinct economic formation. It possessed a particular economic and historical ordering, with its own profile and dynamic. This phase of economic development should not be consigned to a "proto-industrial" form, nor more pertinently should it be situated as the precursor to the industrial state of the twentieth century. By the same token, however, the economy of manufacture was differentiated from the economy of the sixteenth and seventeenth centuries by its size and dynamism. From the late seventeenth century, consumer markets expanded more or less continuously and (a new feature, this) international linkages grew increasingly sophisticated and complete. The central purpose of this chapter is to describe the key elements of the economy of manufacture.[1]

---

[1] See Maxine Berg, *The Age of Manufactures 1700–1820* (London, 1985), for the use of the notion of "manufacture" to understand the economy of this period. See Karl Marx, *Capital: A Critical Analysis of Capitalist Production* (Moscow, n.d.; repr. of English-

The argument that I shall make rests upon a notion of economic change and development that requires some initial explanation – although it will be immediately obvious to the specialist reader. The period c. 1680 to c. 1880 has not typically been regarded as a discrete stage in Britain's economic history. Indeed, the conventional treatment would be still to divide it between a period of "apprenticeship" to industrialization and a period in which the prometheus of industrial capitalism was unbound. In the traditional narrative of British economic history, this transition took place around the end of the eighteenth and the beginning of the nineteenth centuries when an "industrial revolution" set free the forces of unrestrained growth. This produced a composition unimagined before, and it marked the birth of the modern economy and the modern world. In this account, everything that precedes this transformation is but prologue to industrialization, and everything that succeeds it is but the corollary of its consequences.[2]

Until recently this narrative organization of economic history remained virtually unquestioned. Yet it was never entirely convincing. When Sir John Clapham wrote his three-volume economic history of modern Britain in the 1920s and 1930s, for example, he made no use of the term "industrial revolution." Indeed, Clapham argued that Britain was only halfway toward an "industrial state" by 1850, and not until the 1880s did industry move to a dominance over the economic relations of the society and its politics.[3] Contemporary economic historians have picked up on

language edn., 1887), vol. I, pp. 318–65, for his categories of manufacturing and modern industry, and pp. 432–72 for his attempt to reconcile the persistence of the domestic manufacturing system into the period of modern industry. It is worth noting that there is much evidence in Marx for the argument that modern industry was not a dominant economic form during this period. Like most other commentators, Marx read the evidence in a way that did not allow him to extend the period of manufacture much beyond the early nineteenth century. Thus, he spent quite a few pages trying to reconcile the deep interpenetration of his categories of manufacture and modern industry.

[2] David Landes, *The Unbound Prometheus: Technological Change and Industrial Development in Western Europe 1705 to the Present* (Cambridge, 1969). This book was perhaps the culmination of a narrative that began with Arnold Toynbee, who entered the industrial revolution into the historiography in a series of lectures published as *The Industrial Revolution* (London, 1884). Other notable works in this tradition, of course, include Paul Mantoux, *The Industrial Revolution in the Eighteenth Century: An Outline of the Beginnings of the Modern Factory System in England* (London, 1928); T. S. Ashton, *The Industrial Revolution 1760–1830* (1st edn., Oxford, 1948); Peter Mathias, *The First Industrial Nation: An Economic History of England 1700–1914* (New York, 1969). Transformation was also the theme of the modern leading Marxist economic historians; see E. J. Hobsbawm, *Industry and Empire: An Economic History of Britain Since 1750* (London, 1968), p. 1: "The Industrial Revolution marks the most fundamental transformation of human life in the history of the world recorded in written documents." Charles Wilson's *England's Apprenticeship 1603–1763* (London, 1965) remains a wise and important book.

[3] J. H. Clapham, *An Economic History of Modern Britain* (2nd edn., Cambridge, 1930), vol. I, pp. 211, 213; (1st edn., Cambridge, 1932), vol. II, pp. 22, 110, 105. Clapham fully

this analysis and have deployed the mysteries of econometric analysis to the scant and bare statistics that survive from the period to demonstrate a view of economic growth as a more continuous process.

As a result of their labors, it is now clear that by the middle of the eighteenth century the key departures had been achieved from an agrarian-based economy to a manufacturing-based one. The balance of labor and productivity had tilted away from agriculture and per capita national income had been lifted to the level of an industrializing society. A more continuous model of economic change suggests a view of "industrialization" that diminishes the importance of the factory, though it does not deny its growing presence throughout the eighteenth century. Nevertheless, the overall effect of this approach to economic change is to downgrade the importance of a "modern" sector in favor of the "traditional" sector of the economy. Indeed, it was this section, characterized by the domestic workshop, hand labor and nonmechanized technologies like water power, that lay at the center of innovation and growth and must therefore be placed at the heart of the process of economic development.[4]

Yet it is quite simply misleading to describe the system of manufacture as "traditional." It was a dynamic economic organism; innovation and

realized that "no single British industry had passed through a complete technical revolution before 1830" (vol. I, p. 141). The phrase "industrial revolution" does not appear in the index (or the text as far as I can tell) in volume I, and only once in volume II. In the latter case it is in a quote from L. L. Price, the late nineteenth-century economic observer. Clapham does, however, occasionally use the word "revolution." Usually this is employed as a rhetorical device contrasting the social fate of various groups, sometimes capitalizing it, in other places not. Thus, the "handloom weavers, marked by the Revolution [sic] for death" and the "seamen of the 'twenties were untouched by the revolution." Similarly, Ephraim Lipson was quite explicit in his *Economic History of England* that it was dangerous to draw sharp distinctions between the different phases of economic growth. Lipson recognized that the industrial revolution "constituted no sudden breach with the existing order, but was part of a continuous movement which had already made marked advance": E. Lipson, *Economic History of England*, vol. III, *The Age of Mercantilism* (London, 1931), pp. 53–54.

[4] The revisionist literature on the industrial revolution is very considerable, and will be well known to the specialist reader. Perhaps the best statement is N. F. R. Crafts, *British Economic Growth During the Industrial Revolution* (Oxford, 1985); but see also C. Knick Harley, "The State of the British Industrial Revolution: A Survey of Recent Macroeconomic Reassessment," Research Report 9012, Department of Economics, University of Western Ontario, 1990; Harley, "British Industrialization Before 1841: Evidence of Slower Growth During the Industrial Revolution," *Journal of Economic History*, 42, 2 (June, 1982), pp. 267–85; Peter Lindert and Jeffrey Williamson, "Revising England's Social Tables 1688–1812," *Explorations in Economic History*, 19 (1982), p. 390; and Williamson, "Debating the British Industrial Revolution," *Explorations in Economic History*, 24 (1987), pp. 269–92. For an excellent survey that is mildly skeptical of revisionism, see Pat Hudson, *The Industrial Revolution* (London, 1992); and Patrick O'Brien, "Introduction: Modern Conceptions of the Industrial Revolution," in Patrick O'Brien and Roland Quinault (eds.), *The Industrial Revolution and British Society* (Cambridge, 1993), pp. 1–30.

growth were integrally configured in its architecture. Local studies of long-term economic change have demonstrated the dynamism of this system and its capacity for accommodating a wide range of organizational forms.[5] The small-scale and often domestic basis of industrial production was as capable of change, expansion and contraction as were its descendants in the twentieth century. It was a system of mass production by means other than those of factory industry. The main agency of change in this economic system lay in the *intensification* of preexisting forms already well established by the early eighteenth century.

But merely to reverse the focus of historical explanation from heavy industry to the traditional workshop only begins to describe how the British economy may be understood in its historical context. Many historians remain reluctant to abandon the concept of an "industrial revolution." This reticence is perfectly logical. Whatever conception is used to frame the economic history in the period must have a way of explaining change.[6] The econometric case for continuity in economic growth rests upon aggregate statistics and macroeconomic trends, and necessarily ignores, therefore, the regional and local levels. Yet it was in the regions that the locus of transformation was situated and experienced. Manchester moved from sleepy market town to pulsating industrial center from 1720 to 1800 even if the country as a whole did not. Still, the question is not which category – change or continuity – can present the most "facts" for our inspection. The question is how we position our understanding of the process of this change. It is not enough to point to continuity in the economic structures and leave it at that. To reject the notion of a transformative caesura around a fifty-year period is not to deny the fact of economic growth.[7]

---

[5] As Charles Sabel and Jonathan Zeitlin have pointed out, this form of industrial production provides a historical alternative to Fordist-style production which can also be found in twentieth-century economies. The difference between that situation and what I am describing is its centrality to the system of production. See Sabel and Zeitlin, "Historical Alternatives to Mass Production," *Past and Present*, 108 (1985), pp. 133–76; David Rollison, *The Local Origins of Modern Society: Gloucestershire 1500–1800* (London, 1992), pp. 32–34.

[6] There is no denying that a remarkable series of transformations marked the period of the eighteenth and nineteenth centuries as a whole. This fact is the reason why someone like McCloskey believes it is necessary to continue to search for explanation of the "industrial revolution." See, for example, Donald McCloskey, "The Industrial Revolution 1780–1860: A Survey," in McCloskey and Roderick Floud, *The Economic History of Britain Since 1750* (Cambridge, 1980), vol. I, pp. 108–23.

[7] For the response to the revisionist scholarship around the industrial revolution, see Joel Mokyr (ed.), *The British Industrial Revolution: An Economic Perspective* (Boulder, 1993); Maxine Berg and Patricia Hudson, "Rehabilitating the Industrial Revolution," *Economic History Review*, 45, 1 (February 1992), pp. 24–50; Berg, "What Difference Did Women's Work Make to the Industrial Revolution?," *History Workshop Journal*, 35 (Spring 1993),

Cycles of acceleration and deceleration were well established by the middle of the eighteenth century. A slowdown in the 1740s was followed by periods of growth from the 1750s and then again from the 1780s.[8] The pace of economic growth quickened in the late eighteenth century. This wave of growth, dating from the 1780s, continued a preexisting pattern that customarily secured great productivity gains using conventional methods of labor and resource utilization. Undoubtedly, this was a more rapid spurt of growth than previous ones. Economic historians are much divided as to exactly when it began, how rapid it was and what its effects were on the distribution of wealth.[9] One of its highlights was to intensify some of the innovations of the previous hundred years, such as the steam engine modified by James Watt, and the factory. Shifting our angle of vision to slow the speed, soften the impact and qualify the distinctiveness of this particular phase of economic growth provides a perspective that better fits the different elements of the economic history of modern Britain. Attempts to attach the quality of modern industry to any portion of the years between 1680 and 1880 deflect our gaze from those features of the economy that are central to understanding its dynamic. Identifying those elements and describing their character is the central purpose of the remainder of this chapter.

I shall use three routes into my discussion of the economy of manufacture. The first and broadest avenue of approach is to explain how the factors of production were dynamically configured in the economy of manufacturing. In this respect, the following aspects will be discussed: how land and agriculture continued to set the foundational limits to the conception and reality of domestic growth; how innovation and technological change were embedded in the context of slow growth; how the expansion of the domestic market was limited by the pattern of demographic regime and the class basis for consumption; and, finally, how the relationship was configured between the dominant technically primitive and small-scale sector and the sophisticated and large-scale sectors. Secondly, attention will be drawn to the central role the women's labor market occupied in this system, and the way it was increasingly con-

pp. 22–44; and Javier Cuenca Esteban, "British Textile Prices 1770–1831," *Economic History Review*, 47, 1 (February 1994), pp. 66–105, which, using textile prices, argues for a restoration of the estimates of Phyllis Deane and W. A. Cole in *British Economic Growth 1688–1959* (Cambridge, 1962) against those of Crafts.

[8] Anthony J. Little, *Deceleration in the Eighteenth-Century British Economy* (London, 1976).

[9] For a survey of these issues, see R. V. Jackson, "Rates of Industrial Growth During the Industrial Revolution," *Economic History Review*, 45, 1 (1992), pp. 1–23; Joel Mokyr, "Is There Still Life in the Pessimist Case?: Consumption During the Industrial Revolution 1790–1850," *Journal of Economic History*, 47, 1 (March 1988), pp. 69–92.

strained by the state. And, thirdly, I shall discuss the ways in which regionalism shaped and defined the economy of manufacture.

The dynamics of manufacturing

The economy of manufacture was a terrain of dynamic change that was contained within boundaries of ever visible constraints. The origins of the economy of manufacture lay in the opening years of Elizabeth I's reign. Certainly by the middle of the seventeenth century what Charles Wilson called a "production economy" had emerged. The key feature of this economy was that it afforded society the means to escape from the demographic catastrophes of starvation or population decline. A series of continuous improvements had revolutionized English agriculture from the middle of the sixteenth century to lift the shadow of general subsistence crisis. Few people starved in Tudor England. Yet this did not mean an end to crises and uncertainty. Local emergencies replaced cataclysmic failures. Harvest failures could have quite devastating local consequences among the young and the elderly. Bad harvests led to falling birth rates and opened the way for the increased virulence of disease. A succession of bad harvests occasionally coincided with plague epidemics (which were conspicuously absent in the middle of the sixteenth century) to create widespread crisis. Only the economic collapse of the late 1590s came close to marking a return of the classic subsistence crisis. Yet even that time of dearth was not enough to trigger an emergency of Malthusian proportions and to throw into reverse the generally upward trend of population growth.[10]

A series of dichotomies permeated the manufacturing economy. The certainty of survival was increasingly assumed. Thus, innovation and expansion were natural qualities. Yet the problematic of subsistence had not been forgotten and the sense that there were limits to economic growth was a central fact of economic consciousness. In particular, of course, manufacture was bounded by agriculture and cultivation. As Adam Smith pointed out, it was from the land that the manufacturing sector derived both its raw materials and its sustenance. The economics of land exploitation, therefore, determined the extent to which manufacture could advance. The economy remained, in E. A. Wrigley's words, an "advanced organic economy" rather than the "mineral-energy based" economy of an industrial system. Land and its resources composed the

---

[10] See Rollison, *Local Origins of Modern Society*, pp. 1–18, for the long-term origins of this economy; Charles Wilson, *England's Apprenticeship*, pp. 236–37, 378; Eric Kerridge, *The Agricultural Revolution* (New York, 1968), esp. pp. 15–40, 326–48; Joyce Youings, *Sixteenth-Century England* (Harmondsworth, 1984), pp. 148–49, 151–53.

ultimate limits to change. These limits were never approached, let alone reached, of course, yet the awareness of their presence conditioned all economic discussion and action.[11]

It was dichotomies such as this that provided the inherent tension within the system of manufacture between constraint and change. On the one hand, the system was capable of considerable gains. It was, after all, within these constraints that the transformation occurred from an economy based on the land to one based on the resources of minerals. On the other hand, such gains were achieved through a long and (relatively) slow pedigree of change. "The date at which the new regime [of a mineral-based energy economy] began to make a substantial general impact on English economic life was later than many accounts of the industrial revolution would suggest, and . . . the advanced organic economy remained the mainstay of economic life until well into the nineteenth-century."[12] Two centuries elapsed, from the middle of the seventeenth to the early to middle years of the nineteenth, before this shift was effected.

Historians have found in this period the origins of the era of exponential growth. Yet it is important to reflect that none of the political economists of the day possessed that understanding. Neither Adam Smith, Robert Malthus nor David Ricardo spotted the transition to a new level of economic growth. This is not to say, of course, that they failed to recognize the facts of economic expansion. The perception that economic growth was altering the dynamic of society itself was a constant fact of economic thought, and reached a level of frenetic intensity in the early nineteenth century. It was a major purpose of Adam Smith to understand how the substantial gains in output had been achieved since Tudor times. The importance of securing increased productivity, and the various devices to reach this end were commonplace concerns of economic commentators. Yet neither Smith nor Parson Malthus – to take two particularly pertinent examples – believed themselves to be the cusp generation of economic revolution.

Classical political economy was well named the dismal science. It was inherently pessimistic about the economic process. The essential focus of political economy settled on the constraints to continued expansion. There was little optimism that economic growth contained the key to a better life for all in society – which is the basis of a modern economic culture. Indeed, any economic advance was qualified by the expectation of economic theory that the constraints on growth would soon be

[11] E. A. Wrigley, *Continuity, Chance and Change: The Character of the Industrial Revolution in England* (Cambridge, 1988), pp. 50, 80; see chs. 2 and 3 for the meaning of advanced organic economy and mineral-energy-based economy.
[12] *Ibid.*, pp. 68–82 (quote, p. 82).

reached and a cycle of decline and deprivation would reassert itself. The duty of economic science was constantly to remind society of these limits and to identify the warning signs of their appearance. For Malthus, Mill and Ricardo the stationary state economy was the natural model for understanding economic processes, however delayed was the arrival at those ultimate boundaries. It was not until the 1860s that political economists began to realize that the era of exponential growth might have dawned. As late as the 1870s basic textbooks of political economy were still operating on the assumption that available land was the ultimate arbiter of growth.[13]

This view of the economic world mirrored the boundedness of the economy of manufacture. Growth remained firmly within the bounds of a dynamic that was familiar and traditional. Thus, the constraint of a finite amount of usable land remained a fundamental economic preoccupation in the period, yet agriculture remained the most important site of innovation until the early nineteenth century. By the 1740s over half the laboring population had been shifted from agriculture into at least some working relationship to the manufacturing sector. This release of labor from agriculture occurred earlier than the other European countries, but it was no faster.

Agriculture yielded up the necessary labor supply for manufacturing reluctantly, partially and in a protracted manner. It took over a century for manufacturing employment to outweigh agricultural occupations in the labor market. In 1688 the percentage split of the labor force between agriculture and industry was about 60–40. This proportion was not reversed until around 1800, and even afterwards agriculture remained the largest single sector of employment until 1851. The early movement of labor from agriculture into production neither broke the tie between manufacture and land nor diminished the importance of agriculture to the economy and the political economy. The interpenetrations between agriculture and manufacturing remained close and complicated well into the nineteenth century. Factories continued to be established in the countryside in the 1850s, and domestically based proto-industry – straw plaiting and lace and nail making, for example –

[13] Wrigley, "The Classical Political Economists and the Industrial Revolution," in his *People, Cities and Wealth: The Transformation of Traditional Society* (Oxford, 1987), pp. 21–45; John Stuart Mill, *Principles of Political Economy* (London, 1848), vol. I, pp. 211–25. Historians have not sufficiently grasped the implications of the way that classical political economy worked within an understanding of the constraints on growth. These were not economic theorists of an age that conceived of limitless economic advances that were characteristic of economic modernism. They worked within assumptions that were commonplace to the eighteenth century. Thus, Malthus, writing at the time of the "industrial revolution," is entirely concerned about the natural limits to growth.

continued to demonstrate the connection well into the later nineteenth century.[14]

The same combination of growth and constraint ran through the manufacturing sector. Well before 1680 the expansion of industries like coal, salt, shipbuilding and glass had been stimulated by the massive property transfers of the Reformation, changes in property law and shifts in consumer demand. This phase of economic growth was of the same order as that of the later eighteenth century; they were part of the same pattern. Both were placed in a context of gradualism and continuity and both possessed similar markers of development. In the early seventeenth century, for example, coal occupied the place that cotton was later to assume as a leading industry. Indeed, if the rudimentary statistics from the period have any value, they demonstrate a rate of expansion in the coal industry comparable to that of the nineteenth century.[15]

At the turn of the eighteenth century, Britain was already producing between two and a half and three million tons of coal. This was *five times* the production of the rest of the world. By this measure, Britain's economic weight had sharply diminished by 1840 when it produced only two-thirds more tonnage than the rest of the world. The availability of coal encouraged significant changes in other industries in exactly the same knock-on pattern that underlay the expansion of the early Victorian iron and textile industries. In the copper, tin and lead mines of the South West of England, for example, the accessibility of energy sources altered smelting techniques to make this area a hive of heavy industrial activity and technological innovation. Indeed, it was from this inventive culture that the principle of steam condensation was first applied by Savery and Newcomen in the 1680s and which Watt was to improve greatly in the 1760s.[16]

---

[14] Wrigley, *Continuity, Chance and Change*, chs. 2, 3; Michael Turner, "Enclosures in Britain 1750–1830," in L. A. Clarkson (ed.), *The Industrial Revolution: A Compendium* (Atlantic Highlands, NJ, 1990), pp. 218, 236–37; Michael Turner, "Agricultural Productivity in England in the Eighteenth Century: Evidence from Crop Yields," *Economic History Review*, 35, 4 (November 1982), pp. 489–510; Crafts, *British Economic Growth*, pp. 12–14, 54, 66; Hudson, *Industrial Revolution*, pp. 80–81; Ivy Pinchbeck, *Women Workers and the Industrial Revolution 1750–1850* (London, 1981), pp. 202–26.

[15] It is important to note that the claims of J. U. Nef about the expansion of the coal industry in this earlier period have tended to be confirmed by subsequent research: Nef, *The Rise of the British Coal Industry* (London, 1932), vol. I, pp. 123–26, 133–64, 176–79; John Hatcher, *The History of the British Coal Industry* (Oxford, 1993), vol. I, pp. 8–10, 547–56. Nef's claim that this was an industrial revolution of equal significance to that of the eighteenth century was, however, an unnecessary and diversionary claim. See Coleman, *Myth, History and the Industrial Revolution*, pp. 55–58, for the reservations regarding Nef's claim for an industrial revolution of the sixteenth century.

[16] Wrigley, *Continuity, Chance and Change*, p. 54; David Levine and Keith Wrightson, *The Making of an Industrial Society: Whickham 1560–1765* (Oxford, 1991), pp. 2–4, and ch. 2.

The elements that composed the "industrial revolution" of the late eighteenth century were embedded in this earlier period, and not disjunctive to it. The much celebrated increase in patents issued at the end of the eighteenth century can be matched by the 100 percent increase in the final two decades of the seventeenth century. New industries, like calico cloth printing, emerged just as they were to do in the late eighteenth century and early nineteenth century. Older industries were changed by the fusion of new technology and large-scale organization. The shift of brewing from a household to an industrial enterprise was, of course, a classic example of "industrial" development before industrialization. Soap boiling, glass making and the salt industry were similar examples of industries where specialization and concentration into large units were the basis for immense output. In these industries the rate of progress matched anything that was to be achieved during more celebrated periods of economic growth. Throughout the course of the sixteenth century, for example, the output of the salt industry in the North East increased from 300,000 bushels to over one million bushels. Similar examples could be easily multiplied. Factories with complicated divisions of labor were common by the 1730s in industries like silk production and calico printing. Some employed over 150 workers and others belonged to conglomerates of outworking establishments owned by one master.[17]

The rhythm of economic growth in the age of manufacture moved by spasmodic lurches within an overall pattern of gently protracted upward advance. Although per capita income growth jumped significantly in the first two-thirds of the nineteenth century, for example, it had been at a relatively high level compared to other European countries since 1700. Britain's per capita income in 1700 was the same as Sweden's in 1870, for example. Yet it took Britain one hundred years to move to the level that, in the late nineteenth century, Sweden and other countries could achieve in twenty years. Even without the mechanized sector, national annual income per head would have doubled between 1780 and 1860 from £11 to £22; the technologically advanced sector added only another £6 to this total. Domestic rates of capital accumulation were typically quite low. As a percentage of gross domestic product, fixed capital had reached 10 percent by 1800 and remained there until the 1850s. Growth in real output did not reach 3 percent (the level reckoned

---

[17] Charles Wilson, *England's Apprenticeship*, pp. 83, 187, 195–96, 198, 202–05; Nef, *Rise of the British Coal Industry*, vol. I, pp. 174–84; J. Parakunnel Thomas, "The Beginnings of Calico-Printing in England," *English Historical Review*, 39 (1924), pp. 213–14; Christian Simon, "Labour Relations at Manufactures in the Eighteenth Century: The Calico Printers in Europe," *International Review of Social History*, 39, suppl. 2 (1994), pp. 115–44.

to mark an industrializing economy) until the 1830s, about the same time as Belgium.[18]

Productivity growth – a key economic index – demonstrates the unity of the eighteenth and nineteenth centuries.[19] No significant difference distinguished the two centuries in total factor productivity growth, with the partial exception of the middle of the nineteenth century. There was no decisive upward shift in the rate of total factor productivity, although individual sectors provided clear exceptions to this rule. Yet this had always been true. At no time during the industrial revolution did Britain attain 1.5 percent productivity growth per year, and the nineteenth century as a whole continued to be characterized by low growth rates. Even during the "great Victorian boom" of the midcentury (when growth rates were higher than ever before), the pattern of growth was highly variable and contained many indicators of ossification and early senescence. The point is that this pattern was extended and enlarged during the late eighteenth century and early nineteenth century; its basic designs were not fundamentally altered.[20]

These figures suggest another constraint upon the economic dynamism of this period: productivity gains were sought through the more extensive

[18] Crafts, *British Economic Growth*, pp. 46–48, 61, 66, 87, 160.
[19] This raises the whole question of Britain's comparative international economic performance and the explanations for it. The various explanations for low growth rates in twentieth-century Britain are of variable quality. The argument about the destructive impact of the world wars has more to recommend it than the suggestion that Britain somehow "lost" the "industrial spirit" that had produced the innovations of the industrial revolution. As early as the 1840s Palmerston was being warned that the Germans were in front of Britain in design, metal working and chemicals. By the 1850s British watchmaking was exhibiting all the signs of "entrepreneurial failure" that was to obsess observers forty years later. Britain's productivity rate has always been at variance from that of other nations. As early as the middle of the nineteenth century, productivity rates in the United States were twice that of Britain. Long-term differentials in productivity are a function of the different histories of manufacturing structures and resource constraints. The pattern that Britain revealed in the late nineteenth and twentieth centuries was a product of the period of this book. Yet it is important to point out that economic "failure" was not predetermined by this history. See Clapham, *Economic History of Modern Britain*, vol. II, p. 111; Alun Davies, "British Watchmaking and the American System," *Business History*, 35, 1 (1993), pp. 40–54; S. N. Broadberry, *The Productivity Race: British Manufacturing in International Perspective, 1850–1990* (Cambridge, 1997), chs. 5, 10; Corelli Barnet, *The Audit of War* (London, 1988); Martin Weiner, *English Culture and the Decline of the Industrial Spirit 1850–1980* (Cambridge, 1981).
[20] P. L. Payne, "British Entrepreneurship in the Nineteenth Century," in Clarkson, *The Industrial Revolution*, p. 101; McCloskey, "The Industrial Revolution 1780–1860," p. 116; Hudson, *Industrial Revolution*, p. 25. See C. H. Lee, *The British Economy Since 1700: A Macroeconomic Perspective* (Cambridge, 1986), pp. 10, 12, for tables registering the contribution of various sectors to the growth of gross domestic product. See also R. A. Church, *The Great Victorian Boom 1850–1873* (London, 1975); Esteban, "British Textile Prices."

use of labor rather than through harnessing the technology of the machine. This reflected an economic practice that was embedded in the economic structures and in cultural attitudes. It was a practice inherited by Britain's nineteenth-century economy, with significant consequences for that in the twentieth. The transfer of labor from agriculture to manufacturing at an early historical stage was a significant achievement for Britain. Yet this did not imply an ability or desire to capture high rates of productivity from the industrial labor force.

Productivity gains remained firmly tied to innovations in which muscle power counted for more than technological efficiencies. This was true, most revealingly, in the massive textile industry. The rapid expansion of output and varieties of cloth production in the middle of the seventeenth century was facilitated by extending the use of labor on the hand-driven Dutch loom and stocking frame. In the late nineteenth century, low-cost and experienced labor allowed Britain to meet competitive pressures by moving to the cheaper cloth markets without the expense of adopting new technology. Until about 1860, 50 percent of all productivity growth came from the unmechanized sectors of the economy. The building industry's contribution to total net capital formation, for example, continued to surpass the contribution from factory textiles until the 1860s. Over the same period the traditional, nonmechanized sector of the economy grew at a faster rate than either the high-tech iron industry or the well-organized woolen industry.[21]

Manufacture was not a factory-based activity. The factory sector was a presence throughout the eighteenth century and it became more important as the nineteenth century progressed. This was especially true in specific sectors like cotton spinning. But factories remained a relatively uncommon site of employment. In 1831, only 10 percent of males worked in machine-based manufacture, 32 percent in handicraft and retail. As late as 1851, only 27 percent of the male and female labor force worked in industries that were dominated by technology and factory organization. This was an economy which produced goods using labor rather than labor-saving technology; it was to prove very difficult to break free from that legacy.[22]

---

[21] Similarly, productivity increases were achieved by increasing the division of labor on the model of Adam Smith's famous pin-factory example, rather than by adding to the technology at each worker's elbow. See Maxine Berg, "Small Producer Capitalism in Eighteenth-Century England," *Business History*, 35, 1 (1993), pp. 17–39; Berg, "What Difference," p. 27.

[22] There was enormous variation of factory size even within the same sector. In the 1830s the woolen mills employed an average of 43 workers; it was 93 in linens, 125 in silk and 175 in cotton. See Berg, "Small Producer Capitalism," p. 23; Crafts, *British Economic Growth*, pp. 63–68, 155–56; Joel Mokyr, "Introduction," in Mokyr, *British Industrial Revolution*, p. 15; Charles Wilson, *England's Apprenticeship*, pp. 184–95.

Steam power and machinery were widely applied during this period. Yet their engagement was determined by their relevance to manual labor – another example of how the pulses of change were checked. Mechanical processes were understood to be subordinate to the needs of hand labor; they were not generally intended to revolutionize it. The manufacturing phase in the history of steam power opened in the 1690s when the Savery patent opened its use for mechanical uses. This stage closed when Charles Parson successfully developed the steam turbine in 1884. The turbine ended the dominance of the reciprocating mechanism that had hitherto provided the central driving force of all steam engines. It made obsolete the technology that James Watt had adapted from Newcomen in the 1760s.[23]

In the meantime, many modifications had been made to steam technology. Yet its energies were harnessed as an ancillary source of motion for a fairly narrow range of uses. As late as 1800, the steam engine was principally employed to fulfill its original purpose of pumping water from the mines. Fifty percent of all steam engines were used in the mines; only 21 percent were used in textiles. Most of the latter were secondary to water power, which into the 1840s and 1850s continued to be a cheaper source of energy than steam power. Steam did not become the prime energy source for manufacturing until the 1870s. Machines in the early factories were often driven by hand or horses; it was the exception that required steam power. Furthermore, the use of steam power in factories was restricted largely to the textile industry. As late as the 1870s textiles used one-half of all the steam power engaged in British manufacturing. Even in textiles the application of steam power varied greatly, both sectorally and geographically.[24]

Like all other mechanical inventions, steam-driven machinery remained a novelty much longer than was theoretically necessary. The lag time between invention and adoption is a product of forces wider than technology alone. Steam was adopted in the framework knitting trade only from the 1860s. In both the advanced and dynamic Yorkshire and the sleepy, more restrained West Country woolen cloth industry, machines of all sorts did not begin to penetrate until the 1830s and 1840s. For

[23] The turbine was still a *steam*-driven engine, of course. It opened a new era primarily because it enabled machines to be driven by electricity rather than by pulleys, belts and drive axles. See A. Stower, "The Stationary Steam Engine 1830–1890," in Charles Singer et al., *A History of Technology*, vol. V, *The Late Nineteenth Century, c. 1850 to c. 1900* (Oxford, 1958), pp. 124–26, 138–40.

[24] G. M. von Tunzelman, *Steam Power and British Industrialisation to 1860* (Oxford, 1978), pp. 289–95; Dolores Greenberg, "Power Patterns of the Industrial Revolution: An Anglo-American Comparison," *American Historical Review*, December 1982, pp. 1237–61; Phyllis Deane, *The First Industrial Revolution* (Cambridge, 1969), pp. 128–29.

twenty-five years after Edmund Cartwright had developed the power loom, they were introduced at the rate of fewer than 100 per year. (It is fair to note, however, that the water frame and the spinning jenny spread much more quickly.)[25]

Thus steam power was integrated in British industry through a prolonged and lengthy accretion rather than a sudden transformation. Ironically, the progress of steam power was somewhat more rapid in agriculture, although it got a much later start. In the 1860s only about 200,000 acres of the fifteen million acres of arable land in England were ploughed by the steam plough. This decade marked the moment of breakthrough to a mechanized agriculture, however. Artificial fertilizers had begun to be developed by the 1830s; by the 1860s Peruvian guano was a well-established aid to soil fertility. At the end of Victoria's reign, English agriculture was the most highly mechanized in Europe.[26]

What was true on land was even more true on the seas. The tea clippers remained the fastest ships in the world until the 1870s. The tonnage of ships powered by steam surpassed those driven by wind and sail only in 1882. The steam engine and the sail represented the technological duality of the age of manufacture with its uneasy blend of old and new, change and constraint. By the 1870s the limits of this combination were in sight. The compounding steam engine developed by Watt and subsequently improved by marine engineers had arrived at the boundaries of its technological and economic potential. The use of sail for many marine purposes was finally doomed by the quantum leap of the turbine, although steam did not become more cost-effective than sail for voyages over 5,000 miles until almost the twentieth century. The steam turbine was an emblem of the age of industry. Unambiguously technological, the turbine was autonomous of hand labor and superordinate to it.[27]

The dynamism of the manufacturing economy was fueled by a high level of internal consumer demand. Indeed, it is possible to speak of eighteenth-century Britain as a "consumer society." Consumer markets depend on a growing population ready and able to spend money. Britain possessed both qualities. Yet there was a particular pattern of population growth that was peculiar to this period of Britain's history. The demo-

[25] Duncan Blythell, *The Sweated Trades: Outworking in Nineteenth-Century Britain* (London, 1978), pp. 88–90; J. de L. Mann, *The Cloth Industry in the West of England From 1640 to 1880* (repr., Gloucester, 1987), pp. 187–88.

[26] Hugh Prince, "Victorian Rural Landscapes," in G. E. Mingay (ed.), *The Victorian Countryside* (London, 1981), vol. I, p. 18.

[27] Charles K. Harley, "The Shift from Sailing Ships to Steamships, 1850–1890: A Study in Technological Change and Its Diffusion," in Donald McCloskey (ed.), *Essays on a Mature Economy: Britain After 1840* (Princeton, 1971), pp. 215–31; Clapham, *Economic History of Modern Britain*, vol. II, pp. 61–72, vol. III (Cambridge, 1938), pp. 133–34.

graphic regime of the age of manufacture balanced a capacity for growth within definite limits and expectations. Three elements were central to the demographic regime of this period: its evident escape from the mortality trap that linked population growth to food prices; the constraint of the "preventive check" that inhibited a breakthrough to a thoroughly "modern" demographic system; and the gestation of a new pattern of nuptiality from the middle of the nineteenth century that only came to term from the 1870s.

By 1690 Britain had moved well beyond the "pre-industrial" demographic trap that linked mortality to food prices. Indeed, with the benefit of hindsight we can see that the decisive escape from the determination of population by harvests had begun as early as the 1590s. Yet this was a slow and tentative process. Thus, the 1690s registered a favorable shift in the ratio of births to deaths that broke the previous tendency toward a static balance between the two. Still, the new pattern remained fragile. The birth rate fell and the death rate rose during certain years in each decade until the 1730s when the full demographic potential of the deliverance from a subsistence regime began to be realized. After the late 1740s, births begin to outpace deaths consistently. The escape to a demographic world free from natural calamities had been achieved.

There was little perception at the time that this was so, however, and this demographic regime can in no way be considered "modern." It was a regime that went through several modifications, especially around the end of the eighteenth and beginning of the nineteenth centuries. Well into the nineteenth century the "preventive check" remained a powerful and real constraint on the demographic growth. Mortality was no longer linked to natural disasters. Nevertheless, the age and rate of marriage and therefore the rate of fertility continued to be constrained by fluctuations of real income and expectations of economic opportunities. This was not altered even during the economic expansion of the later eighteenth and early nineteenth century, when the Malthusian model of linking family size to changing food prices or real wages was first formulated.

Economic expansion was by no means neutral to population patterns, of course. The eighteenth-century expansion had strengthened the "positive feedbacks" in the demographic regime by allowing rising population to be compatible with falling food prices. The spurt of expansion in the late eighteenth century was critical to this process. This undermined Malthusianism, yet it did so only in theory and in retrospect. It took quite some time for this lesson to permeate into popular consciousness and thus decisively change behavior. Marriage rates continued to be highly sensitive to real wages in the expectation that falling real wages presaged a decisive downturn in living standards and a collapse of expansion. This was a lesson well learnt from population theory, in which the possibility was discounted that populations could continue to grow in conjunction with economic expansion. At the national level the demographic dynamic of the early and mid-Victorian years suggested a basic continuity with the past. National evidence indicates relatively little movement in fertility rates until the onset of a modern demographic regime was heralded by their dramatic decline after the 1870s.[28]

The possibility of self-sustaining economic expansion was only just beginning to be glimpsed in this period. There was nothing irrational about behaving as if Malthus lived when the major script of economic discourse still broadcast the stationary economy as the natural state of affairs. If John Stuart Mill continued to regard the available land as the ultimate limit to economic growth, how can we expect lesser mortals to have displayed greater insight about the dynamics of economic change? Not until the 1870s was the Malthusian link finally abandoned in general behavior and perception. Like other significant changes in this period, the transition from a pre-industrial to a modern demographic regime was prolonged; it did not happen until the end of our period. Only by 1870, when "the classic pre-industrial system [was] on the point of disintegration," does the link between real wages and nuptiality snap, and family size is finally divorced from the prospects of demographic survival.[29]

[28] National demographic statistics gathered from parish records will not produce a model of population growth that can be replicated at the local level. Local evidence does not undercut the picture presented here, but it does suggest the importance of local modifications. Evidence from Kent suggests a sharp response to the installation of the new poor law after 1834 with an almost immediate decline in fertility in the following decade. This indicates that social policy achieved some success in its intention to limit family size and it reveals the sensitivity of local society to changing socioeconomic circumstance. See, for example, Barry Reay, *Microhistories: Demography, Society and Culture in Rural England, 1800–1930* (Cambridge, 1996), pp. 39–67.

FNNPTXDemographic possibilities were also altered by changes in the deployment of labor and the form of wage payment. In the rural areas the decline of farm servants living in the farmer's house began in the middle of the eighteenth century and extended well into the second third of the nineteenth century. As living-in declined, so the possibilities for nuptiality changed, since the pressure to delay the age of marriage disappeared. This applied especially to men. At the same time, however, the tendency of enclosure to diminish the opportunities for female employment pushed women also to contemplate earlier marriage. Similarly, the increased importance of urban living tended to undermine the presumptions of the old demographic regime. Urban dwelling made irrelevant the prudential check of delaying marriage and family until the resource of land or small holding was available. The expansion of waged labor therefore worked to lower the age of marriage. See Hudson, *Industrial Revolution*, pp. 136–40; Martin Daunton, *Progress and Poverty: An Economic and Social History of Britain 1700–1850* (Oxford, 1995), pp. 387–401; Geoffrey Holmes, *The Making of a Great Power* (London, 1993), pp. 44–48; K. D. M. Snell, *Annals of the Labouring Poor: Social Change and Agrarian England 1660–1900* (Cambridge, 1985), pp. 210–11, 345–48.

[29] Michael Teitelbaum, *The British Fertility Decline* (Princeton, 1984), pp. 220–25; E. A. Wrigley and R. S. Schofield, *The Population History of England 1541–1871* (London,

An expanding population was a basic foundation for the exponential growth of the internal consumer market in the eighteenth century. The value of the home market tripled in the first seventy years of the century, and tripled again in the final thirty. The origins of this particular stage of consumer markets appeared first in the late seventeenth century. Retail shops had first appeared at the end of the sixteenth century, yet there was a significant departure in the size and sophistication of the consumer market structures at the end of the seventeenth century. In the urban areas, networks of retail shops joined the system of chapmen, peddlers and markets (still the most common source of consumer items) to serve consumer needs. Retail tailoring shops were well established in London by the 1680s, for example. The increasing complexity and sophistication of the consumer markets were reflected in the dramatic increase from the 1670s in the inventories of household goods. Items that had not been present in households before, such as clocks, china, curtains, prints and utensils for drinking hot liquids, began to appear in large numbers.[30]

The consumer market was driven by the demands of the burgeoning middle classes. Aristocratic patrons remained very important to certain trades, particularly in London, but consumer markets were no longer responsive solely to the demands of this social segment. A mass market for middle-class consumer durable goods clearly existed by the middle of the eighteenth century. This reflected the sharp increase from the first half of the century in the numbers of households with incomes between £50 and £400 per year. In 1750 such households constituted 15 percent of the population; by 1780 they had grown to 25 percent of the population. In addition, there was a reorientation of middling-class consumption away from necessities, like kitchenware, for example, and furniture, toward a whole new range of "luxury" goods that were designed to enhance domestic comfort. East India calicoes were an early example of a product to attract this sort of attention. Clocks were an-

1981), pp. 458–78; Wrigley, "The Growth of Population in Eighteenth-Century England: A Conundrum Resolved," *Past and Present*, 98 (May 1983), pp. 143–50. The findings of this earlier work by the Cambridge group has been confirmed by their recent work on family reconstitution. See E. A. Wrigley, R. S. Davies, J. E. Oeppen and R. S. Schofield, *English Population History from Family Reconstitution 1580–1837* (Cambridge, 1997).

[30] McKendrick et al., *Birth of a Consumer Society*, pp. 9–10, 28–29; Lorna Weatherill, *Consumer Behaviour and Material Culture in Britain 1660–1760* (London, 1988), pp. 24–28, 77, 195–98; T. H. Breen, "An Empire of Goods: The Anglicization of Colonial America, 1690–1776," *Journal of British Studies*, 25 (1986), pp. 467–99; John E. Wills, Jr., "European Consumption and Asian Production in the Seventeenth and Eighteenth Centuries," in Brewer and Porter, *Consumption and the World of Goods*, pp. 131–47, for the international dimensions; Peter Earle, *The Making of the English Middle Class* (London, 1989), p. 45.

other, as technical advances enabled them to be produced in greater numbers.[31]

This was a consumer economy, but it was not a *mass* consumption economy. The consumer market did not embrace the working classes. The economic stimulant of demand derived almost entirely from the body of the middling classes, and the limits to the territory claimed by the consumer market were sharply defined at the boundary between the middling and working classes. Yet this did not mean that opportunities to dabble in the consumer economy were denied to the working classes; they were not. There are reports in the late seventeenth century of working-class consumption of minor luxuries like shoe buckles and ribbons. Such items were undoubtedly purchased as fluctuations in income allowed. Working-class consumption of household items was also a feature of the period. Yet the main class distinctions regarding consumer purchases must have lain – as they always have – in the amounts and types of goods that were owned. Until the middle of the nineteenth century, working-class consumption of "luxuries" like tobacco, tea and coffee remained at a fairly low level. This is hardly surprising. Working-class budgets contained no margin for expenditures beyond rent and food.

This did not change until after the 1870s. Class was a key factor in a series of changes that enter into play in the last quarter of the nineteenth century. Class was not the only element, however. Advertising strategies begin to segment consumer markets by gender, for example. Still, the important point is that working-class men and women were identified as potential consumers for goods other than household necessities or the noxious luxuries of drink and tobacco. Only after c. 1870 is it possible to speak of a working-class consumption market that paralleled the middling class's ability to purchase nonessential goods. Items such as the sewing machine, the bicycle and the piano were the markers of this (mainly upper) working-class consumer market which served as the scouting party for the truly mass consumerism of the twentieth century.[32]

Such a market could not have been imagined within the demographic regime of the age of manufacture. A mass consumption market could not be installed until reproductive behavior ceased to be constrained by the fear of the Malthusian trap. The manufacturing economy was certainly capable of producing relatively simple goods for a world market through its myriad of workshops. But it was not equipped to produce the typical

---

[31] John Styles, "Manufacturing, Consumption and Design in Eighteenth-Century England," in Brewer and Porter, *Consumption and the World of Goods*, pp. 537–38; Holmes, *Making of a Great Power*, pp. 52–53.

[32] McKendrick et al., *Birth of a Consumer Society*, pp. 23, 29, 31; Daunton, *Progress and Poverty*, pp. 437–39; Mokyr, "Is There Still Life in the Pessimist Case?"; Lori Anne Loeb, *Consuming Angels: Advertising and Victorian Women* (New York, 1994).

products of a mass consumption economy where sophisticated technical devices have to be produced in large numbers. It was hardly a historical coincidence that the shift to a modern demographic regime after 1870 overlapped both with the arrival of a mass consumption market, and the transition from a mode of production dominated by the workshop sector to one that was dominated by the large-scale factory unit.

I have already referred to the way production in the age of manufacture contained both factory and workshop organization. There is a continual tendency among historians to represent these different forms of economic organization as competing alternatives. Thus, there is a tendency to place both in a process of linear development which sees the big progressively moving to displace the small. This is not a helpful perspective for our period. Both the large and small, mechanized and hand-labor sectors were integral to the productive process of the period. It is the functional relationship between the two that is the key to understanding how production was organized in the age of manufacture.

Factory and workshop were locked in a relationship of close interdependence. Mechanization and larger-scale units complemented rather than displaced small-scale production. Many of the machines were ancillary to hand labor, rather than its substitute. But machines were also usually relevant only to one part of the manufacturing process; they tended to have the effect, therefore, of increasing the demand for those parts of the work performed in the domestic setting where hand labor was the sole source of productive energies. When production was concentrated into the factory, it tended to cause an expansion of the domestic sector, not its demise. As early as the 1730s, Birmingham and Sheffield were dotted with workplaces that employed hundreds of people in one place and were surrounded by satellite congeries of small workshops. These cities presented the characteristic profile of production processes, therefore, before the shock cities (like Manchester) of the purely factory towns began to occupy industrial geography from the early nineteenth century. At the heart of manufacturing lay a combination of small and large units of production bound together by many layers of subcontracting with labor processes that were highly subdivided and dominated by hand technology.[33]

---

[33] Clive Behagg, *Politics and Production in the Early Nineteenth Century* (London, 1990), pp. 40–43; Berg, "Small Producer Capitalism," p. 23; Eric Hopkins, *Birmingham: The First Manufacturing Town in the World 1760–1840* (London, 1988), p. 10. In Birmingham, for example, Alcock and Kempson's toy works employed between 300 and 400 people in one place. John Taylor's button factory gave work to 500 in 1755. And the famous Solo mills built by Matthew Boulton in the early 1770s opened with 700 employees, and within a year later advertised itself as the largest hardware manufactory in the world with 1,000 workers.

The heart of industrial change in the period 1680–1880 was the shifting equilibrium between the small and large sectors of the economy. The significance of the growth of the factory sector of production was that it altered the balance of interdependency between the small and large units in favor of the latter. This process is common to the whole period, and sweeps well into the middle of the nineteenth century – which in fact was likely *the* crucial period for the final subordination of the small-scale units to their larger partners. In textiles the advantage tilted to the large-scale sector in silk in the 1720s, flax in the 1780s, cotton in the 1790s, lace in the 1810s and hosiery in the 1860s. The shoe industry, for example, moved from a proto-industrial form to a factory-industry form in the 1860s and 1870s.

Framework knitting is a particularly well-known example of the manufacturing form of industrial change because of the chronically depressed conditions of the trade in the later eighteenth and early nineteenth centuries. From around the 1680s it assumed the characteristic form of a domestic industry where the frames were rented to the workers by middlemen who controlled the distribution of the raw material and the finished product. A large percentage of the workers were women and children. These features intensified over the period, most notably in the 1830s, and were not finally displaced by mechanization until the 1850s. Even then, the mechanization of knitting followed the pattern familiar to the age of manufacture. The knitting section of the production process was concentrated into centralized factories staffed by men. This created a heightened demand for hand labor to seam and stitch the hosiery; these tasks were performed by women in domestic workshops. The experience of framework knitting was by no means unique. It was an experience that would be replicated many times over during the period.[34]

The story of economic change in this period is a story of a tightening web that drew the small into a greater dependency upon the large. Technology was by no means the only agent in this process; it was not even the major one. Changes in the credit structure, for example, were another common nexus of dependency. Economic downturns pulled the

[34] Berg, "Small Producer Capitalism"; Blythell, *Sweated Trades*, pp. 31–33; Marie Rowland, *Masters and Men in the West Midland Metalware Trade Before the Industrial Revolution* (Manchester, 1975), pp. 150–52; Sonya Rose, "Proto-Industry, Women's Work, and the Household Economy in the Transition to Industrial Capitalism," *Journal of Family History*, 13, 2 (1988), pp. 181–93; Nancy Osterud, "Gender Divisions and the Organization of Work in the Leicester Hosiery Industry," in Angela John (ed.), *Unequal Opportunities: Women's Employment in England 1800–1918* (Oxford, 1986), pp. 48–49, 63–64; F. A. Wells, *The British Hosiery Trade: Its History and Organization* (London, 1935), esp. chs. 5 and 8; A. F. Moseley, "The Nailmakers," *Journal of West Midlands Regional Studies*, 2 (1968), p. 6; Alan Fox, *The National Union of Boot and Shoe Operatives 1874–1957* (Oxford, 1958), pp. 12–16.

small into a more subservient relationship with the large. The key to economic survival in an increasingly complex domestic market structure was access to distribution networks both for the raw material and the product. The most successful firms were those that employed salesmen directly. There was an inexorable tendency for small producers to be separated from their markets and for middlemen and merchants to control the channels of distribution. Such developments had long pedigrees, of course. In the corn trade, the growing influence of the metropolitan market had created a class of middlemen from the middle of the seventeenth century. In the small iron trades the process was evident by the 1770s when the notorious "foggers" first appeared in the directories.[35]

Many elements constituted the process of economic change in this period; not least among those were the pace and rhythm of this pattern of interdependency. A quickened pace of economic expansion, such as that in the late eighteenth and early nineteenth centuries, reinforced and deepened the interdependence of large and small units, mechanized and nonmechanized. During the period of the "industrial revolution," this process reached a new level of intensity. Artisans were particularly subject to its consequences and their experiences have been fully recounted in such cases as the tailoring or shoemaking trades of London or the metalware trades of Birmingham. Yet artisans were not alone in feeling the full force of the shifting relationship between large and small units of production. Different variants of the process were also to be found even in the large-scale cotton sector. For every cotton-spinning factory, there were many smaller units of production filling in key aspects of the preparatory or finishing processes. Even in the most highly mechanized sector of textiles, the small units retained a clear numerical predominance over the large beyond the 1840s. Yet they were enjoined to follow the rhythms and priorities of the large.[36]

[35] Alan White, ". . . We Never Knew What Price We Were Going to Have Until We Got to the Warehouse': Nineteenth-Century Sheffield and the Industrial District Debate," *Social History*, 22, 3 (October 1997), pp. 307–17; Clive Behagg, "Custom, Class and Change: The Trade Societies of Birmingham," *Social History*, 4, 3 (October 1979), pp. 456–71; Ray Bert Westerfield, *Middlemen in English Business Particularly Between 1660 and 1760* (New Haven, 1915), pp. 150–51; Rowland, *Masters and Men*, pp. 150–52. Foggers were agents of the central warehouse – the large unit in the trade – who controlled the distribution of the raw material and the collection of the finished product from the domestic workshop workers, scattered over the countryside.

[36] V. A. C. Gatrell, "Labour, Power and the Size of Firms in Lancashire Cotton in the Second Quarter of the Nineteenth Century," *Economic History Review*, 30, 1 (1977), pp. 95–125; E. P. Thompson, *The Making of the English Working Class* (Harmondsworth, 1968), pp. 280–88; Behagg, *Politics and Production*, pp. 20–70, for the fullest explanation of the dynamic of this interdependence; Richard Price, *Masters, Unions and Men: The Struggle for Work Control in Building and the Rise of Labour 1830–1914* (Cambridge, 1980), pp. 22–39.

In the economy of manufacture, then, economic expansion was manifested in two ways. Smaller units of production proliferated, but often within the context of a deepening subordination to the mandates of the large. The wave of factory building that Birmingham experienced between the mid-1820s and mid-1830s, for example, drew the small workshops into an ever closer dependence on the large. At the same time, however, expansion offered new opportunities for new small businesses to be established to feed specialized needs that it was not economic to complete in the factories. This variety of economic growth cruelly nourished the artisan dream of graduating to independent small master. Yet, in reality, these possibilities were notably slim and even if they were attained they were soon discovered to be a trap.[37]

The Birmingham metalware trades were awash with just these kinds of opportunities and closures. A centralized core fed half-finished goods for completion to the small workshops that swarmed around the periphery. In this highly competitive environment, small producers were given the opportunities to become "larger" masters. Yet to achieve independent master status in this setting required that small masters discard the artisan culture that governed their worldview. It was necessary to abandon the labor practices of customary standards on apprenticeship, for example, and grind down wages and conditions as economic circumstances demanded. The functional purpose of this small-scale sector was to provide the cushion for the larger masters to expand or contract their output as the market conditions demanded. In good times, overhead cost to the large master was nonexistent. In bad times, labor could be shed easily with no continuous charges for plant, machinery and the like to the large master. For the worker with any kind of skill, subcontracting promised servitude, not social mobility.[38]

The years from about 1790 to 1840 were a false dawn for the revival of the old dream of artisan independence, and also the moment when its demise was finally accepted. It is not surprising, therefore, that the artisans broadcast a language of protest in this period that targeted "middlemen" rather than "capitalists." Indeed, from the seventeenth century to the end of the nineteenth, the meaning of "capitalist" most frequently was confined to middleman. Nor is it surprising that artisans put enormous efforts into the struggle to protect their working conditions against exposure to competition. Groups like the London silk weavers in the 1820s who pleaded for the restoration of statutory control of their working conditions were not a trade anachronism. They were at the cutting edge of economic change. Their trade was progressively

[37] Hopkins, *Birmingham*, pp. 13–15.   [38] Behagg, "Custom, Class and Change."

dominated by large "wholesale" merchants who forced small masters into fierce competition with each other. Lowered wages and worsened conditions of work were the natural consequence for the workmen who bore the brunt of this competition.[39]

The proliferation of small units of production meant that the age of manufacture was also the age of outworking. Putting out the work to a cottage factory or to a domestic household was of ancient provenance. There was a vast increase in outwork from the middle of the seventeenth century and it tended fluctuate in conformity with the economic cycles. Outwork was integral to economic change in this period; it was the predominant form of industrial organization of the age. Nor did outworking suddenly disappear at the end of the nineteenth century; it continued to exist in some sectors of the economy. Nevertheless, the status of outworking in the dynamic of economic growth certainly changed at the end of our period. Beginning in the 1870s, it was rapidly displaced from the center of the industrial process. By the early twentieth century, outwork had been categorized as sweated labor performed by the vulnerable and the poor in their garrets. As a decaying and degenerate industrial form, therefore, it was the duty of the state to regulate it if not to abolish it entirely. The rise and fall of outwork matches the beginning and end of our period almost exactly.[40]

The gendered division of labor

Outwork was always associated with women's work. The growing interdependence of the small and large units of production in this period increased the demand for cheap unskilled labor that could be performed either in the workshop or at home. This translated into a continued, and growing, demand for women's labor. But women's labor extended beyond outwork. Women occupied a key role in the labor market system of manufacture in both the large- and the small-scale sectors. Technical change reinforced rather than altered this pattern. The first factories employed women and children, not men. Indeed, the high-tech sectors of the economy were also those sectors where women's labor was most intensively employed as a way of avoiding artisan standards of payment

[39] Marc W. Steinberg, "The Great End of All Government . . .': Working People's Construction of Citizenship Claims in Early Nineteenth-Century England and the Matter of Class," *International Review of Social History*, 33, suppl. 3 (1995), pp. 463–66.

[40] Blythell, *Sweated Trades*, pp. 12–19, 27–30, 68–74, 83, 143, 147; Raphael Samuel, "The Workshop of the World," *History Workshop Journal*, 3 (Spring 1977), pp. 6–72; Clapham, *Economic History of Modern Britain*, vol. I, pp. 172–84. For the late nineteenth century, see James Schmiechen, *Sweated Industries and Sweated Labour: The London Clothing Trades 1860–1914* (Urbana, 1984).

and working conditions. This was not a new phenomenon. The pattern of confining women to the less skilled areas of work had long been visible in manufacturing.[41]

The gendered labor market differentiation in manufacture created gendered forms of proletarianization. Women were progressively marginalized and displaced to lower skilled occupations; there were different labor markets for married and single women; and state policy actively assisted the gendering of the labor market. The tendency to relegate women to the unskilled sector was not an invention of the age of manufacture. Women generally had not been excluded from guilds in medieval times, although neither had they been entrusted with governing authority. Throughout the sixteenth and seventeenth centuries, however, women were progressively excluded from those skilled sectors of employment they had previously occupied. Much attention has been given to the proletarianization of women in nineteenth-century industry, yet there was nothing new about the increasingly subdivided labor process in which gender was a key component.[42]

The class dimension to this process differed from the gender dimension. Working-class women suffered most from the material effects of displacement. Ironically, however, working-class women were probably better placed than their middle-class counterparts to find new areas of opportunity. Until the middle of the nineteenth century, the cultural constraints on working-class women in employment were not particularly powerful. The same was not true for upper- or middle-class women. Upper-class women had been excluded from a public role in business and the professions by the late 1600s. The late seventeenth century and early eighteenth century marked a critical transition in the closure of spheres of business opportunity to such women.

Yet this pattern of exclusion was not the whole story. Women's employment opportunities did not continuously erode nor constantly decline in status. The pattern of exclusion is more accurately conceived of as

---

[41] Pat Hudson and W. R. Lee, "Introduction," in Hudson and Lee (eds.), *Women's Work and the Family Economy in Historical Perspective* (Manchester, 1990), pp. 20–21; Berg, "What Difference"; Berg, *Age of Manufactures*, pp. 131–32; Judy Lown, *Women and Industrialization: Gender at Work in Nineteenth-Century England* (Cambridge, 1990), p. 20.

[42] There are many examples that could be used to illustrate this. But the glovemaking trade and the hosiery trades provide nice examples because they are drawn from the early eighteenth and the middle of the nineteenth centuries respectively. In both, the expansion of the industry saw a regendering of the labor process which did not depend on technology, but on the expansion and subdivision of women's labor into the least skilled sections of the trade. See Pinchbeck, *Women Workers and the Industrial Revolution*, pp. 222–26; Sonya Rose, "Proto-Industry, Women's Work and the Household Economy"; Osterud, "Gender Divisions."

exclusion from an overt and accepted public role. It was still possible for Defoe in the early 1700s to register the opinion that women should be ready to take over their husbands' businesses if necessary. In fact, in the 1720s up to one-tenth of all businesses in London were owned by women. Artisan wives continued to be effective partners to their husbands. Women continued to be economic actors in business as they were in work. The expanding discourse of domestic ideology effectively disguised the contribution of women, even when it was visible. Throughout the whole period certain retail trades like milk selling were controlled by women. There were many women like Sarah Vye, who established Vye's grocer's shop in Ramsgate High Street in 1817. Nevertheless, the overall picture is clear. By the beginning of our period, the process of gender differentiation in business and employment around the notion of "separate spheres" was well established.[43]

The actual place of women in the economy, then, changed much less than the ideological representation of their role suggested. The same was true as regards women and the home. The "industrial revolution" may have pushed some women into factories, but it also greatly increased the demand for women's domestic labor. Household labor began to dissolve as manufacturing processes became more specialized and subdivided, and moved into cottage workshops. The progress of this development varied greatly. In certain sections of the textile industry the process was in train by the seventeenth century; in others it appeared in the late eighteenth century. Similarly, women were used in areas where new production methods were being introduced well before modern industrial forms were developed. What was new and shocking to contemporaries at the end of the eighteenth century and beginning of the nineteenth, of course, were the potential transgressions of domesticity and femininity threatened by the transfer of female proletarianization to the factories.[44]

The history of the gendered labor market in agriculture followed a similar trajectory to that of manufacture. In the Midlands and the South

---

[43] Kay E. Lacey, "Women and Work in Fourteenth- and Fifteenth-Century London," in Lindsey Charles and Lorna Duffin (eds.), *Women and Work in Pre-Industrial England* (London, 1985), pp. 24–82; Leonore Davidoff and Catherine Hall, *Family Fortunes: Men and Women of the English Middle Class, 1780–1850* (Chicago and London, 1987); Earle, *The Making of the English Middle Class*, pp. 161–73; Margaret Hunt, *The Middling Sort: Commerce, Gender and the Family in England 1680–1780* (Berkeley, 1996), pp. 124–28; Pinchbeck, *Women Workers and the Industrial Revolution*, pp. 282–85, 298–99, 303–05; Peter Mathias, *Retailing Revolution: A History of Multiple Retailing in the Food Trades Based upon the Allied Suppliers Group of Companies* (London, 1967), p. 37. Vye's later became one of the first multiple chain stores concentrated in the South East.

[44] Hudson and Lee, "Introduction," pp. 8–10; Pinchbeck, *Women Workers and the Industrial Revolution*, p. 121; Berg, "What Difference," pp. 34–35.

of England, the female labor market was increasingly casualized and marginalized throughout the eighteenth century. The division of labor was regendered to diminish the numbers of tasks that were regarded as women's work. Many forces worked to effect these changes. Technical innovation in the form of larger, heavier tools like the scythe played a role. The decline of apprenticeship closed off areas of skilled employment to women: in 1748 perhaps 34 percent of parish apprentices were women; by 1800 virtually none were. Women's wages began falling after 1760, earlier than those of men, and after 1750 there were higher rates of seasonal unemployment for women, which signified the casualization of female employment.

These changes heralded a new employment regime in agriculture for men as well as women. Throughout the eighteenth century, the stability of agricultural labor was undermined by a variety of forces. It became impossible to shield agricultural labor from national market fluctuations, for example. In addition, variable labor conditions that responded to economic movements were matched by poor law policies that increasingly reflected the labor needs of farmers. The enclosure movement of the late eighteenth century reinforced these trends – it did not invent them. Much scholarly effort has been devoted to disproving what was obvious to both supporters and opponents of enclosure at the time: that enclosure's social consequences were deleterious. Irregularity and instability of employment increased as a corollary of enclosure. Enclosure encouraged the end of yearly labor hirings. In the early eighteenth century over half of hirings were for more than two years; by 1830 only 15 percent ran that term. For women this pattern was starker and more extreme than it was for men. Just as in manufacturing, women's labor was progressively marginalized and casualized. The characteristic form of female employment in agriculture at the end of the eighteenth century was as an unskilled, low-paid day laborer.

The most obvious division of the gendered labor market, then, was along the line of skill. Yet this was not the only distinction that was drawn in the labor market of manufacturing. Divisions on the basis of status and age began to appear. The end of yearly hirings and of live-in servants shifted the bias in the labor market away from single men or women. This had the effect of removing women from areas that previously had been under their control. Dairy work, for example, was displaced into male hands – the milkmaid being a figure of nostalgic pastoralism. Similarly, preference in hiring now began to be given to families with children which meant changes in the marriage and family structure. In the past, living-in women farm servants had an incentive to marry late. Under the new labor market of the eighteenth century, it was in their interests to marry early as a protection against the greater danger of unemployment. In manufacturing, married women were increasingly likely to be confined to outworking as it became more and more a low-paid and low-status appendage of the more highly organized sector. Conversely, the place of single women in the formal sector of employment – such as the cotton mills – was reinforced.[45]

The labor market was not shaped by economic forces alone, however. The division of labor was gendered both by ideology and by social policy. The growth of separate spheres ideology will be addressed more fully in chapter 6. Here it is important to note that as the evangelical middle-class ideal of the family captured the national discourse, so social policy became more obviously directed toward gendering the labor markets. Throughout the eighteenth century, poor law administration became increasingly cognizant of the need to reinforce patriarchal authority. The first large-scale efforts to use the state to gender the labor market, however, came with the movements to control hours and conditions of work in the factories in the early nineteenth century. These efforts were to play an important role in establishing gendered boundaries of work that projected into the working classes the prime responsibility of the woman for internal family life.[46]

The legislation of the 1830s and 1840s did not introduce a new labor market system to the economy of manufacturing. The effects of this legislation were more ambiguous and contradictory. On the one hand, it reinforced the labor system of manufacturing, especially as it affected women, and, on the other hand, it began to erode its very foundations. The employment of married women and children in the factories was discouraged and, as a consequence, the confinement of women to the small-scale sector of the economy was promoted. Yet precisely because married women were excluded from factory employment, the legislation began to undermine the structure of the labor system of manufacturing, by defining the large-scale sector of employment as primarily a masculine domain.

In this respect, as in others, the acts spoke the language of domesticity. The ideology of domesticity was the keystone of the political coalition that pressed for regulation of factory conditions both inside and outside Parliament. The purpose was to install an ideal of domestic family life among the working class by putting wives and children back in the home.

---

[45] The above paragraphs are drawn from Hudson and Lee, "Introduction," pp. 20–23; Snell, *Annals of the Labouring Poor*, pp. 345–52, 375.

[46] Laws governing entitlements to benefits, for example, were changed so that the right to settlement – which identified the parish responsible for the claimant – could be obtained only through the father: Snell, *Annals of the Labouring Poor*, pp. 116–31, 334.

Unmarried women continued to work in the mills and came to dominate the female sector of factory employment. Once they married, however, it was expected that they would leave such work and attend to the cares of family life. Some factory employers actually dismissed married women on the passage of the 1844 act. Naturally, married women continued to work in industry in large numbers, but increasingly they did so in the small-scale sector where their presence was already well established.

Indeed, the exclusion of women from what the state defined as "factories" meant that more women were available for employment in the small-scale sector. Outwork, garret and domestic labor almost certainly increased as a result of protective legislation. In addition, this legislation undoubtedly contributed to the trend noticeable by the 1850s for female employment to shift away from work in manufacturing toward sectors like domestic service. From the 1850s a declining proportion of women were employed in manufacturing. In fact, it is probable that women contributed more to manufacturing output *before* 1850 than they were to do afterwards.[47]

By the 1870s, therefore, the terrain of the gendered labor market of manufacturing was beginning to erode. The agricultural depression of the 1870s dissolved the remains of the old rural labor market (and much else in rural society). The competitive pressures unleashed by the depression – and particularly the challenge to arable farming from the new world imports of wheat and meat – hastened the trend for pastoral farming to replace arable. In the process the labor market was reshaped. Pastoral farming required a smaller labor force with a much lower casual component. Arable farming could survive only by severe cost cutting and mechanized rationalization. At last the reaping machines that the Captain Swing riots had halted in 1830 resumed their progress. The changes introduced by the agricultural depression should not be exaggerated; they did not burst unheralded on an unsuspecting universe. Nevertheless, it was the case that the labor needs of agriculture changed from a reliance

[47] Sylvia Walby, *Patriarchy at Work* (Cambridge, 1986), pp. 100–17, 130–31; Lown, *Women and Industrialization*, pp. 160–64, 181; Robert Gray, "The Languages of Factory Reform in Britain," in Patrick Joyce (ed.), *The Historical Meanings of Work* (Cambridge, 1987), pp. 143–79; Marianna Valverde, "'Giving the Female a Domestic Turn': The Social, Legal and Moral Regulation of Women's Work in British Cotton Mills, 1820–1850," *Journal of Social History*, 21, 4 (Summer 1988), pp. 619–34; Jane Mark Lawson and Anne Witz, "From Family Labour' to Family Wage'?: The Case of Women's Labour in Nineteenth-Century Coalmining," *Social History*, 13, 2 (May 1988), pp. 151–70; Jane Humphries, "Protective Legislation. The Capitalist State and Working-Class Men: The Case of the 1842 Mines Regulation Act," *Feminist Review*, 7 (Spring 1981), pp. 13–28; Berg, "What Difference," p. 40. As many as 67 percent of married women were employed in 1780; by 1911 only 10 percent were recorded as employed outside the home.

on a year-round casual labor availability to a smaller, more specialized labor force that was entirely male.[48]

Outside agriculture, the changes in the female labor market are more difficult to capture in simple terms. Domestic service continued to expand; the new clerical sector of employment saw the gradual replacement of male clerks by women. The latter development involved the familiar process of women moving in with new technology – the typewriter – and the deskilling of a previously high-status, middle-class occupation. In the manufacturing sector the most significant development was the designation of "sweated labor" as a category to be rooted out by state action. This was a political decision, not an economic one, and, while it resulted in the further restriction of women and child labor, it also had the consequence of driving some of them deeper into the recesses of the small-scale sector.

The role of the state in regendering labor market boundaries in the late nineteenth century was even more important than it had been in the earlier period. The introduction of elementary schooling in the 1870s, with compulsory schooling coming in the 1880s, did much to remove child labor from the labor market pool. The Workshop Acts in 1867 and their extension in the 1870s reinforced the reshaping of the female and child labor markets. These acts represented an extension of the legislation of the 1830s and 1840s into the small workshop sector. It is important not to overstate their effects. The acts of the 1870s did not extend to work in dwelling quarters which were precisely where the worst sweating was to be found. They had little impact, therefore, in urban concentrations of outwork, like the East End of London.[49]

Yet their importance lay in the way they continued the pattern of the earlier measures in regendering a division of labor that had remained intact for at least two centuries. These legislative efforts to define the meaning of labor markets undercut the remaining strongholds of family labor in industrial production. Brickmaking, for example, ceased to be an industry in which families could work together once the acts of the 1870s prohibited girls under sixteen from working in the yards. Since the family economy demanded that they work before this age, the net effect of these measures was to push young women into domestic service – often to their

---

[48] See Pinchbeck, *Women Workers and the Industrial Revolution*, pp. 53–110; Snell, *Annals of the Labouring Poor*, pp. 22, 37, 50, 52–56, 74, 120–22, 139–69, 272–78; J. M. Neeson, *Commoners: Common Right, Enclosure and Social Change in England, 1700–1820* (Cambridge, 1993), pp. 27–35, 243–51; Alun Howkins, *Poor Labouring Men: Rural Radicalism in Norfolk 1870–1923* (London, 1985), pp. 2–13: F. M. L. Thompson, *English Landed Society in the Nineteenth Century* (London, 1963), pp. 308–16.

[49] For a graphic picture of sweating in the East End, where it became imbricated in immigration politics in the 1880s, see William J. Fishman, *East End 1888* (Philadelphia, 1988), pp. 60–81.

parents' dismay. Such measures therefore tended to move women out of these traditional industries. They went either deeper into the small-workshop or home-production sectors, or into the newer areas of domestic service, retail shop service or clerical work.[50]

Regionalism in the system of manufacture

Economies are arranged spatially in geographical units as well as through the categories of production and labor. Each phase or period of economic growth contains particular geographical divisions of labor. In this respect, the economy of manufacturing was a collection of *regional* economies. The regional level was the key location for economic growth and change. As David Rollison has suggested in his study of Gloucestershire in the period 1500 to 1800, the origins of modern society were embedded in local changes. The initiative for change, the locus of economic development and the institutional base for economic growth were above all local.[51]

The spatial organization of the economy of manufacturing rested on the keystone of the region. In the sixteenth and seventeenth centuries, zonal economic organization took the form of a mosaic of similar regions existing side by side. For the most part, these regions were only weakly integrated. Throughout the seventeenth century, the center of economic gravity progressively shifted from the local community to the region, where it remained until the end of the nineteenth century. By the end of the nineteenth century, however, a new spatial arrangement of the economy was coming into focus which marked off the age of manufacture from the age of industry in the twentieth century. In this economy, specialized regions were nationally integrated. The Midlands produced cars, the North East produced steel and so on.[52]

[50] For brickmaking, see Parliamentary Paper, *Report of Commissioners Appointed to Inquire into the Factory and Workshop Acts*, 1876 [C1443–1], vol. XXX, Part II, qq. 7273–75, 9279, 9302–05, 13979–80, 14630–33, 15581–83. It is interesting to note that brick-makers protested the restriction against girls under sixteen by arguing that the work was very light and that the regulation broke up the family unit of employment. In this trade, machinery made employment of really young people unnecessary, but increased the need for the employment of youths of both sexes. Family labor did not disappear completely, of course. It remained a feature of the pottery industry well into the early twentieth century. See Richard Whipp, "The Stamp of Futility: The Staffordshire Potters 1880–1905," in Royden Harrison and Jonathan Zeitlin (eds.), *Divisions of Labour: Skilled Workers and Technological Change in Nineteenth-Century Britain* (Brighton, 1985), pp. 113–50; Whipp, "Work and Social Consciousness: The British Potters in the Early Twentieth Century," *Past and Present*, 19 (May 1988), pp. 133, 138–41.

[51] Rollison, *Local Origins of Modern Society*, esp. ch. 1.

[52] For the geography of economic regionalism, see Doreen Massey, *The Spatial Divisions of Labour: Social Structures and the Geography of Production* (London, 1984); John Langton, "The Industrial Revolution and the Regional Geography of England," *Transactions of the Institute of British Geographers*, 9, 1 (1984), pp. 145–67.

Regions were transformed by economic change throughout this period, of course. Indeed, the "industrial revolution" was a characteristic example of the regional process of economic growth during this period. It is at the regional level that the strongest case can be made for retaining the traditional formulation of the idea of an "industrial revolution."[53] Yet this particular phase of economic growth did not create a modern integrated economy. To the contrary, the "industrial revolution" intensified rather than diminished the economic regionalism of the age of manufacture. The process of sectoral specialization accompanying the industrial revolution reinforced the trend toward regional integration that was a familiar attribute of economic growth long before the last years of the eighteenth or early years of the nineteenth centuries. In the economy of manufactures new regions regularly displaced old ones as the locational centers of activity.

This process had first presented itself in agriculture. The sectoral division between pastoral and arable areas had been essentially completed by the late seventeenth century, thus laying the basis for the productivity gains of the eighteenth.[54] Industry, too, had experienced shifting regional specialization from the sixteenth century. The rise of the North East coal industry and the locational shifts in the salt industry in the sixteenth century were such two cases.[55] By the later seventeenth century, however, the profile of the regional distribution of industry for the next 200 years was beginning to take shape. Regional specialization in the textile industry was already well advanced by 1680, for example, and its main outlines were to remain fixed until the later nineteenth century.

Thus, by the 1680s Yorkshire had achieved importance as a center of textile production. From the outset, the textile industry in Yorkshire was organized differently than the traditional centers of production in the South West and East Anglia. Yorkshire was not at this point in competition with either of these older areas; increasingly it concentrated on producing cheaper worsteds. Competition between the South West and

[53] The regional interpretation of the industrial revolution has been most persuasively argued by Pat Hudson (ed.), *Regions and Industries: A Perspective on the Industrial Revolution* (Cambridge, 1990); Berg and Hudson, "Rehabilitating the Industrial Revolution."

[54] Ann Kussmaul, *A General View of the Rural Economy of England 1538–1840* (Cambridge, 1990), esp. pp. 100, 170. A further phase in agricultural specialization was not to occur until the depression of the late nineteenth century undermined the viability of these prior structures of agriculture and brought to rural society a new sectoral (and sociopolitical) differentiation.

[55] On salt, see Charles Wilson, *England's Apprenticeship*, pp. 201–02. See Edward Hughes, *Studies in Administration and Finance 1558–1825* (repr., Philadelphia, 1980), pp. 377–432, for the fluctuations in the fortunes of various regions of this industry and the shift from brine to rock salt as the source of the product.

the Yorkshire cloth industries developed gradually over the period. Not until the 1830s did the South West began to lose market share to the more efficient industry of the Northern county. Indeed, throughout most of this period the South West and Yorkshire developed in parallel rather than in counterpoint. Machine production was introduced at about the same rate in both regions. Yorkshire was not notably more progressive in this respect than the South West. It was undeniable that the balance between the South West and Yorkshire and between Yorkshire and the East Anglian regions shifted in favor of the Northern county during this period. Yet it is important to remember that the demise of the textile industry of South West England did not occur until the 1880s when the American tariff closed off the lucrative American market for the more expensive goods that the region produced.[56]

Between the late seventeenth and the late nineteenth century, the facilities and the initiatives for the development of manufacturing were a function of the opportunities that presented themselves to particular localities. It is not possible to speak of a nationally integrated economy whose imperatives dictated regional development. Equally, this is not to suggest the complete absence of nationally unifying tendencies; regions did not exist in a vacuum. Product markets were increasingly national and, indeed, international in scope. In the East Midlands, for example, imperial and domestic markets in the eighteenth century stimulated the development of new industries like lace and the expansion of older ones like hosiery. Yet economic growth in this region was realized through the small-scale methods of manufacture. The industrial revolution arrived in the East Midlands in the wagons of the railways only toward the end of our period in the 1870s. Railways were always a force for national integration; they transformed the potential of the region beyond the local market. In the East Midlands, the local textile industries suddenly gained access to new markets and were rapidly led to adopt technical innovations that they had hitherto avoided. The workshop basis of the manufacturing sector gave way to larger industrial structures as heavy industry made its appearance. The Nottingham coal industry was transformed by the linkages of a rail network to a national market for coal.[57]

[56] Clapham, *Economic History of Modern Britain*, vol. II, p. 27; Berg, *Age of Manufactures*, pp. 52–53; Charles Wilson, *England's Apprenticeship*, pp. 192–93; Mann, *Cloth Industry in the West of England*, pp. 123–31, 187–89, 194–222. A similar pattern of regional specialization marked cotton textiles where the ground had been prepared by the extensive production of fustians, linens and woolens in Lancashire in the seventeenth century. The quickened pace of the late eighteenth-century economy reinforced a pattern in cotton textiles that had been etched out over the previous hundred or so years.

[57] The railways, of course, were a key agent of national economic integration in the twentieth century: J. V. Beckett and J. E. Heath, "When Was the Industrial Revolution in the East Midlands?," *Midland History*, 13 (1988), pp. 87–90.

Until the end of the nineteenth century, the processes of production and the institutional structures that facilitated the operation of markets were insistently local. The highly localized nature of labor markets provides an apt illustration of this. Thus, the characteristic patterns of labor migration were designed in response to the regional variation in labor market conditions. The artisan habit of "tramping" was the most highly developed form of this labor market strategy. Tramping involved moving from town to town along fixed circuits to remove surplus labor from one labor market and seek employment in another. The rise and fall of tramping was exactly coincident with the boundaries of the age of manufacture. By the 1870s it had virtually disappeared, as labor markets became more integrated even in trades such as building which continued to possess a local economic cycle. The same generalizations apply to the capital and credit markets which were almost entirely based on a particular region or industry. During our period, for example, a national capital market for manufacturing industry did not exist, although, as will be shown later, there were links at several steps removed between local banks and national channels of capital flows.[58]

When we speak of manufacturing in this period, then, we are speaking of a process that was intensely local. Yet manufacturing was not only for local uses. Increasingly the products of manufacturing were for export both within the domestic national market and abroad. Manufacturing alone does fully encompass the meaning of the economy of the period 1680–1880. The economy of Britain in this period involved more than just the manufacture of goods. The growth of trade has long been recognized as a key economic marker of the period. Indeed, the British economy was well practiced at moving goods and exchanging capital with, first, its European partners – like the Dutch – and then with its North American empire and, finally, with all quarters of the world. In a word, it was an *imperial* economy, with a refined and sophisticated network of commercial and financial procedures and institutions.

What was the relationship of this imperial economy to the manufacturing economy of the domestic society? How did these various parts of the

---

[58] François Crouzet, "Capital Formation in Great Britain During the Industrial Revolution," in Crouzet (ed.), *Capital Formation in the Industrial Revolution* (London, 1972), pp. 162–222; Pat Hudson, *The Genesis of Industrial Capital: A Study of the West Riding Wool Textile Industry c. 1750–1850* (Cambridge, 1986); R. A. Leeson, *Travelling Brothers: The Six Centuries' Road from Craft Fellowship to Trade Unionism* (London, 1980); E. J. Hobsbawm, "The Tramping Artizan," in his *Labouring Men: Studies in the History of Labour* (London, 1964), pp. 42–63. A strategy like tramping can work only in an economy that is not entirely driven by national trends. Although it was known in medieval times, the creation of a system of regular "tramp" circuits occurred in the late seventeenth century. It was refined throughout the eighteenth century. By the middle of the nineteenth century, it was falling into disuse and after c. 1870 disappeared.

economy relate to each other? These questions have tended to divide economic historians into two camps. On the one hand are those who emphasize the centrality of *production*. Such an accent writes the familiar story of Britain's economic history as a narrative of industrialization. This is the story, of course, that I have been concerned to modify in this chapter. On the other hand, there are those historians who favor an account of the British economy as an economy of commerce and trade. In this version, commerce, trade and finance constituted the true "leading sectors" of the economy. Cotton was a mere upstart compared to the enormous riches generated by trade. This perspective argues that Britain's comparative advantage did not lie in being the first industrial nation. Britain's distinction and privilege over other nations, historically speaking, lay in the commercial capitalism that rested on the trading networks of the British sphere of influence.[59]

There is no doubt that Britain's status as an imperial nation is fundamental to understanding its history. The importance of the imperial dimension in economic history, as in other areas, has often been elided.[60] Traditional economic history scholarship focused on technical change and failed to treat trade flows in the context of political economy. Revisionist econometric scholarship has explained economic expansion largely by emphasizing the processes of demand and supply in the home market. A narrative that focuses on commerce, trade and imperialism has much to recommend it, therefore. Yet it is not adequate to propose that an imperial narrative replace the narrative of domestic industrialization as a superior storyline for economic history. Any framework for understanding British economic history in this period must accommodate *both* the abiding presence of manufacturing and the restless spirit of commercial imperialism.

There is a long tradition in British economic history, however, to treat the economy of manufacture and the economy of commerce and finance as mutually exclusive alternatives. By this account, if industry is dominant in the political economy, then commerce and finance must suffer. And the reverse is true. It is undeniably true that each of these sectors historically tended to have differing visions of the ideal political economy for

---

[59] See in particular W. D. Rubinstein, "Wealth Elites and the Class Structure of Modern Britain," *Past and Present*, 76 (1977), pp. 99–126; Rubinstein, *Capitalism, Culture and Decline in Britain 1750–1990* (London and New York, 1993); Lee, *British Economy Since 1700*; Geoffrey Ingham, *Capitalism Divided?: The City and Industry in British Social Development* (London, 1984).

[60] Throughout our period, the service and commercial sector of the economy contributed a constant and large share to national income: 42 percent in 1700 and 47 percent in 1870. This was not entirely an imperial sector, of course, but its economic and political orientation increasingly was. See Lee, *British Economy Since 1700*, pp. 125–41, 93–106.

Britain. Manufacturers favored protectionism and the domestic market. Commercial merchants and financiers gradually came to favor free trade and the foreign market. Yet it is neither helpful nor necessary to designate either of these options of industry or commerce as the dominating hub of the British economy in this period. It should be noted that the case is very different for the twentieth century. Indeed, it is entirely from a twentieth-century perspective that the notion derives of an incompatibility between the interests of manufacturing and the interests of finance. The priorities of finance capital governed Britain's twentieth-century economic policy. These priorities installed institutional rigidities; they raised severe impediments to the ability of British industry to adjust to the economic world that opened with the "second industrial revolution." Yet to read this as a long-standing disease of British capitalism is to misread the past radically.[61]

In the period covered by this book, the major sectors of the economy did not stand in institutional opposition to the other. The economy of manufacturing and the empire of commerce and finance were complementary and integral to the economy of Britain. The relationship between these spheres was functional and effective. Economic development and growth were facilitated – not frustrated – by the relationship between manufacture, commerce and finance. In order to locate the economic history of Britain in this period in a more satisfactory framework, therefore, it is necessary to complement the foregoing chapter with two additional emphases. First, it is necessary to address the commercial and imperial dimensions of the economy. Secondly, it is also necessary to suggest how those dimensions were compatible with the manufacturing and industrial sectors of the economy. Those questions form the subject matter of the next chapter.

[61] The argument that British capitalism was historically unable to break free of its aristocratic and feudal past began with Perry Anderson in "Origins of the Present Crisis." E. P. Thompson's hilariously polemical response, "The Peculiarities of the English," reprinted in his *The Poverty of Theory and Other Essays* (London, 1979), pp. 35–91, effectively closed off what was in fact a very fruitful line of inquiry. Recently, of course, the Anderson argument has been revived with some modifications by mainstream archival scholars like Rubinstein and Cain and Hopkin who have restored its credibility. See, in particular, P. J. Cain and A. G. Hopkin, *British Imperialism: Innovation and Expansion 1688–1914* (London, 1992), ch. 1, where they argue that the aristocratic–financial capitalist alliance was the dominant fraction of capital from the beginning. For an excellent account of the fusing of capitalist social relations within a "pre-capitalist" political structure and discourse, see Ellen Meiksins Wood, *The Pristine Culture of Capitalism* (London, 1991).

2   A universal merchant to the world: the political economy of commerce and finance

A distinct system

The political economy of Britain in the period covered by this book was a political economy of commercial imperialism. What do I mean by "commercial imperialism"? I mean that commercial activity was the central, integrating practice of the economy. And furthermore I mean that commerce in the old seventeenth-century sense of trade was the defining property of British imperialism. The scope of commerce was not a function or result of Britain's manufacturing base – although this is how it is usually presented – and it did not depend solely upon what the domestic society cared to produce. Commerce did not imply merely a pathway along which the textiles, buttons, nails or steam engines manufactured in the industrial sector moved to the rest of the world. The importance of commerce was precisely that it was an economic activity the reach of which extended beyond the home market. Explaining the profile of commerce in this sense is the first purpose of this chapter.

Commerce presumed above all an *imperial* presence. It was a presence the first interest of which lay in the ability to carry goods. The origins of these goods mattered far less than the opportunity to transport them to their destination, which could be around the corner or at the ends of the earth. This fact determined the interests of commercial imperialism. It followed as a natural consequence that commerce was inseparable from the structures of financial capitalism. And this is the second purpose of this chapter.

The expansion and development of financial institutions were essential to the projection of imperial commerce; it was their duty to mobilize and deploy capital in the aid of commerce. This had not been their original purpose. Initially, the key financial institutions were a product of the policy of war that had brought William of Orange sailing into Torbay in 1688 in the first place. The genteel institutions of British finance were conceived to facilitate war and conquest in the Protestant cause in Europe. This was particularly true of the foundational body of British finance capitalism, the Bank of England. The Bank was the center of the system of finance capitalism, upon which all the other institutions of national finance were ultimately dependent. From the moment of its creation, however, the Bank was also at the heart of the political establishment. The Bank was indelibly marked by its association with the state, whose banker it was originally designed to be. Yet this did not remain its main function. The function of the Bank shifted from being the administrator of the national debt to the guardian of a disciplinary fiscal orthodoxy secured by the gold standard. This evolution paralleled the changing shape of the political economy itself, which will be the third major focus of this chapter.

This third part of my argument is, perhaps, the most important. I wish to emphasize the functional rationality of the interrelationship between the main sectors of the political economy. My argument here is that the political economy of the two centuries from the late seventeenth century composed a system in which the key elements of the commercial, the manufacturing and the financial sectors were linked together in a configuration that met the needs of each. I wish to make plain that to center the political economy of the period around commercial imperialism does not relegate other aspects of economic activity to a lesser order. In practical terms, for example, it would be difficult to draw a clear or consistent distinction between commerce and manufacture in this period. The two were both functionally and practically related.[1] Commerce both encompassed and surpassed the limits of domestic manufacturing; its interests were neither divorced from nor exactly convergent with those of the manufacturing sector that I discussed in the previous chapter. And the same imprecision was surely true between commerce and the landed interest, even though that relationship is now commonly regarded by historians as the determinate axis of British capitalism.[2]

[1] The origins of the famous bill brokerage firm of the middle of the nineteenth century, Overend and Gurney, lay in banking, commerce and merchant capitalist activity in Norwich, for example. They began to emphasize the first function – after 200 years in wool dealing and merchant capitalist manufacture – only in 1800. See W. T. C. King, *History of the London Discount Market* (London, 1936), pp. 17–18.

[2] I refer here, of course, to the argument that this political economy was one of "gentlemanly capitalism" dominated by the alliance forged in the 1680s between the landed gentry and the financial elites of the city of London. See Cain and Hopkin, *British Imperialism*, esp. pp. 1–104; and Rubinstein, *Capitalism, Culture and Decline*. This framework provides a good way to understand the enduring persistence of aristocratic styles and conventions in modern Britain and is a healthy counterweight to overestimating the power of industrial capital. It does not explain the historical relationship between the sectors of capitalism, however. And it is an argument that reads that relationship back from the twentieth century. The interests of commerce, finance and industry were not always mutually exclusive priorities in the British political economy.

It is obvious that the relationship between the various segments of the political economy was inherently ambiguous and contradictory. Each one had its own interests and priorities. A complex process of negotiation and struggle marked the history of the political economy. Historians have ceased to be much interested in this story, although the competition between economic interests for political access surely remains one of the most signal features of eighteenth-century politics.[3] Some of this will appear in my narrative, but it is not my main interest. My concern lies more in the evolving relationship between the main divisions of economic activity during this period. I am particularly interested in the changing affiliations between manufacture and finance. This story will form the fourth and final theme of this chapter.

As I have suggested, an integrated balance between the principal sectors of economic activity marked the political economy of commercial imperialism. Yet by the middle of the nineteenth century the conditions that maintained this balance were fast disappearing. This was a key development in the history of British capitalism. It meant the demise of a political economy that accommodated the interests of each main category of economic enterprise. In its place emerged a fragmented political economy, in which it was more difficult to harmonize the policy interests of the various sectors. This was especially true of the relationship between the financial and the manufacturing sectors. From the late nineteenth century these two sectors became more and more separate and alienated. On the one side of the political economy lay the behemoths of twentieth-century industrial factory-based production whose priority for finance was low interest rates. On the other side were the suave and shadowy centers of finance whose priority was maintaining the attractions of London as a center by offering sound, high-interest finance. There has been a tendency to treat the segregation between finance and industrial capital as an endemic reflex of British capitalism, as the product, perhaps, of its feudal and aristocratic roots. The argument here will be that it was a construction of the late nineteenth century.

The political economy of commercial imperialism

The first glimmerings of the political economy of commercial imperialism came into view during the difficult economic decades of the 1620s through the 1640s. Economic crises and depression forced a fundamental

[3] I am thinking here, of course, of the older work of Lucy Sutherland such as her "City of London in Eighteenth-Century Politics," in Aubrey Newman (ed.), *Politics and Finance in the Eighteenth Century* (London, 1984), pp. 42–66, and Sutherland, *The East India Company in Eighteenth-Century Politics* (Oxford, 1952).

reorientation of the trading patterns of the economy. Old markets were collapsed and closed by war; new markets opened in the Mediterranean and East Asia. Within the domestic economy, pioneering industries – the new draperies, for example – provided new centers of economic growth and dynamism. Established merchant oligarchies were thrown into disarray as fresh commercial and financial groups and interests competed for access to the networks of trade. Monopolies suddenly came under pressure, not simply because self-interested interlopers sought to break their exclusive grip, but also because economic theory began to question the wisdom of organizing commerce in that manner.[4]

The prolonged economic crises from the 1620s initiated some fundamental rethinking about the principles of economic policy. A sharp debate about the causes of economic depression began to move economic theory to a new level of secular complexity. The most important contribution came from Thomas Mun. Mun challenged the idea that hoarding bullion was the key to economic plenty. He proposed that the secret to national wealth lay in foreign trade and trade balances with other nations. It followed that competition was the key to healthy trade surpluses. The key to dealing with competitors was to undercut their selling price, and not (as most of his contemporaries believed) to use various forms of trade restriction to gather more bullion than their competition possessed. Thus, the trick for economic policy was to find ways of cheapening the cost of exports rather than keeping the unit price high.[5]

This unorthodox view did not remove the need for state policy to secure and protect the interests of English trade. But it did suggest a more dynamic view of the economic world than was typical of most bullionists. The implications of this focus on trade flows and trade balances suggested the necessity of sweeping as much trade through England as possible. Thus, the idea of England as the world's entrepôt was born. The Navigation Acts beginning in 1651 and extended and refined in 1662 and 1663 were a consequence of that perception. For the next century and a half they formed the basis of a political economy that aimed to direct as much trade as possible through the ports of England.[6]

[4] Charles Wilson, *England's Apprenticeship*, pp. 52–65; B. E. Supple, *Commercial Crises and Change in England 1600–1642* (Cambridge, 1959), esp. chs. 3, 6 and 7.

[5] Supple, *Commercial Crises and Change*, pp. 212–24; Joyce Appleby, *Economic Thought and Ideology in Seventeenth-Century England* (Princeton, 1977), pp. 37–40, 74–93. See Jacob Viner, *Studies in the Theory of International Trade* (repr., New York, 1965 [1937]), pp. 1–51, for an extensive discussion of various strands of early economic thought.

[6] Charles Wilson, *England's Apprenticeship*, pp. 61–64, 163–65; C. A. Pincus, *Protestantism and Patriotism: Ideologies and the Making of English Foreign Policy 1650–1668* (Cambridge, 1996), pp. 446–49. Although Pincus is concerned to displace economics in favor of religion as an explanation for the wars with the Dutch in the seventeenth century, he admits that out of these struggles came a secularization of the political culture and the

A renewed debate over economic policy was galvanized by the political and economic crises that were sparked by the wars of the 1690s. This debate produced an extensive and important pamphlet literature which placed economic matters firmly in the public sphere.[7] It disclosed a discourse which laid out, however incompletely, many of the economic ideas that were to be current until the late nineteenth century. Bullionist theories that Mun had challenged were still to be found, of course.[8] But the function of trade as a way to exchange goods rather than merely as a way to acquire and hoard money was well understood. A merchant like Sir Dudley North, for example, who had wide experience in the trade of the eastern Mediterranean, possessed a sophisticated economic intelligence. North believed that expanding trade was the key to increasing national wealth; that economic efficiency was driven by market forces, the division of labor and the profit motive; and that individuals should be free to compete in trade with as little restriction as prudent national interest allowed. North opposed the protective regulations of guilds and others for their distorting effect on trade and he rejected a bullionist view of the national economy in favor of one that recognized the interdependence of the world economy.[9]

The idea and the reality of trade lay at the center of this economic discourse, therefore. National wealth depended on expanding England's control of the circulation of goods. Sir Walter Raleigh had expressed this recognition in 1600 when he was reported to have said that "whosoever commands the sea, commands the trade of the world; whosoever commands the trade of the world, commands the riches of the world, and consequently the world itself." Raleigh was a premature commercial

expansion of the definition of the national interest to include economics. It is quite shocking to realize that the last book on the Navigation Acts was written before the Second World War: Lawrence A. Harper, *The English Navigation Laws: A Seventeenth-Century Experiment in Social Engineering* (New York, 1939). Sarah Palmer, *Politics, Shipping and the Repeal of the Navigation Laws* (Manchester, 1990), is very good on the politics of repeal in the 1840s.

[7] The pamphlet literature of the 1690s has been used to good effect by Joyce Appleby in *Economic Thought and Ideology*. There is, of course, a large and mainly older literature on the history of economic theory that was quite fascinated with the debates of these years, largely because of their relevance to issues like tariff reform and protection in the early 1900s and 1930s. See, for example, E. A. J. Johnson, *Predecessors of Adam Smith: The Growth of British Economic Thought* (New York, 1937); Viner, *Theory of International Trade*; Eli Heckscher, *Mercantilism* (London, 1935), 2 vols.

[8] The idea of the balance of trade as a total balance of the sum of all trading activity of the nation was not universally accepted. Versions of the old bullionist argument about the need to ensure a favorable balance of trade using protectionist measures if necessary were also current. See Peter Marshall, *Mercantilism and the East India Trade* (London, 1963), pp. 21–24.

[9] Richard Grassby, *The English Gentleman in Trade: The Life and Works of Sir Dudley North, 1641–1691* (Oxford, 1994), p. 239.

imperialist, however. What had been a buccaneering view in 1600 was a respectable consensus by 1700. Indeed, it was geography that dictated this fact of life for the British Isles. Like the Dutch – from whom they learned so much about these matters – the British were closed off from easy access to the sources of mineral wealth. They could acquire wealth only by trade. In this they possessed the good fortune to sit athwart one of the busiest trade routes in the world. Tapping into the trade that flowed besides its shores was England's great opportunity. It was this recognition that lay behind the general understanding that the economic future of the nation lay in its aspiration to be the "universal merchant to the world."[10]

Contemporaries understood that the political economy that emerged in the late seventeenth century was composed of the three complementary segments of manufacture, commerce and finance. As one writer in 1722 put it:

> though our lot is so fortunately ordered for us, that in manufacturing of many of our own commodities (which are the product of our nation only) and which we are risen to a great degree of perfection in; yet the balance of our treasures and riches must be produced from a free and flourishing trade; otherwise we shall soon become as poor and defenseless as the most barren, arbitrary country in Europe. Our trading in all ages past, sufficiently has demonstrated, that the opulence of the kingdom can only arise from hence.[11]

There was a clear insight as to the key importance of the balance of trade and of the complexities of its various elements. In 1713 Charles King listed a series of measures that constituted good and bad trade. Among the former were exports of manufactured goods, imports of materials to be made into goods for either home or export consumption, the imports of commodities to be exported, the exchange of various manufacturers and commodities and the carrying of goods from one country to another. According to this schema, bad trade consisted of trade that diminished rather than increased the circulation of goods, such as the import of luxuries that diminished the demand for home products.[12]

---

[10] These were the words of William Stockton quoted in Harper, *English Navigation Laws*, pp. 12–13; Sir Francis Brewster, *Essays on Trade and Navigation: In Five Parts* (London, 1694), p. 1; Sir Walter Raleigh quoted in Lawrence Stone, "Introduction," in Stone (ed.), *An Imperial State at War: Britain from 1689 to 1815* (London, 1994), p. 25; Josiah Child, "Great Honour and Advantage of the East India Trade," in Child, *Selected Works 1668–1697* (Farnborough, 1968), p. 16.

[11] *The Nature and Weight of the Taxes of the Nation* (London, 1722), pp. 18–24 (quote, pp. 18–19).

[12] Charles King, *The British Merchant* (repr., London, 1743 [1713]), vol. I, pp. 2–3, 18–19, 24–27; John Cary, *An Essay on the State of England in Relation to Its Trade, Its Poor and Its Taxes for Carrying on the Present War Against France* (Bristol, 1695), p. 178; [Henry Martyn], *Considerations upon the East India Trade* (London, 1701), pp. 36–37. There was a sophisticated attitude toward trade deficits on particular accounts. It was pointed out in

Naturally, there was disagreement as to where the maximum benefit was to be gained in trade – in home or foreign markets – and how the circulation of trade could best be encouraged – by protection or various forms of free trade. These controversies led to arguments as to whether one particular segment of the trade universe should receive special consideration over others. There was continual tension between the interests of land, commerce and manufacture, as the spokespersons for each pressed their respective cases. Such arguments were recognized as the legitimate pleading of special interest groups. Trade was understood to comprise diverse elements that were interconnected and mutually dependent.[13] Within this context, manufacture was only one segment in the wider system of trade and commerce. The importance of a vital manufacturing sector was generally accepted, but its frequent claims for protection were always subject to the skepticism of economic theorists. Protecting industries in Britain that could produce goods more cheaply in India, for example, was disapproved of because it diminished the general circulation of trade upon which national wealth was recognized to depend. The most powerful argument for protecting industry was its employment of the poor.[14]

Exports from domestic manufacture played an important but limited role in the political economy of commercial imperialism. Indeed, the British economy was not an export-led economy until after 1870. Over the years 1700 to 1851 the share of exports in the national output increased from about 8 percent to over 19 percent, and the contribution of industrial output to national product remained steady at about one-quarter. Yet there was no linear pattern to the place of exports in the national product; their proportion ebbed and flowed over the different

the case of the East Indian trade that trade deficits were not a drain on the national wealth if they brought increased numbers of goods into circulation which either were used in Britain or which it sold abroad. Similarly, sending money abroad for pitch and tar for the navy was beneficial because it enabled a large shipping industry to be supported which employed large numbers of people as well as adding to the carrying trade.

[13] Thus, for example, clothing manufacturers argued that the ability of manufacturing to sell abroad was the basis of national prosperity and therefore justified legislative protection of local industry. John Cary, a Bristol merchant and worthy, argued that the importance of the wool trade as a source of domestic employment should lead England to prevent the development of such an industry in Ireland – whose land and people, he argued, were much better suited to husbandry and agriculture. Still, he went on, if it was felt necessary for the Irish plantation to have industry, a linen manufacture should be developed that would attract French refugees and in which Ireland would possess a comparative advantage: Cary, *Essay on the State of England*, pp. 90–93, 102–03, 109–10.

[14] [Martyn,] *Considerations upon the East India Trade*, pp. 60–61. But in other contexts, particularly relations with France, Martyn was not a free trader. See Cary, *Essay on the State of England*, p. 178, for the protectionist case. Yet even Cary recognized that the "interest of England doth consist in improving its trade, product and manufactures" (ibid.).

periods. Until 1780 the export portion of national output remained basically stable. The final twenty years of the eighteenth century saw a rapid growth that increased their share to over 15 percent. This was partly, though by no means wholly, due to the expansion of cotton industry exports in the 1790s. However, there was no breakthrough after 1800 to a new kind of export economy. The contribution of the export sector to the national economy retained its eighteenth-century pattern well into the nineteenth century. Until the 1860s the contribution of exports to national income hovered between 15 percent and 19 percent. But then a new pattern appeared which signaled the key role that exports were to play thereafter in the wellbeing of the British economy. During the 1870s the ratio of exports to national income leapt to over 25 percent, and by 1914 this figure had grown to over 30 percent, where it was to remain.[15]

British exports drew from a very narrow range of industries. Cloth and iron were the key export categories in the eighteenth century as they were to be in the nineteenth. The reliance on a small number of industries for exports was reinforced dramatically by the sectoral growth of the textile industry in the late eighteenth century. But dependence on one or two leading export industries was not a creation of the industrial revolution. Furthermore, by the middle of the eighteenth century, an imbalance of trade between imports and exports was apparent. It was a gap that was bridged, of course, by invisible exports.

Invisible exports earned 30 percent of the value of exported products by 1820. By the end of our period they were earning over 50 percent of the value of exports – another sign that the contours of the political economy were being redrawn. Equally worthy of note were the changes in the source of these invisible earnings between the early and later parts of our period. Until the 1870s returns from the shipping trade were the major contributor of invisible earnings. This proclaimed the commercial bias in the national economy and the importance to national wealth of the earnings on the movement of physical goods. After the 1850s, however, with the coming of free trade, the more purely financial element in the

[15] For this, see François Crouzet, "Toward an Export Economy: British Exports During the Industrial Revolution," *Explorations in Economic History*, 17 (1980), pp. 48–93, and Crouzet, *The Victorian Economy* (New York, 1982), pp. 114–19; S. B. Saul, "The Export Economy, 1870–1914," *Yorkshire Bulletin of Economic and Social Research*, 17 (1965), pp. 5–18; Saul, *British Economy Since 1700*, pp. 107–08, 218–19; Albert H. Imlah, *Economic Elements in the Pax Britannica: Studies in British Foreign Trade in the Nineteenth Century* (New York, 1958), pp. 20–41; Crafts, *British Economic Growth*, pp. 130–31; Daunton, *Progress and Poverty*, pp. 375–79. In comparison to other countries, of course, manufacturing always occupied a prominent place in the pattern of Britain's trade. In France, for example, exports made up a mere 6 percent of the national output in the 1840s – less than half that of Britain at the same moment.

balance sheet of invisible earnings displaced these returns from commerce. The export of capital for investment overseas began in earnest after midcentury. By the 1870s it was the return on capital invested in the empire and elsewhere that constituted the main source of invisible earnings. A political economy of financial imperialism had replaced the political economy of commercial imperialism.[16]

Commerce meant trade and the root of commerce was the carrying trade. During the seventeenth century, the British had learnt from the Dutch the importance for economic power of controlling the transit of goods. There was a fundamental difference, however, between the Dutch carrying trade and the British carrying trade. The Dutch had used their control over trade flows to stimulate manufacturing activity such as a processing industry in tobacco or coffee. The British interest in the carrying trade was limited to simple warehousing. With the exception of calico printing, little industrial activity was ignited by the British carrying trade. Indeed, the commercial policy of the state discouraged goods from staying in Britain long enough for them even to be unpacked. An ever increasing number of "drawbacks" were written into customs regulations that allowed revenue on goods that were imported to be recovered if they were subsequently reexported. The aim of British commercial imperialism was to exploit its geographical location and its empire and thereby to become the warehouse of the world. Only then was there an interest in also becoming the workshop of the world.[17]

The reexport trade was the key to understanding the political economy of commerce during this period. From 1660 (and particularly from the early 1700s) the reexport trade became the most significant economic development. This was a sudden and very sharp growth. In about forty years at the end of the seventeenth century reexports grew from virtually nothing to about one-third of total exports by 1700. By the middle of the eighteenth century, reexports were nearer to 40 percent of total exports. Indeed, during the first half of the eighteenth century reexports grew faster than foreign trade as a whole. Throughout the eighteenth century reexports trebled in value, whereas domestic exports doubled. Until the

---

[16] Charles Wilson, *England's Apprenticeship*, pp. 263–65; Ingham, *Capitalism Divided?*, pp. 96–97; Imlah, *Economic Elements in the Pax Britannica*, p. 49. In the case of India, for example, there was very little British capital invested until after 1850. Indeed, in the 1820s and 1830s over £20 million was withdrawn from the Indian money markets. See C. A. Bayly, *Indian Society and the Making of the British Empire* (Cambridge, 1988), p. 119.

[17] The reexport trade has been largely ignored by historians, yet its importance to both economic activity and the political economy seems to be undeniable. The reexport trade likely tended to divert goods away from home consumption. Calico printing was one of the few exceptions to this rule, as an industry that was stimulated by the reexport trade in this period. For a useful study, see David Ormrod, "English Re-exports and the Dutch Staplemarket in the Eighteenth Century," in D. C. Coleman and Peter Mathias (eds.), *Enterprise and History: Essays in Honour of Charles Wilson* (Cambridge, 1984), pp. 89–115.

middle of the eighteenth century, the import trade was dependent upon reexports, after which it became more an autonomous reflection of domestic needs. The rise of the reexport industry was a significant revolution in trade. Yet its effects were not to stimulate British industry. The imperative of reexports lay in finding large amounts to commercial capital to finance trade flows, not in finding investment for British industry.[18]

The reexport trade was at least a two-way street. It was fueled by the explosion of demand in European markets and also by the rapid development of the North American markets for manufactured products. The concentration of trade flows on Britain meant the creation of a large sterling area that involved intra-European trade which was otherwise unconnected with Britain. But since all flows went through Britain, so all credits and debits were settled in sterling. Two-thirds of the calico imported from India in 1700 passed through on its way to the Netherlands, and this figure was about the same forty years later. Similarly, between one-third and one-half of imported linen was reexported. Exotic products like tobacco and sugar went to Europe in equivalent proportions. Reexports thus became integral to Britain's economic makeup and made a crucial contribution to its wealth and balance of trade. This continued throughout the nineteenth century. Indeed, the coming of free trade reinforced the preexisting patterns established from the late seventeenth century. Increases in yearly reexport values outstripped those of exports or imports as Britain took advantage of the general European economic expansion of the period.[19]

The reexport trade implied that Britain should become the warehouse of the world. From the introduction of the Navigation Acts in the 1650s, the tariff policy of the state was consistently designed to facilitate the diversion of trade through British ports. The Navigation Acts were crucial to the development of the Atlantic economy, which accounted for 60 percent of British trade by the 1770s. "By these means England created for herself a great confluence of commodities out of flows in both directions, which otherwise need not have touched her shores at all."[20]

[18] Charles Wilson, *England's Apprenticeship*, pp. 161, 169–70; Deane, *The First Industrial Revolution*, p. 63; Lee, *British Economy Since 1700*, p. 116; Ralph Davis, "English Foreign Trade, 1660–1700," *Economic History Review*, 7 (1954), p. 162. Ralph Davis, "English Foreign Trade, 1700–1774," *English Historical Review*, 15 (1960), pp. 291–92, has slightly different figures for the eighteenth century.

[19] Jacob Price, "What Do Merchants Do?: Reflections on British Overseas Trade, 1660–1790," *Journal of Economic History*, 49, 2 (June 1989), pp. 267–84; N. B. Harte, "The Rise of Protection and the English Linen Trade, 1690–1790," in Harte and Keith Ponting (eds.), *Textile History and Economic History* (Manchester, 1973), p. 85; Cain and Hopkin, *British Imperialism*, p. 64; Mathias, *First Industrial Nation*, pp. 93, 97, 101, 307; Imlah, *Economic Elements in the Pax Britannica*, pp. 169–71.

[20] D. W. Jones, *War and Economy in the Age of William III and Marlborough* (Oxford, 1988), pp. 49–51.

No export from the empire could go to an extra-European area save from a home port and all important imports had first to be landed in Britain. The Navigation Acts were of particular relevance to British shipping, of course. Other legislation addressed the issue of warehousing more precisely.[21]

As early as 1700 an act was passed establishing bonded warehouses for the reexport of Indian calicoes. This act began London's rise as "the great warehouse for the store of goods destined for other parts of the world." Walpole's trade policy was entirely designed to encourage the expansion of the warehouse system. It was to this end that he removed most export duties in the early 1720s, and his general excise proposal of 1733 was partly motivated by the same considerations. In the 1730s, the cumbersome means of collecting and then rebating duties on reexports was reformed. An act of 1803 removed all responsibility from the merchant for the bonding of goods and a bill of 1823 removed transit duties on linens and silks in the hope that it would encourage the trade in these goods to flow through London.[22]

This political economy had been constructed with blood and calculation. Markets needed to be created, and trade required protection, and these demanded the mobilization of state power, either directly or through surrogates like the great trading companies. The recognition by economists from the 1690s that a long purse rather than a long sword was the surest guarantee of military victory did not imply a pacifist policy. It implied the need for deterrence through a strong navy and command of the seas. The idea that peace and trade were two sides of the same coin was a luxury that the nineteenth century could afford only because of Britain's success in removing all effective competitors to its position as warehouser to the world by the early nineteenth century. When Cobden talked about the wastefulness of expenditure on empire – and when modern-day historians naively pronounce him right – he was privileged to

[21] There were many suggestions as to how to make Britain the warehouse of the world. In a very early statement of what was to become free trade policy, for example, it was proposed that customs duties be abolished and replaced by an excise tax payable only when goods were sold, and not assessed, therefore, on goods passing through Britain. Other ideas were even more "modern" and proposed the establishment of certain ports that would be tax-free zones. See Brewster, *Essays on Trade and Navigation*, pp. 33–34; Harper, *English Navigation Laws*, pp. 12–13, 43–44. Marshall, *Mercantilism and the East India Trade*, pp. 114–15; Daunton, *Progress and Poverty*, pp. 536–37.

[22] Paul Langford, *The Excise Crisis: Society and Politics in the Age of Walpole* (Oxford, 1975), pp. 31–33; James Henderson, *Some Observations on the Great Commercial Benefits That Will Result from the Warehousing Bill* (London, 1823), p. 13 (quote). The debate over the bill of 1823 replayed similar debates over the course of the previous century. The home manufacturers were largely opposed to removal of the duties – which they had secured in the first place as a protectionist measure. The supporters of this version of free trade argued that the aim of policy should be to make Britain the emporium of the world.

speak from the security of a "free trade empire" that rested on the basis of an already established commercial imperialism.[23]

The system of commercial imperialism was built upon coercion and war. Slavery was the ultimate form of coercion. The importance of slavery to Britain's economic development has, of course, been a matter of deep controversy.[24] Yet, in the final analysis, the matter should not be decided by the economic returns that slavery may or may not have generated. Slavery was integral to the imperial and the domestic economy, as eighteenth-century observers like Joseph Gee and Malachy Postlethwayt clearly recognized. Slavery may not have directed a stream of surplus capital into new technologies, but it was hardly without a presence in the dynamics of national finance. West Indian mortgages were a major part of the London financial market. The £37 million invested in the West Indies in the 1770s produced returns that were then expended domestically. The consequences of slavery were particularly evident at the regional level. This was true not only for the generation of goods, but also for the development of networks of credit and fiscal exchange in Lancashire, lowland Scotland and the Bristol region.[25]

Slavery was a system of managing and controlling labor. Yet even after the end of chattel slavery in 1833, coercion continued to play a central role in the labor system of commercial imperialism. Indeed, emancipation tended to make the problem of labor discipline even more intractable. Throughout the middle of the nineteenth century the difficulties of securing output from ex-slaves remained a central preoccupation of colonial policy. Thus, a variety of coercive labor systems continued to be employed that were not seriously disrupted until the very end of our period – and in some cases not until well beyond that date. Indentured

---

[23] Cary, *Essay on the State of England*, p. 170; Brewster, *Essays on Trade and Navigation*, p. 5. See also Lance Davis and Robert Huttenback, *Mammon and the Pursuit of Empire* (Cambridge, 1988), which argues the unprofitability of empire in general but also shows that empire was extremely profitable to certain upper-class interest groups.

[24] The denial of the imperial context of Britain's economic development is argued in Patrick O'Brien, "European Economic Development: The Contribution of the Periphery," *Economic History Review*, 35, 1 (February 1982), pp. 1–18; and Patrick O'Brien, "The Costs and Benefits of British Imperialism 1846–1914," *Past and Present*, 120 (August 1988), pp. 163–200.

[25] Eric Williams, *Capitalism and Slavery* (Chapel Hill, 1944); Hudson, *Industrial Revolution*, pp. 194–99; David Eltis, *Economic Growth and the Ending of the Transatlantic Slave Trade* (Oxford, 1987), pp. 1–16, and *passim*; Seymour Drescher, *Capitalism and Antislavery: British Mobilization in Comparative Perspective* (Oxford, 1987), pp. 1–24; Barbara L. Solow and Stanley L. Engerman, *British Capitalism and Caribbean Slavery* (Cambridge, 1987), pp. 4–11, 72–73, 103–05. For a revealing study of the interpenetration of the credit networks of slave trading with other kinds of trading, see B. L. Anderson, "The Lancashire Bill System and Its Liverpool Practitioners: The Case of a Slave Merchant," in W. H. Chaloner and Barrie M. Ratcliffe (eds.), *Trade and Transport: Essays in Economic History in Honour of T. S. Willan* (Manchester, 1977), pp. 59–97.

labor was the most common substitution for slavery, although it was by no means universally successful in saving plantation economies. Nevertheless, where it was successful – as in Mauritius, which received over 300,000 Indians between 1842 and 1857 – indentured labor allowed the plantations to be run on the same lines as in slave days.[26]

Indentured labor meant coerced labor. Thus, the august institution of the law was trundled in to replace a system of social authority that rested on the ownership of human bodies. Liberal politicians fondly imagined that they were breaking with the past in prohibiting slavery in the empire and in propagating its abolition elsewhere. Yet at the height of the age of laissez-faire, the state was more deeply involved in regulating the social relations of empire than at any time before. The regulation of the supply and demand of labor, the conditions under which indenture could be practiced, even the subsidization of immigration from India itself were all willingly fathered by the noninterventionist liberal state. After emancipation master-and-servant law was widely adopted in the colonies. It remained a crucial technique of labor management throughout the colonial period. Indeed, this body of legal control was often the first application of British law to indigenous populations.[27]

[26] As undersecretary of the colonies, Herman Merivale pointed out: "in civilized countries the laborer, though free, is by a law of nature dependent on capitalists; in colonies this dependence must be created by artificial means." The classic work on indentured labor is Hugh Tinker, *A New System of Slavery: The Export of Indian Labour Overseas 1830–1920* (London, 1974). See also David Northrup, *Indentured Labor in the Age of Imperialism 1843–1922* (Cambridge, 1995); Marianne D. Ramesar, "From Slavery to Indenture: Forced Labour in the Political Economy of Mauritius 1834–1867," in Kay Saunders (ed.), *Indentured Labour in the British Empire 1834–1820* (London, 1984), p. 42 (quote); M. D. North-Coombes, "From Slavery to Indenture: Forced Labour in the Political Economy of Mauritius 1834–1867," in Saunders, *Indentured Labour in the British Empire*, p. 92; C. A. Bayly, *Imperial Meridian: The British Empire and the World 1780–1830* (London, 1989), pp. 150–55, 220–22.

[27] In Mauritius, for example, ordinances in 1849 and 1862 progressively regulated the length of labor contracts and in 1867 a labor code was issued that imposed regulations on the behavior and movement of those who had served out their indentures and were now nominally "free." For Mauritius, see North-Coombes, "From Slavery to Indenture," pp. 78–125. In the Hong Kong colony it was embodied in the ordinance of 1847, and in the Ceylonese tea plantations it was introduced in the 1860s initially to deal with the troublesome issue of absenteeism. See Anthony Woodiwiss, "Labour Law in Hong Kong: From Laissez-Faire to Enforceable Benevolence," in Marcel van der Linden and Richard Price (eds.), *Collective Labor Law in Historical Perspective* (Bern, forthcoming).

The domestic economy was no exception to the tightening bonds of labor coercion over the period 1690 to the 1870s. Master-and-servant law became *more* coercive over the period and was widely used in the nineteenth century. See D. C. Woods, "The Operation of the Master and Servant Law in the Black Country 1858–1875," *Midland History*, 7 (1982), pp. 97–111. See also Christopher Tomlins, "Subordination, Authority, Law: Subjects in Labor History," *International Review of Labour and Working-Class History*, 47 (Spring 1995), pp. 56–90; Trygve Tholfsen, *Working-Class Radicalism in Mid-Victorian England* (London, 1976), pp. 180–84.

War is coercion under a different name. And war was a crucial agent in the growth of this imperial economy. Yet war was fraught with ambiguity. Its losses and risks frequently seemed to far outweigh its potential gains. The origins of the Cobdenite and Gladstonian conviction of the economic wastefulness of war lies deep in the experience of the eighteenth century when national bankruptcy seemed to loom with every imperial adventure. Nevertheless, historically speaking, if war posed clear dangers to commercial imperialism, it also offered opportunities and stimulants to economic expansion.

The successful development of the reverbatory furnace for nonferrous metals in the 1690s was a direct result of the military needs for copper and it was a process that could be applied to processing other minerals such as lead. The war of the Austrian succession in the 1740s was important in expanding the demand for iron and in seeing the replacement of charcoal-smelted iron by pig iron. The Seven Years War had the same effect in the textile trades. The wars against revolutionary France marked the most intensive development yet experienced by the British iron industry. Naturally, the impact of these wars extended beyond demand for heavy goods. The shipbuilding industry benefited greatly from the demand for ships. Each war tended to result in markets gained and an expanded commercial empire.[28]

This expansion was not just a function of successful treaty making by the British. In the early 1700s, for example, while Marlborough was rampaging around the continent, British traders were taking advantage of the crippled state of most European competitors and were busy enjoying an export boom to Portugal, Russia, the Low Countries and Germany. The successes of the allied armies were used to shut the French out of the areas conquered. Further east the disruption in Poland and the Baltic region caused by the Swedish wars opened up more opportunities. In addition, the gold boom in Brazil provided opportunities for Britain to enter that expanding market while its competitors were occupied elsewhere. Under these circumstances the balance-of-payments problems that had accompanied the wars of the 1690s were avoided. The ultimate consequence was that access was guaranteed to markets that were to fuel a trading expansion greater than anything that had been achieved over the previous century.[29]

The general pattern until the end of the nineteenth century was for Britain to benefit in terms of economic development from the wars. They were the essential ancillary to an expansive commercial imperialism and

[28] See A. H. John, "War and the English Economy 1700–1763," *Economic History Review*, 7 (1955), pp. 329–44.
[29] D. W. Jones, *War and Economy*, pp. 160–97, 210, 311.

the one seeming exception – the loss of the American colonies – in fact turned out to prove that rule. Although the wars of the last half of the eighteenth century are often thought to have retarded economic growth and depressed standards of living, there is much uncertainty about this. Capital markets were decentralized and regionalized (an issue to which we shall return), and there was considerable space between central institutions of finance and local ones. In this context, government spending would not necessarily suck up savings that otherwise would be productively employed elsewhere. Government spending reached unprecedented levels during the French wars and heavy new taxes were imposed to meet the expenses. Yet even then there is little evidence that price levels were adversely affected and on the whole government spending probably worked to stimulate and maintain aggregate demand. In any case, internal development was not much affected by wars; the capital markets continued to supply capital needs and interest rates were not increased.[30]

Nevertheless, war threatened the fragile edifice of commerce. The effects of war were not to be foreseen, and contained a dangerous ambiguity for a trading nation. If war was sometimes necessary to protect and expand commercial relationships and markets, it was also true that war could disrupt the increasingly complex networks of trade and commercial exchange that produced national wealth. The wars of the second half of the eighteenth century probably had the effect of retarding growth at home and depressing living standards. As soon as William III was placed on the throne and enlisted England in his various warring enterprises in Europe, wails of anguish wafted up from port towns like Great Yarmouth protesting the difficulties that were caused by the consequent "stop of trade."[31]

Even more seriously, war imposed new fiscal demands upon the state. Financial crisis tended to converge with war. Only one of the financial crises of the eighteenth century was not attributable to war. Similarly, recessions were initiated by the interruption of commerce by war and by the accompanying price inflation, especially of manufactured goods. Indeed, the fear of national bankruptcy as a result of the fiscal strains of war is a theme that began in the 1690s and reached its apotheosis in Gladstone. Certainly the events of the 1690s provided ample evidence of the threats to fiscal stability. Trade was interrupted, credit and transfer

[30] Gary Hawke, "Reinterpretations of the Industrial Revolution," and Patrick O'Brien, "Political Preconditions for the Industrial Revolution," in Patrick O'Brien and Quinault, *Industrial Revolution and British Society*, pp. 73–74, 125, 148; J. L. Anderson, "Aspects of the Effect on the British Economy of the Wars Against France, 1793–1815," *Australian Economic History Review*, 12, 1 (March 1972), pp. 1–20.

[31] Perry Gauci, *Politics and Society in Great Yarmouth 1660–1722* (Oxford, 1996), p. 186.

difficulties were endemic, exports to Europe suffered greatly. Too many resources were evidently being directed away from trade by the war. Severe balance-of-payments problems in the 1690s were resolved only – it is guessed – by clipping coins, trade in which made up the deficit. The experience of the early 1700s was, as we have seen, quite different. Still, war was both the handmaiden of and the damoclean sword for a commercial and trading imperialism, although throughout our period its much feared apocalyptic consequences were deferred.[32]

The structures of finance

War invented the institutions of finance capitalism in Britain. Financing war had always been a challenge for the state. The prolonged wars that William brought with him to England in the 1690s generated an insatiable appetite for money. The strategy of the "double forward" involved a huge land army in Flanders and various naval offensives in the Mediterranean and Northern Europe and, later, actions in the Americas. Although we can now see the 1690s as the crucial turning point in the creation of the institutions of national finance, it was by no means obvious at the time that the financial revolution had occurred. There was a frantic search for initiatives that would effectively mobilize capital to meet the fiscal strains of war. And there were moments in the desperate years of the 1690s when the fiscal structures teetered on the edge of collapse.

The scale of fiscal demands was unprecedented, and no devices that could easily satisfy them stood readily to hand. Thus, a groping experimentation ran through the proposed means of mobilizing capital to fund the wars. Proposals for various lotteries were floated. The Tories were very keen on a Land Bank which would use the security of land to raise money, but this soon failed due to the absence of liquidity. The great trading companies were tapped for public loans. The annuity was invented as a form of public investment in the state. The ultimate linchpin in the system of finance came to be the Bank of England. Yet it established itself only after a long period of insecurity when its very survival was at times threatened and it had to jostle hard to secure its status as banker to the state. It took the crisis of the South Sea Bubble – which was actually a struggle for control of the national debt – in 1720–21 and the effective destruction of its rival, the South Sea Company, to ensure the primacy of

---

[32] D. W. Jones, *War and Economy*, p. 65; John Brewer, *The Sinews of Power: War, Money and the English State 1688–1783* (London, 1989), pp. 190–99; Richard Shannon, *Gladstone*, vol. I, *1809–1865* (London, 1982), pp. 286–87; Olive Anderson, *A Liberal State at War: English Politics and Economics During the Crimean War* (London, 1967), pp. 195–97.

the Bank. The function of the Bank was to superintend the raising of capital for state finances and to administer the national debt. From the beginning, then, the sector of public finance was inextricably tied into war and imperial expansion.[33]

The national debt was the fundamental fact of public finance. Throughout the eighteenth century, the national debt grew exponentially until it swallowed about half of all public revenue in service charges. As much as three-quarters of the annual budget by the 1780s was absorbed in the distribution of dividends on loans raised in the City. Small wonder, then, that the state was the fastest-growing sector of the economy in the eighteenth century. Throughout most of this period the national debt and the needs of state finance shaped the role of the City of London. The City had long been a center of financial transactions and exchange and a close relationship to government was nothing new. But the content of the relationship changed after the 1690s when the City was bestowed with the permanent function of administering the state's fiscal needs and mediating the relationship between the government and its financiers. This role runs throughout the period, although there are important changes in the role of the Bank once the pressure to fund war had been released after the defeat of Napoleon.[34]

The relationship between the Bank and the state was marked by a reciprocal dependence colored by mutual suspicion. This was true, also, of the relationships between the state and the other great trading companies. If government needed the networks of the "monied interest" to fund its policies, so the men of finance needed the patronage of government to gain access to the loan calls, as well as government support for the periodic renewal of their charters. Yet even on the matter of charter renewal, the advantage did not lie with the state. Chatham failed to push the East India Company into a fair sharing of its Bengali *diwan* in 1767, for example. And until 1781 renewal of the Bank's charter was

[33] John Briscoe, *A Discourse on the Late Funds of the Million Act, Lottery Act and the Bank of England* (London, 1696); J. H. Clapham, *The Bank of England: A History* (Cambridge, 1958), vol. I, pp. 24–26; H. V. Bowen, "The Bank of England During the Long Eighteenth Century, 1694–1820," in Richard Roberts and David Kynaston (eds.), *The Bank of England: Money, Power and Influence 1694–1994* (Oxford, 1995), p. 4; D. W. Jones, *War and Economy*, pp. 11–12, 24–25, 289–98; Charles Wilson, *England's Apprenticeship*, pp. 313–14; Brewer, *Sinews of Power*, pts. 2, 3; P. G. M. Dickson, *The Financial Revolution in England: A Study in the Development of Public Credit 1688–1756* (London, 1967), pp. 387–89; D. W. Jones, "London Merchants and the Crisis of the 1690s," in Peter Clark and Paul Slack (eds.), *Crisis and Order in English Towns 1500–1700* (London, 1972), pp. 321–25; E. L. Hargreaves, *The National Debt* (London, 1930), pp. 4–9; Philip Lawson, *The East India Company: A History* (London, 1993), pp. 54–55.

[34] Ingham, *Capitalism Divided?*, p. 106; Cain and Hopkin, *British Imperialism*, pp. 62–63, 66–67, 71–72, 74.

always negotiated on its own initiative during war, which was exactly the moment when it could extract the best concessions from government.[35]

Tension between the government of the day and the Bank was persistent. Yet once the Bank had been granted the right of virtual monopoly note issue in 1709 it occupied in effect a very strong position. The new monetary policy of the gold standard introduced at the end of the Napoleonic wars presented an opportunity to redefine Bank–government relations, with Peel clearly asserting the primacy of the state. Yet the Bank continued to possess a wide area of autonomy, and negotiations between the two tended to resemble those between two sovereign powers. The tradition of hostility to the overweening power of the Bank was to be found well into the middle of the nineteenth century, especially among radicals. It was one of Gladstone's hopes that the Post Office Savings Bank would establish an alternative channel to the Bank for government access to capital. As late as the 1890s, Chancellor of the Exchequer Sir William Harcourt was alarming his officials with talk of looking outside the Bank for cheaper money to tide government operations over. Such threats, of course, were largely empty.[36]

The Bank was a force to be reckoned with from the beginning of its history. Within a year of its foundation, for example, the king himself was reduced to appearing before the Court of Governors to protest at the harsh bargain it was trying to drive for a new loan. In 1710 Anne was politely told to her face that it would be a bad idea to replace Sunderland as lord treasurer with Godolphin – just as Ramsey Macdonald was provided with sensible policy advice by Montague Norman over 200 years later. Although Anne, unlike Macdonald, rejected the Bank's counsel, the important fact is that the Bank felt free enough to make it in the first place. Obviously, accommodation required give and take: in 1742, for example, during negotiations for the renewal of its charter, the Bank was pressured into lowering the interest rate for government loans. These kinds of negotiations were, presumably, commonplace between the state and the purses of finance. Certainly, all three major companies – the Bank and the East India and South Sea Companies – cooperated in 1737 to block Walpole's attempt at a rate reduction and again in 1749 when Pelham successfully negotiated one.[37]

---

[35] H. V. Bowen, *Revenue and Reform: The Indian Problem in British Politics 1757–1773* (Cambridge, 1991), pp. 48–66.

[36] Bowen, "Bank of England," pp. 5–8, 17; David Kynaston, "The Bank of England and the Government," in Roberts and Kynaston, *Bank of England*, pp. 24–25.

[37] Dickson, *Financial Revolution*, pp. 201–04; Clapham, *Bank of England*, vol. I, pp. 38–48, 73–80, 94–95; Sutherland, *East India Company*, p. 23. The Bank established an early primacy over the other companies. Between 1694 and 1744 it held ninety loans totaling £8 million from the East India Company.

The ambiguous reciprocity of the relationship between the state and the Bank followed quite inevitably from the Bank's role as administrator to the finances of government. Initially responsible for the temporary loans and advances (the floating debt) that the government needed, the Bank soon took over the long-term annuities (the funded debt) that had proved so effective a method of raising money. In 1710 it took over administration of the government lottery. By the 1750s both the long- and short-term loan market were controlled by financial institutions led by the Bank. There was no original intention that the Bank would ascend to this fiscal hegemony. Still, when Lord North made his famous declar- ation about the Bank in 1781 that "from long habit and usage of many years, [the Bank] was part of the constitution," he was merely registering what – in fact, if not by intention – the Bank had been from the very beginning.[38] Although it was seldom free of political tension, the process of mobilizing capital for state needs was originally a relatively open process. In 1693 over 1,200 individuals were making advances to the government on the guarantee of the land tax; by 1750 this was down to 106. In the beginning Parliament had issued the call for loans which was intended to avoid the suspicion of cabals. The disadvantage, however, was that it complicated negotiations, and any failure to raise the required loan threatened the credibility of foreign policy. A more discrete conduct, therefore, began to be instituted, which removed the process from the public view. Before any public announcement of a float, private contact and discussions between the treasury, the Bank, the trading companies and certain leading financiers would allow the conditions of the loan to be prenegotiated. Each financier represented a list of others whom he would recruit, usually including a goodly number of members of Parliament. Once it was clear that all parties could be satisfied by the conditions, the subscription lists would be closed and the loan publicly announced.[39]

This system had the advantage of avoiding the risk of embarrassment. Equally it created the basis for oligarchy. Those outside the magic circles

[38] D. W. Jones, *War and Economy*, p. 13; Hargreaves, *National Debt*, pp. 11–12, 16–18; Clapham, *Bank of England*, vol. I, p. 73. We should also note that the stock exchange too was a product of this expanded financial sector, and also intimately connected to the body of the state. Until the 1690s the London stock market had existed only in embryonic form for the purchase and sale of mainly great trading company securities. But in 1692, even before the Bank was created, the practice of selling annuities to raise money had been introduced. Combined with the various other paper securities – such as lotteries – that were floated in the 1690s, this greatly increased the business of the stock exchange which from the beginning was the major market for government securities.

[39] See Clapham, *Bank of England*, vol. I, pp. 54, 58, 64, for the case of William Lowndes as instructive in the interpenetration of personnel between finance and politics. Lowndes moved between banking, the treasury and Parliament from the 1680s through the 1730s and was in on most of the major developments of state fiscal policy over those years.

were excluded from the opportunities of this business: thus the importance of patronage to secure access, or of a seat in Parliament where votes
could mesh nicely with admission to the subscription list. As Lucy
Sutherland remarked of a slightly later period, "the fortunes of the richest
of the monied men would seem at this time to have been largely made by
satisfying the credit needs of the state, in subscription to government
loans, in government remittances and in financing government contracts." Naturally, doing business in this way tended to disquiet those
individuals and interests excluded from the honey pot. This was the
reality, of course, behind the radical discourse of an interlocking set of
interests parasitically feeding at the public trough that was named "old
corruption." From the 1730s insistent calls began to be heard for an
opening of this process – a campaign that presaged the city radicalism of
the 1760s. Bending to such pressure in 1748 led to a rather neat formulation whereby one agent took care of the traditional inside subscribers and
another dealt with the interlopers. Still, the numbers always remained
quite small. In the 1780s the interests of the 17,000 fund-holders were
presided over by a committee of about sixty merchant bankers.[40]

The structures and procedures of the institutions of state finance
therefore contained an implicit tendency to oligarchy. At the time of the
financial revolution, of course, the City of London was a fairly small
place. In 1696 just over 400 merchants accounted for about two-thirds of
both the import and export trades of London. Thus, the tendency to
oligarchy was strongly developed from the very beginning. Merchant and
political hierarchies were deeply interlocked from the outset, and they
were to remain so in one form or another throughout the period. Between
the years 1734 and 1832, for example, the great London banking families
of the Barings, Drummonds, Martins, Childs, Mackworth-Praeds and
Williamses provided one scion after another for seats in the House of
Commons. Thirty-two bankers who were directors of the Bank of England were also members of Parliament. And from the 1760s, 6 percent of
the House of Commons were in the East India Company interest.[41]

Naturally, the shape and form of oligarchy did not remain unchanged
over the two centuries. The late eighteenth and early nineteenth centuries, for example, were a period of comparative social openness in the

---

[40] Dickson, *Financial Revolution*, pp. 220–26; L. S. Sutherland, "Samson Gideon and the
Reduction of the Rate of Interest, 1749–1750," *Economic History Review*, 1st ser., 16, 1
(1946), pp. 18–24; Sutherland, "City of London," pp. 42–48 (quote, p. 42); Ingham,
Capitalism Divided?, p. 106.

[41] Gerrit Judd, IV, *Members of Parliament 1734–1832* (New Haven, 1955), pp. 62–63, 65. I
should just note that the largest single category of members of Parliament in this period
were those in commerce or trade who outnumbered the manufacturers by forty to one –
or 897 to 29.

City. This was the moment when the institutions of old corruption were being dismantled in accordance with the new political economy of free trade. But the opportunities of gentlemanly capitalism for new members was distinctly limited. And from the middle of the nineteenth century there was a renewed consolidation of the merchant banking sector around a oligarchy whose families bore names that were familiar to such circles in the eighteenth century. The Barings, Grenfells and others continued their prominence on the Court of Directors of the Bank and their representation in political circles. After the 1870s a further process of renewal was instituted. Much attention at that time was given to the few Jews who attained prominence, or the new South African millionaires. But the real story was the close family ties that were forged by marriage alliances of merchant bankers and financially distressed sections of the aristocracy. This was merely a new version of an old pattern. Over the 200–year period covered by this book, the core institutions of financial capital revealed a persistent disposition to consolidate and centralize power within a narrow circle.[42]

The oligarchic tendencies in the world of finance capital did not speak only to the closed nature of this particular segment of the political-economic elite. They were symptomatic also of a functional and geographical separation between the constituent elements of that elite. From the national perspective, the financial, commercial and manufacturing elites were separated by metaphorical and real distances. Geographical location played a very important role in this. London was far removed from the provinces. The heart of commercial and financial capitalism was geographically, socially and politically confined to London. It was true that the eighteenth century saw the growth of regional centers of trading activity which in cities such as Liverpool established a comparative advantage in some sectors. Yet the overall predominance of London is quite notable. In 1700 about three-quarters of overseas trade was conducted through London; by 1800 this had diminished to about two-thirds. Customs revenues tell the same story. Between 1530 and 1730 London paid between 70 and 90 percent of the total customs revenues. In 1750

---

[42] Anthony Webster, "The Political Economy of Trade Liberalization: The East India Company Charter Act of 1813," *Economic History Review*, 43, 3 (1990), pp. 404–19; Michael Lisle-Williams, "Beyond the Market: The Survival of Family Capitalism in the English Merchant Banks," *British Journal of Sociology*, 35, 2 (June 1984), pp. 248–57; Lisle-Williams, "Merchant Banking Dynasties in the English Class Structure: Ownership, Solidarity and Kinship in the City of London, 1850–1960," *British Journal of Sociology*, 35, 3 (September 1984), pp. 331–62. The problem with this analysis is that it treats the emergence of merchant banking oligarchy as a new feature in the late nineteenth century instead of being a particular stage in an older story. The leading families in Lisle-Williams's analysis were prominent also in the eighteenth century; so the case is even stronger, or worse, than he imagines.

London's share of export revenues was 66 percent and, for imports, 71 percent.[43]

The case of finance capital was even clearer. In the 1730s there were probably about 25,000 holders of the public debt. These were drawn mainly from the middling classes – only a minority of the peerage invested in the funds. This large total disguised the small number of large investors, however. Such investors constituted less than 50 percent of the total, but controlled between 70 and 80 percent of the stock. The home addresses of the 2,000 voting proprietors of the Bank of England in 1791 was heavily weighted to London or the Home Counties. Over 1,200 lived in these locations. Only two had Liverpool addresses and only one was a resident of Manchester. This is a fairly stark and simple demonstration of the well-known tendency of finance capital to develop separately from manufacturing capital. The system of finance capital stood apart from and at a goodly distance from the manufacturing sector of the economy.[44]

Finance capital was centered on London, and from the beginning it was intertwined with the structures of the state. It dominated the personnel of elite institutions. Between 1734 and 1832, for example, only twenty-nine members of Parliament belonged to the manufacturing interest and of those only eight entered before 1800. By contrast, in the same period nearly 900 members were engaged in commerce and trade, over 200 were bankers (virtually all of whom were from London) and 700 were drawn from the law.[45] The "monied interest" could rival the landed interest in ease of entry to the centers of policy making. Friction and affinity were therefore inherent in the social relations between land and finance, and it is too easy to assume that the relationship between the patrician landed gentry and the patrician gentlemen of the City of London was unproblematic.

The perpetual needs of the landed interest for access to the resources of finance bound both elites together in a healthily self-interested alliance. Yet this alliance was not without its tensions and it is a mistake to see "gentlemanly capitalism" as unproblematically deploying its power.

---

[43] Penelope Corfield, *The Impact of English Towns* (Oxford, 1982), pp. 71–73; Elizabeth Evelynola Hoon, *The Organisation of the English Customs System 1696–1786* (repr., Newton Abbott, 1968), p. 122.

[44] But it was not entirely a matter of geography. There were further distinctions to be drawn between commerce and finance. In the middle of the eighteenth century virtually all of the aldermen of the City of London were engaged in commerce; relatively few of them were in banking, the orientation of which tended to be more toward the state itself. See Clapham, *Bank of England*, vol. I, p. 288; D. W. Jones, *War and Economy*, pp. 262–66; Dickson, *Financial Revolution*, pp. 300–03; Nicholas Rogers, "Money, Land and Lineage: The Big Bourgeoisie of Hanoverian London," *Social History*, 4, 3 (1979), p. 437.

[45] Judd, *Members of Parliament 1734–1832*, pp. 56–57, 61, 69.

Tension between the landed interest and the merchants of the City of London was a constant theme of the economic literature in the eighteenth century, as it was in the politics of the period where it formed the basis of the country Whig ideology. A sector that fed on the public debt and that possessed its own infrastructure of power separate from that of Parliament threatened to ruin the landed economy by sucking up all funds to service the national debt, reducing the value of land and harming manufacturing by making interest rates too high. This was essentially the critique of the financial sector that was to develop in the twentieth century – except that industry substituted for land as the section that was harmed by the priorities of finance. By the early eighteenth century, the critique of the "monied interest" (as finance capital was called) had developed into the litany of "old corruption" that was to be heard well into the early nineteenth century. It was argued that those who participated in the financial markets and lived off servicing the public funds held a disproportionate influence over the course of the economy which they manipulated to their own advantage.[46]

This scenario possessed more than a grain of truth. Yet it explained only so much of the political reality. It is a mistake to attribute hegemonic status to the financial sector of the economy, even though we can see their dominant presence in certain key institutions. Manufacturers may have had only a minority voice in Parliament, but they hardly went unheard in the corridors of national political power. When a particular trade or industrial interest needed protection, its claims could be brought to the attention of the state by one means or another. The system of virtual representation did not deny middling-class economic interests a voice in Parliament, even if it refused them membership. Local county members, for example, regarded it as their duty to speak for the towns in their constituencies, and manufacturing towns like Birmingham or Manchester had no difficulty in getting matters of concern to local industry on the Parliamentary agenda.[47]

The manufacturing interest did not have the same purchase on the levers of national power as the financial interest. Yet it would be quite

---

[46] H. V. Bowen, "The Pests of Human Society: Stockbrokers, Jobbers and Speculators in Mid-Eighteenth-Century Britain," *History*, 78, 252 (February 1993), pp. 38–53; Briscoe, *Discourse*, pp. 33–35, for an early critique of the monied interest as harmful to land; Charles King, *The British Merchant*, vol. II, pp. 125–26; John Broughton, *The Vindication and Advancement of Our National Constitution and Credit* (London, 1710); *A Short View of the Apparent Dangers and Mischiefs from the Bank of England* (London, 1707); *Englishmen's Eyes Open'd; or All Made to See, Who Are Not Resolved to be Blind: Being The Excise Controversy Set in a New Light* (London, 1734); J. G. A. Pocock, *Virtue, Commerce and History* (Cambridge, 1985), pp. 108–09, 175.

[47] Paul Langford, "Property and Virtual Representation in Eighteenth-Century England," *Historical Journal*, 33, 1 (March 1988), pp. 83–115.

wrong to conclude from this that manufacturing suffered from a marginalized status in the political economy. There are good reasons to argue that the twentieth-century priorities of the political economy have been increasingly distorted by the overweening dominance of finance over industry. Yet the central place that finance and commerce occupied in the political economy did not disable manufacture in the two centuries 1680–1880. Indeed, there was nothing dysfunctional in the relationship between finance and manufacture in this period. To the contrary, the needs of manufacturing were well served by the way the financial sector was structured and operated. By the end of our period, however, this convergence was eroding. The logic of internal and external pressures was beginning to overwhelm the boundaries and constraints of the old system.

Separate but functional: finance and manufacture in the political economy 1680–1880

Britain was a collection of geographical and specialized regions. The financial world was headquartered in the few square miles of the center of London, and this endowed the city with a supreme importance. Yet in the global sense London was just one locality among many. Furthermore, it was a locality whose main tendrils snaked around the Palace of Westminster and then ran outward beyond the shores of the British Isles to the empire. In addition to this grand world of state finance and international commerce, however, there were many provincial worlds whose links to the metropole, while not insubstantial, were incomplete and tenuous. At this level of the region and the locality, a political economy prevailed that allowed finance and manufacturing to collaborate in a responsive and coherent system. Thus, the political economy of this period operated at two levels in a way that was adaptive to the conditions of the time. At the local level the major theme is the regionalization of banking and finance, and at global level the various parts of the political economy were separate and distinct. These two levels expressed a system in which the various elements of the political economy complemented rather than contradicted each other.

The system of public finance centered on the City of London was only weakly linked to the funding of manufacturing enterprise. Industrial finance in the eighteenth century was a local matter, facilitated by associational networks of friends and family and coordinated by attorneys. Such strategies seem to have been particularly important in the early stages of an enterprise or during expansion. They remained the major source of financing of industry throughout our period. At the same time there was a growing need for access to capital markets and sources of credit. In this way manufacturing was increasingly brought into closer contact with the organized sources of capital. It was in response to this need that country banks grew at such rapid rate in the second half of the eighteenth century. In the 1750s there were estimated to be about fifty country banks in England. By 1784 this number had grown to over 100, and from then on expansion was very rapid, so that in the second decade of the nineteenth century there were over 600 country banks in England and Wales. This was a major institutional shift. But it was primarily a local and regional development.[48]

At the regional level, finance capitalism was no stranger to manufacturing industry. Contrary to what used to be thought, British industry did not rely on ploughed-back profits as a source of capital investments. The most important business of the local banks was in supplying short-term credit lines on current accounts. Yet this was not their only function and provincial banks were well accustomed to granting long-term loans on the security of stock or buildings. Indeed, some local banks in this period were created and owned by manufacturing enterprises. Thus there were strong and vibrant connections between the worlds of finance and manufacturing. On the other hand, the regional and local bias of this relationship does indicate the strongly specialized character of the British capital markets. This system was well suited to the typically small-scale needs of manufacture. Large-scale investment for infrastructural needs such as the railways could not be accommodated within this regional banking system and had to seek other sources of capital. German banks were initially drawn into the German industrial arena by the need to fund railway development. In Britain, by contrast, funds for railways were raised on the private capital markets.[49]

In the early and middle years of the nineteenth century, provincial banking continued to grow apace. As the pace of economic growth quickened, the banks' traditional relationship with local industry tightened. Parliamentary legislation worked to strengthen this relationship. The Bank Act of 1826 stimulated local banking by extending note-issuing rights beyond the Bank of England. One of the results of this

[48] Briggs, *Age of Improvement*, p. 31; Elie Halevy, *England in 1815* (New York, 1968), p. 339; L. S. Pressnell, *Country Banks in the Industrial Revolution* (Oxford, 1956).

[49] Hudson, *Industrial Revolution*, pp. 25–26, 95–96; Hudson, *Genesis of Industrial Capital*, pp. 211–17, 219–34, 254–55, 265; M. Miles, "The Money Market in the Early Industrial Revolution: Some Evidence from West Riding Attorneys c. 1750–1800," *Business History*, 23, 2 (July 1981), pp. 127–46; Crouzet, *Capital Formation in the Industrial Revolution*; P. L. Cottrell, *Industrial Finance 1830–1914: The Finance and Organization of English Manufacturing Industry* (London, 1980), pp. 210, 244; Rondo Cameron, with the collaboration of Olga Crisp, Hugh T. Patrick and Richard Tilly, *Banking in the Early Stages of Industrialization* (New York, 1967), pp. 23–27, 35–58.

act was to create local branch networks in the provinces. The late 1820s to the late 1870s was the golden age for provincial banking and the highpoint of their traditional role as financiers for local industry. The London capital market continued to be almost totally uninvolved in industrial floatings and capital formation. Nevertheless, since credit instruments needed to be circulated, there were always pathways between the credit networks of the provinces and the funds of the metropole.[50]

From the early nineteenth century, the institution of bill brokering was the most prominent manifestation of this exchange. The function of the bill broker was to ensure a smooth and reliable circulation of provincial credit by discounting local bills in the metropolitan market. In this bill brokers followed a longstanding tradition of agents in London acting to grease the wheels of provincial commercial credit. Banking remained fragmented throughout this period, with national economic needs being met by local structures and London feeding international commerce. Yet a functional integration between the various levels of the financial and credit systems was created and refined.[51]

This system held good throughout the middle of the nineteenth century. Between about 1820 and the 1870s, however, a different dynamic appeared that was ultimately to displace the procedures and priorities of these structures. Simply stated, the main theme of this transition was the emergence of a liberal political economy. Economic activity came to be regulated by the gold standard, which was monitored and guarded by the Bank of England. Yet the road to that particular (and twentieth-century) economic Jerusalem was hardly straightforward. To the contrary, it was a process of evolution and development in which the implications for the structure of banking and its relationship to manufacture were not implicit, but unfolded only under the pressure of events. In order to make sense of this reorientation it is necessary to begin with a brief consideration of the shifts in the political economy and in economic policy that began to be apparent from the end of the Napoleonic wars.

The defeat of Napoleon ended the century-long struggle between Britain and France for primacy over world commerce. It was hardly surprising, therefore, that a liberal trade policy rapidly came to dominate economic theory and practice in Britain. A liberal trade policy could mean many specific things, of course. But, as it was formulated in the

[50] Daunton, *Progress and Poverty*, pp. 347–52; Hudson, *Genesis of Industrial Capital*, p. 234; Cameron, *Banking in the Early Stages of Industrialization*, pp. 27–31; Charles W. Munn, "The Emergence of Joint-Stock Banking in the British Isles: A Comparative Approach," *Business History*, 30, 1 (January 1988), pp. 69–83; Michael Collins, *Banks and Industrial Finance in Britain 1800–1939* (Basingstoke, 1991), pp. 26–31.

[51] Leland H. Jenks, *The Migration of British Capital to 1875* (repr., New York, 1971 [1927]), pp. 21–22, for the origins of bill brokers; Cottrell, *Industrial Finance*, p. 268.

political world after 1815, two central elements lay at its core. On the one hand, the complex system of trade regulation was adjusted, often with the intention of stimulating reciprocal responses from other nations. And on the other hand a renewed importance was accorded to the gold standard as the arbiter of national economic value. Neither of these strategies was new to the nineteenth century. But the political context and implications for trade liberalization were fundamentally transformed after 1815.

The removal of the threat of constant war transformed public finances. In particular, it diminished the importance of the national debt in state finances. Until 1815 the main function of the financial system was to fund the national debt. After 1815 that constraint was removed and the expertise of the financial system could be shifted to other purposes. Most immediately, however, the removal of the national debt as the main concern of state finance also meant the end of old corruption. The system of institutional alliances between finance, trading companies and the state that was described as old corruption was no longer required to mobilize the fiscal resources of the state. Thus, the institutional and ideological architectures associated with old corruption began to be dismantled in earnest only after 1815. This was a more protracted process than we tend to assume, although the ideological battle against the "protectionism" associated with old corruption was won fairly quickly after the Napoleonic wars. As early as 1813, for example, a majority of the key players in the City of London had declared against the regulative protections of the old trading companies – but the centerpiece of trade regulation, the Navigation Acts, was not actually dismantled until 1849–52.[52]

The dismantling of old corruption, however, from the second decade of the nineteenth century, did not mean that the financial institutions of the City of London were to become redundant. It may be said that as they lost the empire of old corruption, they simultaneously found the promised

---

[52] Cain and Hopkin, *British Imperialism*, pp. 78–79, 83, 142; Philip Harling and Peter Mandler, "From Fiscal-Military' State to Laissez-Faire State, 1760–1850," *Journal of British Studies*, 32, 1 (January 1993), pp. 44–70; Webster, "Political Economy of Trade Liberalization," pp. 404–19. Over the period 1815 to 1870 (which is the key period of transition), government expenditure itself fell from about 29 percent of gross national product to about 9 percent. Although the national debt now occupied a diminished position in state finances, it still played its accustomed role as a corrupter of public virtue in the fiscal imagination. Evangelical Whigs and Tories regarded the national debt as sinful. Gladstone tended toward this position and endeavored (albeit unsuccessfully) to avoid adding the cost of the Crimean war to the debt account. Not until the 1860s and 1870s did attitudes shake the patina of moral disapproval that had been fixed to the debt from the beginning. New legislation on limited liability and joint stock companies in the 1860s and 1870s suggested more accepting attitudes toward adventure capital and credit. See Boyd Hilton, *The Age of Atonement: The Influence of Evangelicalism on Social and Economic Thought 1785–1865* (Oxford, 1988), pp. 119, 128, 203–05, 262–63; Hargreaves, *National Debt*, pp. 11–12, 169.

land as the financial marketplace of the world. As the function of the City
as financier to the state diminished, so it became the arena for the
flotations of international finance. After 1850 this function was accelerated and reinforced with a further inflection to finance capitalism that was
to be of the utmost importance: the rise in importance of capital exports
and the return flows of investment income. The Bank of England's role in
this shift was central. From being banker to the state, it now became the
guardian and protector of the gold standard, which was the key icon of the
liberal political economy.[53]

The gold standard was the cornerstone to London's role as financial
market to the world. As a mechanism to measure the value of a currency,
the gold standard was the brainchild of John Locke. Locke was searching
for policies to meet the wild fluctuations of economic crises of the 1690s.
He was searching for a means that would assure economic stability
through self regulation. The great advantage of the gold standard, Locke
claimed, was that it was one way of measuring the value and esteem of a
particular currency. The gold standard operated free from artificial constraints of government or other collectivities; it was therefore an essential
component to a free trade political economy. Although the gold standard
had been a *de facto* presence from the early eighteenth century, it became
an economic orthodoxy only in the early nineteenth century when evangelical Tories like Huskisson were looking for ways to displace protectionism with free trade.[54]

The prime advantage of the gold standard was that it deposed a
self-acting economic judgment with neither fear nor favor. It was both
scientific and mystical, and thus well suited to an age where science and
religion were seen as mutually supportive. Depending on one's epi-
stemological bias, the gold standard could be taken to reflect a true,
scientific verdict of economic virtue; or, alternatively, it could be seen to
be transmitting the moral ruling of providence. The gold standard was as
much a moral conduit as an economic mechanism. It fitted well, therefore, in a liberal political economy whose vocabulary and frame of reference continued to speak the language of sin and atonement. But this
functioning of the gold system was true only if an arbiter existed to ensure
that fiscal discipline was upheld. Someone had to guard the gold standard
itself. As controller of the nation's money supply, this responsibility fell
naturally upon the Bank of England. The Bank was therefore trans-

[53] Cain and Hopkin, *British Imperialism*, pp. 149, 170–84, 189; Jenks, in *Migration of British Capital*, p. 333, claims that two-thirds of the capital exported between 1815 and 1873 moved after 1850. For the displacement of domestic by foreign issues in the discount market from the 1860s, see W. T. C. King, *London Discount Market*, pp. 264–71.
[54] Appleby, *Economic Thought and Ideology*, pp. 237–41.

formed from an institution tainted by the odor of old corruption into the old lady of Threadneedle Street – the prim guardian of a fiscal orthodoxy whose moral code preached the lessons of just deserts and divine retribution for economic mismanagement.[55]

Yet if the Bank of England was no longer the banker to the state, this did not mean that it became the bank of the nation. The Bank had not been created to serve as the lender of last resort in the event of commercial crisis. There was no intent that the Bank of England protect the social equilibrium of the nation. It was not, in that sense, a central bank with the duty of monitoring the waves of economic fortune in the interests of political and social peace.[56] Indeed, protecting the gold standard meant maintaining sound finance, and sound finance was basically incompatible with allowing such priorities to enter into consideration. As a consequence, until the 1860s the Bank demonstrated the greatest reluctance to intervene in either the London or the provincial money markets. There was no question that it would easily countenance intervention in local business ventures, even though some branch managers did indulge in such practices. Thus, although the Bank of England was represented in the provinces through its branches until the end of the 1880s, it was largely passive in regional economic life. The most important activity of the local branches of the Bank was limited to easing the remittance of notes from the provinces to London agents. Local banks were allowed to crash unless it was judged that a general crisis was threatened by local failures.[57]

Control over currency issue, however, was a different story. This was a matter that touched most intimately on the Bank's role as guardian of the gold standard and it was therefore sensitive to anything that impeded its

[55] Hilton, *Age of Atonement*, pp. 129–30. The treasury served this role within government, extending its control over public expenditure throughout the nineteenth century. See Henry Roseveare, *The Treasury: The Evolution of an Institution* (London, 1969), pp. 183–86, 199–210.

[56] Obviously what the Bank did on such matters as discount rates for bills affected the money markets. But it made no attempt to control credit policy. See W. T. C. King, *London Discount Market*, pp. 73–82.

[57] Viner, *Theory of International Trade*, pp. 254–56; Dieter Ziegler, *Central Bank, Peripheral Industry: The Bank of England in the Provinces 1826–1918*, trans. Eileen Martin (Leicester, 1990), pp. 77–78, 84–87, 129. The Bank had been badly burned in the 1820s by the naivete of some local managers in Norwich, which drove home the lesson that it was unfamiliar with the morality of local business cultures. See David J. Moss, "Business and Banking: Ethics and White-Collar Crime in Norwich 1825–1831," *Albion*, 29, 3 (Fall 1997), pp. 373–98. The distrust of local business culture by the bank was reciprocated in the localities themselves. Considerable resistance was mounted to the establishment of a branch of the Bank of England in Manchester in the mid-1820s. See Michael Turner, "Before the Manchester School: Economic Theory in Early Nineteenth-Century Manchester," *History*, 79, 256 (1994), p. 226; Michael Collins, "The Bank of England at Liverpool, 1827–1844," *Business History*, 14, 2 (July 1972), pp. 144–59.

ability to influence the money supply. The Bank had been unhappy with the provisions of the 1826 act precisely because note-issuing authority was dispersed from its control. Thus, branches of the Bank were established in the provinces after 1826 in order to maintain the Bank's issuance authority. In 1844 the Bank acted to secure the Charter Act, which laid the foundations of its modern authority by securing its right to be the sole note-issuing authority. The act of 1844 separated the issuing and lending departments of the Bank and further reinforced the Bank's guardianship of the currency by limiting the circulation of notes to the gold supply.[58]

The Bank was thus awarded the weapon to enforce fiscal discipline. Yet in fact it seldom used the power that it did possess and throughout the middle of the nineteenth century sought nothing more than an indirect power over the monetary system.[59] Provincial bank note issues were not seriously affected by the greater restrictions of the 1844 act. It was only after the 1870s that the Bank moved to enforce its issuance authority and to extend its grip on the monetary policy of the economy by ending provincial bank note issuance. Neither macroeconomic nor microeconomic policy was subject to the control of the Bank of England, therefore. This was due more to circumstances than to the failure of the statutory weapons at its disposal.[60]

Given the conditions of economic growth of the middle of the nineteenth century, there was no pressing need for the Bank to exercise its power. In addition, it is important to realize that the Bank did not have the political credibility it was later to attain. As an institution that had only recently escaped from the maws of "old corruption," it was regarded in some circles as a relic of feudalism. As a consequence, until about 1860 the Bank of England did not display the directive power or influence normally expected of a central bank. Thus, the regional autonomy of the

---

[58] The linking of the rate to the gold reserves became an article of faith in the Bank following the crisis of 1847. In the tradition of intimacy between the Bank and the state, this act was not only proposed by the Bank, but actually drafted by it in the form of a memo to Peel which he then used as the basis for the bill. See Clapham, *Bank of England*, vol. II, p. 179; Ziegler, *Central Bank, Peripheral Industry*, pp. 31–33, 77–78; W. T. C. King, *London Discount Market*, p. 167.

[59] The actual result of the act of 1844 was to lead the Bank to behave like a commercial bank and treat its bank rate as a competitive weapon in the discounting business. It was firmly held Bank policy to disabuse the public of any notion that the Bank was a lender of last resort. This led to an interesting paradox: that the Bank gained practice in using the bank rate – which was the key weapon of a true central bank – at a time when it decisively rejected the role of a central bank. See W. T. C. King, *London Discount Market*, pp. 109–12.

[60] Ziegler, *Central Bank, Peripheral Industry*, pp. 79–82, 34–38. It was true that following 1844 the Bank instituted a restrictive money supply which stimulated a petition of protest from manufacturing interests for the damage to industry that would follow from a deflationary policy. And there were occasional complaints to be heard from the provinces and industry about the Bank's delight in restricting currency issue.

provincial system of commerce and banking remained essentially unaffected by the new political economy from the 1820s. Although the structures were in place for the Bank to infringe on that autonomy, it was rare for it to do so. The consequence was that the system of a functional integration between finance and industry at the local level remained intact throughout this period.[61]

The first cracks in the old system began to appear in the 1860s with a disruption of the bill brokerage system which had provided the link between provincial banks and the credit networks of London. The collapse of the discount brokerage firm of Overend and Gurney in 1866 sparked a renewed wave of criticism about the foundations of the credit system and the practice of banks extending overdraft credits to local industries. Bill brokers retreated to discounting only short-term bills. In response to this, companies began to look to the limited liability option (which had lain virtually unused since the acts of 1856 and 1862) as the means of raising long-term capital.[62]

Limited liability was a tactic that modernized the traditional method of raising money through associational groups. It provided statutory protection to partners in an enterprise against unlimited debt. Thus, limited liability reinforced the customary funding of industry through small-scale groups just at the very moment when the objective needs of industry required access to large sources of capital. In the late nineteenth century between 60 and 70 percent of industrial capital formation derived from this more primitive source. This was not a case of the loss of an industrial spirit, nor of entrepreneurial failure. It was a matter of the disruption of a particular structural relationship between finance and industry that had formerly performed well in providing the necessary capital resources.[63]

At the same time, the old system of local financing of industry was further damaged by spectacular crashes of banks associated with local industrial enterprise. Thus, the collapse of the City of Glasgow Bank in 1878 and the Cumberland Union Bank in Carlisle, both of which were closely linked to local industry, eroded the credibility of autonomous provincial banking. The Bank of England began to pronounce with greater confidence its conventional wisdom that industrial investment

---

[61] Marcello de Cecco, *Money and Empire* (Oxford, 1974), pp. 77–86.

[62] W. P. Kennedy, "Institutional Response to Economic Growth: Capital Markets in Britain to 1914," in Leslie Hannah (ed.), *Management Strategy and Business Development* (London and Basingstoke, 1976), pp. 159–77. For the bill broker system, see W. T. C. King, *London Discount Market*, pp. 112–23, 242–56, and *passim*.

[63] Jenks, *Migration of British Capital*, pp. 259–62. Small-scale associational groups were not unknown, of course, in the commercial sector, and they too experienced the need to move into a more corporate style of financing and organization. This was not always easy; see M. J. Daunton, "Firm and Family in the City of London in the Nineteenth Century: The Case of F. G. Dalgety," *Historical Research*, 62, 148 (June 1989), pp. 161–74.

was contrary to sound banking practices. Yet, the increasingly large scale of industry and its growing demands for vast infusions of capital made it apparent that "the entire system had either to be reorganized to withstand the greater risks of steadily enlarging industrial requirements or the system had to withdraw from long-term industrial involvement." By the early 1890s, therefore, some distinct policy on the relationship between the Bank and local enterprise could no longer be avoided. There was really no contest for the Bank's soul. Since the late 1870s the Bank had been engaged in a series of moves that imposed a new structure of banking in which the relationship between finance and manufacture was severed and the space for industrial finance was much reduced.[64]

The Bank used the failures of the late 1870s to encourage what was known as the amalgamation movement in banking. This marked the end of the independent local bank and of provincial autonomy over banking practices and loan policies. Banking power now was gathered into chains of national banks, headquartered in London, which were subject directly to the priorities and outlook of the Bank of England. Before the 1880s only the National Provincial Bank had branches outside London. During the 1880s the Midland, Lloyds, National Provincial, Barclays, London and County reached out from their London bases and established networks in the provinces. By 1913 Midland had over 800, Lloyds had 673 and Barclays had 600 branch offices.[65]

The advantages to be gained from the consolidation of banking were not to be denied. The most sophisticated remitting and check system in the world was established. A deeply cautious business philosophy presided over by the Bank of England confined the banks to the specialized sector of deposit banking. As a consequence British banking possessed a stability that was absent from the money systems of the United States and Germany. Still, the demise of local banking broke the traditional tie between the financial sector and industry. The centralization of monetary policy in the City of London subjected lending practices to national standards. It was not surprising, therefore, that the amalgamation movement was followed by more restrictive, bureaucratized and centralized lending policies. Precisely at the moment when the industrial structure needed access to new supplies of capital, banks became "very reluctant either to supply working capital on a continuous basis or more particular-

---

[64] Cottrell, *Industrial Finance*, pp. 104–62, 210–36; Kennedy, "Institutional Response to Economic Growth," p. 160 (quote); Ziegler, *Central Bank, Peripheral Industry*, pp. 100–28. A particularly nasty scandal in the Bank's Birmingham branch in 1894 which involved some dubious dealings between the manager and local businesses (including the Chamberlain family) confirmed the distaste of Threadneedle Street for financial involvement in industry.

[65] Collins, *Banks and Industrial Finance*, pp. 26–41.

ly to support investment in plant and machinery for any length of time."
Although most traditional industries adapted silently to this closure,
complaints were heard from new industries like electrical engineering that
banking practices were unfriendly toward industry.[66]

This move, of course, was convergent with the strong preference of
the financial system for government-backed issues, either domestic or
foreign. The other institutions of the financial system failed to offer
support to industry in the face of the Bank's withdrawal. The focus of
the capital markets was directed away from domestic industrial issues,
and this bias was encouraged by the preference of the Bank of England
for low-risk securities rather than venture capital. Government securities
of one kind or another continued to dominate the exchange markets. In
1913 industrial securities composed only 10 percent of the new issues.
The City of London was extremely knowledgeable in handling foreign
issues; it was extremely efficient at sorting through the low-risk, high-
yield securities from overseas. The same expertise or function was not
replicated for domestic issues. It is an amazing fact to contemplate that
by the late nineteenth century there was virtually no active involvement
by the established financial institutions in the formation of industrial
capital.[67]

These developments disrupted the boundaries of the political economy
of commercial imperialism. Previously, the relationship between finance
and manufacturing had been functional to the needs of both. Now those
linkages had been decisively disconnected. By the end of the nineteenth
century, finance and manufacturing occupied clearly demarcated separate spheres. One way of understanding this process of disruption is to see
it as the removal of constraints that had previously kept the various
sectors of commerce, finance and manufacture in balance. The sources of
this disruption were not, however, entirely internal to the dynamic of the
political economy itself. The changing landscape of the political economy
was convergent with the opportunities and challenges that the British
economy faced at the turn of the era. From c. 1870 the interface between
Britain and the world political economy was transformed.

The emergence of industrialism was one such agent of transformation.
Although this period is quite commonly termed the "*second* industrial
revolution," it is more appropriate to regard it as the beginning of the era
of heavy, urbanized industry. The profile of this phase of economic
growth was very different from the phase of economic growth that began

[66] Cottrell, *Industrial Finance*, pp. 194–244, 248–70; Kennedy, "Institutional Response to
Economic Growth," pp. 169–70.
[67] Collins, *Banks and Industrial Finance*, pp. 38–44; Kennedy, "Institutional Response to
Economic Growth," pp. 162–77.

in Britain in the late eighteenth century. As we have seen, economic growth in the earlier period was regionally based, small-scale and not dependent upon complex science or highly capitalized technology. It was an economy of manufacturing, not industrialism. Only from the late nineteenth century did industrial revolutions occur in such countries as Germany, United States, Italy, France and Sweden.

Britain did not stand aside from the economic trends that unbound prometheus in the later nineteenth century. Large-scale industry, integrated production, scientific management, reconfigured social relations and the fusion of science and technology all appeared in the British economy as elsewhere. These were the properties that were to shape the economic history of the next 100 years; they were not the properties that had defined the economic rhythms of the previous 200 years. This was a new phase of capitalist expansion, therefore, and its implications for Britain included a sharpened competition for markets in which Britain's traditional advantages (low wages and stable politics, for example) counted for much less. What counted for more now, it was widely recognized at the time, was size of internal markets and the ability to mobilize the internal resources of a society.

Where did Britain's comparative advantage lie in this new political economy? Britain could seize readily the opportunities provided by the expansion of the world market to become the center of international finance. Two centuries of experience in discounting bills and capital movements provided an indisputable advantage for Britain to play the role of international banker. As I have noted, from about the middle of the nineteenth century the role of capital exports in the national wealth of the country began to assume a critical importance. After 1870 this shift was reinforced by the explosion of demand for investment capital from all quarters of the world. Returns on foreign investments now became the critical element to the surplus on Britain's balance of payments. Whereas in the past the perpetual balance of trade deficit had been covered by reexports and commercial services, by the Edwardian period the deficits were covered by returns on capital invested abroad. Between the three elements of finance, commerce and industry, the first became even more important. The traditional importance of commerce remained, but it shrank relatively as priority in the political economy moved decisively to a financial capitalism that was focused on the export and movement of capital flows.[68]

[68] Cain and Hopkin, *British Imperialism*, pp. 170–84; Ingham, *Capitalism Divided?*, pp. 96–97. Capital exports did not begin in the 1850s, of course. Jenks, in *Migration of British Capital*, began his account in 1815. But it was not until the 1870s that capital exports and returns on foreign investments became the dynamic center of British finance imperialism.

The Bank of England's guardianship of the gold standard was the primary guarantee of probity and reliability in this political economy. The gold standard finally came into its own as the prime determinant of economic policy. This meant, among other things, high interest rates and sound trade balances, both of which inherently disadvantaged industry but encouraged the flow of money into and through London. Yet it is quite clear that even this preference in the political economy was not entirely inconsistent with the current circumstances of industry. Although Britain was now facing serious competition from more efficient industrial economies, for example, it was not obvious that investing huge sums of capital to meet this competition could satisfy a profit-and-loss calculation. Existing market opportunities in the empire and elsewhere were quite sufficient to absorb much industrial output. There were far greater returns to be gained from investment in service industry (which now became an extremely important sector) or in the infrastructural needs of empire – railways in Argentina or sewers in Johannesburg for example. Whether or not this new configuration of the political economy diverted much-needed capital from domestic investment is a question that has preoccupied historians. The answer is that industrial investment almost certainly did suffer. Yet this mattered only in the very long term. Not until after 1918 could the consequences of this new political economy be seen to be disadvantaging Britain in the world economy. Nobody in 1880 or 1890 could know this and it is of little value for historians to impute to the late Victorian world things it could not know.[69]

A retrospective fixation on explaining the particular course of the twentieth-century economy also detracts from an accurate historical appreciation of the political economy of commercial imperialism. How can we best locate the political economy of commercial imperialism in the long scope of British imperial presence? The commercial imperialism of the period 1680–1880 was the era when the pax Britannica was most nearly a reality, when British power rested most clearly upon a commer-

[69] On the question of the starving of capital from domestic sphere, see Lance Davis and Huttenback, *Mammon and the Pursuit of Empire*, pp. 33–38. This book focuses on the issuance and sales of stocks and bonds, "not on the amount raised by the British savers, nor on the level of the accumulated total of overseas finance" (p. 34), which might be thought to miss the point. It does, nevertheless, establish that this phase of imperialism was economically rational. On the supposed entrepreneurial failure of the late nineteenth century, see Weiner, *English Culture and the Decline of the Industrial Spirit*; Donald McCloskey, "Did Victorian Britain Fail?," in McCloskey (ed.), *Enterprise and Trade in Victorian Britain* (London, 1981), pp. 94–110, for the argument that Britain was using its existing productive resources and techniques as efficiently as possible. For the case of cotton spinning, see William Lazonick, "Factor Costs and the Diffusion of Ring Spinning in Britain Prior to World War One," *Quarterly Journal of Economics*, 96, 1 (February 1981), pp. 91–106.

cial supremacy, backed up by a powerful state and a healthy manufacturing sector. In this system, trade, manufacture and finance were interdependent; it was not a system that was conditional on industrial power.

By contrast, industrial power *was* critical to the imperial role in the world economy after 1870. Before the 1880s Britain could aspire to a free trade empire – meaning that it could trade anywhere and it could aim to gather a major proportion of the world's commerce and carrying trade. After the 1880s this aspiration was closed out by a wave of protectionism abroad, the establishment of formal empires and industrial competition from countries whose ability to mobilize internal resources outpaced that of Britain. For the financial capitalism of the City of London, however, the aspiration to a free trade empire remained valid. The possibility that it could be banker to much of the world was realized for the first time during the course of the nineteenth century. This possibility held serious consequences for the history of twentieth-century British society. More narrowly, it also explains one of the more amazing alchemies of the period: the historical transformation of the City of London from an identification with the protectionism of the monopoly companies to the most unambiguous champion of the doctrine of free trade.

3   The ambiguities of free trade

Free trade and the Victorian age

Free trade is one of the defining notions of nineteenth-century Britain. It is as Victorian as the whatnot, the piano or self-help. Of course, historians no longer treat free trade as the economic calling card of the industrial bourgeoisie. Yet until quite recently the idea that the urban middle class·marched onto the political stage with the repeal of the protectionist corn laws in 1846 lurked close to the surface of historical interpretation. Few historians would now argue that class analysis is the best way to understand the repeal of the corn laws and the arrival of free trade in 1846, although the idea has not entirely died out in other sectors of the academic world. More important in contemporary interpretations of free trade is its cultural dimension, the close relationship it bore to the evangelical religion that was believed and practiced by many of its most prominent advocates in the nineteenth century. Nevertheless, whatever the interpretive nuance, in nineteenth-century history, 1846 is a key date which is taken to mark a genuine passage from one economic regime to another. This chapter seeks to problematize that assumption.[1]

What was the content of free trade; what did it mean? To ask these questions is to encounter ambiguity and uncertainty. Free trade as both idea and policy defies straightforward treatment. Using certain economic measurements it can be argued that Britain's distinctive nineteenth-

---

[1] For older perspectives, see Briggs, *Age of Improvement*, pp. 321–25; Perkin, *Origins of Modern English Society*, pp. 315–16; Llewellyn Woodward, *The Age of Reform: England 1815–1870* (2nd edn., Oxford, 1962), pp. 118–25; Norman McCord, *The Anti-Corn Law League 1838–1846* (London, 1958). For more recent approaches, see Hilton, *Age of Atonement*, pp. 108–10, 246–50, 352, and *passim*; Daunton, *Progress and Poverty*, pp. 533–57. Anthony Howe, *Free Trade and Liberal England 1846–1946* (Oxford, 1997), pp. 1–2, treats free trade as beginning in 1846, but is good on the internal political history and the diplomatic history of free trade. Douglas Irwin, *Against the Tide: An Intellectual History of Free Trade* (Princeton, 1996), accepts the superiority of the free trade argument and tracks its expression in the literature of economic analysis. Corn, of course, in the British context refers to wheat; the corn laws imposed a customs duty on imported wheat.

century image as a low-tariff nation is a chimera. If tariffs are measured as a percentage of the value of imports, Britain after 1846 was more protectionist than France. The reductions in tariff levels inaugurated by Lord Liverpool's government in the 1820s were so dramatic because they started from such a high level. By 1860 both Britain and France were at a comparable level of trade regulation. This remained the case until after 1880 when French tariffs begin to rise again while Britain's remain low. Such a perspective suggests the irony that the true era of British free trade came after our period when it alone among the major powers of the world remained obstinately committed to nonprotectionism.[2]

This particular argument is not entirely convincing for technical reasons. Yet it is a useful reminder that free trade was always a partial reality. It was a particular version of free trade that came to define its meaning. This version defined free trade as a tariff policy that taxed for revenue purposes only and did not discourage domestic enterprise. By this iteration an impressive list of import taxes protecting certain economic sectors remained after 1846. It was twenty years before most of these taxes were finally removed. The long-standing duty on wine was protectionist of the British brewing industry, for example. Even some industries remained protected. The ban on silk imports was removed in 1826, but the industry continued to be protected by a 30 percent duty until 1860. The same was true of corn, which was protected by a (fairly modest) "registration duty" of one shilling per pound. This was not abolished until 1869, at which date it was generating nearly £1 million in revenue.

Duties on foodstuffs could be argued to be purely revenue creating; they were not protective of local business. Britain did not produce sugar, for example. Yet the empire did produce sugar, and although the duties on foreign and colonial sugar were equalized throughout the 1820s, 1830s and 1840s, they effectively protected the West Indian sugar planters whose free labor costs were higher compared with their slave labor competitors. This was a protection that remained in effect until 1874. The same was true of pepper, the duty on which went back to the middle ages and was not repealed until 1866. The coffee duty was made uniform between foreign and colonial rather than abolished in 1851, and was not reduced until 1872. Even the repeal of taxes on manufactured

[2] John Vincent Nye, "The Myth of Free-Trade Britain and Fortress France: Tariffs and Trade in the Nineteenth Century," *Journal of Economic History*, 51 (March 1991), pp. 23–46. This argument may be contested, however, by the fact that it fails to draw a sufficiently sophisticated distinction between tariffs that protect domestic manufactures and those that merely tax goods for revenue purposes. The dominant definition of free trade in the nineteenth century did not rest on the notion of a tariff-free fiscal regime.

goods was spread over a long period and the list of such products that were still subject to import taxes in the early and mid-Victorian period is a long one, which includes glass, soap, timber, playing cards, dice and medicines.[3]

If free trade was an incomplete tariff policy, it was also a contested policy. There were always important differences between the proponents of free trade, and the idea that free trade meant tariffs for revenue purposes was not unchallenged in Victorian Britain. Indeed, for some Victorians such a notion was highly problematic. William Gladstone's brother, Richard, for example, was a leading light in the Financial Reform Association, an organization which was formed in 1848 and which lasted until 1914. The Financial Reform Association advocated the abolition of all tariffs, regarding them as distorting trade and as polluting business morality by encouraging tax evasion. In their place, the association wanted to substitute income and property taxes. This was not a view of free trade that held much appeal for Gladstone or Cobden.[4]

Tariff reduction cannot be understood outside the context of expected revenue flows. The nineteenth century was no exception. At one level free trade was merely a rationalization of the tariff structure which cleared items that had become obsolete and worthless as sources of revenue. High-yield customs duties were left untouched. Thus, of the 700 dutiable items in the 1840s over 500 produced only £80,000 in revenue; seventeen alone produced £21.8 million. Needless to say, it was the former that were removed. The latter tended to be reduced on the correct assumption that the stimulant to commerce would produce more revenue. Lowered rates was as much the signifier of free trade after 1846 as abolished duties. Apart from silk, no manufacture had more than a 10 percent duty protecting it and many like iron, coal and wool had none at all. Higher duties remained on lace, carpets and some other fabric products, and the duty on paper was overtly protective. Even so, there was constant tinkering with the level of duties to cover the special expenses that seemed to recur every year after 1846. Thus, in 1860, the repeal of duties on silk, gloves, watches, oils, leather and some other items meant customs duty losses of £1m. It was expected, however, that most of this would be recovered from increased consumption of articles

---

[3] These various data are drawn from Stephen Dowell, *History of Taxation and Taxes in England* (London, 1884), vol. IV, pp. 30–51, 162–76, 241–51, 295; Lucy Brown, *The Board of Trade and the Free Trade Movement 1830–1842* (Oxford, 1958), pp. 179, 149; O. Williams, *The Repeal of the Customs and Excise Laws* (Liverpool, 1859).

[4] See Financial Reform Association, *Tracts 1848–1851* (Liverpool, 1852) and Financial Reform Association, *The Cost of Customs and Excise Duties* (Liverpool, 1852). Note that most historians treat free trade as uncontested. Howe, for example, in *Free Trade and Liberal England*, treats Cobden as the authoritative free trader.

still subject to taxation and the shortfall was filled by new duties on chicory and other products.[5]

Free trade was a process, not an event. Tariff reduction of the sort I have described above began in the 1820s and continued throughout the 1860s. Along the way there were few more significant moments than the Cobden–Chevalier treaty of 1860 between Britain and France. Indeed, this date may more properly be claimed over 1846 as the moment of free trade. In 1860 there were still over 400 items subject to the customs tariff; the budget of that year reduced this number to forty-eight. Colonial preference decisively disappeared in 1860 with the equalization of duties on foreign and colonial timber. From 1861, when the treaty took effect, "no foreign manufacture whatever appeared in the British tariff except flour, alcoholic drinks, manufactured tobacco and sugar, gold and silver plate, playing cards and dice . . . flour was no longer taxed after 1869, nor sugar after 1874."[6]

The tariff negotiations with France in 1860 drew the curtain on a major theme of international economic relations since the late seventeenth century. France had been one of the main targets of British trade policy in the eighteenth century, and the politics of tariffs were judged in terms of their impact on the commercial struggle with France. Thus, the treaty of 1860 possessed a major symbolic significance. Yet it also opened an era of restructured tariff relations which for twenty years held out the promise that a free trade world could be constructed. Aside from its reduction of duties on French wine and the like, the treaty inaugurated a series of reciprocal trade agreements throughout Europe that lowered tariffs all round. Britain alone concluded eight such agreements in the 1860s. Cobden could be forgiven for believing that the utopia of international free trade was around the corner. Alas, it was not to be. The treaty of 1860 established the pattern of European trade policy only until the mid-1880s, after which Europe spiraled into a new round of protectionism, leaving Britain as the sole champion of free trade.

The ambiguities of free trade extended beyond its definition and meaning, however. What was the relationship of free trade to the historical development of Britain's political economy? Nineteenth-century free

---

[5] John Noble, *Fiscal Legislation 1842–1865* (London, 1867), pp. 7–8; Noble, *Fifty Three Years' Taxation and Expenditure, 1827–28 to 1879–80* (London, 1882), pp. 25–26; Clapham, *Economic History of Modern Britain*, vol. II, pp. 1–2, 242–44. The duties on timber (which were as intricate as any eighteenth-century duty) continued to produce a very high revenue even at the low rate of one shilling per ton. The low level of duties on foreign china, grand pianos, machinery, cutlery and iron and steel manufactures were not likely to have made much difference.

[6] Clapham, *Economic History of Britain*, vol. II, pp. 244–47. Howe, *Free Trade and Liberal England*, pp. 92–105, emphasizes the diplomatic importance of the treaty in opening a new phase of reciprocity treaties – although they were not given that name.

trade was not simply the product of the environment of the nineteenth century alone – although this is often how it is contextualized. The liberalizing trade policies of the 1820s and the repeal of the corn laws in 1846 were not only the beginnings of Victorian conventional economic wisdom. They were also particular moments in the historical development of the political economy. Nor was free trade the predestined outcome of the historical forces of the period. The relevance of free trade as a trade policy, like the relevance of protectionism, depended upon an estimation of the best means by which markets could be captured and commerce protected, enhanced and controlled.

Free trade and protectionism were strategies in the system of commercial imperialism. The interlude of a free trade fiscal policy is generally taken to reflect the economic harvest of the previous century and a half of mercantilist protectionism and manufacturing development. After a long period of debate and struggle, free trade came to be regarded by key policy-making groups as the strategy best suited for British commercial interests at one particular moment from c. 1840 to c. 1880. Its advocates proudly touted its freedom from self-interest, in contrast to protectionism. Yet free trade did not signify an anti-imperial alternative to protectionism. In a context in which Britain could trade freely worldwide, a policy that advocated empire was a protectionist policy that meant a diminution of potential markets. In the nineteenth century, free trade was an imperialist policy precisely because it claimed the right to expand its reach everywhere. Its ideal was a world imperium without the bother of a formal empire.[7]

The ancestry of free trade is commonly regarded as unproblematic, beginning with Adam Smith and moving through to the classical political economists of mid-Victorian Britain. Yet matters were more clouded than this. Free trade was an outgrowth of the debate over trade policy in the system of commercial imperialism. Free trade possessed the same genealogy as protectionism; it existed on a continuum with protectionism rather than in binary opposition to it. The intellectual lineage of free trade was a historical phenomenon that was ambiguous, contingent and contested. This will be the first theme of the chapter.

The second theme to the chapter will follow from this. I will suggest that free trade was itself a contingent phenomenon, and did not progress inevitably toward the defining trade doctrine of the Victorian age. Free trade was a contested site. This was most obviously true before 1846, and especially before 1815. Yet it was also true after 1846. Historians have

---

[7] J. Gallagher and R. E. Robinson, "The Imperialism of Free Trade," *Economic History Review*, 7, 1 (1953), pp. 1–15.

been rightly impressed with the way a particular version of free trade (low revenue-raising tariffs) closed out all other alternative trade policies after 1846. What has escaped notice is how unstable that hegemony was. Free trade discourse in the middle of the nineteenth century was inherently fragile and uncertain.

The hegemony of free trade is taken to rest on its superior intellectual merits to any other theory on offer. Yet the power of free trade did not derive solely from its intellectual merits. Free trade was also a cultural force. The hegemony of free trade over the discourse on trade policy was a function of its ability to moralize economics. Free trade's cultural resonance in the early nineteenth century derived from its convergence with the discourse of evangelicalism that shaped the Victorian representation of the world. Popular economics rested on notions of divine providence and the ideology of free trade could easily be fitted into this vocabulary. Protectionism had no such advantages; its overtly materialist and instrumental purpose and rationale could not be disguised. Thus, free trade as a cultural discourse will be my third theme.[8]

The role of sectoral economic interest groups in the coming of free trade will be my fourth and final theme. Mid-Victorian free trade appealed to a wide cluster of economic interests. This was the hard political reason for its dominance. The sector I shall focus on is that of commerce. There was an increasingly convergent relationship between commerce and free trade after 1815. This connection was hardly surprising. The relationship between trade policy and commerce was one of the major continuities in this period. It was to be a prescient connection for the future of British history. By contrast, the commitment of the manufacturing sector to free trade was both more recent and much weaker. Yet, once again, these intersections were contingent in ways that tend to be forgotten by historians. This is especially true for the coming of a free trade economic policy in the 1840s. It is important to emphasize that the repeal of the corn laws in 1846 and the dismantling of the Navigation Acts in 1849 were not an offensive to realize the promise of trade hegemony for British commerce. They were defensive responses to external challenges.

---

[8] Free trade as a cultural phenomenon is a running theme of Frank Trentmann's important work on political economy in the late nineteenth and early twentieth centuries. Naturally, the moralizing discourses of free trade were different in the two periods, although there are some interesting continuities to be found in the Labour Party, especially in the later period. See Trentmann, "Civil Society, Commerce and the Citizen-Consumer: Popular Meanings of Free Trade in Late Nineteenth- and Early Twentieth-Century Britain," Working Paper No. 66, Center for European Studies, Harvard University, n.d. (? 1997); Trentmann, "Political Culture and Political Economy: Interests, Ideas and Free Trade," *Review of International Political Economy* (forthcoming).

The protectionist origins of free trade

When the history of free trade began to be written in the early part of the twentieth century, it was noted with some surprise that the first free traders in the late seventeenth century were Tories, not Whigs. Yet it was the Whigs and their allies, of course, who claimed ownership of free trade doctrine in the nineteenth century. The faultlines that ran between various economic schools at the end of the seventeenth century followed different trajectories than those proposed and imposed by Manchester School propaganda in the nineteenth century. Who was a free trader and who was a protectionist, and when they were combined in the same person, were not the simple matters that they later became. Both protectionism and free trade were forged in the heart of the mercantilist system. They were formulated from the arguments about trade policy that were promulgated by different interest groups. This was true across the whole spectrum of economic activity, and not just in economic theory. Good liberal measures such as rationalization of the tax system and elimination of archaic customs and trade barriers were as likely to be mouthed by protectionists in the early eighteenth century as by free traders. Attempts to differentiate sharply between free trade or protectionist ideas or to assign exclusive labels on particular thinkers tend to falter on the common context that both these positions shared. The irony of nineteenth-century free trade is that it is inextricably interwoven with the genealogy of protectionism.[9]

Free trade was spawned in the womb of old corruption. The free trade argument was developed and initially articulated by the supporters of the East India Company in the 1690s.[10] Naturally such arguments did not immediately coalesce into the fully fledged doctrine of free trade as it came to be defined in the nineteenth century. Yet many of the reforms later identified with a free trade position were pioneered by mercantilists in the seventeenth century. The first free traders were men like Josiah Child operating within the bosom of the East India Company who argued

[9] Johnson, *Predecessors of Adam Smith*, pp. 144–46; Richard F. Teichgraeber III, *"Free Trade" and Moral Philosophy: Rethinking the Sources of Adam Smith's Wealth of Nations* (Durham, 1986), pp. 18–19; Appleby, *Economic Thought and Ideology*, pp. 158–98, 248, and *passim*.

[10] This is not to suggest that free trade ideas were absent before; they were not. Throughout the seventeenth century, resistance to monopoly trading companies had spawned calls for open trade. Indeed, on occasion the right to membership in the trading companies was thrown open to all comers – the Merchant Adventurers (who handled three-quarters of London textile exports) were thus opened in 1621 and 1624 to provincial merchants trading in kersies and the like. But such moves were always forced by government policy to preserve social peace in the face of economic crisis. See Supple, *Commercial Crises and Change*, pp. 238–43.

against the import duties or tariffs that domestic interests wanted to impose on Company goods. I have already noted the significance of this economic debate in the 1690s and early 1700s. Its relevance here is how it forged the key elements of the nineteenth-century free trade case.[11]

Defenders of the East India trade had to contend with the argument that it operated at a net loss for Britain and therefore drained the nation of silver and gold bullion to cover the deficit. In meeting this argument a line of theoretical inquiry was opened up that argued the necessity of looking beyond the specific balance of trade in order to properly gauge national wealth. Thus, out of the debate around the East India trade came the most complete statement of the free trade case before Adam Smith – a pamphlet by Henry Martyn, *Considerations upon the East India Trade*, published in 1701. In this work, Martyn advocated opening India to all traders and dismissed (as others like Davenant had done before him) the value of restrictions on the importation of Indian goods. He controverted the bullionist position by positing a highly sophisticated vision of trade as a constantly expanding exchange and circulation of goods which, uninterrupted and unimpeded, would increase wealth whatever the bullion holdings of a particular country. Martyn attacked the notion that wealth was increased by taking it away from others. In an early statement of the theory of comparative advantage, he bruited the possibility that British manufacturers should be driven out of business if Indian ones could produce the same goods more cheaply. Martyn anticipated Adam Smith in recognizing the relationship between international trade and an increased, more efficient division of labor. Indeed, in place of Smith's famous example of the division of labor in pin making, Martyn had instanced the case of watchmaking.[12]

At the same time defenders of the East India trade had to face another line of argument which attacked the practice of monopoly. There was nothing new about the complaints over monopolies. Struggles between various interest groups to secure monopoly rights were a constant feature

[11] Josiah Child, *A Treatise Wherein Is Demonstrated...* (London, 1681), and Child, *The Great Honour and Advantage of the East India Trade to the Kingdom, Asserted* (London, 1697). For an example of the way in which this debate resulted in legislation that attempted to balance the interests of domestic manufacturers against the trading claims of the East India merchants, see J. Parakunnel Thomas, "Beginnings of Calico-Printing in England," pp. 206–16, and Marshall, *Mercantilism and the East India Trade*, pp. 23–24, 102–11, 114–15, 120–28. See also Irwin, *Against the Tide*, pp. 52–57.

[12] *Considerations upon the East India Trade* has in the past been attributed to Dudley North, but it is now generally accepted as Martyn's. Many of Martyn's arguments had been prefigured by others, of course, notably Josiah Child. But see Johnson, *Predecessors of Adam Smith*, p. 348, n. 31, for accusation that Martyn plagiarized these arguments from Sir William Petty. See also Appleby, *Economic Thought and Ideology*, pp. 167–68, 182–83; Irwin, *Against the Tide*, pp. 57–59.

of court politics from the early seventeenth century. The general explosion of trade and the particular fiscal crises that followed the Glorious Revolution ensured that the issue featured prominently in the politics of the 1690s. For a variety of reasons, the political advantage began to tip toward those who urged greater trade liberalization. Attempts to establish new monopolies – as in paper manufacture, for example – were unsuccessful and the renewal of company charters met fierce counterpetitioning of Parliament. The attempt to renew the Russia Company monopoly in 1697 established the pattern of contestation around this issue. A compromise agreement threw open the trade to all merchants on payment of a £5 membership fee. A similar solution was followed in the case of the African Company.[13]

The big prize in the monopoly stakes, however, was the East India Company. By the mid-1690s two East India Companies vied for monopoly rights. Neither was able to establish a clear supremacy in the snake pit of Westminster politics, however. Ultimately, protracted negotiations produced a merger between the two companies with the result that in theory all merchants with an interest in eastern trade were granted access. In practice, however, the London merchants continued to dominate the trade and provincial merchants continued to be shut out. Each time the charter of the company was revised over the next century, the issue of access was a central issue of debate. In 1793, for example, the Company was forced to grant space to private merchants in its larger ships. Similarly, the act of 1813 permitted the Company to retain its monopoly on the China tea trade in return for further measures of trade liberalization.[14]

All the staple economic arguments that constituted the nineteenth-century definition of free trade were to be found somewhere in the literature of economic discourse by the 1740s. The relationship between the level of taxation and economic growth and expansion was understood. Proposals were issued to end all prohibitions on trade activity and substitute a property tax for the excise. The distorting effects of the state on economic growth were condemned in a pamphlet of the 1740s which argued for the repeal of all protectionist acts with the exception of the Navigation Acts. These were lauded as "the most glorious bulwark of our trade." This exception to the free trade sentiments of the writer – in this case the influential Matthew Decker – did not reflect a lapse of logic. It reflected the absence of clear demarcations between free trade and pro-

[13] George Cherry, "The Development of the English Free Trade Movement in Parliament, 1689–1702," *History*, 25 (June 1953), pp. 103–19.

[14] Phillip Lawson, *The East India Company: A History* (London, 1993), pp. 55–57; Halevy, *England in 1815*, pp. 321–23; Hoh-cheung Mui and Lorna H. Mui, *The Management of Monopoly: A Study of the East India Company's Conduct of Its Tea Trade 1784–1833* (Vancouver, 1984), pp. 134–37.

tectionist arguments. The definition of free trade had emerged from debates around the economic value of monopolies and the positive effects of expanding exchange and circulation of trade. This did not necessarily lead to the logical conclusion of full economic individualism.[15]

Thus, free trade did not spring into being fully formed. The meanings of free trade or protectionism were neither fixed nor unchanging and the boundary between them was mobile. Indeed, free trade and protectionism existed on a continuum. Free trade arguments could be combined with protectionist sentiment in the same person or theory. The case of Henry Martyn is instructive here. As I have noted, Martyn published an early statement for free trade. Yet by the standards of nineteenth-century free trade doctrine, Martyn's beliefs were unstable and ambiguous. Thus, a decade after his famous pamphlet Martyn was to be found consorting with a group of protectionist writers who argued ardently against liberalized trade provisions of the Treaty of Utrecht (1713). Although this has typically been attributed to the time-serving opportunism of the political and journalistic worlds of the early eighteenth century, it is more accurately regarded as disclosing the difficulty of maintaining a consistent meaning to free trade or protectionism. There was hardly an expression of free trade belief that was not qualified in some way with protectionist sentiments – and vice versa. Indeed, protectionist sentiments were present in Martyn's early *Considerations upon the East India Trade* which suggested that an end to the monopoly of the East India Company would require the state to take over its responsibilities. Free traders did not intend for India to be opened to *any* merchant irrespective of national origin.[16]

If free trade meant low tariffs, the first free traders were the great monopoly companies. If free trade meant access to markets, the first free traders were those opposed to monopoly who also tended to be in favor of protecting domestic industry. Equally, protectionists were not opposed to certain free trade tariff policies. Joshua Gee, for example, was fully in favor of imposing sharp duties on foreign goods to encourage home manufacture and bounties to encourage the production of strategic goods. Yet he was also supportive of a liberal policy regarding the

[15] The quote is from Matthew Decker, *Some Considerations on the Several High Duties Which the Nation in General Labours Under* (London, 1743), an influential and much reprinted pamphlet of 1743. See also Decker, *The Nature and Weight of the Taxes of the Nation* (London, 1722). William Horsley, *Serious Considerations on the High Duties Examined* (London, 1744), repeated Decker's arguments one year later but with a special emphasis on the need to replace indirect taxes with taxes on property, an argument that was to be central to the debate on fiscal policy in the middle of the nineteenth century. Appleby, *Economic Thought and Ideology*, p. 158, has pointed out that many of Decker's arguments could be also found expressed 100 years earlier.

[16] Johnson, *Predecessors of Adam Smith*, p. 348; [Martyn,] *Considerations upon the East India Trade*, p. 28.

exemptions from customs duties that could be claimed by goods warehoused for reexport. It was similarly the case with John Cary, the Bristol merchant, who combined a belief in freeing trade from monopoly control, removing all duties and reducing the excise with support for the Navigation Acts and monopolies that ensured the employment of the poor and furthered British commercial imperial power.[17]

Protectionism and free trade were different answers to the question of how to increase the national wealth. In this enterprise few believed that state responsibilities were minimal. Understanding the importance of the market did not automatically lead to the intellectual condition of advanced liberalism. This was only one position that could be occupied across a whole spectrum of belief. Nineteenth-century ideologues imposed a consistent clarity on free trade and protectionism that was absent before 1850. A merchant like Dudley North, for example, active for many years in the Mediterranean trade and a commissioner of excises, believed firmly that individual freedom to compete in the unrestricted market sphere was essential to the efficient allocation of resources. Yet he also recognized that discrimination and interference to help and support merchants was a legitimate role for government. Which part of North's well-thoughtout approach do we privilege in categorizing him as free trader or protectionist?[18]

Like free trade, protectionism was largely an invention of the later seventeenth century. Import duties, for example, previously had played a fairly small role in the fiscal system. In the 1690s, however, the convenience and ease of the tariff for revenue creation was discovered. Legislation in 1690 and 1693 quadrupled import duties over the decade. At this moment the English tariff structure was transformed into a "high level system which, although still fiscal in its purposes, had become in practice protective." Export duties were not touched in this exercise, and it was soon recognized that this oversight was highly beneficial to the balance of payments. Thus, those industries that had export duties began to plead for their removal – just as others were urging the imposition of import duties. Walpole's celebrated customs reform of 1722 which abolished virtually all export duties while retaining import duties represented an official acceptance of this policy.[19]

[17] Joshua Gee, *The Trade and Navigation of Great Britain Considered* (repr., London, 1969 [4th edn., 1738]), pp. 207, 214, 229–30; John Cary, *Essay on the State of England*; see also Cary, *An Essay Towards Regulating the Trade and Employing the Poor of This Kingdom* (London, 1717), pp. 22–24.

[18] Grassby, *English Gentleman in Trade*, pp. 238–41.

[19] Appleby, *Economic Thought and Ideology*, pp. 100–13; Ralph Davis, "The Rise of Protectionism in England, 1689–1786," *Economic History Review*, 19, 2 (1966), pp. 307–13 (quote, p. 307).

Protectionism may have started as a fiscal device, but it was immediately adopted by manufacturing interest groups. Free trade in raw materials
was beneficial for manufacturers: competition from finished goods was
more problematic. The textile trades – later the epitome of free trade
manufacturing – were at the center of this tension from the very beginning. The remaining export duties and the duties on raw materials like
silk and flax were removed in the 1730s and 1760s. Of more significance
was the matter of direct competition. In the 1690s, when the protectionist
case had been formulated, the textile industry was reeling from the
fashion craze for Indian calicoes and muslins. It was in this context that
protectionists argued that trade policy should be directed toward encouraging cheap imports of raw material to provide employment for the
manufacture of exports that would then be fed into the British carrying
and commercial system. Like most free traders, protectionists wanted
some element of trade regulation, specifically in the interests of home
manufacturing.[20]

Self-interest obviously informed the protectionist argument of various
manufacturers. But the argument for protectionism also proceeded from
a conception of the national interest that was hard to dispute. The social
question underlay the power of the protectionist case. Manufacturers
were more likely to support protectionist measures on domestic industry
than merchants, because they were closer to the dangers posed by the
laboring poor. Protectionism's most persuasive appeal was that it ensured
the proper employment of the poor and thereby preserved the social
balance. The potential damage done to home industries by the free
trading instincts of the monopoly companies was a major issue of political
concern and fed the continued vitality of protectionism as a trade policy.
The need for some kind of regulation and control over the violent fluctuations that came from unalloyed competition was widely recognized.
Protectionists, therefore, focused primarily on the domestic consequences of economic policy. Free traders, on the other hand, as befitted
their function in the great trading companies, attended more to the
international dimension. As a consequence, free traders tended to be
more open to protectionist measures that served the international ends of
commerce. The line between protectionism and free trade, once again,
showed itself to be a moving and unstable boundary.

The intellectual fathers of free trade were themselves walking models of
this plastic meaning. John Locke, the inventor of the gold standard, for
example, recommended government regulation to ensure favorable trade
balances. The case was similar with Adam Smith, whose place in the

[20] Ralph Davis, "Rise of Protectionism," pp. 313, 315–16.

economic literature is generally regarded as the launching pad for Malthus, Ricardo and the other classical political economists. Yet Smith was the intellectual heir to the pamphlet literature of the eighteenth century. Indeed, there is less discontinuity in eighteenth-century economic theory between Smith and his mercantilist forebears than between Smith and those classical political economists of the nineteenth century who claimed his parentage. Smith was openly pragmatic about the continuing relevance of protection, for example. It was true that Smith was more definitive than many of his contemporaries on the theoretical advantages of liberal free trade. Yet he regarded the Navigation Acts as "perhaps, the wisest of all the commercial regulations of England" because their original purpose of defense against the naval power of the Netherlands now served as security against any power that tried to challenge British commercial supremacy. In the final analysis, Smith recognized that "defense . . . is of much more importance than opulence." Although Smith saw control of the colonial trade as distorting and ultimately dangerous, he also recognized that a sudden dissolution of the connection would be extremely disruptive and could only propose to leave the question "to the wisdom of future statesmen and legislators."[21]

Smith was similarly practical on monopolies. He argued that, although monopolies ultimately distorted the "natural distribution of stock of the society," in the British case these effects were generally countered by the liberal aspects of British trade and rule. He recognized that, in the early years of an enterprise, monopoly could be both necessary and justified. Problems arose once the enterprise became more than just a trading company and obtained political interests which were then used to preserve its monopoly position and divert attention from trade. Once this point had been reached there was no possible advantage in the maintenance of a trade monopoly. Similarly, Smith's perspective on the balance between free trade and protection within the political economy was close to that which prevailed in the 1690s. He thought that "to expect . . . that the freedom of trade should ever be entirely restored in Great Britain is as absurd as to expect that an Oceana or Utopia should ever be established in it." He doubted that free trade could ever completely dominate because of the ability of the industrial interest groups to secure protection for themselves through Parliament. At the least he

---

[21] Adam Smith, *An Inquiry into the Nature and Causes of the Wealth of Nations*, ed. R. H. Campbell, A. S. Skinner and W. B. Todd (London, 1976), vol. I, pp. 464–65, 471 (quotes); Appleby, *Economic Thought and Ideology*, pp. 254–55; Pocock, *Virtue, Commerce and History*, p. 123; Viner, *Theory of International Trade*, p. 108; Donald Winch, *Adam Smith's Politics: An Essay in Historiographic Revision* (Cambridge, 1978), pp. 4–5, 180–81, 184–85; Winch, *Riches and Poverty: An Intellectual History of Political Economy in Britain 1750–1834* (Cambridge, 1996), p. 161.

expected that free trade would be introduced very slowly, which in fact it was.[22]

Adam Smith's version of free trade, then, allowed for a judicious element of protectionism to accommodate various interests groups and to protect Britain's commercial health. In this respect Smith was more in the tradition of the eighteenth-century economic debate than he was a pre-cursor of the hegemony of nineteenth-century free trade ideology. Con-trasting prescriptions for trade policy could be drawn from the authority of Smith, unlike Malthus, Ricardo or Mill. Lord Shelburne claimed in the 1780s that during a carriage ride with Smith he had the inspiration for a bill that would follow the recommendation in the *Wealth of Nations* and drop all trade regulations with the colonies. On the other hand, at about the same time, Smith's defense of the Navigation Acts was being used to justify a more moderate measure that would preserve the West India trade for Britain while freeing trade between Britain and the United States themselves. Both positions were held by Smith.[23]

Thus, Smith's own economic writings were largely within an eight-eenth-century tradition of a continuum between free trade and protec-tionism. Nevertheless, it was Smith's accomplishment to separate out mercantilist and free trade theories from ideas that had previously over-lapped. What divided protectionists and free traders by Adam Smith's time was less the technicalities of economic logic and more the political import of particular policies. Whereas protectionists looked to political intervention to reconcile public and private interest, free traders were increasingly suspicious of this and saw it as unlikely to foster either social virtue or economic enterprise. The ultimate result of the growing separ-ation and tension between protectionists and free trader was a closure of the economic debate that had marked eighteenth-century discourse. The exuberant literature of eighteenth-century economic debate, for example, contained the space to contest Smith himself. Neither Ricardo nor Mill were subject to the same kind of challenge. This was the real significance of 1846: it marked the capture of the economic discourse by a particular interpretation of free trade which contained no room for other alterna-tives. A trade policy was implemented which aimed to reduce tariffs and to rely on indirect taxes for revenue. This was then *named* free trade. The duties that remained were somehow not considered relevant to this interpretation, as they have not been deemed relevant in the historiogra-

---

[22] Adam Smith, *Wealth of Nations*, vol. II, pp. 606 (quotes), 608–14, 631, 637–41.
[23] Ralph Davis, "Rise of Protectionism," p. 314; Langford, *A Polite and Commercial People*, pp. 631–34, for the way American independence raised the question as to whether protectionism was now necessary. See also Winch, *Riches and Poverty*, pp. 158–59, 161–62, 205, 211.

phy. Protectionism as a fully fledged doctrine was decisively ruled out of court by the repeal of the corn laws and the succeeding repeal of the Navigation Acts in 1849. With the exception of Robert Torrens, no reputable economist dared call himself anything other than a free trader.[24]

But it would be a mistake to leave the matter there. While nineteenth-century free trade came to be far less problematic than it had been earlier, it remained subject to different meanings. Free trade continued to be rent with ambiguity after 1846. The Gladstonian version of free trade was the governmental version. Yet it was not the only rendition. Nor was its dominance quite as solid as historians have assumed. Beneath the seeming universality of its intellectual hold lay a greater diversity of opinion than we tend to assume. The consensus around free trade in the middle of the nineteenth century was more fragile than it appears at first sight.

Furthermore, the relatively sudden triumph of free trade as the hegemonic – the only *possible* – economic doctrine in the early nineteenth century was not the result of a spectacular epiphany by the intellectual and political classes. The ideas of Victorian free trade had been available for many years. Yet it was only after 1815 that they began to sweep all other notions aside. Why was this? It was because free trade was never solely a matter of economics. Free trade was also a cultural construct whose power derived from its legitimating the market system of economic individualism. In addition, free trade began to possess more relevance to key sectors of the political economy after 1815. This was particularly true for the finance capitalism of the City of London, previously the home of protectionism and old corruption. More hesitantly and then only at the last minute did key sectors of manufacturing capital join the free trade caravan.

A fragile hegemony

The progress of free trade was extremely uneven until its triumph in national politics in the 1840s. This was particularly true in the industrial and commercial communities. We might expect this in the City of London with its long association with the trading companies and its fiscal entanglement with the state. Yet it was true even in Manchester where opinion on trade policy remained divided well into the 1840s and even beyond. At the end of the Napoleonic wars free traders attained a significant presence in Manchester through their control of a section of the local press. The progress of their ideas and their political power were not to be

---

[24] For the challenge to Smith, at a much lower level of intellectual achievement, see Thomas Mortimer, *Lectures on the Elements of Commerce, Politics and Finances* (London, 1801); Winch, *Riches and Poverty*, pp. 332–35.

taken for granted, however. Indeed, the presence of a vocal free trade group within the city's bourgeoisie stimulated debate and contention rather than paving the way for their hegemony. The success of free trade beliefs within the Manchester business community depended, as it always had, on the particular needs of commerce. In this respect, of course, circumstances smiled on the fortunes of the free traders and legitimated their discourse. With the cotton industry poised on the edge of a significant world dominion, the remaining taxes on textile imports and exports were an unnecessary burden. The same was true of assessed taxes such as the stamp duties and protectionist customs like the sugar duties which increased the cost of living and, therefore, wages. Similarly, trade policy continued to be discussed in terms of monopoly because Manchester goods needed to gain access to the Indian and China markets controlled by the East India Company.

On other issues, where the interests of commerce pointed to a different trade policy, there was far greater diversity of opinion. Different sectors within the same industry had different fiscal policy interests. There continued to be support for the regulation of emigration by skilled artisans and controls on the export of machinery, for example. The export of yarns and twist caused divisions within the cotton industry. Master spinners wanted to be free to sell yarn and twist abroad, but those engaged in other branches of the cotton trade opposed their export as depriving handloom weavers of work. Nor was there ever unanimity on the corn laws. As elsewhere, there was no great cry from Manchester industry for free trade in corn. The special place of agriculture in the economy was accepted. From the 1820s the free trade ideologues faced strong opposition for their position on repeal, and the most they could get was agreement on a moderate fixed duty rather than a sliding scale. In December 1838, for the first time, free traders secured enough support for a resolution supporting repeal of the corn laws. But the Chamber of Commerce remained largely protectionist. And the free trade group in Manchester triumphed only in 1845 when the conservatives walked out to form their own Chamber of Commerce.[25]

Industrial Britain's ambiguity about free trade should not surprise us. It is useful to be reminded that the debate over economic theory involved more than just the elegance of theory. One of the basic sectoral divisions in the economy was between those directed toward the home market and

[25] See Michael Turner, "Before the Manchester School"; William D. Grampp, *The Manchester School of Economics* (Stanford, 1960), pp. 11–12; A. C. Howe, *The Cotton Masters 1830–1860* (Oxford, 1984); Lucy Brown, *The Board of Trade and the Free Trade Movement*, pp. 53–54, 161–63. Not enough attention has been paid to the sectoral differences on fiscal policy even within the same industry. For this in twentieth-century free trade debates, see Trentmann, "Political Culture and Political Economy."

those whose interests lay in foreign markets. This divide had also formed one of the shifting boundaries between protectionist and free trade policies. Thus, manufacturing interests tended to favor protectionism and those involved in commerce – even monopolistic commerce – tended to favor free trade. If the creation and the distribution of wealth was to lie primarily in the domestic markets, manufacturing industry must be protected. On the other hand, if wealth was to be derived from trade, policy should focus on the foreign market.

It was obvious that these were not mutually exclusive positions, nor were they arguments that could be generalized for all commerce or manufacture. Still, it was the argument of classical political economy to have effectively integrated these divergences. This may have been true at the purely theoretical level. Yet it hardly resolved the matter in terms of practical politics because different trade policies implied different social policies within the domestic regime. It was traditionally argued that trade policies that privileged commerce threatened social stability by exposing the price of goods (and especially food) to the vagaries of market fluctuations. And this explained why the political establishment was very cautious about embracing a free trade policy. On the other hand, policies that protected the home market were prized because they stimulated employment and were thought to guarantee a greater degree of social peace. By the early nineteenth century, however, such policies were increasingly seen as intellectually unrespectable and economically short-sighted.

The differing claims of the home or foreign market in the making of trade policy were not an invention of the early nineteenth century. They were a permanent fixture to the economic literature of the eighteenth century. Indeed, the competing positions were first formulated in the 1690s, were an issue of hot debate around Walpole's policies, reappeared in the French treaty of 1786 and were part of the critique that had been launched by Thomas Mortimer against Adam Smith and Thomas Malthus in the 1790s. It was not surprising, therefore, that the contrasting priority of the home versus the foreign market became a contentious issue again as Britain moved to return to the gold standard between 1819 and 1821.[26]

---

[26] Johnson, *Predecessors of Adam Smith*, pp. 147, 152–56; Appleby, *Economic Thought and Ideology*, pp. 202–07, 226–41; [Martyn,] *Considerations upon the East India Trade*; William Pulteney, *Some Considerations on the National Debt* (London, 1729), pp. 80–83; R. J., *A Woollen Draper's Letter on the French Treaty* (London, 1786); Mortimer, *Lectures*, pp. 69–72, 83–85; but note that both Pulteney and Mortimer provide good examples of the overlapping nature of this body of argument because they also emphasized the importance the reexport trade. It is worth speculating that the bias against mass consumption and high wages that is a major theme in British economic policy and culture in the twentieth century can be traced to this period.

This was the crucial moment in the debate between these two tendencies in economic thought. The nineteenth-century version of free trade as an economic, cultural and social construct was forged in the crucible of this debate. More than just economic theory was at issue. What was at stake was the social order that was to underlie the fiscal policy. Yet economic theory was central to this wider import, for the social order could be argued to be mandated by economic theory. And so it was. Commitment to the gold standard possessed very precise implications for domestic policy. A trade policy that rested on the gold standard presumed some version of free trade as the preferred economic policy – although which version was not implicit. Reliance on the gold standard for economic virtue also implied a low priority for domestic manufacturing and (partly as a consequence) a low-wage policy. A protectionist policy implied a strong home market and (also partly as a consequence) a high-wage policy. This issue was an old one. In the context of the post-Napoleonic war period, however, it became a debate over how to reshape the political economy. On the one side were the "Birmingham School" of economists (although it reached outside Birmingham, into *Blackwood's Magazine*, for example, and crossed class lines to find slightly different forms of development in the Owenite socialists). And on the other side were the political followers of David Ricardo and the younger ranks of the intelligentsia.

The Birmingham School tended to place the agricultural interest at the center of their conception of the social order. They argued that the true index of national prosperity should be grain prices – which, of course, was exactly the kind of perception that classical political economists were trying to get away from. At this point the Birmingham School arguments met the interests of the landed gentry whose concerns went beyond the simple material advantage of a protected agricultural market. Gentry spokespersons had long developed a consumptionist argument to justify protection. As early as 1717 it had been pointed out that the laboring people represented the only mass market available to the economy. The less the lower class spent, the worse off the farmers and shopkeepers would be, and the more it cost the landed gentry to support the poor law and give to charities. British society had no economic or cultural place for a mass market composed of the working classes, however, until the later nineteenth century. Thus, in retrospect, these arguments presented easy targets to the superior intellectual firepower of the Ricardians. But it is important to remember that the protectionist system was still intact, had widespread popular support and was not without allies. Indeed, the Birmingham School could point to the many "practical" men like Sir John Sinclair, Arthur Young and Patrick Colquhoun who supported its position. The Ricardians by contrast were self-consciously theoretical. Ricardo himself always disclaimed any knowledge of practical economics. Indeed, his main contribution was precisely to remove economics from the political economy focus of Smith into a more abstract theoretical discourse that claimed the status of a science separate from political intention.[27]

For the Birmingham School (as for Smith), the purpose of economic activity was consumption. Yet their view of consumption was tied more closely to the goods produced by industry and consumed by the working classes. Like earlier commentators who favored privileging the domestic market, the Birmingham School saw the function of economics as furthering the interests of social balance and peace. Monetary policies that rested on a metallic currency were seen by the Birmingham School as imposing too many limitations on economic expansion. They believed that industrial production would tend to outrun the available supply of gold. The result would be cycles of deflation and industrial depression, unemployment and the consequent transfer of resources from producers to nonproducers. This could be avoided, however, using the state's control of the money supply to maintain high domestic demand. Thomas Attwood, for example, wanted to use the income tax to redistribute income to increase working-class consumption.[28]

The Birmingham School held an optimistic view of economic potential. By contrast, restraint was the watchword of classical political economy. The Malthusian proposition that population would outstrip resources unless human behavior was constrained was a fundamental tenet of belief. This fit well with the class preferences of classical political economy which had been refined somewhat since Adam Smith's time. Smith's emphasis on the cost of corn and the role of supply and demand as the ultimate determinants of market value had been displaced by Ricardo's attention to the role of labor in the economic system. Everything in Ricardo's schema revolved around the centrality of labor costs, from the rate of profit to the price of gold to the value of the product of the land. Ricardo believed that only by saving and retrenching expenditure could national capital be increased. It was precisely the

[27] David Moss, *Thomas Attwood: Biography of a Radical* (Montreal, 1990), pp. 55, 63, 66; S. G. Checkland, "The Birmingham Economists, 1815–1850," *Economic History Review*, 2nd ser., 1, 1 (1948), pp. 9, 13–14; Richard Wiles, "The Theory of Wages in Later English Mercantilism," *Economic History Review*, 2nd ser., 31, 2 (1968), pp. 113–26; Ingham, *Capitalism Divided?*, pp. 102–03, 107–09.

[28] Checkland, "Birmingham Economists"; Moss, *Thomas Attwood*, pp. 55–84; Appleby, *Economic Thought and Ideology*, pp. 238–41; David Ricardo, *On the Principles of Political Economy and Taxation*, ed. Piero Sraffa (Cambridge, 1982), pp. 246, 296, 352, 382. Harold Perkin puts "Birmingham School" economics in the context of a paternalistic "aristocratic revival." See his *Origins of Modern English Society*, pp. 246–52.

need for restraint that made the gold standard so attractive to Ricardians, because it delivered an automatic assurance of equilibrium which would correct sudden fluctuations in the exchanges and thereby bring the economic system back into a balance between resources and demand. For the classical economists consumption was inherently inflationary. And the most effective prophylactic against inflation, therefore, was low wages.[29]

The social policy implications of these two positions – the Birmingham School and the Ricardians – demonstrated a significant continuity with the past. An emphasis on the foreign market and the use of the gold standard to regulate the economy implied a lower priority for manufacture and a willing acceptance of a low-wage economy. This had been apparent from the very beginning when the idea of the gold standard had first been floated in the 1690s. The Birmingham economists were the descendants of those who opposed the free trade merchants of the 1690s on the grounds that free trade exposed the poor to the caprice of market forces. Their emphasis on the home market was underpinned by a social conviction that a managed currency was the best way to fuse economic growth and the responsibility of government for the wellbeing of the people. Their analysis implied a high-wage and mass-consumption economy. This, too, had been a commonplace among many of the protagonists in the debates of the 1690s. Commentators such as Daniel Defoe, John Cary and Henry Davenant had argued that high wages promoted efficiency in the division of labor and – most importantly – social stability. Similarly, Thomas Mortimer in his critique of Smith had argued that a high-wage labor force would be more cooperative and productive, and that wages should be indexed to the cost of living.[30]

It is not surprising that the Owenites and Ricardian socialists picked up on these arguments and integrated them into their analysis that the cause of economic instability lay in the deleterious effects of competition and overproduction. Working-class spokespersons like William Newton, the engineering union leader, were continuing to make these arguments well into the 1850s, long after respectable opinion had consigned them to the dustbin of bad economics. Historians have been much too willing to endorse such a trashing. And considerable attention has been given to the deep loyalty of the working class to free trade ideology. It would be well to remember that there was once another

[29] Ricardo, *Political Economy and Taxation*, pp. 247–49, 253–54, 296, 352, 382.
[30] Mortimer, *Lectures*, p. 69; J. E. King, " 'Perish Commerce!': Free Trade and Underconsumption in Early British Radical Economics," *Australian Economic Papers*, 20, 37 (December 1981), pp. 235–50.

analysis whose disappearance from working-class politics would also be a tale worth recovering.[31]

The triumph of free trade was a political process that was built on the charred ruins of its competitors. By the early 1820s the alternative political economy offered by the Birmingham School had been intellectually marginalized and politically crippled. The economic knowledge system was captured by the Ricardians with the assistance of their liberal Tory allies. The story of why the Birmingham School failed to secure the discourse of political economy has not been satisfactorily told, and cannot be attempted here. But this failure cannot be attributed to intellectual inadequacy. The Birmingham School undoubtedly suffered serious theoretical shortcomings – such as how the currency would actually be managed. Ricardian economics, by contrast, was a much sweeter theory. Obviously, a theory has to be persuasive for it to achieve credibility among political and social groups who matter. On the other hand, the success of a particular viewpoint also depends on its political resonances and implications and, more simply, on the success of the particular theory in capturing key citadels of intellectual and sociopolitical power. How free trade and gold standard orthodoxy successfully captured the knowledge system of the nineteenth century has also not been adequately disclosed. Still, a key moment in the process can, perhaps, be glimpsed when Huskisson and Ricardo managed the evidence presented to the Select Committee on Agricultural Distress in 1821 in such a way as to discredit Attwood's Birmingham School theories and allow only the view of the Ricardians. No doubt the years from the 1820s through the 1840s were full of such episodes, as free trade doctrine seeped into the bastions of opinion and power.[32]

The intellectual and political victory of free trade orthodoxy against the putative alternative of the Birmingham School, however, was less complete than has been traditionally allowed. Even in the middle of the nineteenth century when it faced no major economic competitor, the

[31] R. J., *A Woollen Draper's Letter*, pp. 19–21; Boyd Hilton, *Cash, Corn and Commerce: The Economic Policies of the Tory Governments 1815–1830* (Oxford, 1977), p. 293; Gregory Claeys, *Machinery, Money and the Millennium: From Moral Economy to Socialism, 1815–1860* (Cambridge, 1987), pp. 192–94, for the continuities between economic theory in the seventeenth and eighteenth centuries and Owenite theory. For working-class liberalism, see Biagini, *Liberty, Retrenchment and Reform*, pp. 95–100. For the revival of this tradition, see Frank Trentmann, "Wealth Versus Welfare: The British Left Between Free Trade and National Political Economy Before the First World War," *Historical Research*, 70, 171 (February 1997), pp. 70–97.

[32] Another moment would be when the Whig chancellor, Lord Althorp, tried to manage the committee to' renew the charter of the Bank of England so as to exclude alternative theories to those represented by its wisdom. See Hilton, *Cash, Corn and Commerce*, pp. 306–14; Moss, *Thomas Attwood*, pp. 96, 304–05; Checkland, "Birmingham Economists," pp. 15–18.

meaning of free trade was contested. There were very real differences, for example, between Richard Gladstone, Cobden and the more extreme free traders organized into the Financial Reform Association. The case of John Ramsay McCulloch is instructive as an illustration of the tensions within the free trade camp.

McCulloch was an enormously prolific writer who published his first essay on the national debt in 1816 and went on to see five editions of his textbook on political economy, the last in the year of his death in 1864. He is frequently regarded as a crude free trader who was more Ricardian than Ricardo. Yet, in fact, he was a sharp critic of the Cobden–Gladstone school of free trade and of those in the Financial Reform Association who favored the substitution of a property tax for all duties. McCulloch's definition of free trade was that all commodities be treated alike rather than the removal of all duties. He favored the fixed duty on corn in recognition of the special status of agriculture, and supported moderate import duties for revenue purposes and export duties, which he believed transferred costs to the foreign consumer. He criticized Gladstone's 1860 budget as going too far in the free trade direction. McCulloch opposed a system which imposed heavy duties on selected items while admitting others free of charge for its restriction of choice and its artificial channeling of trade. Such a policy, he believed, possessed "all the worst features of the old protective policy, being a mere tissue of preferences and *quasi* prohibitions."[33]

Free trade, therefore, continued to be subject to different meanings. It was not to be confused, for example, with laissez-faire. Free traders could contemplate government intervention in market structures – to counter the effects of monopoly in the railways, for example. Furthermore, free trade's intellectual and political hegemony was deceptively shallow. A subterranean stream of protectionist sentiment persisted throughout the period. Even in Manchester some cotton masters were proclaiming free trade a failure by 1850, at least in its Cobdenite version. And in the mid-1850s the indictment was heard from the same quarters that free trade produced an adverse balance of trade, an increased dependence on foreign food and raw materials and depression in industry. This was exactly the case that was to be made by the Fair Trade and Tariff Reform movements from the 1870s. Liverpool was unusual in being the home of both extreme protectionism and extreme free trade

[33] J. R. McCulloch, *A Treatise on the Principles and Practical Influence of Taxation and the Funding System*, ed. D. P. O'Brien (Edinburgh and London, 1975), pp. xlii, xliii, xlv, 224–29. For McCulloch, see D. P. O'Brien, *J. R. McCulloch: A Study in Classical Economics* (New York, 1970). See also Bernard Holland, *The Fall of Protection 1840–1850* (repr., Philadelphia, 1980 [London, 1913]), pp. 322–33.

positions. Yet Liverpool's popular politics in the 1840s and 1850s remained staunchly protectionist. There was a brief national skirmish in the late 1860s when Lord John Manners, commissioner of public works, called for Peel's work to be reversed. An "Association of Revivers" was formed by industries suffering from foreign competition which sponsored a flurry of discussion in towns as diverse as Macclesfield, Coventry, Spitalfields, Preston, Manchester, Derby and Nottingham.[34]

What is striking is the speed with which protectionist sentiments entered the public discourse with the appearance of economic depression in the 1870s. The first serious rumblings of discontent with free trade from the nether regions of the provinces began to catch the attention of the world of high politics in the early 1870s. Later in the decade this questioning spilled over into the chambers of commerce in the industrial towns as they began to discuss the implications of the depression for trade policy. With the formation of the National Fair Trade League in 1881, the issue of imperial preference was once again placed on the political agenda. The short-lived hegemony of free trade – however it was defined – as a trade policy was decisively broken, even as its enormous power and appeal still remained.[35]

Free trade, however, was not simply an economic theory. It was also a cultural construction. Indeed, to understand properly the intellectual hegemony of Victorian free trade, it is necessary to move beyond economics. Nineteenth-century free trade derived its cultural power from its moralization of economics. The moral discourse of free trade afforded a legitimation of the social order as a natural phenomenon and a framework for individual behavior that was consistent with pure market economics. This provided the singular advantage of free trade over protectionism, for it fused economics and morality into a system that met the needs of a political economy of commercial imperialism. This was not inherent in free trade economics; it had to be constructed. It is to that question that I shall now turn.

The moral economy of free trade

At the beginning of our period a political economy designed by free trade held no moral advantage. Indeed, the difficulty with free trade lay precise-

---

[34] Howe, *Free Trade and Liberal England*, pp. 86–87; John Belchem, "Introduction: The Peculiarities of Liverpool," pp. 9–13, and "Liverpool in the Year of Revolution: The Political and Associational Culture of the Irish Immigrant Community in 1848," pp. 60–67, both in Belchem (ed.), *Popular Politics, Riot and Labour: Essays in Liverpool History 1790–1940* (Liverpool, 1991); John Noble, *Free Trade, Reciprocity and the Revivers* (London, 1869).
[35] Benjamin Brown, *The Tariff Reform Movement in Great Britain 1881–1895* (New York, 1943), pp. 2–17.

ly in its failure to provide a moral compass for market behavior. For economic exchange to work effectively, honor and trust were essential. Yet it was obvious that these virtues clashed with the search for advantage and profit which were the great motors of economic change for the economic individualist. The logical premises of economic individualism were exposed to devastating satire by Bernard Mandeville in his renowned *Fable of the Bees*, published in 1714. Mandeville identified the moral vacuity that lay behind the arguments for economic individualism. If self-interest was the motor of economic advancement, then questions of morality were irrelevant to actions that brought economic gain. Private vices were, therefore, the necessary basis of public progress and prosperity. Mandeville's argument was deeply troubling at a time when virtue and vice were seen in competition for the public mind and it is hardly surprising that Mandeville met with a fiercely negative response. Yet it was an argument that revealed the inability of individualism and free trade to provide a morally reassuring way of understanding economic processes.[36]

By contrast, both the moral and the political advantages seemed to lie with the protectionist point of view. The advantage of protectionism was that it allowed domestic social stability to be combined with the pursuit of increased trade balances. Protectionism offered a superior trade policy because it promised to provide the poor with employment in the nation's industries, thereby securing domestic peace and as a consequence protecting the class hierarchy. The transformation of free trade and economic individualism into a morally superior theory of economy is, therefore, one of the more astounding events of our period.

It was John Locke who had first attempted to explain how economic growth was best secured by individual freedom. Locke placed great emphasis upon the market as the arbiter and judge of economic rationality. To this end, as we have seen, he invented the gold standard. Locke's theory that money had value only in relation to the esteem placed by men in gold and silver was an attempt to complete the logic of a system of economic individualism. Yet this was not a theory that met with much approval at the time. It was not particularly convincing empirically, nor was it a theory that projected a particularly attractive social order. In later years the trumping force of an argument for economic individualism was to be that it legitimated the social hierarchy and the distribution of power

---

[36] Bernard Mandeville, *The Fable of the Bees*, ed. and intro. Phillip Harth (London, 1970). The same horror, of course, greeted Hobbes. John Locke recognized the contradiction highlighted by Mandeville and recommended, for example, that merchants not be made to swear oaths as to the truthfulness of their customs accounts because the temptations to perjury would be so great as to threaten the credibility of the state.

as natural products of market relations. At this particular moment in time, however, this strength of free trade economics was well hidden.[37]

It was Adam Smith's achievement to establish this advantage. Smith authorized free trade theory in two ways. In the first instance, he laid out with greater erudition than ever before the theory of economic liberalism. And, in the second instance, he provided the necessary *moral* case for free trade and individualism. Smith was by no means the first to identify economic analysis as integral to moral philosophy. But he was, perhaps, the most uniquely qualified to speak on both accounts because he was above all a moral philosopher. Indeed, *Wealth of Nations* can best be read as an extension, a working through, of the economic implications of Smith's earlier work on the *Theory of Moral Sentiments*. In his moral philosophy Smith gave credence to a providential distribution of economic justice: adversity and reward were generally found to accord with bad and good behavior. Smith's argument in *Wealth of Nations* provided the economic justification for that system.

Smith treated property and material needs as historical constructions and argued that freedom was demonstrably the best way to assure the proper distribution of these qualities. Free trade was thus placed firmly on the side of the angels of natural justice (meaning freedom of property and politics) and prosperity. The moral advantage that protectionism had possessed was that it was the only way to secure a fair degree of subsistence for the poor. This was undermined by Smith's argument that only individualism could satisfy the claims of both property (through freedom) and the poor (through fair distribution). This notion was a crucial breakthrough for the free trade argument; it provided a convincing intellectual framework for economic development. Even more profoundly, Smith's argument secured the moral high ground for free trade. It allowed the possibility that the results of the market could serve as the arbiter and judge of individual morality. This was precisely the intellectual footing to the argument for economic individualism that had been lacking in Locke.[38]

---

[37] Appleby, *Economic Thought and Ideology*, pp. 188–89, 191, 221–36.

[38] For these two paragraphs, see Istvan Hont and Michael Ignatieff, *Wealth and Virtue: The Shaping of Political Economy in the Scottish Enlightenment* (Cambridge, 1983), pp. 42–43, 261; Winch, *Riches and Poverty*, pp. 21–23; Teichgraeber, *"Free Trade" and Moral Philosophy*. See Adam Smith, *The Theory of Moral Sentiments*, ed. D. D. Raphael and A. L. Macfie (6th edn., Oxford, 1976), pp. 21–25. The economic discourse was hungry for Smith's arguments, as the contrast with James Steuart, the Jacobite theorist of protectionism, reveals. Steuart's *Political Oeconomy* was published seven years before Smith's *Wealth of Nations*, yet it disappeared into oblivion almost as soon as it appeared. Smith played a quite nasty role in this. Although he had drawn quite significantly upon Steuart's work, he discredited it in private and ignored it in public. Perhaps a reason for Smith's hostility to Steuart lay in the fact that Steuart believed as much as Smith that the economy was a

Smith argued that only unnatural human intervention distorted the natural workings of economic exchange. It was but a short step from this to see free trade economic theory as divinely ordained. This was where the discourse of high economic theory, the language of political economy, met the discourse of economics as an expression of providential will. In popular and political parlance, economic trends and developments were expressed through a theology of evangelicalism which emphasized the role of providential judgment in life. This was tremendously functional in Victorian society where the explanatory power of religion was fast eroding because it allowed faith in the invisible hand of providence to be retained through Smith's invisible hand of economics. Until the 1870s the major authorities for the conceptions that guided popular economics were early eighteenth-century sources such as the philosophical divine Bishop Butler. Both William Gladstone and Peel subscribed fully to Bishop Butler's conception of economics as a balance between virtue and retribution. Such a notion would have particular psychological appeal to Gladstone, of course, with his highly developed sense of moral fragility. Gladstone had been converted to the ethical precepts of Bishop Butler in the 1830s and continued to regard him as a major moral authority throughout his life. Indeed, when Butler was dropped from the Oxford University syllabus in the mid-1850s, Gladstone was outraged. As late as 1896, he published an edition of Butler's works.[39]

Underlying the theories of free trade and the gold standard as they tightened their hold in the political culture lurked the hell-fire and damnation of the old testament. Both religious conception and economic theory could be joined in a notion of an active providence working through the natural functioning of individual wills. Economic outcomes and events could therefore be seen as judgments by God on man. This was a line of reasoning about economic prospects that fit well with the main themes of the dismal science to impress upon the working classes the limits to growth and the necessity for sexual abstinence and political

natural process. He believed, however, that it was the duty of government to correct the unnatural results of that process. This is not to deny that *Wealth of Nations* is a more impressive work; it is merely to remark that its very publication was a political as well as an intellectual step in the validation of the theory of free trade individualism. See Johnson, *Predecessors of Adam Smith*, p. 209, and *passim*; Hont and Ignatieff, *Wealth and Virtue*, p. 19.

[39] Hilton, *Corn, Cash and Commerce*, pp. 312–13; and more particularly, of course, Hilton, *Age of Atonement*, pp. 15–16, 25–32, 53–67, 75, 170–79, 341, and *passim*. Cobdenite free trade internationalism was an aspect of this moralizing of economics; see R. F. Spall, "Free Trade, Foreign Relations, and the Anti-Corn Law League," *International History Review*, 10, 3 (August 1988), pp. 405–32. There were, of course, variations among Victorian free traders to their attachment to this version of divine economics – Cobden was much less committed to Butler than Gladstone or Peel. In Gladstone's case, the need to explore the boundaries between virtue and retribution in his relations with women led to frequent self-flagellation to subdue his sexual temptation.

restraint. Deflationary tendencies were morally good because they purged the economic system of ill-gotten and immoral wealth, taught the working classes that economic salvation could come only from self-restraint and forced men to be responsible for their own destinies. Nineteenth-century free trade was, therefore, underpinned by a moral framework of sometimes quite frightening darkness. The economic views of William Huskisson, the initiator of tariff reduction in the 1820s, are described by Boyd Hilton as

a state of moral trial, avarice and original economic sin, and economic man in a condition of probation. It was a system of temptation and retribution, conversion and self-restraint, whose sanction was the shame and gains of debt, and whose hope lay in the atoning sacrifice of bankrupts.[40]

This religious vision of the world of economics was perfectly designed for the key tenets of free trade individualism. Religion moralized economics and provided a providential discipline to the natural corruption of man's character. As we have seen, the gold standard could serve as a neutral regulator of economic behavior, but it suffered from the absence of a moral arbiter. This absence was filled by the development of evangelical economics. A religious dimension was accorded to the economic fluctuations that followed from adherence to the gold standard. Economic results attained the status of the self-acting rewards and punishments of a divinely inspired nature.

In chronological terms the early and mid-Victorian years stand at the tail end of that eighteenth-century habit of categorizing public life through the values of corruption and virtue. Yet, oddly, a moralized conception of political economy rooted in the eighteenth-century notion of consumption as luxurious vice was never a stronger presence in the culture than during the Victorian years. Indeed, the last exponents of this image of economic action were certainly the most eloquent and powerful. Gladstone's obsessional faith in the moralizing nature of free trade made him the last liberal Tory. Economic theory was not to shake the moralizing mantle of the eighteenth century until the 1850s and 1860s. Measures such as limited liability law were the mundane instruments of this renunciation, as they moved debt and bankruptcy out the realm of morality and into the (new) procedure of accountancy. By then, too, Christian theology was in the process of transforming its vision of Hell from a geographical location into a metaphor. And by the 1880s the purpose of economics was no longer believed to be to explicate a theory of ethics and morality. Ricardo had aspired to create the new science of economics. Yet it was not until the application of a positivist methodology

[40] Hilton, *Cash, Corn and Commerce*, pp. 313–14.

to the study of society that economics could claim to have become a scientific procedure rather than a set of religio-moral prescriptions. The theory of marginal utility had no room for the theory of moral sentiments.[41]

The cultural power of free trade would not have been enough to account for its capture of the discourse of political economy, however. In addition to its economic and cultural dimensions, there was a compass to free trade which was both political and contingent. From the 1820s the passage of free trade ideology through the worlds of politics and business was eased by the growing convergence between the moralized economy of free trade with two more material influences: the changing shape of commercial interests and the need to respond to economic challenge from abroad. This final piece must now be fitted into the puzzle of nineteenth-century free trade.

Free trade and commerce: convergence and contingency

Free trade is commonly associated with the contest between a protectionist-inclined agricultural sector and a free trade-leaning middle-class sector. In reality the affinity of free trade was closest to the commercial and financial sectors of the economy. Manufacturing industry possessed a natural empathy for protectionism, and the primal instinct of the landed classes was to follow whatever policy promised social peace. These attachments remained alive into the nineteenth century. The social location of the ideology of evangelical economics was not in the North of England, but in the South. In spite of the looming presence of the dissenting middle classes in the social history of the nineteenth century, Northern industrialists did not espouse this ideology. Their tendencies moved more on the spectrum of a Christian paternalism. Evangelical economics was the ideology of commercial interests in the City of London, the service economy, the professions and progressive Whig aristocrats. Thus, in addition to the power of economic theory and cultural persuasion, the story of how free trade became a dominant trade policy in the nineteenth century is also a story of the changing interests of commercial and financial capital.[42]

As I have suggested previously, the key moment in this process followed the end of the Napoleonic wars. It was increasingly apparent that commercial exchange was impeded by the protectionist apparatus that

---

[41] Hilton, *Age of Atonement*, pp. 64–70, 120–30, 248–50, 321, 335–39; H. G. C. Matthew, *Gladstone* (Oxford, 1986), vol. I, *1809–1874*, p. 76; Alon Kadish, *The Oxford Economists in the Late Nineteenth Century* (Oxford, 1982); Winch, *Riches and Poverty*, p. 414.
[42] Hilton, *Age of Atonement*, p. 375.

had previously served Britain so well. The experience of the war had suggested (as war always did) protectionism's dangers especially to the reexport trade. It was the reexport trade that was at the forefront of free trade thinking after the war years. The return to the gold standard after 1815 was made with the intent to strengthen the entrepôt trade rather than to assist the manufacturing sector of the economy. At this juncture neither free trade nor the gold standard were seen as the keystones to a world liberal economic order. At the same time, however, the manufacturing sector's commitment to protectionism was slackening. Indeed, by the end of the wars the major supporters of the protectionist system were the major beneficiaries of the Navigation Acts – the shipping interest and the great trading companies.

Industry was quite indifferent to free trade, too, of course. Yet the fact was that the markets for manufactured goods were about to grow exponentially, and manufacturers in Manchester and elsewhere were very conscious of this prospect. The traditional tie between the manufacturing sector and the home market was about to be broken. What was necessary now was a political economy that, on the one hand, accommodated these changing world conditions and, on the other hand, extended free market principles to social discipline domestically. Free trade as a slogan and a trade policy met those requirements. Protectionism stood in the way of both sides of this political economy. Thus, the steady move by the liberal Tory government of Lord Liverpool in the 1820s to dismantle protectionist structures moved in tandem with the elevation of the gold standard and the first serious moves to reduce tariffs. Similarly, the erosion of the edifice of the fiscal-military state began almost immediately. The installation of a free trade regime and the waning of the structures of "old corruption" were part of the same historical movement.[43]

Given the theoretical implications of the protectionist and free trade positions, it is unsurprising that the decisive shift toward a free trade policy was first registered in the City of London. Nor is it surprising that the context was provided by debate about the East India Company's trading monopoly when its charter came up for renewal in 1813. Provincial merchants pressed for a freer trade that would give them access to Company markets. The London merchants were divided on this issue, although a solid core supported the Company. Over the previous thirty years the case for monopoly had been severely weakened by the growing acceptance of the theoretical arguments for free trade and also by the government's progressive chipping away at the Company's powers as part

[43] See Ingham, *Capitalism Divided?*, pp. 97, 113–14; Briggs, *Age of Improvement*, p. 204, for the cotton industry's support of the gold standard.

of the effort to resolve the perpetual political and financial crises of Company rule.[44]

By 1813, therefore, the Company's political position was much weakened. In addition, core support for the Company among the London merchants had eroded. Since the 1790s the changing trading interests of the City companies encouraged the movement of opinion away from the protectionism of the trading companies and "old corruption" and toward free trade. In the 1790s, for example, much of Barings's business had been with the East India Company and they were strong supporters of the monopoly. By 1813 Barings had developed other interests superseding their Company business, and they were genuinely divided as to where their true interest lay. This was typical of the position of the City merchants and it marked the movement toward free trade sentiment in the London financial class.[45]

This, then, was a moment of opening toward free trade. The presence of a powerful free trade lobby was signaled in 1820 when the famous petition in support of free trade organized by Thomas Tooke was presented to Parliament. The Tooke petition received strong backing from those City merchant groups who traditionally had supported free trade. Yet the shifting balance of opinion was suggested by the fact that 50 percent of the directors of the Bank of England signed the petition. The mercantile community mobilized by Tooke was primarily involved in the reexport trade which, as usual, was seen as the main beneficiary from free trade. And the select committee of the Commons that was set up in response to the petition recommended abolition of most transit duties and the modification of the Navigation Acts to encourage trade with Germany and the Low Countries.

Nevertheless, the progress of free trade in the City of London, as elsewhere, remained hesitant and gradual. The merchant community of the City contained powerful interests such as the shipping and sugar lobbies that remained committed to protectionism. It should be remembered also that the reexport trade benefited from the protectionism of the Navigation Acts. But although protectionist interests remained prominent until the 1840s, the growing weakness of their position was exposed by the relative ease with which sugar duties were equalized in 1846 and

---

[44] Lawson, *East India Company*, pp. 124–25, 137–43. For examples of the growing involvement of the state in Company affairs, see Sutherland, *East India Company*, pp. 138, 177, 248.

[45] Halevy, *England in 1815*, pp. 321–23; W. R. Brock, *Lord Liverpool and Liberal Toryism 1820–1827* (Oxford, 1929), p. 194; Webster, "Political Economy of Trade Liberalization," pp. 404–19. Webster argues that the decision to open India to free trade was not taken in response to these provincial pressures or London divisions, but as part of a deliberate policy by the government.

the Navigation Acts repealed three years later. Contingent chance played a big role, however, in the erosion of the protectionist political economy. The financial crisis of 1847 bankrupted many of the firms prominent in the protected colonial trade and so removed them from the centers of power. Likewise, the 1847 crisis bankrupted 20 percent of the directors of the Bank of England and – it is not clear if the two were connected – was the occasion of a withdrawal of the East India Company from a central role in the Bank's affairs. Given the history of the relationship between the Bank and the great trading companies, this was a major event which signified the erasure of the structures of "old corruption" from the heart of the City.[46]

"Old corruption" also began to be divorced from the state. I have already noted the changing structure of state finances and the consequent shift in the function of the Bank of England from government financier to international banker. Yet free trade could not win the heart of the state until the politics of food supply had been transformed. The politics of trade policy continued to be driven by the social and domestic implications of the state of agriculture. The corn law of 1815, for example, was ample demonstration that the final determinant of economic policy remained food supply. The adoption of the corn law of 1815 was due less to the self-interest of the landed interest and more to a widespread assumption that agriculture was too important to leave to the vagaries of free trade. The fear was that an influx of imports from Europe would destroy agriculture and thereby threaten the social order. Free trade could not be installed until it was evident that agriculture did not need protection from large European surpluses waiting to pounce on the British market. The final element in the story of free trade that needs to be stressed, therefore, is the international dimension. This was a context in which the Navigation Laws were a far more important issue than the corn laws. It was a setting, too, which casts free trade more as an act of self-preservation than the fitting climax to a commercial and industrial imperium.[47]

Trade policy had long been about seeking reciprocal advantage. The arguments over the various trade treaties in the eighteenth century revolved around differing judgments as to the extent of reciprocal advan-

[46] See Ingham, *Capitalism Divided?*, pp. 97, 113–14; Howe, *Free Trade and Liberal England*, pp. 13–18, 50–56; A. C. Howe, "Free Trade and the City of London c. 1820–1870," *History*, 77, 251 (October 1992), pp. 391–410. Howe suggests that the initiative for the adoption of free trade by the City came from the shift in state policy by Peel and the Conservatives, but the lack of resistance suggests that shifts in the balance of interest of commercial and mercantile capital were also a part of this story.

[47] Hilton, *Corn, Cash and Commerce*, pp. 292–301. For the controversial nature of all corn laws in the eighteenth century, see Donald Grove Barnes, *A History of the English Corn Laws from 1660 to 1846* (London, 1930), chs. 2–5, 7.

tage that British manufacture and commerce gained. Every time there was a peace treaty with France or Spain it was scrutinized for the relative advantage each party obtained from the trade provisions. There was always sharp debate about the consequences of such trade politics. The Navigation Acts were not only about grabbing more trade for Britain; they were also a strategy in the reciprocity of Britain's trade agreements. Throughout their history, the acts had been manipulated in quite arbitrary ways to meet the needs of particular trading interests. The result was that the acts were a maze of exceptions, qualifications and dispensations.

Reciprocity was also at the heart of the campaigns for free trade. Free trade was seen as the most effective general answer to foreign reprisal for Britain's commercial progress or for the trade policy of its Navigation Acts. Thomas Tooke's petition of 1820, for example, had argued that a major reason for freer trade was precisely the growing threat of foreign retaliation. Similarly, when the Manchester Chamber of Commerce presented its petition for free trade in 1838, it opened with the claim that the "rapid extension of foreign manufactures" and the "consequent diminution of a profitable trade with the Continent" was been noted "with great alarm." Indeed, a powerful argument for free trade among Manchester men was their early experience of competition from economies like the United States. Free trade, they believed, could help impede the development of competitors. Thus, free trade was not simply something that Britain could now pursue because of its economic supremacy; it was a necessary response to the development and the policies of other countries.[48]

The economic diplomacy of the 1820s inaugurated by Huskisson was designed not so much to *free* trade as to preserve and protect Britain's commerce. Exceptions to the Navigation Acts were offered to aggressive or successful competitors who threatened to damage Britain's position. Indeed, the purpose of Huskisson's reforms was to update rather than to undermine the Navigation Acts. General revisions of the Navigation Laws in 1825 and 1833 continued the policies of the past by enumerating which goods had to be imported in British ships or those of the country of origin. The general purpose of these acts was to liberalize trade with

---

[48] Harper, *English Navigation Laws*, pp. 53, 350–56; Harte, "Rise of Protection and the English Linen Trade," pp. 85–91; Palmer, *Politics, Shipping and the Repeal of the Navigation Laws*, pp. 42, 50–54, 68–69; Norman McCord, *Free Trade: Theory and Practice from Adam Smith to Keynes* (Newton Abbott, 1976), pp. 51–52, 64–65; Michael Turner, "Before the Manchester School," pp. 233–34 (quotes); Grampp, *The Manchester School*, p. 113. Reciprocity was also at the heart of the revival of protectionist sentiment at the end of the century; see Trentmann, "The Transformation of Fiscal Reform: Reciprocity, Modernization, and the Fiscal Debate Within the Business Community in Early Twentieth-Century Britain," *Historical Journal*, 39, 4 (1996), pp. 1012–15.

Europe and retain control over long voyages for British ships. Alongside this liberalization an ambitious policy of economic diplomacy was launched of negotiating reciprocal treaties with countries like the United States, France, Prussia, Austria, Sweden and the South American republics. Between 1824 and 1844 twenty-six such treaties were negotiated. Reciprocity was at the heart of the technical attempts by economists to guess the effects of free trade. A sharp debate occurred in the 1840s between those who believed that unilateral tariff reduction would adversely affect the balance of trade and those who argued for tying reductions to reciprocal privileges. It was expected that reciprocity would remain a weapon in trade negotiations. It was not anticipated, for example, that repeal of the corn laws in 1846 implied repeal of the Navigation Acts. In common with many others within the political establishment, Gladstone was fully in favor of retaining the Navigation Acts as a negotiating inducement for other nations to sign reciprocal agreements with Britain.[49]

Thus, the final move toward free trade policies was essentially a *defensive* response. The recognition that British agriculture was not about to be swamped by foreign imports led to the realization that protectionism could work to Britain's disadvantage by impeding European farming efficiency and thereby reducing their ability to feed Britain. The added risk to this was that European nations would be tempted to develop industries behind their own protective tariff walls. It was to Britain's advantage to encourage Europe to adopt the policy of "comparative advantage" through which they would supply Britain with raw materials and food rather than competing with its manufacturing. Finally, in this respect the writing was already in bold script upon the wall. Europe and the United States were increasingly ready to meet British protectionism with protectionism of their own. Free trade was an attempt to put a stop to this policy, and thereby arrest industrial development in other countries.[50]

It was not optimism about the promise of a liberal economic world order that lay behind the drift to free trade from the 1820s, therefore. The key backdrop, rather, was a pessimistic fear that growing resentment in foreign countries at Britain's protectionism would lead to reciprocal action and the loss of markets for British trade. Free trade was necessary in order to save British manufacturing and commerce from being sur-

[49] J. H. Clapham, "The Last Years of the Navigation Acts" (part I), *English Historical Review*, 25 (July 1910), pp. 481–84; Douglas A. Irwin, "Welfare Effects of British Free Trade: Debate and Evidence from the 1840s," *Journal of Political Economy*, 96, 6 (December 1988), pp. 1142–64; Palmer, *Politics, Shipping and the Repeal of the Navigation Laws*, pp. 135, 167.

[50] Hilton, *Corn, Cash and Commerce*, pp. 195–203, 292–301.

passed by other countries. Free trade was a device to stave off a decline that some free traders such as J. D. Hume, a leading civil servant string-puller for free trade, saw as inevitable. In this context, free trade was the somewhat somber attempt of commercial imperialism to enforce on other countries the policy of "comparative advantages" that would keep them in the thrall of the British reexport trade and (increasingly) offering markets for British manufacturing goods. Far from being the symbol of British industrial supremacy, free trade was an attempt to preserve and protect the commercial supremacy of the previous 150 years.[51]

Fear of the loss of markets centered particularly on the rise of Prussian economic dominance over northern Germany. If this posed no immediate balance of power or military threat and thus was not paid much attention by the Foreign Office, the same was not true of the Board of Trade, which monitored closely the economic diplomacy of Prussia. Britain encouraged efforts by Hanover to create an alternative trading bloc to the Prussian-dominated Zollverein because it was feared that Prussian absorption of the great entrepôt of Frankfurt would close the main British gateway to central European markets. Indeed, the central storyline of trade policy in this region in the 1830s and 1840s was the way Prussian diplomacy progressively forced Britain into dismantling the protectionist restrictions of the Navigation Acts. Thus, a reciprocal treaty with Austria in 1838 which negated the Navigation Acts by allowing Austrian ships to bring goods from other countries to Britain led Prussia to demand and be granted the same concessions in 1841.

By the 1840s, then, the Navigation Acts had turned from an asset to British commerce into threat to its imperial interests. They were the excuse and the reason for a growing discrimination against Britain's trade interests. It was recognized that this tendency would likely grow as other countries developed manufacturing sectors. Free trade, therefore, was a trump against foreign protectionism. By 1846 both the United States and Prussia were making threatening noises about the remaining restrictions of the Navigation Acts. In 1846 Prussia refused to renew the treaty of 1841, thus opening the possibility of trade war. In the autumn of 1847 the United States adopted the same position. These threats fell on the receptive ears of the committed free traders in the Board of Trade. Nevertheless, it was ominous that the Navigation Acts were repealed under pressure from the two countries who were to be Britain's future rivals. The economic arguments for free trade may have been contestable, although, as I have pointed out, they were seldom contested at a fundamental level after this date. Yet it was not economic arguments that delivered the fatal

[51] Lucy Brown, *The Board of Trade and the Free Trade Movement*, pp. 195–204.

blow to the protectionist Navigation Acts. Forces far beyond Britain's control dictated the growing irrelevance to British commercial imperialism of these regulations. Arguments about the date when Britain's economic demise began have preoccupied too much of the historiography of the nineteenth century. Nevertheless, we can add another candidate to the list: 1849. The moment when Britain dismantled those legislative controls over trade that had enabled it to build a trade empire may be as good a moment as any other to choose for the crumbling of power.[52]

Free trade, however, as I have indicated, was also a domestic policy. The political economy of free trade contained implications for the internal of social policies that governments could pursue. Most obviously, of course, free trade implied a tax policy that minimized the costs of commerce. Exactly how this should be achieved was a matter for debate, as it had been throughout the eighteenth century. The Gladstonian definition of a free trade tax policy – low tariffs and some combination of excise and property taxes – did not follow naturally, however much he liked to present it as providentially ordained. Nevertheless, after 1846 free trade turned from a debate over monopolies to a debate over taxation. In this, free trade also described the structures of the state. The structures of a free trade state would be different from those of a protectionist state. It is to the history of state structures in our period that I shall now turn.

---

[52] The previous paragraphs draw on Clapham, "The Last Years of the Navigation Acts" (part II), *English Historical Review*, 25 (October 1910), pp. 687–707; Lucy Brown, *The Board of Trade and the Free Trade Movement*, pp. 195–96; Palmer, *Politics, Shipping and the Repeal of the Navigation Laws*, pp. 114–15.

4   The reach of the state: taxation

Defining the Victorian state

In 1888, at the end of a series of lectures for the law tripos in the University of Cambridge, the constitutional historian, F. W. Maitland, remarked that modern statutes had vastly extended the powers of "councils and boards and officers, high and low, central and local." England, he claimed, was fast becoming "a much governed nation." This was a curious claim for Maitland to make. Maitland had just treated his students to several months of erudite consideration of the dense fabric of legal regulation that composed the English constitution. Yet this did not seem to count as "government," even though Maitland was well aware that it was impossible to draw clear distinctions between, for example, constitutional law, administrative law, property law and even criminal law. By any account, Britain was a nation of laws that penetrated deep into the fabric of society, and from which it was impossible for even the lowliest to escape.[1]

In proclaiming Britain to be a newly "much governed nation," however, Maitland was reflecting a common conceit of his age. A. V. Dicey was to make the same point, in a different way, ten years later in a series of lectures at Harvard University. The main direction of modern legislation, Dicey argued, was to interpose upon individuals a collectivist regulation by the state. Whereas the main bias of government in the nineteenth century had been to permit the widest possible sphere for individual freedom, at the end of the century government had succumbed to the prescriptive spirit. Civic initiative as the source of social action was being displaced as the state shifted from a minimalist model to an intrusive and proactive force. Dicey was not particularly sympathetic to this shift; he was a more political academic than Maitland. Nevertheless, what Maitland and Dicey were constructing was a view of the twentieth-century state. The twentieth-century state was extensively structured with an

---

[1] F. W. Maitland, *The Constitutional History of England* (Cambridge, 1908), pp. 380–87, 501, 526–39.

intensive reach. The nineteenth-century state existed in faint outline and operated in minimal ways.[2]

This is a view that has continued to sculpt our thinking about the Victorian state. Indeed, it is a persuasive view because it is consistent with a narrative that contrasts the "weak" state of Britain with the "strong" states of Europe. The key signifier of a "strong" state was certainly lacking in Britain until the twentieth century: there was no tradition of a powerfully centralizing agency. In Britain, historically speaking, distinguishing between "government," "the state" and "the law" was notoriously difficult. Indeed, it was a common theme of constitutional theorists to elide the concept of "the nation" with that of "the state." Blackstone and Burke, for example, had used the two as synonymous terms and it remains uncommonly easy to slip them both under the roof of parliamentary sovereignty. Matthew Arnold – who was perhaps as well versed in comparative government as any constitutional theorist – wrote that the British constitution had no place for *the state* as the collective representative of the nation, "entrusted with stringent powers for the general advantage, and controlling individual wills in the name of an interest wider than that of individuals." In place of the "autonomous public power and authority" that exercised sovereignty over European nations, the British state was a collection of institutions bound together only by their subordination to the law.[3]

The British state was the law and how the law was applied determined in particular cases whether the state was strong or weak. The writ of the center ran selectively. In the 1780s, for example, it was reckoned that as much as £2 million per year was lost to the revenue through smuggling. When Sir Robert Walpole, at the height of his prime ministerial powers in the 1730s, tried to impose a general excise tax, the culture of liberty met him head on and he was defeated. A general excise, it was feared, presaged extensive government intrusion. These limits made the fiscal-military state of the eighteenth century a "weak" state. The Victorian state, it is commonly assumed, was even weaker. The state structures that replaced the fiscal-military state once the Napoleonic wars had been

---

[2] See A. V. Dicey, *Lectures on the Relation Between Law and Public Opinion in England During the Nineteenth Century* (London, 1905), Lecture IV, for a summary of the argument. See Henry Parris, *Constitutional Bureaucracy* (London, 1969), pp. 258–83, for a critique of Dicey. W. H. Greenleaf, *The British Political Tradition*, vol. I, *The Rise of Collectivism* (London, 1983), pp. 1–42, is within this tradition, while recognizing its inadequacies. Indeed, volume III, part I, of this authoritative work, which deals with the twentieth century, takes its title, *A Much Governed Nation*, directly from Maitland.

[3] Matthew Arnold, *Culture and Anarchy*, ed. J. Dover Wilson (Cambridge, 1969), p. 75; Barry Jones and Michael Keating, *Labour and the British State* (Oxford, 1985), p. 11.

won were entirely modest in their extent and limited in their purpose. If the Victorian state was not completely a "laissez-faire" state, so the general account goes, it was nevertheless that of a "nightwatchman." This state was a part-time affair, staffed by volunteers, respectful of individual freedom and mindful of the spheres of liberties that John Stuart Mill and Matthew Arnold warned were endangered by democracy.[4]

Yet this historically weak state could also claim to be the most successful in Europe. Measured by rates of survival and by the ability to mobilize resources – both money and personnel – the strength of the British state was without European peer. The "fiscal-military state" that was forged in the wars of the 1690s and lasted until the end of the Napoleonic wars in 1815, when it was no longer needed, coordinated – in fact if not by intention – the empire of commerce and territory that Britain acquired in the eighteenth century. Events proved that it could outrun any other state in its ability to tax and spend without revolution.

By comparison to the eighteenth-century state, however, the Victorian state was intrusive and unrestrained. It surrendered none of the revenue-raising power of the fiscal-military state. In fact, the Victorian state almost certainly did far better in this respect. Smuggling was stamped out by the simple devices of reducing duties and more effective policing. In some respects the Victorian state was more unconstrained than the big welfare state of the twentieth century. Those early and mid-Victorians unfortunate enough to have revenue disputes with the government, for example, were subject to the unaccountable whims of treasury officials. The authority of the state over tax decisions was unchecked until the consolidating Inland Revenue Act of 1874 brought tax disputes under the authority of the courts. Similarly, when necessary, the state was far more willing than any of its predecessors to intervene in the private sphere. Charities were radically restructured by state intervention, as was the structure of women's employment. When the public interest demanded it, private property was trampled on, as with the enforced destruction of diseased cattle during the rinderpest outbreak of 1865–66. The civil service establishment in central government grew quite markedly, from about 21,000 in 1832 to 54,000 in 1871. And if some observers are to be believed, London in the early nineteenth

---

[4] For the fiscal-military state, see Brewer, *Sinews of Power*; for an argument about its dismantling, see Philip Harling and Peter Mandler, "From Fiscal-Military State to Laissez-Faire State, 1760–1850," *Journal of British Studies*, 32, 1 (January 1993), pp. 44–70; Stone, "Introduction," pp. 14–16, 21. Anthony Trollope was able to combine his prolific output of novels with a full-time job in the Post Office thanks to a workday that ended in the early afternoon.

century was more heavily policed than Paris. By eighteenth-century standards this was Leviathan.[5]

Dicey, Maitland and most other historians who succeeded them saw the Victorian state in the shadow of the twentieth-century state. By this account, nineteenth-century state formation was inevitably a weedy growth. More importantly, it was a *different* plant, and our understanding gains little by judgments of comparison. Even less is gained from comparative metaphors of physical strength. The ambiguities and paradoxes of the nineteenth-century state in this respect are legion. Thus, a nineteenth-century workman hauled before the magistrate under the repressive clauses of the Master and Servants Act of 1823, could easily have pointed out "the state" to any political theorist. Nor would that workman have been left in any doubts about its "strength." That same man trying to sue his employer for an injury incurred at work before the Workmen's Compensation Act of 1896, however, would have been equally impressed by the "weakness" of the state to enforce "contracts" in the realm of employment law. No such liability was known to the law. The nineteenth-century state was its own formation; it was not heading inevitably toward the twentieth-century state and it needs to be historicized as part of the state system of the period 1680–1880.

Three principal features marked the outline of the state during these two centuries. The first of these was the extensive reach of the state. This attribute was most evident in the impressive ability of the state to mobilize the economic resources of the nation through taxation, a habit that was first developed during the years immediately following 1688 and continued unabated throughout the period. Nevertheless, the dynamic of the state in this respect was generally constrained by the second characteristic feature of the state during this period: the tension that maintained the balance between central and local spheres of government authority. It was here that notions of "weak" and "strong" state shaded into one another and become redundant. The central structures of the state could be weak precisely because they were so well integrated with the dense networks of local structures upon which the actual business of government rested. This polarity between central and local was also the foundation for the third significant peculiarity of state structure during this period: the definition of what lay within the public sphere and what

---

[5] G. R. Rubin and David Sugarman, *Law, Economy and Society: Essays in the History of English Law 1750–1914* (Abingdon, 1984), pp. 445–46; John Wade, *The Black Book; or, Corruption Unmasked* (London, 1820), pp. 101–02, 109, claims over 3,000 police in the 1820s; Patrick Colquhoun, *A Treatise on the Functions and Duties of a Constable* (London, 1803), p. xiii, claims 1,045 in the late 1790s; Sir Norman Chester, *The English Administrative System 1780–1870* (Oxford, 1981), pp. 167–68; W. L. Burn, *Age of Equipoise* (London, 1964), pp. 212–16.

belonged to the private sphere. The boundary separating these jurisdictions – like all the boundaries in this study – was never cast in stone, but it did move within a common field of force over this period.

Each of these aspects of state structures will be the subject of separate treatment. In this present chapter I shall focus primarily on the reach of the state, especially as it is illuminated in the continuities of tax structure. In the succeeding two chapters my attention will shift first to the relationship between central and local power, and then to the contours that fashioned the private and the public spheres of civil society.[6]

The reach of the state

The state in the eighteenth and nineteenth centuries possessed wide powers to interfere and regulate commercial and social exchange in society. This domain was an expanding field of activity over the period, not a shrinking sphere. Britain, like most liberal states, possessed well-established frameworks for economic regulation. In Britain, of course, the key element was the importance of the law in commercial regulation. This use of the law was not invented in the eighteenth century. But just as the law was professionalized during this period, so its role as the arbiter of commercial exchange was elaborated and extended. The differences between the eighteenth and nineteenth centuries in this regard resided more in the growing complexity of legal regulation than in the fact of its presence.[7]

In this compass of its activity, as in all others, the law worked in mysteriously ambiguous ways which foil any attempt to discern consistent general trends. Even the broad truism that the nineteenth century saw the rise of a law of commercial contract does not apply in the case of stock transactions – which is perhaps one place we would expect to find it. It is a somewhat shocking fact to realize that stock exchange transactions were not enforceable by law because they were mostly illegal under the Stock Jobbing Act of 1733, passed at the height of an anti-monied interest political campaign. This situation held good until an act of 1867 required written contracts of share sales. And although this act, too, was often

---

[6] See the remarks in Martin Daunton, "Payment and Participation: Welfare and State-Formation in Britain 1900–1951," *Past and Present*, 150 (February 1996), pp. 169–72, for the interrelated nature of these three themes.

[7] Economic backwardness is generally regarded as the prime case requiring the regulation of commercial activity by enlightened elites in pursuit of modernization. In fact, the real content of the distinction between countries consists in the different interfaces between the state and economic enterprise, not in the absence or presence of such relationships. See Alexander Gerschenkron, *Economic Backwardness in Historical Perspective: A Book of Essays* (Cambridge, MA, 1962), pp. 5–30; Rubin and Sugarman, *Law, Economy and Society*, pp. 18–20.

ignored, it may be said to begin (if in a very hesitant and unintentioned way) the apparatus of stock exchange regulation by the state. Debt, however, was a different matter. In this respect, the state was less neutral and forgiving. At the very same time that master-and-servant law was being liberalized in the late 1860s, for example, the law on debt as it applied to the poor was being toughened – so much so that it offended the sensibilities even of many a Victorian county court judge.[8]

The growth of the liberal state did not mean an expanding arena of freedom as far as the employment relationship was concerned. The commercial exchange of labor and wages was subject to an extensive and rigorous legal code. Master-and-servant law became more, not less, coercive and regulatory over the period. This body of law had its origins in the Statute of Laborers of 1349 and it remained the most important law regulating employment relations in this period – which makes the absence of any extensive and serious study of this body of law a gaping void in the historiography. Master-and-servant law was only one among several bodies of law that regulated the nature of employment, however. Particular trades were subject to specific legislation which most commonly was directed at trade union activity. Perhaps the most complete and notorious case of direct regulation of the employment relationship was in the worsted trades, where acts of 1777 established a private police force with extensive powers to enter workers' homes on mere suspicion they had embezzled woolen yarn.[9]

We know even less about the legal regulation of internal trade than we do about the actual operation of employment law in this period. Nevertheless, at the local level a dense body of administrative law seems to have regulated the conditions of economic exchange. Exactly how important this law was for sectors like the retail trade, for example, is quite impossible to say. According to John Wade, there were half a dozen laws relating to the packing of butter alone and "innumerable laws [which] have been enacted relative to the woolen, linen, and cotton manufactures, the whale, cod, herring, and pilchard fisheries; cheese, lace, sugar, glass, and almost every article of wear or consumption." Such laws were in part a reflection of how sensitive eighteenth-century politics were to the specific

---

[8] P. S. Atiyah, *The Rise and Fall of Freedom of Contract Law* (Oxford, 1979); Rubin and Sugarman, *Law, Economy and Society*, pp. 14, 191–208, 241–99, 321–48. Legal enforceability was unnecessary in the stock exchange, so strong was the code of honor.

[9] Donald Woodward, "The Background to the Statute of Artificers: The Genesis of Labor Policy, 1558–1563," *Economic History Review*, 33 (1980), pp. 32–44; Tholfsen, *Working-Class Radicalism*, pp. 180–86; Tomlins, "Subordination, Authority, Law"; John Rule, *The Experience of Labour in Eighteenth-Century Industry* (London, 1981), pp. 130–31; Richard Soderlund, "Intended as a Terror to the Idle and Profligate': Embezzlement and the Origins of Policing in the Yorkshire Worsted Industry, c. 1750–1777," *Journal of Social History*, 31, 3 (Spring 1998), pp. 647–69.

needs of particular interest groups. Still, Parliament was quite capable of detailed regulation of aspects of economic activity that were regarded as in the national interest.[10]

The highways and turnpikes, for example, were the subject of an amazing complex of laws which lasted until the parish was removed as the unit of road administration in the 1870s. At the same time, the few remaining turnpike trusts were dissolved by Parliament. The trusts had been Parliament's answer, beginning in the 1660s, to the need for a road system that could nurture economic expansion. They were only one example, however, of the regulation of road usage by Parliament that began in earnest in the 1690s. So extensive had this regulation become by the 1770s that its details filled a handbook of over 300 pages. Many of these pages had to do with pure administration, of course, although even these were surely enough to confound the idea of a "weak" state. The qualifications needed by local surveyors and other officials were spelled out, as was the time of year that trees at the curbside were to be pruned, and who was responsible for keeping the hedgerows in proper shape. Road usage was managed in the interests of preserving surfaces. Between 1695 and 1715 four acts addressed the draft power of wagons. An act of 1719 which laid down law on the width of the iron streaks binding the wheels occasioned many petitions from carriers who protested its cost. It was not repealed until 1740. In 1753 Parliament passed the first of several acts regulating the width of wheels. Other legislation specified the width of cartways leading into the market towns, the number of horses to particular wheel sizes and the maximum weight of particular types of wagons at different times of the year. Even the behavior of draught animals was prescribed by laws from as many as ten different Parliaments. Thus, cattle were to be so harnessed in the shafts that they would follow in each other's footsteps and not straggle all over the road.[11]

When the great reformers of roads administration, Thomas Telford and John McAdam, began to press in the early part of the nineteenth century for a different system of managing the roads, they were concerned not so much to repudiate this matrix of regulation as to change its personnel. I shall address the politics of reform more fully later on; here it merely needs to be noted that reform had less to do with smaller govern-

[10] Wade, *The Black Book*, pp. 207–08; Lee Davison, Tim Hitchcock, Tim Keirn and Robert Shoemaker, *Stilling the Grumbling Hive: The Response to Social and Economic Problems in England, 1689–1750* (New York, 1992), pp. 4–14.

[11] John Scott, *Digests of the General Highway and Turnpike Laws* (London, 1778), pp. 6, 10, 38, 40, 139–46; William Albert, *The Turnpike Road System in England 1663–1840* (Cambridge, 1972), p. 170; Eric Pawson, *Transport and Economy: The Turnpike Roads of Eighteenth-Century Britain* (London, 1977), pp. 68–74; Sydney Webb and Beatrice Webb, *English Local Government: The King's Highway* (London, 1920), pp. 73–75.

ment and more to do with who was actually doing the governing. Thus, in the case of roads, the turnpike trusts had, according to McAdam, "fallen into the hands of the lowest order of society." This was self-evidently contrary to good government: the lower orders were constructed as corrupt. Roads needed to be managed by "gentlemen" surveyors like McAdam who could rise above the corrupting influences of local politics in the hiring and supervision of the staff of "yeomen" below them. Both Telford and McAdam believed that the state of the roads and their economic importance called for *more* legislative oversight of the roads administration, not less.[12]

The Victorian state contained both big and small government. Indeed, more government was a general feature of the Victorian state. The size of government depended entirely upon which corridor of power one wandered into. In those departments that were devoted to directing and mobilizing the military and revenue resources of the state, Victorian government built on and expanded the precedents that had been established from the late seventeenth century. The nineteenth-century state did not direct its fiscal energies to war to the same degree that the eighteenth-century state had done, but it was much more effective in making its reach felt. Outside the departments dedicated to mobilizing resources, of course, the central administrative bureaucracy was small or nonexistent.

The origins of big government lay in the mobilization for war, or the expectations of war from the 1670s. War was the most obvious stimulant to the growth of government in this period. Whenever war broke out, the numbers of employees in the relevant departments jumped sharply. War demanded both a central control to administer an increasingly complex logistical system and a government presence in the naval stores, the roperies, the drydocks and the arsenals. Indeed, the capital and enterprise invested in provisioning for the wars of the 1690s far outpaced the size and expenditure of even the largest industrial manufacturing enterprise. Ambrose Crowley's famous ironworks was capitalized at about £10,000, for example, but in the late seventeenth century it took three times that much to build a superior ship of the line. By the time of the Seven Years War in the 1750s, this had doubled again and the 900 men necessary to build such a vessel far outstripped any of the manufactures of the day. The enormous ongoing expenses of war also required considerable organizational efforts. One has only to consider the huge amounts of food required for both navy and army to realize the scale of organization presided over by the various Boards of Control. In 1710 nearly 300,000

---

[12] John Loudon McAdam, *Observations on the Management of Trusts for the Care of Turnpike Roads* (London, 1825), p. 9; Webb and Webb, *The King's Highway*, pp. 168–74.

were on the British military payroll. Military expenditure, therefore, was the major business of government, and military costs typically ran at between 60 and 75 percent of government expenditure during the eighteenth century.[13]

A professionalized administrative bureaucracy was also stimulated by these developments. The government bureaucracy and administrative culture established in the late seventeenth century was not displaced until the civil service reforms of the 1870s. Both the fiscal and the military needs of the state demanded a professionalization of administration. Thus, the first indicators of a more effective administrative style can be seen in naval administration and in the collection of taxes from the 1670s. Although sinecures continued well into the nineteenth century, drawing money from the various fees attached to office, the actual bureaucracy was run on a more professional basis. During Anne's reign the numbers of place-men in Parliament had been reduced to relatively small numbers. Outside the legal bureaucracy and the monarch's household, there were around 12,000 civil servants by the mid-1720s. These were salaried employees appointed after meritocratic selection through examinations and other professional criteria. The method of selection paralleled exactly that of the bureaucracy of the middle of the nineteenth century. A combination of influence and raw talent were necessary for many positions. Entrance exams were instituted in the customs service as early as the 1690s, although only candidates approved by the commissioners could sit for them. Outright purchase of office irrespective of any qualification had virtually disappeared by 1700.

The large new departments created by the wars of William III were run by commissions that by and large ensured the priority of efficient and independent administration. Standards of professionalism were not universally high, nor did the governing bureaucracy move progressively toward the standards of the twentieth century. There is good reason to think that standards of propriety had slipped by the end of the eighteenth century. Certainly, Pitt's extensive reforms in the 1780s effectively removed a lot of deadwood, particularly in the tax bureaucracy. Pitt's reforms, however, regenerated the old system rather than creating a new system of bureaucratic administration. Efforts to end the prevailing mixture of influence and competition in the recruitment and style of the administration in the mid-Victorian period were generally unsuccessful.

---

[13] Geoffrey Parker, *The Military Revolution: Military Innovation and the Rise of the West 1500–1800* (Cambridge, 1988), pp. 45–81; Brewer, *Sinews of Power*, pp. 29–42. War expenses in the nineteenth century after the Napoleonic wars were obviously much lower, averaging around 30 percent of government expenditure, except during the Crimean war when they rose to around 56 percent.

Yet, of course, when reform did come in the 1870s, it merely replaced one kind of selective screen for civil servant recruitment with another. If the method of recruitment in our period was a combination of influence and competition, the competitive exams installed in 1870s were geared to another kind of influence; they ensured an intake drawn entirely from the Universities of Oxford and Cambridge. Still, however much British administration was open to the blandishments of influence, it never had to resort to methods such as tax farming that were guaranteed to create a system of jobbery.[14]

It is important to get some idea of the extent of central government in this period. Unsurprisingly, good figures are hard to get, and the figures of recent research do not match those of older works. Nevertheless, there is little disagreement about two things: a small central bureaucracy was matched by a revenue bureaucracy that was larger and more efficient than that of the most centralized despotism on the continent of Europe. Thus, in the 1790s even the Admiralty and the War Office together only employed about 100 people, although the Ordnance Department contained triple that number. The civilian departments were even smaller. In 1829 the Home, Foreign and Colonial Offices employed a total of about 100 personnel; the treasury was larger at eighty-two. And these totals had not moved much by 1851. Very different totals characterized the revenue departments, of course. Yet even here the central establishment tended to vastly understate the reality of government presence. Only about 1 per cent of the total revenue officers were employed in the central offices in the 1790s, for example.[15]

Over the eighty years from the 1690s to the end of the American war of independence, there may have been a threefold increase in revenue officers. Two-thirds of this growth occurred in the first two decades of the eighteenth century, and there was another spurt of expansion beginning in the 1760s. The revenue departments included many separate bureaucracies involved in collection of excises and assessed taxes, such as those on stamps, wine and salt. In one of the few detailed studies of the history of taxes, Edward Hughes estimated that the Salt Office (responsible for the salt tax) employed about 600 full-time officers in 1798. The largest and fastest-growing section of the tax bureaucracy, however, was the excise, which expanded fourfold from 1690 to 1780.

The excise composed the most centralized tax system in Europe in the

---

[14] It is worth remarking that, by 1862, open competition had been applied to only twenty-nine posts since the recommendations of the Select Committee of 1855: Emmeline W. Cohen, *The Growth of the British Civil Service 1780–1939* (London, 1941), pp. 35–44, 120.

[15] Chester, *English Administrative System*, pp. 167–68; Brewer, *Sinews of Power*, pp. 65–67; Cohen, *Growth of the British Civil Service*, pp. 34–35.

eighteenth century. At the end of seventeenth century, the excise employed about 40 percent of all revenue officers. A century later this
proportion had grown to two-thirds, and the excise was the largest
employer of government workers. Significantly enough, the excise office
was a model of administrative efficiency, centrally controlled in a way that
was perhaps unparalleled elsewhere in Europe. In the middle of the
eighteenth century, the 700 people employed in the London office over-
saw the work of the fifty-three collection regions. In the regions, taxes
were collected by over 3,000 local officers (called gaugers) whose job it
was to take in the monies on excisable commodities during their "walks"
through their assigned districts. The gaugers were watched by nearly 300
supervisors to prevent collusion or fraud with the traders.

Nineteenth-century government continued and reinforced these
trends; it got bigger and more efficient. The Napoleonic wars saw the
usual bloating of government fed by the needs of military mobilization.
This was a temporary phenomenon, of course, and the most concentrated
growth in government in our period was during the supposedly laissez-
faire dominated mid-Victorian years. Thus, in 1797 about 84 percent of
government employment was in the revenue departments; by 1829 this
had grown to 90 percent. Between 1832 and 1851 the numbers of
government employees grew by 18,000. This was mainly due to an
enormous increase of 10,000 in the Post Office with the coming of the
penny post. The other revenue departments had increased by a more
modest 1,500. Still, revenue activity (now including the Post Office)
continued to occupy 86 percent of all government bureaucrats in 1851.[16]

The customs service was a more decentralized bureaucracy than the
excise. However, customs administration provides further evidence of the
complexity and extent to the fiscal compass of the state. Even if we confine
ourselves to the customs administration in London at the end of the
eighteenth century, the point is illustrated. Aristocratic Bench Officers
supervised the work of clerks and deputies at Customs House, but separate
offices collected the duties on various products and goods. At the London
docks there were about 400 officers in the import division alone by 1780s,
for example. The supervision of vessels into the port of London was close
and detailed. After 1727 every foreign ship was boarded at Gravesend by a
tide surveyor who stationed tide waiters until the ship was cleared at
London in order to ensure that no goods were smuggled. Tide waiters were
also stationed on all outgoing ships carrying debentured goods to guard
against fraudulent landing of cargo that had received exemption from

---

[16] Brewer, *Sinews of Power*, pp. 65–67, 102–10, 126–27; J. E. D. Binney, *British Public
Finance and Administration 1774–1792* (Oxford, 1958), p. 179; Hughes, *Studies in
Administration and Finance*, p. 217; Chester, *English Administrative System*, pp. 167–68.

duties under various provisions of the Navigation Acts. By the 1780s there were over 800 tide waiters and others associated with this part of the work, and this did not include the officers concerned with the East India trade, which had a separate system of managing customs. At the unloading of a ship two land waiters were assigned to clear each vessel, and they then supervised the weighing and registering of the cargo. Land waiters themselves were supervised by the land surveyors who also appointed the lower grades of constable, gaugers and others. Once the cargo had been unloaded and assessed for duties, the ship's records were then referred to the land surveyor for approval and deposited with the jerquers, whose job it was to compare the description of cargo on the master's report with that of the land waiter. In the warehouses another set of procedures prevailed, administered by further classes of workmen. The weighing department of the King's Warehouses, for example, employed over 200 weighers and an almost equal number of casual workers ("glutmen" as they were known) engaged to cope with the fluctuations of trade.[17]

A sophisticated fiscal bureaucracy was required to handle the increasingly complicated nature of the regulations for the import or export of goods. Until the early 1690s the structure of customs was quite simple. It rested on the occasionally revised Book of Rates which was described as "no more than an alphabetical catalogue of goods then usually imported and exported, with their respective valuations, together with twenty-seven rules, which were understood to be sufficient for the officers to govern themselves by in all circumstances of collecting the duties." This changed rapidly after 1690, necessitating a consolidation of duties in 1725, and by the 1780s around 1,200 articles were subject to duties. Complicated by a multitude of exemptions, exceptions and drawbacks, the calculation of duties was no simple matter. Duties on goods imported from France or its colonies, for example, were subject to higher duties than goods imported from elsewhere. It is not surprising that guides to the customs began to appear – in 1702, 1714 and 1724, for example – whose interest to us lies in the way they reveal just how sophisticated and complicated government had rapidly become. By 1757 the current guide was a 600–page book listing all the duties and tables. After 1760 the pace of legislation increased even more. In the seventy years before 1760 about 800 acts of Parliament affecting the customs were passed; by 1813 another 1,300 had been added. The radical pamphleteer John Wade claimed in 1820 that forty revenue acts had been passed in the previous eighteen years alone, and that there were 140 customs and excise acts of Parliament concerning

---

[17] Hoon, *Organisation of the English Customs System*, pp. 140–59; Harper, *English Navigation Laws*, pp. 90–93; M. Dorothy George, *London Life in the Eighteenth Century* (repr., London, 1966 [1926]), p. 263.

spirits alone. So complex were the customs duties that, it was claimed, a lifetime was not sufficient to obtain a perfect knowledge of them.[18]

Wade was certainly right in pointing to the extent of taxation in Britain. An early historian of taxation was prompted to remark that "the intricacy of our fiscal provisions has in certain cases and at certain times been amazing," avowing that the excise and the stamp laws were "a farrago of legislation" resembling "Chinese puzzles." Changing fiscal needs made the tax system the subject of continual attention by the organs of state. This was particularly true with assessed taxes on particular services and occupations. Only a partial list of these taxes is necessary to suggest the true extent of state involvement in all kinds of economic exchange. A probate stamp tax had been introduced in 1694, and from 1780 a legacy stamp tax was imposed. Property sold at auction was taxed from 1777 until 1845 and property insured against fire between 1782 and 1869. Sea insurance polices were taxed from 1795, although this was reduced by both Gladstone and Disraeli. Carriages had been taxed in 1747; saddle and carriage horses and race horses from 1784; women servants from 1785; hair powder had been taxed in 1795 and dogs one year later. For one year between 1797 and 1798 a tax had been imposed on watches and clocks. The window tax lasted from 1696 to 1851; taxes on silver plate from 1756 to 1777; men servants were taxed in 1777; and persons keeping horses were taxed between 1784 and 1874. Even in the era of free trade over seventy acts of Parliament covered these kinds of assessed taxes. Nineteenth-century politicians were eager to simplify the layers of fiscal accretions that had gathered over the previous century. This process was a slow and hesitant business, however, the history of which would repay study. Gladstone began to trim back the assessed taxes in 1853, and Lowe continued his work in the late 1860s and early 1870s.[19]

British taxes were not only complicated; they were also heavy. Between 1660 and 1815, for example, the national income tripled: tax revenue increased sixteen times. Only the Low Countries were more heavily taxed than Britain. Yet Britain avoided the kinds of administrative or political problems that accompanied tax collection in more lightly taxed France. This must be attributed in large part to the fact that tax administration encompassed a wide section of the society. Those employed in the local collection and administration of taxes included people from relatively humble backgrounds. Although the excise was always associated with the intrusions of the state, restrained methods of collection generally ensured

---

[18] Henry Saxby, *The British Customs* (London, 1757), pp. vi–vii (quote); Hoon, *Organisation of the English Customs System*, pp. 25–33, 245–56; Wade, *The Black Book*, pp. 207–08.

[19] Dowell, *History of Taxation and Taxes in England*, vol. III, pp. 20, 180–83 (quotes, p. 180).

a low profile for this highly efficient money-raising machine. The excise was collected at the point of production before the consumer ever saw the product and thus was relatively invisible. In London by the end of the eighteenth century, for example, two-thirds of the beer was produced by eight or nine firms which made collection very easy; and London paid one-third of the national beer excise tax.

In most other European countries the problem of taxation was not just a matter of inadequate revenue collection; it was ultimately a problem of social authority. Britain avoided both of these problems. Indeed, taxation in Britain worked to reinforce social authority, not to challenge it. Thus, the invisibility of excises was true also of the land tax. This tax was notorious for being a tax imposed by the wealthy landowners upon themselves. This was not entirely true, but the share passed on to the tenant farmers through rents, for example, remained unseen. Yet if taxes were not generally a threat to social stability in Britain, this did not mean that the politics of taxation were unproblematic. Tax issues were capable of promoting popular protests. It did mean, however, that on the whole it was the structure of taxation rather than its principle or extent that was the subject of contention.[20]

The structure of taxation

The social politics of taxation were defined by the question of where the balance of the tax burden should lie. What should be the distribution of taxation between the different types of property? How should the weight of responsibility be shared between property and consumption? On what products and services should consumer taxes be laid? Should consumer taxes be pressed on necessities or on luxury items? These were complicated issues because they involved more than the amount and kind of revenue that would be generated by a particular tax. Questions of political responsibility and rights, of the relative contribution of different groups to national wellbeing and even of liberty and freedom were entangled in the prosaic matter of the generation of revenue. The most challenging issue was how the taxation of the poor should be accomplished. There was no question that the poor should remain untaxed. The tax system was consciously constructed to draw all into its net at one level or another. No section of society escaped some kind of obligation, although there were continual arguments about who was bearing how much of the tax burden.[21]

[20] Patrick K. O'Brien, "The Political Economy of British Taxation, 1660–1815," *Economic History Review*, 41, 1 (1988), pp. 1–32; Peter Mathias and Patrick O'Brien, "Taxation in Britain and France, 1715–1810: A Comparison of the Social and Economic Incidence of Taxes Collected for Central Governments," *Journal of European Economic History*, 5 (1976), pp. 601–50.

The excises were the single most important group of taxes. Excises were an old tax dating back to Edward I. They became a favored tax of seventeenth-century economists who took from the example of Holland the capacity of excises to raise large amounts of revenue efficiently. Nevertheless, the excise was historically a controversial tax. It was believed to threaten liberty and its economic implications were problematic, particularly the belief that it discriminated against the poor. Marvel had condemned the excise in verse and an attempt by the Cromwellian Republic in 1651 to impose an excise on home brewing had to be withdrawn after a public outcry. The standard constitutional argument against the excise was laid out in a pamphlet of 1659: that it endowed excise officers with an independent judicial power separate from the authority of the courts. These arguments were replayed in 1733 when Sir Robert Walpole attempted to impose a general excise which, it was feared, would ensure "fiscal independence to the crown [and thus] threaten the revolutionary settlement." Similarly, in the 1760s, an attempt to impose a tax on home-brewed cider roused organized opposition in the West Country because of the prospect that every yeoman's house could be entered at will for inspection "as none but the gin shop is in other countries." These concerns were a continuous part of the political tradition in Britain during this period. Until the end of the nineteenth century the same arguments were heard from those free traders who wanted to abolish indirect taxes and rely entirely upon the income tax for state revenue.[22]

---

[21] William Kennedy, *English Taxation 1640–1799* (2nd edn., London, 1964), pp. 101, 105. The salt tax was always controversial, for example, because it was believed to weigh heavily on the poor and discourage trade. Until the Napoleonic wars, the landed aristocracy probably bore a diminishing burden of the property taxes, due to the decline of the importance of the land tax and to the imposition of highly successful taxes on items like carriages and windows from the 1740s. The French wars may have seen that burden increase somewhat. Certainly the perception that this was so was the excuse for the increased corn duties, and the repeal of the income tax in 1816 probably restored the position of the landed aristocracy.

[22] Brewer, *Sinews of Power*, p. 147 (quote); Edward Raymond Turner, "Early Opinion About English Excise," *American Historical Review*, 21, 2 (January 1916), pp. 314–18; Langford, *Public Life and the Propertied Englishman*, pp. 316–17. Paul Langford, *The Excise Crisis: Society and Politics in the Age of Walpole* (Oxford, 1975), is now the standard work, of course, but his focus is almost entirely on the political dimensions of the crisis. See also E. R. Turner, "The Excise Scheme of 1733," in R. Mitchison (ed.), *Essays in Eighteenth-Century History* (London, 1966), pp. 21–44; William J. Hausman and John L. Neufeld, "Excise Anatomized: The Political Economy of Walpole's 1733 Tax Scheme," *Journal of European Economic History*, 10 (1981), pp. 131–44. On the cider tax, see [David Hartley], *The Right of Appeal to Juries in Causes of Excise Asserted* (London, ? 1764), p. 7 (quote), and, on the political protest campaign that was mounted against it, see Patrick Woodland, "Extra-Parliamentary Political Organization in the Making: Benjamin Heath and the Opposition to the 1763 Cider Excise," *Parliamentary History*, 4 (1985), pp. 115–31.

Both constitutional and social objections to the excise came into full view when Walpole attempted to relieve the tax on land by imposing a general excise on wine and tobacco in 1733. Walpole's argument was that his policy was designed to secure a more reliable and effective stream of revenue, stimulate and encourage commerce and trade and spread the tax burden more evenly among the population. The opposition to Walpole was led, of course, by powerful merchants whose self-interest was offended by his policy. Nevertheless, there was genuine uncertainty about the economic and social effects attached to excise taxes. The social argument against the excise was formulated in terms that would recur until the end of our period: that, as a tax on consumption, it discriminated against the poor, discouraged trade by burdening the mercantile trading classes and encouraged vice by the inducements it gave to smuggling or to evading the law. As early as the 1740s the argument was made that a property tax should replace the excise tax. It was urged that taxes on property – in this case the land tax – impeded commerce less than the "petty inconveniences which the excise would inflict on the inland trade" and, therefore, should bear the main burden of revenue needs.[23]

It was a commonplace assumption that excise taxes were likely to fall most heavily on the poor. The important question was whether this was a bad or a good thing. The general convention among politicians in the eighteenth century was that it was a bad thing and that taxes should avoid burdening the poor. On the other hand, high taxes were also believed to enforce industriousness and curb debauchery among the poor. At the same time there was a widely held conviction that excise taxes increased wages and thus discouraged trade. This argument recurred frequently in the pamphlet literature throughout the period and remained a favorite theory of wage determination into the early nineteenth century. It was well known that the theory contained logical and empirical problems. Yet its popularity in the eighteenth century revealed the disposition of the political culture to tax the domestic luxuries of the wealthy before those of the poor. Thus, financial difficulties in the 1770s and 1780s were met by increased taxes on such things as carriages and man servants. Lord North expressed the typical view when he claimed in

[23] Z. G., *Excise Anatomiz'd* (repr., London, 1733 [1659]). Caleb D'Anvers, *An Argument Against Excises* (London, 1733), was originally published in the anti-Walpole journal *The Craftsman*, but contains a very detailed expression of the anti-excise argument. *Englishmen's Eyes Open'd* contains a debate between a merchant and a landowner on the relative merits of land tax and excise and addresses the tension that the issue involved – and which is an underexplored aspect of fiscal policy debate in the early eighteenth century – between the merchant and landed interests. See also *A Scheme or Proposal for Taking off the Several Taxes on Land* (London, 1733); Horsley, *Serious Considerations*; Decker, *Some Considerations*; Decker, *Nature and Weight of the Taxes of the Nation*.

1776 that normally taxes should fall on the luxuries of the rich and opulent. When Pitt was forced to put a tax on coal, he accompanied it with protestations of deep sorrow (perhaps, though, with earlier events in Boston in his mind) that the urgency of the crisis necessitated this blow to the comfort of the poor.[24]

Victorian political culture, on the other hand, saw moral virtue in taxing the poor. It was one of the great achievements of Victorian public finance to reverse eighteenth-century inclinations and generate the bulk of normal taxation from ordinary people. This shift away from allowing the rich to bear the main weight of taxation began with the bias of classical political economy in favor of indirect taxation over direct taxation. Like Smith, early Victorian economists paid careful attention to which part of the national income a particular tax would affect.[25] The relationship that interested most political economists was that between taxes and trade. The key question was which kind of tax did less damage to trade. In this respect indirect taxes were far preferable. J. R. McCulloch opened the section of his *Treatise* on direct taxation with the dictum that anything that converted capital into revenue would diminish labor and "be a fruitful source of pauperism." The danger of property taxes like the income tax, therefore, was that they discouraged enterprise. On the other hand, a tax on consumables – and beer and tobacco were at issue here – was a tax on luxuries since buying them was entirely a matter of choice. Such a tax also ensured that the burden of supporting the state was shared by all classes in the country. They were the common person's contribution to the national treasury.[26]

---

[24] Charles Davenant in the late seventeenth century had originally made the link between the excise on necessaries and high wages. Adam Smith carried it over into classical political economy by arguing that increased taxes lowered family size by inflating the cost of living, reduced the numbers of laboring poor which disrupted the balance of supply and demand of labor, and pushed up wages. For a sample of this literature, see *Englishmen's Eyes Open'd*; Horsley, *Serious Considerations*; [William Temple,] *Consideration on Taxes as They Are Supposed to Affect the Price of Labour* (London, 1765); A Farmer, *Thirty Years' Observation on the Effects of Taxing Provisions Instead of Income* (London, 1836); W. R. Ward, *The English Land Tax in the Eighteenth Century* (Oxford, 1954), p. 123; Kennedy, *English Taxation*, pp. 108–21, 160–62.

[25] It should be noted in passing that the classical political economists contributed little on such matters as the relationship between capital depreciation and income tax rates. Their economic theory was not adapted to an economy of big industrial capital; it reflected, naturally enough, the trading emphasis of the age.

[26] This balancing act was a delicate matter. Ricardo saw taxes on necessaries as raising wages and thus lowering the rate of profit. This demonstrated in a "scientific" way the case for low taxation and free trade, but it also provided economic justification for a few taxes on high consumption items that could also be regarded as luxuries. And this meant items that were consumed largely by the working class. See Ricardo, *Political Economy and Taxation*, pp. 152, 205, 242–46, 253–54; McCulloch, *Treatise*, pp. xxxiii–iv, xxxvi, 51 (quote).

This, of course, was Gladstone's position, which he had inherited from the liberal Tories of the 1820s. A low-tariff and high-consumption tax policy could be argued to be the least damaging to trade and commerce. Indeed, the early nineteenth-century free traders can be seen as implementing Walpole's excise scheme of 1733 but without the kind of powerful opposition that he had faced. With his preference for high taxes on a few consumer items, Gladstone was the best Walpolean of them all. Yet there was no essential reason why excise taxes should become the staple of a free trade tax policy. The debate about the best balance between direct and indirect taxation continued to echo (somewhat faintly, it is true) within the context of a free trade paradigm throughout the middle of the nineteenth century. In the debate on the malt tax in 1850, for example, Disraeli objected to excise taxes on the grounds that they placed the burden of public taxation on the domestic population. When the Cobden treaty with France was being debated in 1860, the objection was raised that it allowed luxuries in free of charge while continuing to tax the necessities of life for the majority of the people. The various indirect taxes remained extremely complicated and heavy in the mid-Victorian period and formed the core of the complaints that free trade would be incomplete while the excise taxes remained so burdensome.[27]

The eighteenth-century arguments against excise taxes continued to drift through the lulled economic debate of the mid-Victorian period, although how widely they found an audience is not clear. The most prominent spokespersons for that position were to be found in the Financial Reform Association, which argued for a tax policy that rested entirely on property. As has been mentioned, Richard Gladstone was its president in the middle of the nineteenth century and many Liberal members of Parliament were associated with it. In spite of these connections and the large numbers of mind-numbing pamphlets it issued, the association's influence on policy seems to have been negligible. Richard Cobden initially greeted the association warmly. But he quickly distanced himself and never endorsed the association's central program for the abolition of all indirect taxation and a total reliance on the income tax.[28]

[27] Holland, *Fall of Protection*, pp. 331–35. The malt tax was claimed to cause the cost of beer to be more in nineteenth century than in the eighteenth century and to encourage the growth of monopoly brewing by its prohibition against home brewing.

[28] The Financial Reform Association's arguments against the excise were those that were developed in the eighteenth century: that it discouraged trade, discriminated against the poor, encouraged immorality by the stimulus given to smuggling and lying under oath and was integrally connected with the "big state" of old corruption. For the Financial Reform Association, see W. N. Calkins, "A Victorian Free Trade Lobby," *Economic History Review*, 13, 1 (1960–61), pp. 90–104; Financial Reform Association, *Cost of Customs and Excise Duties*.

Why did these arguments fail to resonate more widely in the politics of the middle of the nineteenth century? Why did the Gladstonian position of taxation with its clear class biases fail to attract more criticism? There is some suggestion that working-class listeners were receptive to the critique of indirect taxes. The arguments of the Financial Reform Association about the taxation of necessities undoubtedly found sympathetic ears in some parts of working-class political culture. Yet organizations like the Financial Reform Association extended their understanding of free trade to labor too, and thus vitiated any meaningful connection with the organized labor movement. And, as I have suggested in the last chapter, the knowledge system of free trade and its cultural links with evangelical economics and the whole moral apparatus of a self-help mentality effectively monopolized the ways these kinds of questions were discussed.

Dissenting notions of trade policy occasionally did challenge the public hegemony of the Gladstonian fiscal orthodoxy. Ultimately, however, these were arguments between different definitions of free trade which found a public when finance and taxation were high on the national political agenda. In the 1870s, John Noble – a fairly well-known free trade economist – was still making the argument that complete free trade would not be established until the bias of the tax system was shifted from customs and excise to the income tax. And even more explicitly in line with earlier arguments was the claim of T. E. Cliffe Leslie that the 12,000 customs and excise officers represented an enormous unaccountable power of the state and that free trade remained an ideal even while customs and excise taxes impeded the free movement of commerce. Such reasoning implied that Gladstone's policy be inverted and that direct taxation replace indirect taxation as the main source of revenue.[29]

The reliance on direct taxation as the basic source of revenue, however, was to be a characteristic tax formula of the twentieth century. The structure of taxation throughout the eighteenth and nineteenth centuries was the exact reverse. Indirect taxes provided a steady revenue stream. Direct taxes drawn from property furnished sudden influxes of money to meet particular and temporary emergencies. In the eighteenth century the land tax provided this emergency source, and in the nineteenth century it was supplied by the income tax. The land taxes and income tax were very different kinds of taxes, of course, yet their function in the tax system was very similar. Both came out of the demands of war; both were

---

[29] John Noble, *National Finance: A Review of the Policy of the Last Two Parliaments* (London, 1875); T. E. Cliffe Leslie, *Financial Reform* (London, 1872); Lawrence Heyworth, *Fiscal Policy: Direct and Indirect Taxation* (Liverpool, 1861). For the appeal of this version of free trade for the working class, see Biagini, *Liberty, Retrenchment and Reform*, pp. 101–02, 110.

extraordinary taxes which could be readily adjusted as emergency sources of revenue. Their sociopolitical purpose and justification were similar. As extra taxes that were levied on those in possession of sufficient property, they could be presented as the price the propertied classes bore for the privileged position they occupied in the power structure.

While the wars of the 1690s spawned a large number of new excise and assessed taxes, the chosen instrument of extraordinary taxation at this moment was the land tax. There were both constitutional and fiscal reasons for settling on a land tax. The advantage of the land tax over excise was that it lay firmly under the control of Parliament. In addition, the events of the early 1690s demonstrated the dire need for a steady and reliable flow of revenue. The established method of meeting exceptional needs was to assess aids and subsidies on a county quota system. Yet the one-time nature of this system proved manifestly unable to ensure a sufficient stream of funds. By May 1689, for example, it was obvious that the double monthly assessment voted in February was insufficient to close the gap created by the Irish and French campaigns. By November another £2 million was needed and by October of the following year a further equal amount was required. For the next two years, expenditures of about £4 million per year were maintained. In 1692, therefore, the idea of imposing what was in effect a yearly tax on wealth and income was revived in the form of a four-shillings-in-the pound rate on personal estates as well as on other personal properties. The tax immediately proved its worth by producing the highest yield ever collected in a single annual extraordinary tax.[30]

The advantages of the land tax were social as well as fiscal. Socially, it exemplified the engagement of the key social groups in the country in the fiscal and political process. It was a "modern" tax in that it extended beyond the landed gentry to include a large number of the middling classes, although as the century wore on it certainly failed to capture the taxable wealth of this class. The administration of the land tax through the county commissions and the local collectors was also a way of enlisting large numbers of ordinary people in government service. Indeed, peers were deliberately excluded from the land tax commissions, even though in many counties their estates bore the greatest proportion of the assessments. Nevertheless, inequities in the land tax were built in from the beginning. There were local vagaries of assessment; the tax discriminated against certain kinds of wealth and most notoriously it failed

[30] Ward, *English Land Tax*, pp. 1–6; J. V. Beckett, "Land Tax or Excise: The Levying of Taxation in Seventeenth- and Eighteenth-Century England," *English Historical Review*, 100, 395 (April 1985), pp. 287–306.

to snare the rentier income of the "monied class." Furthermore, the land tax soon acquired serious rigidities from a failure to adjust the county assessments to reflect changing regional wealth. These inefficiencies were accepted in the interests of political peace and thus they tended to accumulate. By the end of the century, barren Cumberland was paying relatively much more in land tax revenues than opulent Middlesex. These kinds of disparities were similar to those that were to face the income tax; they fueled the ongoing debate on how and where the tax burden should fall.[31]

The fiscal advantage of the land tax lay in the predictable flow of revenue it generated. This was of particular value during wartime when budget projections needed to operate within tolerable limits of certainty. Yet almost from the moment of its inception the land tax became of secondary importance to the revenue stream in normal times. Even in the 1690s it was insufficient to fund entirely the extra expense of wartime and was supplemented by an additional list of excises. And from the early 1700s until the end of the nineteenth century, British taxation rested on the keystone of the excise. In 1661 the excise contributed 17 percent to total revenue. By 1740 the excise provided 50 percent of revenue, and it remained at that level throughout the century. Over the same period, the contribution of the land tax fell from 43 percent to 17 percent of total revenue. In peacetime the rigidities in the land tax reinforced this declining share of revenue, and there was a constant search throughout the century for new sources of income which led to the great increase in assessed taxes.[32]

By the 1780s the state of public finances was again a major source of political concern and attention. There were good reasons for this. The Seven Years War and then the American war had exploded the national debt to over £238 million by 1783. Interest payments soaked up more than three-quarters of the annual revenue. This was the background to the cry for "economical reform," and in 1785 William Pitt embarked on a radical program to streamline the administration of the assessed taxes. This was a highly successful enterprise. Indeed, without Pitt's precedent, the work of Peel and Gladstone would have been impossible. The coming of the French wars in the 1790s brought to a halt Pitt's schemes to get the

---

[31] J. V. Beckett and Michael Turner, "Taxation and Economic Growth in Eighteenth-Century England," *Economic History Review*, 43, 3 (1990), pp. 377–403; Beckett, "Land Tax Administration at the Local Level 1693–1798," in M. Turner and D. Mills (eds.), *Land and Property: The English Land Tax, 1692–1832* (Gloucester, 1986), pp. 162–63; Langford, *Public Life and the Propertied Englishman*, pp. 339–47, 525–26.

[32] Brewer, *Sinews of Power*, p. 95; Langford, *Public Life and the Propertied Englishman*, p. 362.

country out of debt, however. Once again, the need for a reliable flow of revenue to fight the war became acute. The solution was obvious: to tap further the greatly increased wealth of the middling classes by means of an income tax. Political and administrative considerations posed serious obstacles to realizing that objective, however, and occasioned a sharp debate that was an important event in the formation of a consciousness of a "middle" class. Thus, until 1797 all sorts of expedients were tried to avoid the income tax, even though it was widely recognized as the most effective answer to the dilemma of public finance. Pitt's policy of placing assessments on a wide variety of items – hair powder, dogs and watches, for example – produced howls of political pain. Such efforts only delayed the inevitable arrival of a tax on incomes. And in 1797–98 Pitt forced through a radical overhaul of the tax system which included the redemption of the land tax and the conversion of its administrative machinery into the apparatus to collect an income tax.[33]

The history of the income tax throughout the first two-thirds of the nineteenth century is not the prehistory of the twentieth-century fiscal state. To the contrary, the income tax of the nineteenth century was an extension of the eighteenth-century system of taxation. The income tax took the place of the land tax in the revenue system. Like the land tax, the income tax was always intended purely as a fiscal device. The income tax was not designed to be an instrument of social engineering. From the beginning, the income tax was a supplement to revenue, available to be turned on and off as the occasion required. Thus, its reintroduction in 1842 (it had been repealed in 1815) was a response to the problem of how to meet the revenue shortfall that rising duties had failed to cover. This was hardly a new predicament. But the experience of 1799–1815 had demonstrated that large amounts of revenue could be secured relatively easily from this source, and cumbersome taxes on items like windows thereby avoided. The Whig government adopted the combination of reducing customs duties and increasing the income tax in 1841 as a solution to an archetypal problem of the eighteenth century: whom to tax to cover revenue shortfalls.

The income tax did not change the eighteenth-century balance between direct and indirect taxation in the fiscal system. Indeed, the cornerstone of Gladstonian finance was to maintain the subordinate position of direct taxes on income to indirect taxes on consumable items. This was partly because of the technical and social difficulties associated with the

---

[33] W. R. Ward, "The Administration of the Window and Assessed Taxes, 1696–1798," *English Historical Review*, 67, 3 (October 1952), pp. 538–42; Halevy, *England in 1815*, pp. 363–72; Kennedy, *English Taxation*, pp. 160–67; Ward, *English Land Tax*, pp. 133–37.

income tax. It was difficult to secure agreement on how to define "income" in relationship to different kinds of property. And this question was a constant irritant in any discussion of how to structure the income tax. These difficulties had attached to the land tax and, in addition, there was another parallel between the two types of taxes: both constituted the boundary of the political nation. The land tax was broadly convergent with the enfranchised classes, and for mid-Victorians, too, the income tax and the franchise went together. It was inconceivable to Gladstone, for example, that a man should pay the income tax *without* being in possession of the franchise. This was one major reason why changes in the franchise always occasioned much poring over the statistics of various property categories. Like the land tax, the income tax was seen as the price the propertied classes bore for their greater political power and responsibility. Thus, the social politics of the Victorian tax structure were consistent with the tax politics of the past.[34]

The same was true of the proportionate contribution of direct and indirect taxes to the revenue. Until the 1880s and 1890s the income tax constituted a small (and generally constant) percentage of the general revenue. In 1873, for example, it produced only £5.7 million out of £77 million of total revenue. By contrast, the customs and excise generated over £47 million. Indirect taxes continued to take in between 60 and 70 percent of total revenue until the mid-1880s. From the 1870s, the contribution of the income tax to the general revenue began to change. In 1876, for the first time, the income tax was used to make up a deficit in ordinary expenditure. The fiscal demands of the Boer war pushed direct taxation to the fore and 1900 was the first time

[34] The funding of the Crimean war, 1854–56, followed quite closely the pattern of eighteenth-century finance. The war was funded by a combination of the income tax and the national debt. There was no question of increasing the income tax to close the gap between expenditure and revenue. Recourse was made to indirect taxation, which raised the old issue of what burden should be placed upon consumables and therefore the poor. The government was forced to resort to war loans raised in a similar way to the past, with a few great contractors – notably the Rothschilds – holding a monopoly on those funds. Even the sinking fund was revived in spite of its poor reputation in the City and among economists. See Olive Anderson, *A Liberal State at War*, p. 194, and *passim*. The specter of "old corruption" was revived. The fiscal politics of the past reentered the political stage during the 1850s to produce a discourse that would have been familiar to the London radicals of the 1750s. After all, old corruption was still a living memory. The old radical cry of the overweening power of the executive over the House of Commons in the formulation of policy was raised by the campaigns of David Urquhart against government foreign policy and the Administrative Reform Association. See Miles Taylor, *The Decline of British Radicalism 1847–1860* (Oxford, 1994), pp. 223, 235–37, 247–49, 250–51; Miles Taylor, "The Old Radicalism and the New: David Urquhart and the Politics of Opposition 1832–1867," in Biagini and Reid, *Currents of Radicalism*, pp. 23–43.

a larger revenue was secured from direct as opposed to indirect taxation.[35]

Like the land tax, the income tax was a product of the needs of war and, even when it was restored in peacetime, it was not intended to be a permanent addition to the fiscal system. Although some thought the income tax had been repealed in haste in 1815, when it was revived in 1842 it was initially extended only on a year-to-year basis. The expectation that the income tax would be a purely temporary tax was not some wild delusion. It was anticipated that the commercial success of free trade would permit adequate revenue from the excises. Thus, the practice of renewal for predetermined periods of time was designed to provide sufficient opportunity to bring the finances of the country to the ultimate fiscal version of free trade. This objective was accepted by all politicians. In 1853 Gladstone launched a fully worked-out plan to abolish the income tax within seven years by substituting revenue from increased spirit and succession duties. As late as 1874 both Gladstone and Disraeli included its abolition in their election manifestos, although neither specified how this was to be done. (Gladstone later claimed that he had planned to replace the income tax with death duties.) Such ambitions did not begin to sound distinctly old-fashioned until the 1890s. In 1894 Sir John Lubbock, the prominent backbench Liberal who had in the past strongly opposed the income tax, expressed the new reality when he accepted that "we must recognize it as a permanent portion of our fiscal system."[36]

In fact, the conditions had long since passed that would allow the income tax to remain a purely temporary fiscal device. Yet this recognition was to be excluded from political reality throughout the mid-Victorian period. The reason for this was the control of the discourse on fiscal policy that was exercised by the wisdom of William Gladstone. Until very

[35] Matthew, *Gladstone*, vol. I, *1809–1874*, pp. 120–28; 221–22; H. C. G. Matthew, "Disraeli, Gladstone and the Politics of Mid-Victorian Budgets," *Historical Journal*, 22, 3 (1979), pp. 615–43; Sidney Buxton, *Finance and Politics: An Historical Study 1789–1885* (repr., New York, 1966; [London, 1888]), vol. II, p. 368; B. E. V. Sabine, *A History of Income Tax* (London, 1966), pp. 110, 123–25. Sample percentage contributions to the revenue of indirect to direct taxation were as follows:

	Indirect	Direct
1836–40	78.7	21.3
1846–50	69.8	30.2
1856–60	64.8	35.2
1866–70	66.6	33.4
1876–80	65.3	34.7
1886–90	56.1	43.9
1896–00	52.4	47.6
1906–09	48.3	51.7

[36] Edwin A. Seligman, *The Income Tax* (New York, 1914), p. 180.

late in the nineteenth century, it was Gladstone's version of fiscal reality that determined the limits of political possibility. This command had been demonstrated as early as 1851 when considerable interest was expressed in Liberal circles in the possibility of introducing a graduated and differentiated income tax – a modern income tax in other words. This opportunity was forbidden by Gladstone as the price of throwing his political support to the Whigs and Liberals: "it was the first, and not the least remarkable, occasion on which Gladstone was able to convert his minority view [that the income tax not be graduated or differentiated] into financial orthodoxy."[37]

As the mid-Victorian years wore on and as the income tax became more entrenched, there was a growing gulf between reality and rhetoric. The permanence of the tax was effectively ensured by the demands of the Crimean war. Changes in the policy of administering the income tax in the 1860s reinforced this tendency. Traditionally, for example, the income tax rate had been moved only in conjunction with the movement of indirect taxes. This kept the balance between the two in a steady equilibrium. In 1867 this practice was quietly abandoned and for the first time an increase in revenue was derived from the income tax alone. Robert Lowe, chancellor of the exchequer from 1868 to 1873, was probably the first leading politician to believe that the income tax should be a permanent part of the financial structure. There was little he could do to change the orthodoxy in the abiding presence of Gladstone. Nevertheless, we are not bound by the same silence, and from the late 1860s a variety of forces can be observed shifting the traditional balance in the tax structure away from a terrain that was constrained by eighteenth-century precepts and into a twentieth-century mode.[38]

Disruption of the traditional tax balance

In the late nineteenth and early twentieth century, tax policy underwent a significant transition that contained three key elements. First, the lip service paid to the temporary nature of the income tax was abandoned, and the income tax was accepted as *de facto* permanent. Secondly, the purpose of taxation acquired another component. In the past, taxation had been relevant mainly to the concerns of trade and fiscal policy. To this was now added the relationship between taxation and the social engineering priorities of government. And, thirdly, direct taxation re-

---

[37] P. R. Ghosh, "Disraelian Conservatism: A Financial Approach," *English Historical Review*, 391 (April 1984), p. 276.

[38] Buxton, *Finance and Politics*, vol. I, pp. 94–95, 114, 166, 188, 330–33; vol. II, pp. 147, 171.

placed indirect taxation as the prime source of government revenue. Like most transitions, the emergence of these new axes of tax policy was slow, untidy and incomplete. Nevertheless, the direction in which tax history was moving in this period can be illustrated through the issues of differentiation and graduation of the income tax.

Differentiation and graduation were really questions about how the burden of taxation should be distributed and how tax policy should treat different kinds of wealth. Differentiation referred to the question of how to evaluate disparate kinds of property for tax purposes. Differentiation was an extension of the old debate about how to judge income derived from the very different sources of land, money and real property. This was a perpetual issue of controversy in assessing different property for the poor rate, for example. Graduation, of course, referred to the relationship between the tax rate and income level. Neither differentiation nor graduation was a new issue to politics. Yet the debate around these issues at end of the century signaled the junction between a phase of tax history which had opened in the early eighteenth century and the introduction of the tax discourse of the twentieth century. Both graduation and differentiation, but particularly graduation, signified a different conception of the income tax than that which the nineteenth century had inherited from the eighteenth century. Both proclaimed a view of the income tax that confronted more openly the complicated sectional needs of the different social classes and economic interests.

It was not the original ambition of the income tax to interfere with the political or the social hierarchies. The initial intent was that the income tax be neutral in terms of income distribution. This was the underlying purpose of the practice of moving the income tax only in line with other taxes. The objections to an income tax that distinguished between different kinds of property and was graduated according to income were various. The idea that the state should inquire into individual circumstances in order to differentiate effectively between kinds of incomes was regarded as morally obnoxious and administratively infeasible. The great classical political economists had deemed a graduated tax as implicitly confiscatory and as explicitly discouraging investment. Thus, until the later part of the century, the income tax was frozen in a constrained discourse as to its possible limits. There were some administrative changes in the 1870s, but political resistance remained strong and change in the principles of taxation itself was halting and slow.[39]

A major reason for this stasis, of course, was William Gladstone.

---

[39] Michael Veseth, *Mountains of Debt: Crisis and Change in Renaissance Florence, Victorian Britain, and Postwar America* (Oxford, 1990), pp. 116–20; Seligman, *The Income Tax*, pp. 177–78; McCulloch, *Treatise*, pp. 126–50.

Gladstone adamantly opposed a graduated or differentiated tax. Either one, in his view, would disturb the balance between direct and indirect taxes and thereby undermine the fiscal basis of free trade. Equally significant was the disruption both would threaten to the social compromise between property-owners and non-propertyowners upon which Gladstonian politics rested. Gladstone saw the income tax as the extra share of the tax burden borne by property. Excise taxes were paid by everyone, of course, but specifically they were the share borne by the working class. The income tax defined the political nation, therefore. Graduating the income tax had the great disadvantage of undermining its status as a boundary marker for the enfranchised classes. Similarly, Gladstone opposed differentiation because it implied setting one propertied interest against another and threatened unwarranted intrusion into private lives.[40]

Nevertheless, graduation and differentiation had been implicit from the moment the income tax was introduced. A graduated income tax had been a Chartist demand. And a crude kind of graduation was instituted in 1842 by the adoption of £150 as the level of income exemption; this was reduced in the 1850s to £100. There were some adjustments to this during the 1860s and 1870s under Lowe and Stafford Northcote in order to ease the burgeoning lower middle class into the tax-paying ranks. Thus, incomes over £150 and between £200 and £400 got various kinds of abatements. As the income tax moved toward permanent and central status in the tax system, so the question of the principles of equity and distribution that should guide its operation acquired major significance.[41]

By the 1870s discussion had shifted away from whether the income tax would be continued or not to the question of the principles of differentiation between various kinds of property and graduation between different levels of wealth. It was recognized in New Liberal circles at least that fully fledged graduation made more sense than trying to tinker with a system that had remained essentially unchanged since the days of William Pitt. The acceptance by Joseph Chamberlain in his unauthorized program of 1886 of a graduated and progressive element to the income tax was a signal that things were about to change. In the budget of 1894 Sir William Harcourt imposed a small death duty which was the first time a graduated

[40] Daunton, "Payment and Participation," p. 176; James E. Cronin, *The Politics of State Expansion: War, State and Society in Twentieth-Century Britain* (London, 1991), p. 22; Matthew, *Gladstone*, vol. I, *1809–1874*, pp. 122–27. Gladstone estimated (correctly) that the £100 income level in the 1860s corresponded generally to the necessary range of property-ownership that also qualified a man for the franchise. It should be noted, however, that Gladstone himself had introduced a form of differentiation in an allowance for life assurance and deferred annuity premiums. He justified this as giving recognition to the need to protect against precarious incomes.

[41] Cronin, *Politics of State Expansion*, pp. 4–11, 28–30, 54–55.

element to the income tax had been formally inscribed in policy. A Select Committee of 1906–07 reported in favor of a graduated and differentiated income tax. And the 1907 and 1909 budgets mark the clear and unequivocal – though still immensely controversial – link between tax policy and social welfare. It was only at this moment that Herbert Henry Asquith, on behalf of the political establishment, conceded that the income tax had indeed become a permanent and integral part of the tax system.[42]

These issues of differentiation and graduation were of considerable significance for the way the income tax, and tax policy generally, was understood. Both differentiation and graduation of the income tax were technically very complex and possessed a tangled political sociology. Yet, as has been suggested, they carried profound implications for state formation. Once they were entered into the political debate and accepted as principles of tax policy, they moved tax policy beyond its previous primary relationship with trade policy. Acceptance of differentiation and graduation as organizing principles for the income tax involved dividing the nation along very different lines than the simple axes of property-holders or consumers. The moment when these issues gained admission to the political discourse is therefore of some significance, and it is a moment that can be located in the local taxation debate of the late 1860s and early 1870s.

At the beginning, the local taxation debate was a debate about tax differentiation that proceeded along familiar and traditional lines. It was initiated in 1868 by the Central Chamber of Agriculture through its parliamentary spokesperson, Massey Lopes, the member for South Devon. Lopes stated the case that had been made many times before about the unfair burden of rates carried by the landed interest. It was claimed that the large increases in rates since the 1830s had fallen disproportionately on the landed interest because they were a tax on real property that allowed manufacturing, merchant and rentier income to escape lightly. A committee was established to press for the relief of real property from the rate burden and attempts were made to forge an alliance between rural and urban property-owners. This argument was reminiscent of many since the 1690s about the distribution of tax burden between land and other forms of property. Equally, it was a debate that aroused all the old radical distrust of the claims of the landowning class for special fiscal privileges. Objection was taken at what was believed to be the attempt to relieve property at the expense of industry. Inquiry into the distribution of

---

[42] Jose Harris, *Unemployment and Politics: A Study in English Social Policy 1886–1914* (Oxford, 1972), pp. 269–70; Harris, *Private Lives, Public Spirit: Britain 1870–1914* (London, 1994), pp. 120–22; Buxton, *Finance and Politics*, vol. I, pp. 309–12.

the tax burden by George Goschen led him to conclude that the claims of land were unfounded, that the increase in local taxation since the 1830s had been borne most particularly by the urban areas rather than the land and "that it is a mere chimera . . . to speak of land being so heavily burdened with rates and taxes that capital is flying from the land and seeking other investments." Indeed, he argued, there had been a general decrease in the burden on land. It was upon houses that relief was most justified because of the way the rating burden fell most heavily upon occupiers rather than owners.[43]

The implications of the debate eventually stretched well beyond the confines of this traditional tension between land and other forms of taxable property, however. The Local Taxation Committee had initiated an alliance between rural and urban property-owners and the campaign came to focus on the idea that relief should be sought by redistributing the tax burden from the local to the imperial exchequer. This proposition propelled the issue beyond the mere question of tax differentiation into the more problematic and sensitive area of which level of government – local or central – was responsible for which taxing authority. When the government agreed to set up a Select Committee on Local Taxation chaired by George Goschen, the issue was immediately taken in a different direction than had originally been intended. Goschen proposed the good Liberal solution of extending the responsibilities of local government by extending their taxing capacities. But there was another tradition which found more sympathy with Disraelian Conservatism. This alternative provided for the exchequer to grant tax relief from local rates. Thus when the Conservatives returned to power in 1874 the practice of awarding grants-in-aid from the treasury was greatly extended; this served to transfer the cost of selective local services to the budget lines of the national exchequer.[44]

Such measures were not without precedent before 1874. Grants-in-aid for prison costs had been assigned to local authorities since 1823, for example. From the end of protectionism in 1846, the agricultural interest had been pressing its claim for some relief from the heavy burden of poor

[43] Christian Gardner, *Local Taxation: An Essay on the Injustice, Inequalities, and the Anomalies of the Present Poor-Rate Assessment* (London, 1869); Sir Massey Lopes, *Speech of Sir Massey Lopes, Bart., M.P., on Local Taxation* (London, 1871); John Noble, *Local Taxation: A Criticism of the Fallacies and a Summary of the Facts* (London, 1876), pp. 38–39, 137; George Goschen, M.P., *Reports and Speeches on Local Taxation* (London, 1872), pp. 50 (quote), 203–05; Dudley R. Baxter, *Local Government and Taxation and Mr. Goschen's Report* (London, 1874).

[44] Christine Bellamy, *Administering Central–Local Relations, 1871–1919: The Local Government Board in Its Fiscal and Cultural Context* (Manchester, 1988), pp. 28–33. This debate put land on the political agenda and fed into the Henry George campaign of the 1880s and Lloyd George's land campaign of 1912–13.

law expenditure. Disraeli had been loud in his support of these claims. Similarly, in the 1830s and 1840s, successful efforts were made to secure some national relief of local expenditures on police and poor law, and funding had been found for teacher training colleges and schools. Capital loan programs had also existed.

Nevertheless, such assistance to local authorities had always been parsimoniously doled out by the national exchequer. The more usual response of central government was to encourage local solutions to local problems. In the 1860s the rising complaints of the localities about poor law expenditure led to the Union Chargeability Act (1865) which redistributed local resources from the rich to the poor parishes. The Conservative government's grants-in-aid in the 1870s were fundamentally different from earlier ones. In the past, such grants had always been tied to improvements in administration – and they were occasionally rejected precisely because they interfered with local autonomy. The Disraeli government's grants were an actual transfer of resources from central to local administration with no guarantees of improved local government efficiency.[45]

Such grants represented a potentially massive rearrangement of the fiscal terrain of the state. They now entered permanently and prominently into the fiscal structure. From being a tiny part of government finance, grants-in-aid grew from £1.7 million in the 1860s to £2.7 million in 1874 and £5.7 million in 1878. By the Local Government Act of 1888, block grants as a percentage of general revenue assigned to local use became a regular part of public finance, and the demands of new expenditure led to the steady increase in grants targeted to specific needs. The significant fiscal legislation of the period, like the Agricultural Rating Bill (1896) and the Education Act of 1902, all contained transfer payments of one kind or another. In 1886 such transfers from the central government to local government had cost £4.5 million; by 1900 these payments had risen to £16 million. Even more significant than the money, however, was the implication of this innovation for the balance between local and central power. At one swoop the possibilities were opened for central government to assume large new fiscal responsibilities.[46]

Taxation had always possessed implications for the structure of the state. The traditional equilibrium between direct and indirect taxes fa-

---

[45] Bellamy, *Administering Central–Local Relations*, pp. 24–35; Josef Redlich and Francis W. Hirst, *The History of Local Government in England* (2nd edn., New York, 1970), pp. 163–66; Buxton, *Finance and Politics*, vol. II, pp. 184–86.

[46] Avner Offer, *Property and Politics 1870–1914* (Cambridge 1982), pp. 180, 214–15; R. J. Bennett, *Central Grants to Local Governments: The Political and Economic Impact of the Rate Support Grant in England and Wales* (Cambridge, 1982), p. 49; Ursula Hicks, *British Public Finances 1880–1952* (London, 1954), pp. 112–13.

vored an equally traditional balance of local over central government. Once the balance of taxation was disturbed, the relationship between the various parts of government was also bound to be displaced. The issue of tax differentiation had thus moved beyond its original confines of the relative tax burden on different kinds of property. The result was that the nature of local government was placed on the political agenda from the early 1870s. This was immediately obvious once the local taxation question was brought into public discussion. As Francis Palgrave pointed out in one of the more considered discussions of the local taxation question, local government's taxing capabilities were severely limited by their reliance upon the rates as a source of revenue. The result was that rating systems had proliferated over the previous half-century as the scope of local government had widened. Palgrave identified twelve principal rates from poor law to the drainage of embankments, each function being performed by a different management body. Overlapping jurisdictions and profoundly inefficient administration were the result. Palgrave was commissioner of the Inland Revenue and therefore had a particular interest in the professionalization of tax collection. Still, he was part of a growing chorus of voices that argued the need to consolidate the structures of local government in the interests of greater efficiency.[47]

The implications for central–local government relations had been obvious to George Goschen, the Liberal expert on these matters, from the moment he entered the local taxation debate. Under his guidance, the Liberals offered a solution to the local tax issue which included restructuring local government. Goschen's proposed solution was to rationalize parish and county administration by consolidating rating taxes into a single fund administered by a parochial board which would be the "superintending authority of the parish," elected on a standard franchise. At the county level, he proposed county boards that would consist of equal numbers of elected representatives of the parishes and the justices of the peace. And, finally, he proposed a Local Government Board in London which would replace the poor law commission and work to foster local government reform. In the event, only the latter proposal was enacted and the main bill was dropped. This abortive reform in the early 1870s was an attempt to restore the balance between local and central government that had been negotiated in the 1830s, and it included various strategies for shoving the problem of ratepayer pressure for tax relief back to the localities. Goschen's proposals were important, how-

---

[47] Robert Harry Inglis Palgrave, *The Local Taxation of Great Britain and Ireland* (London, 1871), pp. 5–6, 11–14, 32–33, 56. The assessment and collection of taxes began at this time to move away from the old voluntarist principles of the past toward the professionalization of the process under central government control.

ever, in prefiguring the reorganization of local government that was to be enacted in the 1880s and 1890s.[48]

This was an ironic denouement to the local taxation campaign. Nevertheless, it demonstrated quite neatly where discussion of tax issues like differentiation would lead. Originally, the campaign had been merely the latest version of the old claims of the landowning and agricultural interests to special consideration in the tax structure because of the particular place they occupied in the social order. It was a reflection of the new calculus of state structures, however, that this turned immediately into a broader discussion of the relationship between property taxes and the nature of local government. And this in its turn revealed how local government now rested on a more complex sociology than the landowners alone. Until the 1880s, governments were reluctant to grasp fully the nettle of local government reform. Its ultimate timing in 1888 and 1894 followed from the franchise extension of 1884. Nevertheless, the reform of local government had entered the realm of national politics with the local taxation crisis.

When reform ultimately came in the 1880s, however, it did not end the influence of landowning interest in county government, nor did it resolve the difficulties of local government finance. Differentiation continued to be a problem. The County Councils Act of 1888 and the Parish Government Act of 1894, however, did signal that the spheres of responsibility between central and local government had been redrawn. The local taxation issue, therefore, opened a dynamic that called into the question the borderline between local and central government that had existed throughout our period. The issues raised by the debate implied that central–local relations were in the process of movement to a new plane. It is to the shifting relationship between the balance of central and local power during this period that we must now turn.

[48] Goschen, *Reports and Speeches on Local Taxation*, pp. 174–76, 207–18.

5   The age of localism

The central and the local in the British state

The relationship between the center and the local is a defining property of state structures. Yet this relationship is never simple or straightforward. Historically, British culture has been antagonistic to centralizing tendencies. Walter Bagehot rightly spoke of the English [*sic*] "dislike of the executive government," as an essential part of English history and the English character. But this was not true at all times and for all spheres. Local governments and provincial elites frequently looked to the center for the assertion of national standards and support. Thus, the relationship between the center and the local is best understood as symbiotic rather than as oppositional. It was a relationship of both balance and instability. There were times when the boundaries between the center and periphery were generally understood and established and there were other times when they were unsettled and required renegotiation.[1]

The events of the late sixteenth and seventeenth centuries had halted the Tudor–Stuart project of restoring the kind of powerful central polity that England had been known for in medieval times. Ironically, however, it was only when the possibility of a directive central government had been blocked that a truly effective institutional, structural (even cultural) unity to the state could emerge. Nation building in Britain happened first at the local level. Indeed, the dysfunctionalism that seized many of England's governmental institutions in the seventeenth century created a vacuum into which local elites were forced to move. Central decrepitude pushed the administration of the country even more firmly into the hands of the local justices in the counties and of local oligarchies in the municipalities. Yet the devolution of authority into the hands of local elites did not impede the efficacy of the center once its vitality was restored. Indeed,

---

[1] Walter Bagehot, *The English Constitution* (repr., New York, n.d. [2nd edn., 1872]), pp. 305–06; Redlich and Hirst, *History of Local Government*, p. 12. I should emphasize that I am not speaking here of the relationship between the different national identities that composed the United Kingdom, but of the bureaucratic machinery of government.

the willing participation of local elites actually enhanced the reach and power of the state.[2]

Local elites furnished the links between the center and the province. This connection was reciprocal and interdependent. The authority of the center endowed local elites with their power. Yet without the cooperation of local worthies the writ of the center could not be served. The local elites transmitted and translated intelligence between the two levels of administration. The emblematic figure of this relationship was, of course, the justice of the peace. Justices were formally officials of the crown whose original responsibility was to supervise police powers. While they owed their authority to the crown, they owed their appointment and their position to their standing in the local community in which they were landowners. Justices were the day-to-day administrative personnel of the state. They were partnered by a dense network of other local agents, however. Without the active cooperation of these cadres the ambition of the center could not prevail. Attempts to impose a tax on birth, marriages, burials and bachelors in 1706, for example, foundered on the displeasure of local elites.[3]

From the late seventeenth century, the reciprocal links between center and locality were facilitated by three prevailing conditions. The first was the weakened condition of the agencies of central authority. Over the course of the seventeenth century the capacity for central direction had been drained out of both the English and Scottish states. Following the Glorious Revolution, of course, new loci of central power had grown rapidly in association with the financial revolution and the demands of war. Yet, in the hubs of this "fiscal-military state," power was both concentrated and diffused and the actual work and administration of government followed local initiative and assent. The needs of government increased as society became more complex and integrated into national and international networks. Yet the expanding government of the late seventeenth century did not flow from the organs of central

[2] Michael Bradelick, "State Formation and Social Change in Early Modern England: A Problem Stated and Approaches Suggested," *Social History*, 16, 1 (January 1991), pp. 1–17; Lawrence Stone, "The Results of the English Revolutions of the Seventeenth Century," in J. G. A. Pocock (ed.), *Three British Revolutions: 1641, 1688, 1776* (Princeton, 1980), pp. 46–50.

[3] Joanna Innes, "Parliament and the Shaping of Eighteenth-Century English Social Policy," *Transactions of the Royal Historical Society*, 5th ser., 40 (1990), p. 67; J. V. Beckett, "Local Custom and the New Taxation in the Seventeenth and Eighteenth Centuries: The Example of Cumberland," *Northern History*, 12 (1976), pp. 105–26; Ward, *English Land Tax*, pp. 42–49; Langford, *Public Life and the Propertied Englishman*, pp. 143–44, 161–62, 339–50, 421–25, 428; Clive Brooks, "Public Finance and Political Stability: The Administration of the Land Tax, 1688–1720," *Historical Journal*, 17, 2 (1974), pp. 281–300.

power; its spaces were occupied mainly by existing and new instruments of local government.[4]

The second influence which facilitated a healthy reciprocity between center and local after the late seventeenth century was the mediating role of Parliament. Parliament was a necessary constitutional defense against executive tyranny. Yet Parliament above all was a place where local power gathered. Parliament was a partner with local elites – in the appointment of local taxing commissions, for example. It was the place where local interests received national validation and arbitration. Parliament's legislation did not reflect the distillation of a national consensus; it mirrored the provincialism of local priorities. Throughout the period, legislation predominantly followed the particularist concerns of regional or sectional interest. In this there was little difference between the 1620s, the 1720s or even the 1820s. Parliament provided an arena for conflict resolution, the coordination of legislation and the arbitration of disputes between and within localities. Even the most parochial legislation required delicate negotiations between a myriad of particularist interests. Parliament was the court of last resort for such tensions and negotiations.[5]

Parliament, therefore, was the guardian of localism. The work of Parliament consisted largely of passing measures and providing resources that were deemed necessary by the localities. Over the course of the eighteenth century, this function tended to increase. Legislation requested by localities to allow environmental improvement – sewers, roads, street lighting and the like – trebled between 1760 and 1789 over the period from 1689 to 1760. Parliamentary power was "deployed in response to the demands of interests, groups, and communities, not so much imposing a sovereign will as providing a legal service" that would rubberstamp what particular localities wanted. Thus, Parliament was a *national* institution that served *local* purposes. Most parliamentary legislation was small-scale and made no attempt to develop national and consistent policy. Nevertheless, since local legislation followed earlier examples of the same kind, it often amounted to *ad hoc* national legislation.[6]

The third influence which reinforced the reciprocity between center and local was the existence of a wide area of agreement on the apportionment of responsibilities between the center and the locality. This division of responsibility was never uncontested, but it was sufficiently well estab-

[4] Joanna Innes, "The Domestic Face of the Fiscal-Military State," in Stone, *Imperial State at War*, pp. 97–104.

[5] Langford, "Property and Virtual Representation."

[6] Conrad Russell, *Parliaments and English Politics, 1621–1629* (Oxford, 1979); Langford, *Public Life and the Propertied Englishman*, pp. 139 (quote), 156–57, 165–66; Innes, "Parliament and the Shaping of Social Policy."

lished to allow the structures of localism to be compatible with the institutions and practices of the fiscal-military state. In 1861 John Stuart Mill prescribed that power should be localized and knowledge centralized. The first purpose of the center was to be the fount of information and wisdom for the localities. There were purely local matters, like street lighting; there were issues of local management under national supervision, like the criminal law; and there were questions of national interest under local control like the poor law. Mill's demarcations did not describe a peculiarly mid-Victorian balance of power, however. They were rather the distillation of the wisdom of the previous 200 years.[7]

Parliament was quite willing to launch inquiries and initiatives to address pressing problems. Special funds were granted to establish schools in the Scottish Highlands after 1715 as part of a pacification effort. Ambitious programs were launched to help reintegrate demobilized soldiers after the wars of the middle of the eighteenth century. Parliament was more active in the eighteenth century than it had ever been before. Over 700 pieces of general legislation passed through Parliament during the course of the century. Social policy was the most common issue they addressed. Indeed, in this area, local governments were quite likely to appeal to Parliament for help and direction in handling often perplexingly complex matters. And although Parliament was willing to cajole and encourage local authorities, it tended to avoid close monitoring of local affairs. There was no general trend toward a greater direction of local government from the center. Both the national and the community levels of the state continued to interact in response to a wide range of domestic issues.[8]

The two centuries from the late seventeenth century were an age of localism, therefore. The structures of the British state were shaped by the primacy of local power and responsibility. Indeed, the outstanding feature of the period stretching from William and Mary to the mid-Victorian era is precisely the expanding reach of local power and authority and the bristling vigor with which it addressed its obligations. It was during the eighteenth century that this localist state was established, and the first issue to be addressed in this chapter will be to provide some indication of the elaboration of the networks of localism during that century.

Localism was not a static formation. The boundaries that demarcated the center from the locality were neither uncontested nor free from stress. Indeed, it was exactly this tension that endowed the contours of the

---

[7] John Stuart Mill, *Considerations on Representative Government* (repr., Chicago, 1962 [London, 1861]), pp. 291, 297–303.
[8] Innes, "Parliament and the Shaping of Social Policy," p. 91; Innes, "Domestic Face," pp. 96, 102, 105–07, 112–18.

localist state with their distinctive character. The second question to be addressed in this chapter, therefore, will be the dynamic of that instability. Particular attention will be directed to the flashpoints of this tension, especially the persistent problem of the poor law. The moment of greatest instability in the equipoise between localism and centralism occurred in the late eighteenth and early nineteenth centuries. During those years the challenge to the existing structures of localism was presented as a series of "reforms" of state structures that presaged new – and better – forms of governing. "Reform" contained multiple meanings, of course, but it was always problematic. In relation to the structures of the state, however, "reform" must be located in the context of eighteenth-century problems rather than nineteenth-century departures. And this is especially so because, in the final analysis, the efforts of reformers failed to displace the equilibrium between localism and centralism in the state structures.

Thus, the salient feature of the reformed mid-Victorian state was precisely the preeminence of localism. Describing this predominance will be the third topic for this chapter. Mid-Victorian localism was cast in a different mould from the eighteenth-century patterns of local control. Yet its revitalized structures of localism reflected more of the past than they presaged the future. Mainstream reform activists in the early nineteenth century had not intended to preside over the reinvigoration of localism. Yet this is what happened and it was a fact which broadcast the failure of the Benthamite reform project. What reform was unable to accomplish in the 1830s and 1840s, however, was beginning to evolve more silently by the late 1860s. The boundaries between the center and the local began to be breached. Localism could no longer suffice to contain the balance between center and periphery. Thus, the fourth issue I shall address will be the disruption of the equilibrium between central and local that had defined the age of localism and the emergence of a new configuration to the state structures.

The localist state of the eighteenth century

The most dramatic evidence of government growth in the eighteenth century was to be found in the localities. This process was first detailed at the beginning of the twentieth century by Sydney and Beatrice Webb in their five-volume study of English local government from the Glorious Revolution to the Municipal Corporations Act of 1835. Their study remains an unsurpassed achievement. But the main thrust of the Webbs' account was to write a history of local government from the perspective of the Benthamite centralizers of the early nineteenth century, whom they saw, of course, as premature Fabian socialists. The Webbs regarded the localist structures bequeathed to the Victorian state as a ramshackle set of institutions in desperate need of reform. In particular, they portrayed the institutions of rural and urban local authority as increasingly dominated by corrupt oligarchies. It is generally true to say that this is the framework that continues to inform our view of the eighteenth-century state. It is, however, a view that is less and less convincing.[9]

It is impossible not to be impressed with the elaboration and proliferation of the localist structures of government. From the late seventeenth century the procedures and structures of both quarter sessions and petty sessions were formalized into effective instruments of government. It was the petty sessions that saw the most substantial empowerment, however, and as a consequence the responsibilities of the justices of the peace rapidly expanded. By the middle of the eighteenth century, justices were devoting on average between one and a half and three days to official business. This amounted to almost a full-time job. In the early 1700s Daniel Defoe had famously remarked on how the power exercised by the justices was sufficient to nullify the will of Parliament. Had Defoe returned a hundred years later, he would have found even more evidence for the truth of his observation.[10]

The judicial portion was only one small segment of justice's work, of course. The justice was the only officer of the state in constant contact with the public across a wide range of activities. Justices were the prime authority for the operation of the poor law and their remit deepened over the course of the century. Under the early Hanoverians the power of the justices was progressively expanded over both the workhouses and the salaried employees who staffed the poor law system. Justices controlled the settlement laws that governed who was entitled to relief in a given parish. In the reign of George III justices were granted singular powers to award relief, a power which was extended in an act of 1815.[11]

The poor law was only one area where justices exercised wide powers of supervision, however. Vestry affairs were a further area of responsibility, and justices either appointed or supervised the highway surveyors, overseers, constables and ale conners, among others. They administered the bastardy laws, maintained the sabbath laws, granted alehouse licenses, arbitrated disputes before they got to court and supervised road and

[9] Alan Kidd, "Historians or Polemicists?: How the Webbs Wrote Their History of the English Poor Laws," *Economic History Review*, 40, 3 (August 1987), pp. 400–17.

[10] Ruth Paley (ed.), *Justice in Eighteenth-Century Hackney: The Justicing Notebook of Henry Norris and the Hackney Petty Sessions Book* (London, 1991), p. xxxi. Justices were not the only officers who worked hard on local government matters. Thomas Turner spent three days investigating a suicide as part of his duties as overseer of the poor law in East Hoathly, Sussex. See David Vaisey (ed.), *The Diaries of Thomas Turner 1754–1765* (Oxford, 1984), pp. 50–54.

[11] Halevy, *England in 1815*, p. 378; Langford, *Public Life and the Propertied Englishman*, p. 263.

bridge maintenance, vagrants and sanitation. These responsibilities multiplied as local government became increasingly complex. One of the more revealing indications of the sophistication and professionalization of local administration during the eighteenth century was the manuals that began to proliferate from the 1750s explaining the relevant parts of law to the predominantly lay justices.[12]

Local administration trawled deeply in the social structure to satisfy its burgeoning need for part-time officers. In Aberdeen 60 percent of the burgh officers turned over each year. Probably one in twelve eligible men could be expected to serve the town government of that city in some capacity in the later seventeenth century. Similar opportunities existed for men of relatively low status and wealth to serve as justices and in other positions in the rural areas of England and Scotland.[13] Nevertheless, the main trend was toward an increasing social exclusiveness.

After the Restoration there had been an influx of the lower social orders into the commissions of the peace. This democratization was short-lived, however, and by 1700 it had gone into reverse. Throughout the eighteenth century the social composition of the county justices became progressively more select. In the early eighteenth century, lesser gentry dominated the rural bench and the leading families of county were almost totally absent from quarter sessions. From the 1750s there was a marked increase in the numbers of clergymen being made justices; by the beginning of the nineteenth century they were joined by the aristocracy of the county. Under the impetus of early Victorian reformers, rural and urban government moved even more decisively away from the lower classes and into the domain of ratepayer elites.[14]

The ballooning responsibilities of the justices forced them to create an increasingly dense administrative matrix. In the counties, quarter sessions – on which a panel of justices sat in rotation – came to approxi-

---

[12] Davison et al., *Stilling the Grumbling Hive*, p. xxxvi. In the first edition of the best known of these manuals, the responsibilities and powers of the justices to regulate traffic, for example, occupied 100 pages – five more than the poor law section; see Richard Burn, *The Justice of the Peace and the Parish Officer* (2 vols., 1st edn., London, 1755). By 1736 the book by W. Nelson, *The Office and Authority of a Justice of the Peace*, was already in its eleventh edition.

[13] R. A. Houston, "Popular Politics in the Reign of George II: The Edinburgh Cordiners," *Scottish Historical Review*, 72, 2: 194 (October 1993), p. 167; for church government in Scotland, see R. A. Houston, "Bustling Artisans': Church Patronage at South Leith in the 1740s and 1750s," *Albion*, 26, 1 (Spring 1994), pp. 55–78; Esther Moir, *Local Government in Gloucestershire 1775–1800* (Bristol, 1969), p. 60. Thus, in the later eighteenth century, the Gloucestershire bench included men of considerable substance such as Joseph Cripps who left £82,000 in bequests to the poor and Charles Morgan who left a mere £1,000 to his wife and £800 in annuities.

[14] See George, *London Life in the Eighteenth Century*, pp. 19, 28, 295, Sydney Webb and Beatrice Webb, *English Local Government from the Revolution to the Municipal Corporations Act: The Parish and the County* (London, 1906), pp. 319–50, 377–79, 385; Gauci, *Politics and Society in Great Yarmouth*, p. 90.

mate an executive arm of government. By the 1830s it was common practice for a series of standing committees to exist under justice supervision with responsibilities for such things as bridges and gaols. Justices were a chief executive officer, with a wide range of part-time and salaried managers reporting to them. Yet, although the justices were the most important figures in the local administration of the country, they were not the only nexus of localism. Aside from the MPs, who were the most important linkage, such offices as high stewards and recorders in the boroughs were chosen not only for their legal expertise, but precisely because of their connections in Westminster.[15]

Nor were the justice-dominated quarter sessions the only network of local legal administration. The responsibilities of the high sheriff, for example, included representing the crown and administering the prisons, elections and various court procedures. There were also the municipal and borough courts and corporations, all of which operated according to special charters, not omitting the various manorial courts that remained in existence until swept away by municipal reform. Finally, there were the nonaccountable bodies created by special acts of Parliament. These were an invention of the eighteenth century and included a large number of miscellaneous bodies set up to cover a wide variety of functions both within and between parishes. By the early nineteenth century, they were very numerous indeed. Since 1748 over 300 improvement commissions had been created, and about 1,800 other agencies with specific local government responsibilities such as sewers and harbors. In addition, the same period had seen the creation of some 11,000 turnpike trusts.[16]

Tension and conflict were rife within this world of local government. Yet conflict was more likely between the various local bodies than it was with the central government. The installation of new authorities challenged the interests of existing bodies, particularly those at the parish and vestry level. Thus, the new special authorities frequently faced strong local resistance precisely because they displaced control from the existing agency of the parish. The creation of the turnpike trusts in the late seventeenth century, for example, was accompanied by a prolonged jurisdictional struggle with the parishes. It took over forty years from the first Turnpike Act of 1663 before the trusts managed to free themselves from justice control.[17]

---

[15] Moir, *Local Government in Gloucestershire*, pp. 89–96, 108–09; Gauci, *Politics and Society in Great Yarmouth*, pp. 49–50; Webb and Webb, *The Parish and the County*, pp. 79–103, 146–72, 483–86, 532–35.

[16] Greenleaf, *The British Political Tradition*, vol. III, *A Much Governed Nation. Part I*, pp. 15–16.

[17] Albert, *Turnpike Road System*, p. 22. The Webbs tended to regard the nonaccountable institutions as a response to the corruption of the old parish and vestry system, but it is not clear that this was true.

Localist administration came to be regarded as corrupt and dilapidated by the Benthamite reformers. Undoubtedly the system had its corrupt and ramshackle side. What system does not? Yet the predominant properties were those of efficiency, improvement and an increasingly sophisticated bureaucracy. Local studies of town government have demonstrated the partiality of the Webbs' views. Even the most closed corporations could hardly operate without keeping in close touch with the interests of the significant factions of the town, particularly the merchant and trading interests. Corporations were not monoliths of self- interested obscurantism. They were evolving institutions that were typically able to respond flexibly to the needs of the town. The responsibility of the corporations to guard the interests of the town and articulate the concerns of its elites to the regional and national authorities was taken very seriously. Reciprocity was the watchword of local government, as it was throughout the system of governing and social authority.[18]

Even the Webbs were willing to concede that the justice system of administration became more professional. The same was true of other areas of local government such as the commissioners of enclosure or the officials who ran the turnpike trusts. In the early part of the century there was a rank amateurism to turnpike administration and some degree of venality associated with toll renting. Over the course of the eighteenth century, turnpike administration became much more proficient and disinterested. One of the first professional groups to emerge from this localist system were surveyors who worked for turnpike trusts. John McAdam, the turnpike reformer, came from a family of trust surveyors. Qualified and experienced people were appointed to the key positions of responsibility in the trust – as clerk, treasurer and surveyor. Such people introduced best practice to the repair and upkeep of roads in the eighteenth century. In the early part of the century, roads were still maintained by statute labor. By the end of the century gangs of wage laborers supervised by qualified supervisors kept the roads passable.[19]

Initiative, improvement and efficiency were integral to the system of local government throughout the eighteenth and nineteenth centuries. Historians have tended to be blinded by the self-promoting claims of a

[18] Gauci, *Politics and Society in Great Yarmouth*, pp. 8, 11, 17, 19, 39–40.
[19] Webb and Webb, *The Parish and the County*, pp. 480–84, 535; M. W. Beresford, "Commissioners of Enclosure," *Economic History Review*, ser. 1, 16, 2 (1946), pp. 130–40. Professionalization did not mean a more even-handed administration for the poor. Justice Norris of Hackney in the 1720s "regularly committed poor men and women to gaol on the flimsiest of evidence. Yet when poor people came to him for the protection of the law, he did his best to discourage them." See Paley, *Justice in Eighteenth-Century Hackney*, p. xxxii; Albert, *Turnpike Road System*, pp. 75–86; Pawson, *Transport and Economy*, pp. 240–42. Statute labor required those without property to contribute six days a year to road repair.

Jeremy Bentham or the self-confident arrogance of an Edwin Chadwick. Yet virtually nothing that these luminaries suggested had not been prefigured in the provinces. Innovations in social policy derived ultimately from the adventurous experiments of local worthies. It was local initiative that led to the search for better ways of delivering relief to the poor, providing education for children, organizing the administration of the roads or the prisons. In these matters the attitude of local magistrates was all-important. The example of Sir George Paul, a leading Gloucester magistrate, who initiated and carried through a reform of the local prisons, was not at all unusual. Indeed, there was a stream of thought at the beginning of the nineteenth century that contested Benthamite centralization by arguing that reformers should look to local government for ideas for how to restructure central government.[20]

The idea of "improvement" was an early eighteenth-century invention. The Victorians appropriated the idea for themselves and fondly propagated the notion that it belonged to their age. Yet the same confidence in material progress and aspiration to moral betterment of the self was a characteristic eighteenth-century attitude. Defoe waxed eloquent on his tour of England about "the improvements in the soil, the product of the earth, the labor of the poor, the improvement in manufactures, in merchandises, in navigation."[21] The eighteenth-century provincial cities were the seedbeds of Victorian urban improvement. Significant advances were made in urban planning and care for the environment in the eighteenth century, particularly in the South and the Midlands. Corporate responsibilities were progressively expanded and moved into the hands of specially created agencies with powers to levy rates to perform specific tasks such as street cleaning. After 1760 improvement commissions secured the power to raise loans. Street lighting was a good illustration of the kind of amenity produced by the spirit of localist improvement. By the 1730s most large towns and many smaller ones had installed some form of public oil lighting. After 1750 corporate responsibility for street paving began to replace individual initiative in such matters.[22]

[20] For some examples of the poor law debate, to which I shall refer again later, see Joshua Child, *A New Discourse on Trade* (London, 1693); Cary, *Essay Towards Regulating the Trade and Employing the Poor of This Kingdom*; Cary, *A Proposal Offered to the Committee of the Honourable House of Commons Appointed to Consider Ways for the Better Providing for the Poor and Setting Them to Work* (London, n.d.); anon., *An Account of Several Workhouses for Employing and Maintaining the Poor* (London, 1725); Henry Fielding, *A Proposal for Making an Effectual Provision for the Poor* (London, 1753); Moir, *Local Government in Gloucestershire*, pp. 113–14.

[21] Briggs, *Age of Improvement*, pp. 1–3, 13, 16, 19, 435–45; Daniel Defoe, *A Tour Through the Whole Island of Great Britain*, ed. Pat Rogers (Harmondsworth, 1971), p. 45.

[22] E. L. Jones and M. E. Falkus, "Urban Improvement and the English Economy," in Peter Borsay (ed.), *The Eighteenth-Century English Town: A Reader in Urban History* (London, 1990), pp. 117–18, 130–137, 144.

Efficient town administration did not depend on the degree of open-ness to the burgeoning middling-class groups. Manchester, the arche-typal city of Victorian progress, was a case in point. Its administrative structure remained a medieval remnant. The council was chosen by the lord of the manor's Leet Court. Yet this "corrupt" old Tory corporation initiated improvement schemes from the 1780s. Similarly, King's Lynn, Wisbech, Leeds and Liverpool were all ripe for political reform by the early nineteenth century, being resolutely closed to access by new groups. Such towns were perfectly well run. Wisbech had been paved by the corporation in the 1680s; by 1700 sewers were being laid and a clean water supply provided. Liverpool's unreformed corporation had im-proved navigation on the Mersey and Weaver Rivers and sponsored an improvement act in 1786 which set about opening new streets and modernizing old ones. The contrast with Bradford, an almost entirely new town where uncontrolled development persisted well into the nine-teenth century, was sharp and telling.[23]

By the early nineteenth century, then, a thick matrix of localist state structures had produced a sophisticated labyrinth of governing institu-tions. These same institutions, however, presented a tempting target for criticism by reformers. Localism was not supported by a theory that could compete with the two major currents of enlightened government: central-ized management and democratic accountability. In Britain, of course, Jeremy Bentham was the most prominent representative of both of these tendencies. Bentham's objection to localist direction of prisons or the poor law was that localism produced dysfunctional inefficiencies. In this account localism was portrayed as rife with corruption from the compet-ing oligarchies that sought to control its forms. Bentham's remedy for this disorder was to fuse accountability with central supervision in local administration. Thus, Bentham favored an elective element to local institutions. Bentham's conception of democratic control was that office-holders answer to informed opinion, rather than to a self-interested corporation oligarchy or the popular democracy of an open vestry. Cen-tral government would monitor the institutions of local administration to ensure the employment of best methods by qualified personnel.

This was the source that informed the "reform" of government in the early nineteenth century. Yet "reform" did not simply flow from a factual description of the infirmities of localism. Bentham's proposals for

[23] Derek Fraser, *Urban Politics in Victorian England: The Structure of Politics in Victorian Cities* (Leicester, 1976), pp. 116–18; Bryan Keith Lucas, *The Unreformed Local Government System* (London, 1980), pp. 15–37; Briggs, *Age of Improvement*, pp. 46–47; Michael Turner, "Gas, Police and the Struggle for Mastery in Manchester in the 1820s," *Historical Research*, 67, 164 (October 1994), p. 303. It is interesting to note that London was fairly late into this fashion for improvement, not getting its first act until 1762.

accountability were a useful discourse for middling-class groups to seize in their constant battle to define themselves against existing power centers and to legitimate their access to institutions of local and national government. Yet the important thing about this component of reform was its predetermined limits. Democracy occupied a decidedly secondary consideration in the critique of localism. Bentham had no objection to justices of the peace being drawn predominantly from one caste. His main concern was how to determine suitability of candidates for the job, and to that end he advocated tests of aptitude as the route to the bench rather than nomination. It was not the class selectivity that distorted the functioning of justices, but the principles of their selection. In Bentham's opinion, vestry government – the tier of government closest to the people – was disabled precisely because of its tendencies to democratic inclusion. The widely differing vestry franchises and governing structures produced inchoate administrative structures. The primitive democracy of the open vestries produced anarchy, corruption and bossism rather than good government and needed, therefore, to be replaced by more formalized and electorally restrictive bodies.[24]

There was nothing particularly novel in much of this theory. Vestry government had long been regarded as a deeply flawed institution. Efforts to reform vestries by redefining their democratic component to include only the wealthier classes were not a Benthamite brainwave. The favorite device of early nineteenth-century reform of vestry government was the select vestry. Yet this controversial formula had been used throughout the eighteenth century.[25] A supervisory function to central government was also well accepted in the eighteenth century. Early nineteenth-century reformers did not invent the model of state structures that contained less room for local initiative and more control from the center. They stood at the tail end of a longstanding historical continuity. The debate as to where the boundary between the authority of the local and the center should lie was a constant theme in eighteenth-century politics. This is the context in which we may situate the movement for the reform of government in the early nineteenth century.

[24] Elie Halevy, *The Growth of Philosophical Radicalism* (New York, 1972), pp. 375, 414, 429–30. I will treat the question of reform of the franchise and the political realm separately, although many of the same considerations discussed below can be seen to apply. See chapter 7 in this volume for a fuller discussion of these themes in the political realm.

[25] For an early statement of opposition to the lack of democracy in select vestries, see Joseph Phipps, *The Vestry Laid Open; Or a Full and Plain Detection of the Many Gross Abuses, Impositions and Oppressions of Select Vestries* (3rd edn., London, 1739). Vestry meetings in the small Sussex village of East Hoathly were often rowdy and contentious affairs and not infrequently ended in one or two of the parish officers the worse for drink. See Vaisey, *Diaries of Thomas Turner*, pp. xxxiv, 19, 35, 75–76, 145, 148, 204, 267.

Reform and the instabilities of localism

The reform debate was a discourse about the structures of government
and administration. It was a debate which addressed the issue of how the
specific institution (whether it be church and state, Ireland or the franchise) should be configured in relation to its own function and in relation
to its place in the national state structure.[26] The climax to this debate was
reached in the 1830s when a large number of adjustments were made in
the various institutional structures of the state. These included the franchise reform in 1832 (to be considered later in this volume, pp. 264–75),
the repeal of the Test and Corporation Acts (1827), the end of civil
disabilities on Catholics (1829), various factory legislation and reform of
the courts and criminal law. There was more than one nexus of reform.
Two are of particular interest for the present discussion, however: the
new poor law of 1834 and the Municipal Corporations Act of 1835,
which reformed town government. The former is of interest as illustrating
the continuities of localism, the latter as showing the reinvention of
localist infrastructures. Both demonstrate how the balance between local
and central power was not decisively disrupted in the early nineteenth
century.

Debate on the poor law was a continuous theme of English and British
politics. One particularly notable phase was the half-century from 1670
when all the issues that were to dominate poor law policy for the next two
centuries made their entrance into the political culture. As early as 1693
Josiah Child put forward the blueprint for the new poor law of 1834.
Child proposed that commissioners in London direct the policy of local
authorities who would build workhouses and govern the poor according
to the procedures established in the center. Similarly, the inventor of the
workhouse test was one Matthew Marryott, a poor law contractor who
made quite a career in the early eighteenth century experimenting with
various poor law policies.[27]

From these kinds of experiences flowed a constant stream of legislation
addressed to specific localities but also serving as models for other areas to
follow. The principle of the poor law union as the basic unit of adminis-

---

[26] The scope of this discussion was not limited to government, of course. It included private
institutions which addressed a national interest such as charities. My discussion here is
limited to government, however.

[27] Marryott established the viability of the workhouse test in 1714. See J. R. Poynter, *Society
and Pauperism: English Ideas on Poor Relief, 1795–1834* (London, 1969), p. 16; Child, *New
Discourse on Trade*, pp. 61–70. This period was a time of considerable experimentation
with poor law methods. For some examples, see *Account of Several Workhouses*. Lynn Lees
describes it as the heyday of the workhouse as miniature factory. See Lees, *The Solidarities
of Strangers: The English Poor Laws and the People, 1700–1948* (Cambridge, 1998), pp.
61–62.

tration was secured in this way, for example, although it was not universally applied until after 1834. There was always a section of opinion which advocated national legislation as the solution to the problems of the poor law. This was hardly surprising given the fact that between 11 and 15 percent of the population were typically in receipt of aid in the eighteenth and early nineteenth centuries. Serious moves to overhaul the poor law completely were launched in the 1730s, 1750s and 1780s. Local particularism successfully resisted these efforts, however, and allowed only two acts (in 1722 and 1783) that truly confronted general problems of administration. These pieces of national legislation are generally accorded a low importance in poor law history. This is certainly a mistaken view.

Sir Norton Knatchbull's act of 1722 was the progenitor of the new poor law of 1834. It brought closure to the previous fifty years of experiment and discussion. Henceforth, discussion of the poor law ranged within the demarcations established at one end by the harsh policy of the workhouse and at the other end by the compassionate practice of out-relief payments. There were no other alternatives. Knatchbull's act sanctioned the workhouse solution. It established the workhouse test and the workhouse as instruments of poor law policy. Both were seen to possess the advantage of regularizing and formalizing poor law policy and reducing local variations. A rapid expansion of workhouses followed the act's passage. Workhouses were no less controversial in the eighteenth century than they were in the nineteenth. The advantages of the workhouse were well recognized to lie in the "apprehensions the Poor have of it. These prompt them to exert and do their utmost to keep themselves off the parish." Similarly, objections were raised to housing the poor in workhouses on the grounds that it would be hard to build structures big enough to hold them. There was considerable experience in the eighteenth century to bear this out (in Shrewsbury for example), although it was an objection that the centralizers of 1834 chose to ignore.[28]

The act of 1783 expressed a more liberal poor law regime than that of 1722. It accepted the legitimacy of out-relief, for example, and was the legislative sanction for the policy of linking relief to the price of provisions made famous by the Speenhamland magistrates in 1798. Yet this act also reflected the belief of its sponsor (Thomas Gilbert) that centralization

---

[28] In 1720 there were only about 3,000 residents of workhouses; by 1777 there were over 90,000 housed in 1,916 workhouses. See Davison et al., *Stilling the Grumbling Hive*, pp. 145–47, 152–60; Innes, "Parliament and the Shaping of Social Policy," pp. 70, 73, 83; David Eastwood, *Governing Rural England: Tradition and Transformation in Local Government 1780–1840* (Oxford, 1994), pp. 170–71; *Account of Several Workhouses*, p. 53 (quote); Halevy, *England in 1815*, pp. 380–81; Vincent Walsh, "Old and New Poor Laws in Shropshire 1820–1870," *Midland History*, 2, 4 (Autumn 1974), p. 227.

was the way forward. Gilbert had little faith in the ability of the parish and its officials to administer the poor law competently, and his impatience with the voluntary traditions of local government prefigured the mood of the reformers of the 1830s.[29] Gilbert reflected a growing sentiment that the problem of the poor law was embedded in its administration. The relationship between poor law administration and poverty itself was conceptualized as the key difficulty. Yet this, too, was not a new insight. In the 1690s John Cary had argued that management of the poor laws encouraged sloth by keeping the poor dependent rather than "raising them to a better way of living." Nothing but good laws, he argued can "restrain this habit of idleness from growing farther." This paralleled exactly, of course, the popular condemnation of the poor laws from the 1790s – that their administration sponsored a culture of dependency. The idea that behavior could be changed through different administrative procedures formed a key part of the debate about the poor law from the 1790s, but it was hardly a new idea.[30]

From the days of Josiah Child, the distinction between relieving the poor and policing them had been a fine one. When Henry Fielding presented a plan for a workhouse for the county of Middlesex that would shelter 5,000 paupers, he had in mind that 600 miscreants would be located in a House of Correction in the same building. Bentham's Pauper Plan was merely his prison design applied to social policy. Those who followed in Bentham's wake, like Patrick Colquhoun, Edward Tremenheere and Edwin Chadwick, were trailing the tradition blazoned by John Cary and Sir Norton Knatchbull. This analysis placed indigence and crime as but two sides of the same coin of the moral deficiency of the poor. The maladministration of localism reinforced the defects of character that were genetically engineered in the working-class body. Thus, it was claimed that the law of settlement and the practice of out-relief produced the very indigence that they were supposed to prevent.[31]

All reformers, whether of the eighteenth century or the nineteenth, were agreed that only the central state could exercise the necessary supervision to combat the vagrancy and mendacity that had grown from the absence of a "systematic superintending policy, calculated to check and prevent the growth and progress of vicious habits, and other irregu-

[29] Langford, *Public Life and the Propertied Englishman*, pp. 156–58; A. W. Coates, "Economic Thought and Poor Law Policy in the Eighteenth Century," *Economic History Review*, 13, 1 (1960–61), pp. 39–47; Eastwood, *Governing Rural England*, pp. 104–07; Poynter, *Society and Pauperism*, pp. 12–13, 15–17, 26.

[30] Cary, *Essay on the State of England*, pp. 153–56 (quotes, p. 156); F. E. Fauquier, *An Essay on Ways and Means for Raising Money for the Support of the Present War* (London, 1756).

[31] Patrick Colquhoun, *A Treatise on Indigence* (London, 1806), pp. 240–41; Fielding, *A Proposal*.

larities incident to civil society."[32] Patrick Colquhoun in the 1790s and Edwin Chadwick in the 1830s saw the supervision and observation of the poor as a necessary condition for order and Colquhoun's concept of crime merged indiscriminately into those offenses against common morality. The duties of the police, both believed, should extend to the supervision of public leisure and other moral purposes as well as fighting crime. Chadwick envisaged policemen as assistant relieving officers in the poor law administration.[33]

Colquhoun and Chadwick were part of a long tradition in the debate over poor law policy. After 1815, however, the assumption that fundamental changes were necessary in the relationship between central and local government was a core belief of reformers. For social policy issues the frontier between the local and the center was widely regarded as needing to be relocated. Two things stood in the way of any reform that aimed to alter the balance of power of localism, however. The first was the structures of localism themselves. It was impossible to contemplate changing poor law policy without encountering these structures, which had grown more powerful over the early nineteenth century. The second obstacle to shifting the boundary of localism was the absence of agencies available to Parliament that could be used to enforce any centralizing measures the reformers might persuade the legislature to pass.

The perception that poor law costs were galloping out of control moved reform of the poor law to the heart of the political agenda after the end of the Napoleonic wars. Control over poor law expenditure could not simply be decreed from London, however. It was subject to the whims and inclinations of local magistrates among others – as the Speenhamland decision had amply demonstrated. In spite of various efforts to reduce magistrate government at the local level, their power had become more sophisticated and effective and their activism had if anything become more intense. They continued to use their traditional powers to intervene in the food market and they persisted in subjecting the administration of the poor law to untidy experimentation. Often these involved wasteful make-work schemes. Nationally, about 69,000 were employed on parish labor schemes by 1831–32, and many more were receiving wages supplements. Bringing the magistrates and other

[32] Colquhoun, *Treatise on Indigence*, p. 82.
[33] See Poynter, *Society and Pauperism*, pp. 117–44, for Bentham and pp. 200–07 for Colquhoun; Colquhoun, *Treatise on Indigence*, pp. 111–20, 187–207; A. P. Donajgrodzki, *Social Control in Nineteenth-Century Britain* (London, 1977), pp. 54–67; Gertrude Himmelfarb, *The Idea of Poverty: England in the Early Industrial Age* (New York, 1985); J. B. Brebner, "Laissez-Faire and State Intervention in Nineteenth-Century Britain," *Journal of Economic History*, 8, suppl. (1948), pp. 59–73; David Roberts, *The Victorian Origins of the Welfare State* (New Haven, 1968).

local institutions under control was to be a major objective of "reform" through the 1830s.[34]

The proliferation of localist structures of government had coopted more people and institutions into its work. Aside from magistrates' power, the other major local government structure that would be encountered in any reform of poor law administration was the vestry. Vestry government and poor law policy were inextricably linked. Controlling poor law expenditure could be achieved only with the cooperation of the vestries. Yet vestries tended to be the most open and democratic institutions of the system of localism. They could hardly be expected to reduce poor law expenditure if they were subject to the influence of the popular classes.[35] Thus, the matter of vestry government was added to the agenda of "reform." The closing down of the open, democratic vestries became a major project for reformers from the end of the Napoleonic wars. There tended to be a close correspondence, therefore, between schemes for poor law reform and the parallel reformation of vestry government.

When Samuel Whitbread introduced a bill into the House of Commons in 1807 for a national reform of the poor law, for example, it included a proposal to reform vestry government. Whitbread sought to replace the popular democracy of the open vestry with a democracy restricted only to the highest ratepayers. After the French wars the major figure in this effort to bridle vestry government was William Sturges Bourne, an obscure but persistently permanent MP and minor government functionary. Appropriately enough, Sturges Bourne was also an avid poor law reformer. Thus, the Select Committee on the Poor Law of 1817 that he chaired prefigured the reforms of 1834 in its bias against the inefficiencies of parochial government, its support of tighter supervision, its greater professionalization of parish officers and its revived workhouse campaign.

This committee also promoted the expansion of select vestries to replace the open vestries. Over the following two years Sturges Bourne implemented this recommendation by acts which established procedures for supplanting the democratic open vestries with select vestries. These vestries were chosen by a ratepayer franchise that allowed plural voting by the larger property-owners. Removing democratic vestries was essential to poor law reform, but it was not the only institution of localism that needed redress. On the very same day that the Vestry Act of 1818 was

[34] Poynter, *Society and Pauperism*, pp. 281–82; Greenleaf, *A Much Governed Nation*, p. 28; Eastwood, *Governing Rural England*, pp. 58–60, 73, 104–07, 150–54, 163.

[35] This is not to imply that resistance to poor law expenditures was new to the late eighteenth century. Difficulties in reaching agreement on the poor rate was a constant feature of the East Hoathly vestry meetings recorded by Thomas Turner; see Vaisey, *Diaries of Thomas Turner*, pp. 267–68, 289.

introduced, Sturges Bourne introduced a bill that captured the several facets to reform. This bill aimed to professionalize the administration of the poor law under central direction, to restrict the relief-giving powers of local authorities who were seen as susceptible to sympathy with their poorer neighbors, and to police the Irish, the "vicious" and children by pressing harsh conditions of relief. The bill failed, but it accurately disclosed the tenor of the age of reform.[36]

The vitality of the structures of localism was not the only constraint facing reformers of poor law government. An additional difficulty was constitutional. Parliament was not equipped with the necessary instruments to enable it to master the localist bias of the state structures. The only device to hand that could impose national legislation was the general public act. Yet there was considerable opposition to this category of statute, and most attempts to pass national poor law legislation were wrecked on this antagonism. Constitutional practice directed Parliament more to specific local matters. The realities of power encouraged this tendency. As has been noted, there were no reliable agents of central government in the provinces. Measures like the new poor law that depended on central direction had either to create such agents or to find ways of enlisting the cooperation of local elites. The formal position of the justices placed them as agents of the center, but they regarded themselves as representatives of the locality to the Home Office. Indeed, many of the efforts at reform before 1834 foundered precisely because they offended the magistrates' sense of the proper or the possible. As it was, the Poor Law Amendment Act caused much concern among the magistrates because it demanded the abandonment of paternalist policies of poor relief.[37]

There was, therefore, a crisis of parliamentary agency during the 1830s. The solution to this crisis was to skirt the constraints that localism placed upon central action by invoking the device of permissive legisla-

[36] It is important to note that there had long been procedures for the replacement of open vestries by select vestries. It would seem that these latest efforts met with the most success. See Elie Halevy, *The Liberal Awakening 1815–1830* (2nd edn., London, 1961), pp. 42–43; Poynter, *Society and Pauperism*, pp. 207–10, 217, 224, 285–86; James Vernon, *Politics and the People: A Study in English Political Culture c. 1815–1867* (Cambridge, 1993), pp. 18–20; Eastwood, *Governing Rural England*, pp. 107, 128–29.

[37] John Prest, *Liberty and Locality: Parliament, Permissive Legislation, and Ratepayers' Democracies in the Nineteenth Century* (Oxford, 1990), pp. 3–6. By the same token, however, the localities could undertake no services without legislative authorization and there were strict limits beyond which they could not stray. Thus, anything the localities wanted to do still had to receive permission from Parliament. This involved private legislation which was both very expensive and extremely cumbersome. A basis existed, therefore, for some convergence of interest between local authorities and the centralizing party of reformers in London. This was especially so when local elites themselves favored reform as was the case by the 1830s. See Hicks, *British Public Finances*, p. 110.

tion. As its name implied, permissive legislation was a compromise between central control and local initiative. It allowed the center to establish general guidelines and the locality to implement policy if it wished. Permissive legislation also held the advantage of allowing technical and expert assistance to the localities from Whitehall, which was traditionally accepted as a legitimate function of central government. Permissive legislation represented no great departure from past practice, therefore. It provided the space for both central and local tendencies in state structures to flourish in a context that was largely familiar. The idea that localities could be forced to a certain course of action remained highly controversial and the consensus practice of government in the middle of the nineteenth century pointed in just the opposite direction.[38]

On balance, permissive legislation was a victory for the traditions of localism. This era contained no significant constitutional or legislative break with the past. Private member's bills continued to outnumber the general public acts in the business of Parliament, as they had during the previous century. There were twice the number of private bills between 1800 and 1884 as there were public acts; indeed, most changes in municipal government were secured by such measures until the local government legislation of 1888. The philosophy of government remained largely unchanged. Governments continued to regard their duties as primarily administrative and not as responsible for initiating and carrying through a specific agenda. Indeed, it was only after the second reform bill of 1867 that an office in government was established to assist members of Parliament in drafting legislation.[39]

The 1830s were the moment of the greatest opportunity to dislodge the defenses of the localist system. Since 1815 the political discourse around key issues such as the poor law had been dominated by those reformers who espoused this shift. Their opening came after 1832 when the language of reform was the prime currency of politics. Indeed, some of the ideas circulating around the corridors of power at that moment were surprisingly radical.[40] The use of central government to clean up the corruptions of governmental and nongovernmental institutions (like the

[38] Prest, *Liberty and Locality*, pp. 7–12, 19.
[39] Ibid., p. 2; Parris, *Constitutional Bureaucracy*, pp. 160–69. Although Parris makes the conventional case that the 1830s marked a decisive shift away from localism, there is much in his book that suggests the continuities between the eighteenth and nineteenth centuries in the structure of government. Thus, the development of a permanent civil service at the national level is detailed as an eighteenth-century phenomenon, even though he argues the case for the nineteenth century.
[40] The Grey cabinet, for example, gave serious consideration to creating a national police force in 1832. See David Philips and Robert Storch, "Whigs and Coppers: The Grey Ministry's National Police Scheme, 1832," *Historical Research*, 67, 162 (February 1994), pp. 75–90.

charities) was integral to this program. Yet the enthusiasm for centralization was not general. It was a condition that lodged itself most comfortably in the group of Whigs around Lord John Russell. Russell was personally sympathetic to extending central control over a wide range of local functions. The prominence of centralizing measures, therefore, tended to rise and fall with the political fortunes of the Russell faction.

The legislative efforts to swing the balance of power toward the center and away from the locality in the 1830s and 1840s were enormously important. Yet the centralizing impulse proved to be a momentary spasm in the body of politics. The recurrent themes were the constraints that limited the success of the reforming tendency. Indeed, even among the Whigs, the traducers of localism were always a minority. The parabola of legislation in the 1830s and 1840s reflected this minority status. Centralizing impulses showed up in the new poor law, and in the various social legislation affecting factories, women and children, but these were contradicted by the confirmation of parish control over highways in 1835 and over constables in 1842 and in the execution of various public health acts. Even Peel's Bank Act of 1844, generally regarded by historians as a statist measure, in fact reinforced the localist structures of British banking.[41]

The high point of the centralizers' influence came in 1848 when Russell used the cholera outbreak to secure an Interments Bill which would have given the Board of Health compulsory authority over London's burial grounds. He hoped that this bill would be the core for a new centrally controlled authority for London. His hopes were sabotaged by the treasury, however, and the Metropolitan Board of Works hardly met his aspiration for an agent of central power. In the same year the Board of Health was created to establish a central direction over public health that the poor law commissioners were supposed to achieve for the poor law. From the beginning of the Board of Health's unhappy and short history the hopes of centralizing reformers were cut short. Although the Board possessed the authority to insist on some municipal action on public health, its powers were always limited and its actual impact was even more shadowy.[42]

During the early nineteenth century, therefore, the boundary between

[41] Eastwood, *Governing Rural England*, pp. 237–39. The Rural Constabulary Act of 1839, for example, facilitated the creation of salaried local police forces, but they remained firmly under magistrates' control. And although there were some 2,800 paid constables in 1846 in England as a result, "in the overwhelming majority of parishes the most visible symbol of police authority remained the parish constable" (ibid., p. 239).

[42] A shift in the 1830s from voluntary associations to bureaucrats as the source of policy innovations has been detected by David Eastwood, in "Men, Morals and the Machinery of Social Legislation 1790–1840," *Parliamentary History*, 13, 2 (1994), pp. 194, 199–200; and Peter Mandler, *Aristocratic Government in the Age of Reform: Whigs and Liberals, 1830–1852* (Oxford, 1990), pp. 171–73, 237–59, 260–66, 270.

localism and centralism was under constant pressure. Yet the dynamic force of the centralizers was contained and the equilibrium that was ultimately established saw no victory for centralism. In national politics the powers of the Central Board of Health were gutted in 1854 and this signaled the denouement of the centralist impulse. Indeed, the flurry of legislation and debate about key constitutional relationships that had been in play since the later eighteenth century produced a curious paradox. The end result of the decade of reform was not simply to restore the balance between centralism and localism in the structures of the state. It was, rather, to permit the reinforcement of localist tendencies and strength. This may be demonstrated by the aftermath of the two most significant examples of centralizing legislation – the new poor law of 1834 and the Municipal Corporations Act of 1835 – and more briefly by the cases of crime and the highways.[43]

Localism in the mid-Victorian state

The state in the middle of the nineteenth century was neither the night-watchman state, nor a twentieth-century state in waiting. It was an extension of the eighteenth-century state.[44] The mid-Victorian state was the result of attempts to resolve the problems of the eighteenth-century state. Specifically, the result (though unintended) of reform was to re-store stability to the institutions of the state that had been under growing threat since the late eighteenth century. This attempt met with some considerable success (in the short term) as far as the question of Ireland was concerned and (in the long term) in respect to the question of church and state, where it restabilized a relationship that had been problematic since the seventeenth century. In future chapters I shall examine the success of reform in the definition of the political nation. The effort to restabilize the relationship between the center and the local through the key institutions of the poor law and municipal government was similarly successful. Yet it was successful within the con-

---

[43] Charity reform provides an interesting example of the limitations of the centralist impulse. Attempts to reform charity administration had recurred throughout the eighteenth century. The reform of 1837 followed many years of discussion and inquiry. Yet like earlier legislation, its provisions were impressively modest and the autonomy of the local charity administration was protected from central direction. The newly established charity commission remained a purely bureaucratic and fact-finding body, making available resources of advice that local authorities could utilize when they so desired. See Richard Tompson, *The Charity Commission in the Age of Reform* (London, 1979).

[44] Equally, it was not a state that followed from a "revolution in government," which is perhaps the oddest category of all that have been invented to describe the mid-Victorian state. For the notion of a revolution in government, see Oliver MacDonagh, *Early Victorian Government 1830–1870* (London, 1977), pp. 9, 11, 13–14, 20–21.

straints imposed by localism. This does not mean that nothing changed in the poor law or municipal government. It does mean that the balance of initiative and responsibility continued to lie where it had lain since the defeat of Stuart absolutism – at the local level. One of the unforeseen results of the reforming legislation of the 1830s was to strengthen the sinews of local power.[45]

It was ambition of the new poor law to introduce a new level of professionalized administration of relief that would be responsive to the dictates of the center. This was proved to be a pipe dream. The old assistant overseers were transformed into the new relieving officers. The new poor law certainly inaugurated a more bureaucratic administration of relief. Yet this was accomplished at the local level. The consolidation of parish workhouses into larger union facilities increased the numbers required to staff them, in addition to the new positions like porters and seamstresses. Local administration became thicker, therefore, often without much real change in organizational structure. Parishes continued to control relief directly long after the new administrative unit of the unions had been formed. All of this was exactly what reformers had railed against in the past. Local administration of the old poor law was regarded as an unredeemed nexus of jobbery. There was considerable truth to this indictment. Old corruption proved a much tougher beast to quell in the localities than at Westminster. The Poor Law Amendment Act of 1834 addressed the venality and inefficiency of local administration through the person of the assistant commissioner.[46]

Assistant commissioners were intended to provide central government with a provincial agency that it had heretofore lacked. The mandate of the assistant commissioner was to bring efficient and virtuous administration

[45] The curious figure of Joshua Toulmin Smith deserves a mention here. Smith was the leading mid-Victorian constitutional theorist of localism, who wanted to restore the primitive democracy of the Anglo-Saxon folkmote. He was the champion of vestry and parish authority against that of Parliament and against the creeping centralism in the towns of the town councils. And he had some influence in the Northern towns in the 1850s. He believed that the proper function of Parliament was to empower institutions of local self-government instead of taking "every pains. . . to fetter all powers of local activity." See J. Toulmin Smith, *Local Self-Government and Centralization* (London, 1851), pp. 87, 148, 236 (quote), 346, 361–64; John Salt, "Isaac Ironside 1808–1870: The Motivation of a Radical Educationalist," *British Journal of Educational Studies*, 19, 2 (June 1971), pp. 183–201; Fraser, *Urban Politics*, pp. 25–28; John Davis, *Reforming London: The London Government Problem 1855–1900* (Oxford, 1988), p. 10; Vernon, *Politics and the People*, pp. 18, 22; Greenleaf, *A Much Governed Nation*, pp. 32–35, for a sympathetic portrayal of Toulmin Smith.

[46] For an interesting study of the continuing role of influence and jobbery in the middle of the nineteenth century, see Dale Porter and Gloria Clifton, "Patronage, Professional Values, and Victorian Public Works: Engineering and Contracting the Thames Embankment," *Victorian Studies*, 31, 3 (Spring 1988), pp. 319–49.

to local administration. Assistant commissioners were imagined as little Chadwicks, sallying forth from Somerset House, armed with the power to invigilate local boards and to dismiss ineffective officials. Under the assistant commissioners' firm guidance, cloddish locals would be cajoled or persuaded into better methods of economy or administration. It was but a short while before the assistant commissioners were brought face to face with the realities of local political life. Assistant commissioners could be effective only with the cooperation of the local power elite and only so long as they exercised their supervisory power with a due regard for "the spirit of local independence and self government which . . . we consider the characteristic excellence of the English people." It proved impossible to remove corrupt or ineffective officials unless the worthies on the local board expressed compliance. Following the abolition of the poor law commission itself in 1847 the influence of the assistant commissioners was further diminished.[47]

Assistant commissioners, however, played a useful role in supporting the adoption of efficient methods of administration by the local elites. They reinforced localism by bringing the best practices of the center to the provinces, or as allies for local reformers. Landowners and farmers hardly needed much encouragement to search for greater savings in poor law costs or more efficient methods of poor law administration. Local elites were fully familiar with the administrative currents of the age and were quite receptive to the use of Benthamite philosophy to bring the poor law more under their control. It had been these groups who had pushed for and implemented the principles of 1834 in the eighteenth century. Instead of being the proxies of central power, therefore, assistant commissioners were more often drawn into struggles between local bashaws. The most significant competition in poor law administration after 1834 was not between the agents of the center and those of the locality; it was between different local interests. This was hardly surprising: struggles between landowners and magistrates were the characteristic struggle of poor law politics.

The new poor law disrupted local power structures. In the countryside, the magistrates were the net losers. In the towns, it was the remnants of vestry democracy that were displaced. Reformers had seen both as the central obstacles to the proper policing of the poor. In this very important respect the reform agenda was a success. Magistrate administration had

---

[47] Philip Harling, "The Power of Persuasion: Central Authority, Local Bureaucracy and the New Poor Law," *English Historical Review*, 107, 422 (January 1992), pp. 30–53 (quote, p. 48); Eric Midwinter, "State Intervention at the Local Level: The New Poor Law in Lancashire," *Historical Journal*, 10, 1 (1967), pp. 106–10. See also Peter Mandler, "The Making of the New Poor Law *Redivivus*," *Past and Present*, 117 (1987), pp. 131–56.

been a major predicament of the old poor law because magistrates tended to operate within the complex world of paternal reciprocities and to view the poor law as a strategy for maintaining social order. The tendency of the magistrates to favor cash payments was a major source of tension with ratepayers – who actually footed the tax bill – in the years leading to 1834. The magistrate-operated old poor law also had more open access than the new. The poor had the right of appeal to the magistrate from the parish overseers who actually administered poor law policies. One of the purposes of the Poor Law Amendment Act of 1834 was precisely to diminish the role of magistrates in the governance of the poor law and install a ratepayer democracy through the institution of the elected Board of Guardians.[48]

The new Boards of Guardians diminished the role of the magistrate. They admitted to the poor law administration tenant farmers and others who now secured equal authority with magistrates. Farmers came to dominate the rural Boards of Guardians after 1834. In some areas they composed three-quarters of the members of the new boards. Even where this was not the case and the Boards of Guardians were merely the old vestry officers in new guise, their constitutional position was different. The 1834 act deliberately specified that guardians be elected on a restricted franchise and meet in closed sessions in order to insulate them from the kind of community pressure that was believed to characterize the vestry. It was this reconfiguration of local authority relations rather than the power of Benthamite philosophy that accounted for the changed tone and spirit of poor law administration after 1834.

The poor law was not simply a system of delivering relief, however. It was also an instrument of the political economy of rural England and the system of social authority that underpinned it. Changing the balance of authority in the poor law was more than just an institutional change, therefore. It bound the poor law more tightly to the rural political economy. The poor law had always been a device to control and respond to labor market conditions and needs. Local poor relief had always been responsive to rural labor market needs. Since at least the middle of the eighteenth century the rights to settlement had been manipulated to meet the labor requirements of the farmers. Under the new poor law this

[48] Anthony Brundage, "Landed Interest and the New Poor Law: A Reappraisal of the Revolution in Government," *English Historical Review*, 82, 48 (1972), pp. 27–48; Brundage, "The English Poor Law of 1834 and the Cohesion of Agricultural Society, " *Agricultural History*, 48 (1974), pp. 405–17; Anne Digby, *Pauper Palaces* (London, 1978), pp. 2–6; Peter Dunkley, "The Landed Interest and the New Poor Law: A Critical Note," *Economic History Review*, 88, 4 (1973), pp. 836–41; Dunkley, "Paternalism, the Magistracy and Poor Relief in England 1795–1834," *International Review of Social History*, 24, 3 (1979), pp. 371–97.

connection was reinforced. The domination of the Board of Guardians by farmers ensured that the political economy of the poor law would be determined by the needs of agriculture for a free and mobile labor force whose subjection was maintained by low wages and reduced allowances. Indeed, the new poor law provided farmers with even more opportunities to tilt labor market conditions in their favor.[49]

The subordination of the rural poor law to the labor market needs of the farmers was the reason for the continuities in practices and policies between the old and the new poor law. Farmers and others rummaged among the offerings of Benthamite ideology for the pickings that suited their taste. Workhouses were used as labor exchanges with farmers visiting them to select labor. Similarly although reformers had consistently condemned the roundsmen system, it continued to be used to send laborers tramping round to a list of farms with tickets to be signed in the event of no work being available. Likewise, the much deplored policy of out-relief remained a popular way of maintaining a rural labor surplus at public cost. In the 1840s, for example, about 70 percent of the able-bodied poor in East Anglia continued to be receive relief outside the workhouse. The Benthamite instructions from the poor law commissioners to disallow outdoor relief to the able-bodied except in the case of illness were widely evaded by the use of that very loophole.[50]

Like all previous national initiatives in poor law policy, the new poor law had been formulated primarily as a response to the problem of rural poverty. Yet it was the cities that were now increasingly the locus of indigence. Almost from the beginning it was apparent that the radical schemes of the commissioners could have no purchase in the cities. It was obvious, for example, that the allowance system would have to continue in the urban areas. In times of real economic distress, like the late 1830s, the numbers of urban unemployed were registered in the tens of thousands and made the possibility of a workhouse test wildly impractical. Even in good times the cost of maintaining a family in the workhouse greatly exceeded the expense of supporting it through out-relief.

---

[49] Midwinter, "State Intervention at the Local Level," pp. 109–10; John E. Archer, "By a Flash and a Scare": Arson, Animal Maiming and Poaching in East Anglia 1815–1870 (Oxford, 1990), p. 50; Snell, Annals of the Labouring Poor, pp. 116–31; Digby, Pauper Palaces, pp. 114–18, 224. As Eastwood points out, this new political economy was not necessarily harsher, but it did replace a system with a political economy that recognized that "economic fluidity which could carry a labourer on and off parish relief without his ever wishing not to work": Eastwood, Governing Rural England, p. 174.

[50] Anne Digby, "The Labour Market and the Continuity of Social Policy After 1834: The Case of the Eastern Counties," Economic History Review, 27, 3 (August 1975), pp. 69–85; Digby, Pauper Palaces, p. 231.

Attempts by the commissioners to formulate a workhouse test policy met with consistent opposition from the localities. In 1844 the order banning relief to the able-bodied outside the workhouse was imposed in the rural areas, but in the urban centers provision was made for an additional labor test. In 1852 opposition from Lancashire and Yorkshire caused the withdrawal of a policy guideline banning out-relief to part-time and casual laborers. Yet if this category of the poor were not subject to workhouse discipline, what hope was there for the others? Thus, in many urban areas, outdoor relief continued to be the main form of welfare. At moments of high unemployment older policies reappeared. Parish labor schemes put men to work in stone quarries or hired them directly for various parish needs. Indeed, it was not until *after* the 1860s that out-relief to able-bodied men declined. This was partly because other relief policies were devised. But it was also a reflection of the tightening of policies that came at the end of the 1860s. As we shall see, the spirit of 1834 was not fully realized in poor law policy until after 1869.[51]

In spite of its radical intentions, therefore, the 1834 Poor Law Amendment Act revitalized the authority structures of localism. Localism was renewed also in town government, although a different kind of continuity characterized municipal forms. Town government was not revolutionized by the Municipal Corporations Act of 1835. Beyond stipulating a uniform system of town councils, the act projected a deeply ambivalent mandate of change. On the one hand it confined the authority of the new town councils to the administration of police and the corporate revenues. On the other hand, the councils were given vague if wide powers to make bylaws for the good government of the borough. The result was that the old structures of municipal government were not swept away. They tended to exist side by side with the new town councils for many years until they were gradually merged into the new arrangements. The act provided for improvement commissions, sanitary commissions and the like to transfer their responsibilities to the town councils. Few did so until the last quarter of the century. In 1850 only 29 of the original 176 municipalities covered by the act of 1835 possessed exclusive powers over sanitation. It took another thirty years for this proportion to be reversed. By 1880 only 14 of the (now) 240 mu-

---

[51] See Michael Rose, "The Allowance System Under the New Poor Law," *Economic History Review*, 19, 3 (1966), pp. 607–20; Michael Rose, "Introduction: The Poor and the City, 1834–1914," in Michael Rose (ed.), *The Poor and the City: The English Poor Law in Its Urban Context, 1834–1914* (New York, 1985), pp. 4–7; Peter Wood, "Finance and the Urban Poor Law: Sunderland Union 1836–1914," in Michael Rose, *The Poor and the City*, pp. 19–56; Midwinter, "State Intervention at the Local Level," p. 110.

nicipal boroughs possessed sanitary authorities independent of the town council.[52]

As was the case with the poor law, the key accomplishment of municipal reform was to reconfigure the social basis of authority in town government. In certain respects, this shift was merely another stage in a process that had been going on in most urban centers since the 1760s. The act of 1835 represented the completion of an agenda that had been first presented by the urban middling classes nearly a century before. The key issue in this struggle was the demand for access by newly empowered groups whose desire for civic power continually bumped up against existing vested interests. The solution offered by the Municipal Corporations Act was to install an urban ratepayers' democracy. Over the next twenty years municipal politics was shaped by the effort to extend the authority of the ratepayers through the chosen instrument of the town council. This was usually accomplished only after fierce struggles around where the boundaries should lie between the town council, the improvement commission or some other authority. Thus, mid-Victorian urban politics were dominated by contests around obscure offices like the highway surveyors or church wardens as old and new, Anglican and dissenting, Liberal and Tory, and middle- and working-class groups jostled for leverage in the new system.[53]

It is generally true to say that before 1835 one main faultline of this contest was between county-based Tory elites and urban-based Whig–Liberal reformers. This rivalry was resolved by the act of 1835. Urban political struggle after 1835 was marked by competition between the town council and the old extra-legal bodies which tended to be responsive to the popular will. Indeed, these bodies were often centers of lower-class political activity; the Chartist presence remained strong in many into the 1850s. Thus, "reform" of the old municipalities was a protracted and contentious process that took several decades to achieve. Town council authority had to meet and defeat the more democratic forces that controlled the police and gas commissions in Manchester, for example, or the

[52] For this general theme, see Derek Fraser, *Power and Authority in the Victorian City* (New York, 1979); Greenleaf, *A Much Governed People*, pp. 51–53; Redlich and Hirst, *History of Local Government*, pp. 136–38.

[53] The process of struggle for political control was as much a matter of *intra-middle class* struggle as it was of middle–upper or middle–working-class contest. One of the consequences of the changes of the 1830s was to create new faultlines within the middling classes. There was much intensive debate, for example, as to whether to increase the poor rates with guardians and others who were part of the poor law establishment favoring this and general ratepayers meetings in opposition. See R. J. Morris, *Class, Sect and Party: The Making of the British Middle Class, Leeds 1820–1850* (Manchester, 1990), pp. 123–39, 165–67; Fraser, *Urban Politics*, pp. 76–78, 103–11.

improvement commission in Leeds and the highway commission in Bradford. From the late 1840s to the mid-1850s the reform faction in Sheffield
fought a running battle against the populist lower-class movement led by
Isaac Ironside whose centers of strength were located in the vestries and
the highway commission.[54]

Nevertheless, after the 1840s the general drift of urban politics was
toward expanded town council control. This involved a new kind of social
politics. The working-class presence in municipal politics had been much
diminished by the 1850s, and to some extent this may be attributed to the
new structures of local government that caused the demise of older offices
of government such as the church wardens. The working-class role had
also been reconfigured, however. The key dividing line in urban politics
now ran between the small retailers – who often sought alliance with
working men – and the large businesses and professionals. Many town
councils, like Birmingham, continued to be dominated by small businessmen who, in the name of economy, firmly resisted the expansion of town
council function beyond that demanded by the act of 1835.[55]

The structures of localism after the 1830s contained many variations.
In most cities the authority of the town council gradually asserted itself
throughout the mid-Victorian period. Yet a major exception was provided by London, where the primacy of localism rooted in neighborhoods
proved unshakable. No acceptable form of municipal centralization was
found to displace the local power of the vestry and parish. Lord John
Russell had desired to create a regional government that would coordinate policy on such issues as public health. The end product was the
Metropolitan Board of Works, created in 1855, whose centralizing potential was quickly subverted into "a triumph for parochial democracy."
Although it did some good work in standardizing procedures for vestry
administration, the Metropolitan Board of Works remained a creature of
vestry interests throughout its life. London was both the target and the
despair of municipal reformers during the mid-Victorian period. Never-

---

[54] In Leeds the Chartists used their control of the improvement commission to turn it into a
democratic institution of local government. In the new improvement bill presented to
Parliament in 1842, the Chartist program was enshrined in the constitution of the
proposed new commission. Whigs and Tories joined to persuade Parliament to abolish
the commission altogether in favor of town council rule. This was a common pattern. In
Leeds the highway commission remained subject to a greater degree of popular control
because it remained under the vestry until an improvement act in 1866 absorbed it into
the town council. See Fraser, *Urban Politics*, pp. 92–96, 105–06, 107–11; for the Ironside
movement in Sheffield, see Dennis Smith, *Conflict and Compromise: Class Formation in
English Society 1830–1914* (London, 1982), pp. 75–78, 83–85.

[55] See E. P. Hennock, *Fit and Proper Persons* (London, 1974), for Birmingham; this is the
main theme, of course, of Asa Briggs, *Victorian Cities* (London, 1968); Fraser, *Urban
Politics*, p. 284.

theless, until the London County Council was created in 1888, London remained governmentally the great wen.[56]

Mid-Victorian localism could thrive because of the limited reach of central government. Institutional links between the center and the regions remained as weakly developed in the nineteenth century as they had in the eighteenth. The only new institutional authority at the center was the Local Government Office, created in 1858 out of the ruins of the General Board of Health. Yet the Local Government Office was not the product of a centralizing revolution in government. Nor was it the advance guard of a modern state bureaucracy. It was, instead, a cruel parody of a Benthamite center, headed by Tom Taylor, whose real claim to fame was his concurrent work as a playwright and theater critic of *Punch*. The office possessed few authorizing powers over the local authorities and those that it did carry were of an office-keeping variety. Even these minimal duties were seldom widely enforced. It was discovered in 1869, for example, that over one-third of local authorities had not submitted their statutory public health returns, and that a similar situation existed with the auditing of the poor law accounts. Likewise, the Local Government Office had made no attempt to enforce the provision that gave it authority over the drawing of local authority boundaries.

The Local Government Act of 1858 which created the office cannot be dismissed as an empty vessel, however. The act was permissive, enabling local governments to engage in a wide variety of public health initiatives. Thus, the act reinforced and energized localism. The new municipal councils welcomed the act precisely because it promised to serve their needs and priorities. Indeed, the most useful work of the Local Government Office was its service as a clearing house and advice bureau for local government. The office provided expertise that were generally lacking in local government. Local governments frequently called upon the services of engineers and other experts available from the office. Yet this was not a new function for central government. The provision of advice and assistance was no innovation of the Victorian state; it was a traditional responsibility of central government.[57]

---

[56] Vestry rule in London was very much a mixed bag. Considerable improvements were made in sewers, drainage and water supply during the period of vestry government in the middle of the nineteenth century. See David Owen, *The Government of Victorian London 1855–1889: The Metropolitan Board of Works, the Vestries, and the City Corporation* (Cambridge, MA, 1982), pp. 223–24, and *passim*; John Davis, *Reforming London*, pp. 10–12.

[57] Prest, *Liberty and Locality*, pp. 42, 166, 167–72; Royston Lambert, "Central and Local Relations in Mid-Victorian England: The Local Government Act Office, 1858–1871," *Victorian Studies*, 6, 2 (December 1962), pp. 121–50. My argument is contrary to that made by Lambert in both the article cited and in his book, *Sir John Simon 1816–1904 and English Social Administration* (London, 1963), that, beneath the surface and in spite of the

The limitations of the Local Government Office were not exceptional. The needs and priorities of local communities continued to mold the shape of state structures in the mid-Victorian era as they had in the past. Attempts by central government to encourage the establishment of proficient police forces in the small towns and counties provides an apt demonstration of this theme. Although the authority of the center for public order policy had always been accepted, efforts to get an act through Parliament in 1854 which contained a measure of obligation on the localities to create police forces was withdrawn on encountering fierce opposition. A similar bill passed through Parliament two years later, but only after local opposition forced the abandonment of provisions that compelled the consolidation of local forces and allowed a broad arena for central government intervention. Counties were obliged to establish police forces where none had existed before, but they remained under the authority of the magistrates. The power of Westminster was confined to the right of inspection in return for a small grant-in-aid for uniforms.[58]

The highways were another instance where localism persisted unchecked. A Highways Act in 1835 was originally intended to remove parish authority over roads administration. In the event, the act retained the permissive, enabling character of most of the other legislation of the period. Parishes were encouraged to combine for administrative efficiency and to professionalize their staff. Yet this merely registered what had already been happening over the previous century. Subsequent attempts to enlarge the administrative unit for road management over the next three decades also fizzled, although local initiative sometimes achieved the same result. In 1862–63, a scheme to force the amalgamation of parishes for highway purposes and remove their control over highways failed. As late as the 1880s about 6,000 parishes maintained their separate authority over the roads, and in Yorkshire alone 90 percent of parishes were in this situation. Legislation in the 1870s began to chip away at what the Webbs described as the "immemorial responsibility of

intentions of people like Simon, central influence grew during this period. It is true that, as medical officer of health to the government, Simon gained increased powers of investigation. But there seems to have been no increase in the ability of Simon and his (often) part-time and (always) few inspectors actually to oblige local governments to do even the things they were supposed to do. Vaccination was a case in point and, although it was not only local obstructionism that played a role in this case, the fact was that it took twenty years before compulsory vaccination of infants provided for in the Vaccination Act of 1853 was actually realized.

[58] Jennifer Hart, "The County and Borough Police Act, 1856," *Public Administration*, 34 (1956), pp. 405–17; W. L. Burn, *The Age of Equipoise: A Study in the Mid-Victorian Generation* (London, 1964), pp. 167–76; Carolyn Steedman, *Policing the Victorian Community: The Formation of English Provincial Police Forces, 1856–1880* (London, 1984), pp. 25–28.

the Parish for its highways," but this obligation was not removed into the new county councils until the Local Government Act of 1894.[59]

Only the prison service provided a partial exception to the general picture of an invigorated localism during the middle of the nineteenth century. Prisons had long been an area where national initiatives and policies were accepted, since they were one of the points at which social policy and policing met. In the 1770s several pieces of legislation were passed that addressed prison discipline. An ambitious attempt to provide machinery to monitor local prison policies passed in 1779, but remained inoperative. A similar act of 1823 laid certain obligations on the running of prisons and required justices to submit frequent reports to the Home Office. Like previous measures, however, the implementation of this act was impeded by the absence of an inspectorate. An act of 1835 plugged this gap and created a prisons inspectorate. Like most other inspectorates, however, its reach was very limited. Its staff of five men hardly made it into a strike force for central government.

Nevertheless, from 1835, the Home Office enthusiastically propagated its favorite systems of prison administration, such as the silent isolation regime. By 1865 the Home Office had issued a list of a hundred rules that were to govern prison administration. In 1839 the inspectors successfully argued for an act that required central approval for all new prisons, and in the case of Scotland went even further in a centralizing direction. Yet the initiatives of central government did not go unchallenged. Local resistance to these centralizing tendencies was constant. Cost-conscious local councils persistently contested Home Office attempts to mandate the construction of new prisons. Again, it was not until the 1870s that the balance of power tipped decisively toward the center, when the Prisons Act of 1877 brought all the prisons of England and Wales under the control of a national commission. By this time the relationships between the center and the local were being reconfigured throughout the structures of the state. The age of localism was about to draw to a close.[60]

The end of localism 1870–1890

The twenty years from the 1870s to the 1890s saw the steady erosion of the structures of localism as they had existed for the previous 200 years. This was not a simple matter of the balance of power tipping toward

[59] Webb and Webb, *The King's Highway*, pp. 204–14 (quote, p. 214).
[60] Bill Forsyth, "Centralisation and Local Autonomy: The Experience of English Prisons, 1820–1877," *Journal of Historical Sociology*, 4, 3 (September 1991), pp. 316–43; Sydney Webb and Beatrice Webb, *English Prisons Under Local Government* (London, 1922), pp. 32–41, 106–12, 201–04.

central government. The key feature of state structures in this period was the multiplication of the functions of local government and the proliferation of its institutions. At the same time there were the first intimations that central government was about to shake off its torpid shell. The faint foreshadowings of a more directive and bureaucratized central state begin to rise cautiously above the horizon of localism from the 1870s. The establishment of the Education Department in 1870 was among the first such harbingers. For the most part, however, the expansion of central government bureaucracy or responsibility did not come until after the 1890s. Likewise, until the 1890s central government remained generally hesitant about *requiring* localities to do certain things, although it was gathering the powers to make such demands. The Local Government Board, the chief link between the center and localities, continued to operate through negotiation and conciliation rather than prescription.[61]

Following in the trail pioneered by Joseph Chamberlain in Birmingham, local government between 1870 and 1890 became more professionalized and bureaucratized, more intrusive and fiscally expansive and expensive. Local government expenditure grew sharply and as late as 1908 remained the largest consumer of all tax revenue. This enlargement of local government reflected a growth in the provision of social services, and in this it presaged the twentieth-century state. Some of these were services that had traditionally lain within the sphere of voluntary association work, such as domestic visiting to poor homes. Others were responses to the definition of new needs, such as school meals for poor children. A few were beginning to be mandated by central government, such as the responsibilities of the Board of Guardians in the area of child neglect which were addressed by the Infant Protection Act of 1896.[62]

Such developments pushed the boundaries of traditional localism beyond their customary locations. The displacement of the voluntary asso-

[61] The Northcote–Stafford reforms of the 1870s introduced a new phase of professionalization throughout the civil service which sharply demarcated it from past practices. The establishment of the Labour Department of the Board of Trade in 1888 was an appropriate signifier of the shifting responsibilities of central government. It enabled strike statistics to be collected for the first time, many years after such figures were available in France or Germany. And the department rapidly expanded its reach, so that by 1910 it assumed a significant conciliatory role in labor disputes. See Roger Davidson, *Whitehall and the Labour Problem in Late Victorian and Edwardian Britain* (Beckenham, 1985); Bellamy, *Administering Central–Local Relations*, pp. 11–12, 118–25, 139–40, 155, 233.

[62] After 1910 the local portion of public expenditure was pushed under 50 percent to begin a continual decline. See Peter Marsh, *Joseph Chamberlain: Entrepreneur in Politics* (New Haven, 1994), ch. 4; Hicks, *British Public Finances*, pp. 107–08; Alan T. Peacock and Jack Wiseman, *The Growth of Public Expenditure in the United Kingdom* (Princeton, 1961), p. 107; Karl Ittman, *Work, Gender and Family Life in Victorian England* (London, 1994), pp. 172–79.

ciation charity worker by the local government social worker moved localism into a different political and social realm. The edifice of localism held fast during the twenty years 1870–90 because ratepayers continued to bear the burden of the expanding sphere of local government. Certainly, the new principle of grants-in-aid and subsidies established in the 1870s presaged a new relationship with the center. Yet central government remained distant from the supervision of local finances until the local authorities secured the right to float their own loans in the 1890s. This introduced a new element into the fiscal equation between center and locality. It also rendered anachronistic the traditional balance of power between center and local.

If local authorities were now to dabble in the capital markets, oversight by the national exchequer was inescapable. The center was bound to take a greater interest in the localities once they possessed the potential and authority to increase the national debt by incurring bond debts of their own. From the 1890s, therefore, the treasury began to exercise a closer charge over local government loan structure. Such developments, neither intentional nor intended, inevitably altered the boundaries between the center and the local. Indeed, the clearest indication of this was the curious inversion of tensions that had colored center and local relations since the seventeenth century. Whereas in the past the local had guarded against the incursions of the center, now the center put forth much effort in "patrolling the boundaries of the central–local divide, limiting the incursions of localities into national politics and, especially, restricting their demands on the national Exchequer and the London money markets."[63]

One part of the dynamic that changed the shape of state structures was to be found, then, in the expansion of the scope of local government. Another part was located in a change at the center. Legislation directed at local authorities began to tilt away from the permissive and toward the mandatory, a tendency first seen in the Sanitary Act of 1866. This act was an attempt to address the question of public health more intensively under the impetus of the last great cholera epidemic to hit Britain. The act greatly increased the power of local authorities to take action over sanitary nuisances and the water supply. If local government failed in these public health duties, the act provided for Home Office intervention. The Sanitary Act, however, was confounded by the lackluster performance of the Local Government Office and Tom Taylor, its dilettante secretary, in implementing its provisions. Thus a sanitary commission was appointed which resulted in perhaps the most successful public health report in the century.

[63] Bellamy, *Administering Central–Local Relations*, pp. 2 (quote), 87–99; Offer, *Property and Politics*, pp. 180–215.

Both the tone and the recommendations of this commission signaled increasing support for an end to the permissive bias in local–central relations in the area of public health. Most of its recommendations were carried directly into law. Henceforth, all sanitary legislation was to be a universal obligation of local authorities who were to create unified departments to handle it. The Local Government Office was abolished and the Local Government Board put in its place. This board centralized all supervisory powers that had previously been distributed between the various parts of government, including the poor law board. The Public Health Act of 1872 followed hard on the heels of this reorganization and reinforced its trend. Under its provisions, the country was divided into sanitary districts by central fiat rather than leaving it to local option. Although this act was not intended to lay a foundation stone of the twentieth-century state, the spirit of Chadwick seemed to be flickering alive again. These measures challenged the permissive element that had defeated all previous attempts at centralization. Local governments could now be charged with a certain course of action.[64]

At precisely the same moment, the central government began to take initiatives in poor law policy that also suggested a renewed assertiveness toward the duties of local government. By the late 1860s it was painfully evident that the economic boom of the midcentury years had failed to abolish pauperism. It was widely believed that many of the abuses of the old poor law had reappeared to obstruct the effacement of poverty. A return to the spirit of 1834 in the administration of the poor law was widely advocated as the answer to the persistence of indigence. Central government endorsed this approach to the poor law and actively encouraged local authorities to bring poor law costs under control. George Goschen issued a famous minute to this effect in 1869 which also sanctioned a partnership between private charities and local administration to address the problems of poverty.

Thus the trend from the 1860s was for tighter and harsher poor law conditions to be imposed. A widespread attack on out-relief, for example, was led by the newly founded Charity Organisation Society. Following Goschen's minute, an alliance was forged in many urban areas between the poor law administration and the Charity Organisation Society, which was to govern a parsimonious poor law policy for the next twenty years. Some spectacular local successes were achieved. Out-relief for the elderly in East London and West Hartlepool was largely eliminated throughout the 1870s, for example – a social reality immortalized in the music hall by

---

[64] Lambert, *Sir John Simon*, pp. 384–99, 501–17; Prest, *Liberty and Locality*, pp. 209–14; Redlich and Hirst, *History of Local Government*, pp. 155–60; *Local Government and Central Control: A West Midland Study Group* (London, 1956), pp. 13–15.

Albert Chevalier's "My Old Dutch." The experience of the poor law by the poor was worse after the late 1860s than it had been throughout the early and middle years of the nineteenth century.[65]

In spite of these efforts, poor law costs continued to soar – virtually doubling in the 1890s, for example. Part of this was due to well-meaning attempts to facilitate local administration such as the Union Chargeability Act of 1865. This act was an attempt to resolve the problem of sharply differing tax receipts for poor law administration across parishes of varying wealth. Such variation was believed to pose an obstacle to consistent and standardized administration of relief. The act shifted the rating basis from the parish to the union, transferred the expenses into a common fund and thus equalized costs across the various parts of the unions. This was a quietly radical measure which undermined some of the major footings of localism. It removed another strut from parish autonomy; it shifted the rating burden onto the wealthier parishes, thus leading them to pay more attention to costs; it contained provisions for unions to incur greater debt to finance buildings; and it made public funds available to the private sector for mortgages, thereby encouraging the contractors who swarmed around local government to urge expenditures. Thus, the poor law unions embarked on a capital-spending spree just at the very moment that they were imposing harsher conditions for relief. The two tendencies were intimately connected. Bigger and better workhouses and other facilities like schools and mental asylums meant a more efficient delivery of welfare relief. They allowed the end of out-relief to be imagined and smoothed the implementation of the principles of 1834 as never before.[66]

---

[65] The alliance between the private Charity Organisation Society and public local government administration epitomizes the transitional nature of the period 1870 to 1890. The COS made a significant contribution to the history of social work. It developed the case study and more "scientific" approach to social welfare. Yet it was ultimately an extension of the voluntary association approach of the earlier period. In its attempt to coordinate the different work of the many individual charities, it represented an attempt to formalize, rationalize and systematize that volunteer tradition. It is this that explains the paradox of the COS as an attempt to combine a return to the tradition of the principle of 1834 with the methods of modern bureaucratized social work. For the COS, see Charles Loch Mowat, *The Charity Organisation Society 1869–1913: Its Life and Work* (London, 1961).

[66] Peacock and Wiseman, *Growth of Public Expenditure*, p. 111; Derek Fraser, "Introduction," in Fraser (ed.), *The New Poor Law in the Nineteenth Century* (London, 1976), pp. 17–21; Mary MacKinnon, "English Poor Law Policy and the Crusade Against Out-Relief," *Journal of Economic History*, 47, 3 (September 1987), pp. 603–25; Michael Rose, "The Crisis of Poor Relief in England, 1860–1890," in W. J. Mommsen (ed.), *The Emergence of the Welfare State in Britain and Germany* (London, 1981), pp. 32–49; Michael Rose, "Introduction," pp. 10–12, Peter Wood, "Finance and the Urban Poor Law: Sunderland Union 1866–1914," pp. 34–40, Keith Gregson, "Poor Law and Organized Charity: The Relief of Exceptional Distress in North-East England, 1870–1910," pp. 96–115, and Pat Ryan, "Politics and Relief: East London Unions in the Late Nineteenth and Early Twentieth Centuries," pp. 142–65, all in Michael Rose, *The Poor and the City*.

By the 1890s, then, the older compasses of localism had been rendered obsolete by the poor law. This was also true of other institutions. The domestic visitor (who was usually female) was no longer an adequate form of social worker; no more was the charity-financed ragged school an appropriate form of education for the masses. It is a significant reflection of the changing tenor of the times that after about 1880 support for vestry government rapidly diminished. Previously, vestry government had been fiercely defended as a sacred principle of self-government against the tyrannies of central interventions. Defenders of the vestry were increasingly hard to find after 1880.[67] Indeed, vestry government was now seen to epitomize the deficiencies of localism – its tendency to spawn a crazy quilt of overlapping jurisdictions, multiple divisions of responsibility, heterogeneous administrative units and a complexity that defied rational organization. Hardly any poor law union, for example, matched the boundaries of the borough it served. These currents now joined others, like the local taxation crisis, to point directly to the need to reconfigure local government and its relationship to the center.

The reform of local government, therefore, was a lurking presence on the political agenda throughout the 1870s and 1880s. It was seriously discussed in Gladstone's cabinet in the early 1880s, for example. The reluctance to grasp this nettle was finally overcome after the franchise reform of 1884 made it unavoidable. The reform of the county franchise in 1884 brought the rule of the rural oligarchs to a dignified end. The counties gained a ratepayer democracy to match that of the urban areas. Reform of the government structures of localism was an inescapable consequence. The Local Government Act of 1888 was the result. This act drew to an end the overlapping administrative and judicial functions of government. The rule of the magistrates through the quarter sessions was brought to a close. A new administrative hierarchy was created from the parishes at the bottom through rural and urban district councils to the county councils at the top. Six years later the final remnant of the old edifice of localism was removed when parish government was restructured by the Parish Councils Act of 1894. Like the act of 1888, this measure was spoken of as an attempt to reinvigorate the traditions of decentralization. But it was not a success in this respect and the parish as a unit of local government rapidly sank into insignificance.[68]

By the 1890s, therefore, at least the outlines of a new relationship

[67] Owen, *Government of Victorian London*, pp. 221–22.

[68] R. C. K. Ensor, *England 1870–1914* (Oxford, 1988), pp. 213–14, 295–96; Matthew, *Gladstone*, vol. II, *1875–1898*, p. 189; J. P. D. Dunbabin, "The Politics of the Establishment of County Councils," *Historical Journal*, 6 (1963), pp. 226–52; Dunbabin, "Expectations of the New County Councils and Their Realization," *Historical Journal*, 8 (1965), pp. 353–79; Redlich and Hirst, *History of Local Government*, pp. 192–99, 216–17.

between center and locality had been drawn. The most important components of this relationship were a greater legislative direction from London, a much more extensive local administration that performed more sophisticated and professionalized functions, and an increasingly entangled fiscal relationship between the center and the localities that necessarily expanded the role of national government. The shape of the twentieth-century state reared into view. There had been no clearly thought-out blueprint for the process that ultimately was to transform the relationship between center and locality. Yet neither was this process a purely arbitrary movement; it was a trend convergent with the logic of other social, cultural and economic forces that all pointed in the direction of greater national integration. One further aspect of this process was the changing boundaries within civic culture between the public and private spheres, which is the subject of the next chapter.

6 The public, the private and the state: civil society 1680–1880

Origins and definition

Civil society is that domain in which public activities of a collective and individual kind may be freely enacted. Civil society is bounded on one side by the jurisdiction of the state and on the other side by the private world of the individual. The kinds of institutions that fill the spaces, define the character and determine the values of civil society vary over different historical periods. Similarly, the relationship between the formal structures of the state, the public world of civil society and the intimate world of the individual will vary over time and place. Understanding the dynamics of civil society in any period requires appreciating the arrangements that govern the relationships between three elements: the institutional state, the public world of civil society and the private world of the individual.[1]

Before the seventeenth century, there was no concept of the "public" as the core of civil society.[2] There was the court, the Lords and an occasional Parliament, and then there were the people. No legitimate space existed for public associations of private individuals. Over the course of the century the role of the court and of Parliament were

[1] It will be obvious that I have found Jurgen Habermas's formulation of the public and private spheres to be extremely useful. There are many difficulties with this schema, however. The tendency to confine it to a bourgeois sphere alone is one such problem. Another difficulty lies in the partial and qualified nature of the framework even in Britain where it fits most closely. I do not need to enter into those arguments. I do not intend my formulation of the workings of the public and private spheres to be a demonstration of Habermasian truth. See Jurgen Habermas, *The Structural Transformation of the Public Sphere* (Cambridge, MA, 1989). For intelligent critiques of Habermas, see Craig Calhoun (ed.), *Habermas and the Public Sphere* (Cambridge, MA, 1992).

[2] The public and private sectors were entangled in each other. For an interesting example of the absence of demarcations between the two spheres in the nearly modern period, see Diane Willen, "Women in the Public Sphere in Early Modern England: The Case of the Urban Working Poor," *Sixteenth-Century Journal*, 19, 4 (1988), pp. 559–75.

transformed. Functional specialization between the political, cultural and economic sectors created a public sphere. By the end of the seventeenth century, the contours of a public sphere were drawn by a greatly expanded associational life. This was primarily an urban phenomenon. Institutions like the coffee shops, the newspapers, the pamphlet literature and various political associations provided the seedbeds for the development and expression of public opinion. Bodies such as charities, theaters, assembly rooms and voluntary hospitals expressed the civic responsibilities of individuals within the public sphere.[3]

The essential quality of public life in Britain from the seventeenth century was its voluntarist disposition. Civil society was not ordered from above by state or monarchical authority. Kingly authority – even a form of divine right – might be invoked to legitimate the hierarchical ordering of society. Yet after the Glorious Revolution it was always understood that authority rested on the consent of those who made up the "public." Begging the question of who precisely composed this public, sovereignty for the social, moral and political ordering of society lay unquestionably in the public sphere. The public sphere did not derive its legitimacy or presence from some integrating national agency or institution. The state did not define the public sphere. In its turn, the public sphere was the private sphere in action, animated by the free engagement of the individuals who belonged to civil society. The purpose of the state was to preserve the voluntarist complexion of the public sphere and, acting at the behest of private initiative, to secure and protect its territory.

Thus, the British state stood in a delicate relationship to action in the public sphere. Parliament established the legal basis for action in society, but the institutions of civil society derived their legitimacy from the voluntarism of private individuals acting as public citizens. To take an extreme example, no powers of taxation could be assumed without parliamentary statute, but it was possible to build a hospital or other institution having a social purpose on the initiative of voluntary association alone. Many activities fell in between these two poles. At Carlisle in 1790, for example, a group of citizens organized a municipal watch that operated on a voluntary basis without legal sanction until an act of Parliament

---

[3] It is not helpful to try to date precisely the emergence of the public sphere. The key shift is the secularization of the public space and the creation of self-conscious institutions that claim to represent "public opinion" in a general, mass sense. This is clearly a function of the late seventeenth century. See David Zaret, "Religion, Science and Printing in the Public Spheres in Late Seventeenth-Century England," in Calhoun, *Habermas and the Public Sphere*, pp. 213–27. For a particularly good description of the public sphere, with an emphasis on the role of print culture in its development, see Kathleen Wilson, *The Sense of the People: Politics, Culture and Imperialism in England, 1715–1785* (Cambridge, 1995), pp. 27–83.

could be obtained to make it permanent. The content and shape of civil society was the responsibility of the public and the private spheres. And although the state was by no means irrelevant to this, the constellation of institutions and actions that composed the public sphere at any one time was not determined by the state.[4]

It will be immediately obvious that this arrangement implied a very different relationship of the state to both public and private spheres than was to be found in the twentieth century. In our period, the collective expression of private wills in the public sphere constituted civil society and determined its priorities. The state was dependent upon this process. As a general rule, for much of the twentieth century this ordering was reversed. The twentieth-century state stands as the collective expression of public wills and it is the state, therefore, that defines the content of the public space. Where the boundaries lie dividing state, public and private spheres constitutes the key difference between the different historical structures of civil society. The contours of these borders mold the terrain of civil society at any particular historical moment.

In this chapter, then, I am concerned with the content of civil society in our period. My argument will be that civil society from the late seventeenth century assumed a particular profile, the outlines of which followed the interconnected boundaries of property, gender and family. I shall proceed, therefore, in three ways. First, I will explain the shape of a civil society which was defined primarily by private voluntarist associations. Secondly, I will discuss how the boundaries of civil society were delineated by gender and how this was a major source of instability within the system of civil society. This will lead me to the third subject of the chapter. I shall suggest how the existing boundaries between the public, the private and the state were ultimately unable to contain the instabilities of domestic ideology and how a new configuration of civil society therefore emerged in the late nineteenth century.

The voluntarist public sphere

Eighteenth-century society was not a society of unqualified individualism. Thick deposits of patriarchalism remained embedded in the social structure and in popular mentality. Kinship ties and obligations remained central to economic behavior at the individual level. Yet equally the relationship between the individual and society rested upon the practice of free contract. This was true not only in the law of the constitution; it permeated the whole of society. John Locke was not the only political

---

[4] Langford, *Public Life and the Propertied Englishman*, p. 212; Langford, *A Polite and Commercial People*, p. 100.

theorist of importance in the eighteenth century, but his model of a contractual society was the best description of how civil society actually worked. The practical expression of social affiliation in this civic order, therefore, was voluntary association.[5]

Voluntary associations denoted the primacy of the private sphere in the shaping of civil society of the period; they were the collective expression of individual interests in voluntary combination. Voluntary associations constituted the arteries of society, achieving purposes that in other countries were the responsibility of the state or of established corporate bodies. Voluntary associations lay at the core of the public space in Britain. We tend to think of them as essentially the property of the nineteenth-century middle class; and, indeed, this was their golden age. Yet they were not a nineteenth-century invention. Voluntary associations belonged to a lineage of social action that stretched back to the late seventeenth century.

As urban growth took hold in the eighteenth century, so the structures of civic community expanded in tandem. Norwich, for example, had three music societies by the end of the century. In Leeds the first voluntary association was a Tory charity, the Pious Uses Trustees, formed in 1680. Others soon followed, providing schools, libraries and infirmaries. Such activity surged in rhythm with changing fashions in social policy. Philanthropic effort in London from the 1740s through 1760s established hospitals, including the famous St. Thomas's. A wave of educational effort crested in the 1820s and 1830s. By that time, of course, a dense network of professional, recreational, political and charity organizations covered the countryside. The expansion of benefit societies alone in the eighteenth century was considerable – they even existed to buy men out of their militia obligation. In London in 1700, for example, there were 2,000 members of benefit societies; by 1800 there were 900 societies with a membership (it has been estimated) of about one-quarter of the population.[6]

---

[5] A major innovation in legal doctrine in this period was the notion of contract freely determined by private wills and not subject to qualification by an outside agency like the state. Coincident with this was the consignment of oath taking to an anachronistic expression of commitment in a society that operated on the basis of free association. "What the solemn oath was to the seventeenth century, the signed agreement was to the eighteenth." See Langford, *Public Life and the Propertied Englishman*, pp. 99–115 (quote, p. 114); Hunt, *The Middling Sort*, pp. 25–26, 29; Atiyah, *Rise and Fall of Freedom of Contract Law*.

[6] Morris, *Class, Sect and Party*, pp. 167–84; Peter Clark, "Sociability and Urbanity: Clubs and Societies in the Eighteenth-Century City," in P. Clark, *8th H. J. Dyos Memorial Lecture* (Leicester, 1986), p. 7; John Brewer, *The Pleasures of the Imagination: English Culture in the Eighteenth Century* (New York, 1997), for the associational organization of cultural life in the eighteenth century; Brewer, "English Radicalism in the Age of George III," in Pocock, *Three British Revolutions*, pp. 358–60; J. R. Western, *The English Militia in the Eighteenth Century* (London, 1965), pp. 252–54.

Voluntary associations took many different forms and we should beware of reducing them to simple meanings. Yet it is possible to identify two key characteristics of the voluntary association in this period. The first was their essentially middling-class quality. Voluntary association was not the exclusive property of the middling classes; yet the middling classes owned it in a more complete way than either the superior or the subaltern classes. There was a lower-class public sphere with its own voluntarist organizations, such as the friendly society. But lower-class efforts to create their own fellowship in the public space met with tremendous suspicion. The landed and titled elite, on the other hand, hardly required the voluntary association to express their social needs. By contrast, voluntary association was the vehicle which propelled the middling-class social, cultural and political presence into society. As such, the voluntary association was a means of middling-class empowerment in a way that was not true for the lower classes.

The second characteristic of the voluntary association that I wish to note is more to our immediate purpose. Voluntary associations served many different functions, of course. Yet the core objective of the voluntary association was to *police* the public sphere. By this, I do not mean policing in the modern sense, although many voluntary associations in fact possessed regulatory tendencies. I mean rather policing in the common eighteenth-century usage of creating civilized refinement – of moral reform, in other words. Voluntary association and moral reform were ineluctably joined.

As the print makers of the eighteenth century were fond of illustrating, the public sphere was imagined to be under constant assault from undesirable forms of social behavior. Spitting in the streets, blaspheming, soliciting for sex and worse were demonstrations of the lack of refinement, order and sensibility in civil society. Collective morality thus required that the public space be purged of transgressive social behavior. From the 1690s coercive policing to enforce higher standards of public behavior became a major preoccupation. It fell to the various societies for the reformation of manners to erase these stains from the public space. These societies were the first voluntary associations of the period.

Societies for the reformation of manners were the characteristic response to the moral panics that dot the landscape of these two centuries. They date from efforts to promote religious piety among the upper classes in the 1670s. By the 1690s, however, a redefined conception of charity (which moved philanthropic effort in a more secular direction) focused attention on the various types of lewd and disorderly behavior that permeated the lower classes. Thus, the parish officers of Tower Hamlets in 1690 created a voluntary policing association to prosecute the bawdy houses that were believed to be seedbeds for the crime wave that was then sweeping London. William and Mary and Queen Anne, also, endorsed moral reform and regularly issued proclamations against profane and lewd behavior. Thus, with monarchical blessing, a phase of moral reform societies was initiated which lasted until the late 1730s. Focusing especially on public vice, they sought to suppress brothels, drunkenness, swearing and cursing in public, and various forms of sabbath breaking. Over 2,500 prosecutions were brought each year in London alone during the period c. 1696–1738, the vast majority being for sabbath trading and lewdness.[7]

This was the origin of the Victorian method of seeking social reform through moral reform. Indeed, when moral reform societies were revived in the 1780s, in the flush of evangelical enthusiasm, they represented the reemergence of the prior tradition of the late seventeenth century. William Wilberforce's Society for the Suppression of Vice, formed in 1801, for example, launched exactly the same kind of prosecutions that its predecessors had pursued a century earlier – notably for breaking the sabbath. Wilberforce's strategies also followed those pioneered in the seventeenth century. In both phases the aristocracy was called upon to set appropriate examples of behavior and the law was deployed to suppress and punish lewdness and other transgressions of the evangelical code.

Nor were the human quarries of these later efforts different from the earlier ones. Children and prostitutes were the favored targets of eighteenth-century social worker volunteers, as were they to be in the nineteenth century. A significant philanthropic mobilization spearheaded by Thomas Coram and Joseph Hanway in the 1730s around the problem of orphaned children led to the creation of the Foundling Hospital in 1738. Mary Carpenter's program for the children of the streets in the 1860s comes straight out of the work of eighteenth-century social reformers like Hanway, or Robert Raikes. Rescue work among the fallen women so prominent in Victorian urban social work first appeared in the 1750s at a time of moral panic similar to that of the 1860s, when public decency was feared to be vulnerable to hordes of prostitutes roaming the streets. Largely because of this fear it was possible to contemplate proposals that went beyond the general rule that intervention for moral reform was the prerogative of the voluntary society alone. In both the middle of the eighteenth century and

---

[7] Edward J. Bristow, *Vigilance and Vice: Purity Movements in Britain Since 1700* (Dublin, 1977), pp. 14–16; for the redefinition of charity, see Donna T. Andrew, *Philanthropy and Police: London Charity in the Eighteenth Century* (Princeton, 1989), pp. 5–6, 198–200, 202; Dudley W. R. Bahlman, *The Moral Revolution of 1688* (New York, 1968), pp. 1–34; T. C. Curtis and W. A. Speck, "The Societies for the Reformation of Manners: A Case Study in the Theory and Practice of Moral Reform," *Literature and History*, 3 (March 1976), pp. 45–64; Hunt, *The Middling Sort*, pp. 114–17, for the distinctions between the various types of societies; Davison et al., *Stilling the Grumbling Hive*, pp. 99–105.

the beginning of the nineteenth century, for example, there were proposals to give magistrates the power to commit prostitutes to state-funded rescue homes modeled on the Magdalene homes.[8]

Intrusion was a growing theme of "social reform" over the period. Intrusion had less to do with new concepts of state responsibility and more to do with protecting the moral safety of the public sphere in the face of subaltern threats to its purity. This was an eighteenth-century obsession which became a nineteenth-century convention. Intrusion demanded the resources and support of the state, however. Moral reform through voluntary associations could operate effectively only with elite support. Yet even though the monarchs were open in their endorsement of moral reform, elite support was not universally awarded in the early years. Tories like Henry Sacheverell saw in moral regulation the revived puritanism of the seventeenth century. In the provinces even some churchmen resisted the establishment of moral reform societies out of fear that they harbored dissenting designs. Queen Anne encountered constant resistance from local authorities to her desire to enforce bans on objectionable plays.[9]

Support from the law was particularly important to the moral reform effort. Indeed, the societies of the 1690s were usually formed by local magistrates and parish officers who hired and trained a staff of professional policemen to root out moral corruption. Yet even in the judiciary it was sometimes difficult for the moral reform advocates to obtain the cooperation of justices for their private initiatives. There was widespread suspicion of the methods used by the societies for the reformation of manners. They were reputed to purvey their prim prudishness by such means as dubious warrants and informers. Lord Justice Holt, the chief justice in the 1690s, was no friend of the moral reform societies. His judgment that it was not lawful for constables to arrest women on mere suspicion of being prostitutes stands in sharp contrast to the judicial climate that allowed the Contagious Diseases Acts to be enforced in the 1860s and 1870s.[10]

[8] See Hugh Cunningham, *Children of the Poor* (Oxford, 1991), pp. 5, 23, 31, 53–55, 87–88; Guy Kendall, *Robert Raikes* (London, 1939); Simon Gunn, "The Ministry, the Middle Class and the Civilizing Mission' in Manchester, 1850–1880," *Social History*, 21, 1 (January 1996), pp. 22–36; Langford, *A Polite and Commercial People*, pp. 142–45; Andrew, *Philanthropy and Police*, p. 96; Bristow, *Vigilance and Vice*, pp. 36–38, 63–66; Jeffrey Weekes, *Sex, Politics and Society: The Regulation of Sexuality Since 1800* (London, 1981), p. 84; Joanna Innes, "Politics and Morals: The Reformation of Manners Movement in Later Eighteenth-Century England," in Eckhart Hellmuth (ed.), *The Transformation of Political Culture: England and Germany in the Late Eighteenth Century* (London, 1990), pp. 72–118.

[9] Bahlman, *Moral Revolution*, pp. 91–96.

[10] Part of the distrust of these societies had to do with the suspicion that they were centers of dissenting activity; see Bahlman, *Moral Revolution*, pp. 35–38, 51–52, 83–85; Bristow, *Vigilance and Vice*, pp. 17, 25–26; Curtis and Speck, "Societies for the Reformation of Manners," pp. 45–46.

There was, therefore, a tradition of suspicion of moral regulation which carried through into the nineteenth century. John Stuart Mill, for example, was a strong opponent of granting police more powers to hunt down prostitutes. Similarly, Lord Shaftesbury's family were regarded with disdain by other aristocrats because of his evangelical views. Yet, by the early nineteenth century, elite opinion had generally moved in favor of the evangelical moral reform agenda. In particular, a close cooperation had been forged between the societies for the suppression of vice and the police. In London in the middle of the nineteenth century, the police looked to the reform societies to identify targets for prosecution. The partnership between the police and the Society for the Suppression of Vice remained active in this way into the 1870s in campaigns against obscene publications and against licensed premises that were covers for prostitution.[11]

The initiative of the private voluntary association remained the main agency for moralizing the public sphere until the late nineteenth century in large part because the powers of the police themselves were embedded in the sovereignty of the private citizen. Until well into the middle of the nineteenth century, anti-vice squads were entirely private organizations. Strict limits restrained the authority of the police to interfere with people in the streets or to enter private houses that might be dens of prostitution. Police policy on moral issues such as prostitution sought only to contain the problem, therefore. Until the 1880s the London police took action against known brothels only when specifically requested by the parish officers. Similarly, there was plenty of evidence in the 1830s that young girls were commonly entrapped into prostitution. But with no publicist like newspaperman W. T. Stead around to work up a voluntarist campaign against the practice, it was a problem that remained within the sphere of rescue work rather than becoming a target of legislative regulation.[12]

Vice and leisure traditionally existed in wholesome combination. It was difficult to draw the line between vice and leisure; yet it was particularly

---

[11] J. M. Winter, *London's Teeming Streets 1830–1914* (London, 1993), pp. 110–12; Stefan Petrow, *Policing Morals: The Metropolitan Police and the Home Office 1870–1914* (Oxford, 1994), pp. 5–10; Robert D. Storch, "Police Control of Street Prostitution in Victorian London: A Study in the Contexts of Police Action," in David Bayley (ed.), *Police and Society* (Beverley Hills and London, 1977), pp. 57–58.

[12] Bristow, *Vigilance and Vice*, pp. 45–47, 55–56, 60–62. This tendency to greater police regulation was also evident in their powers to regulate street commerce. An act of 1867 for London contained the potential to end all street commerce by forbidding the placing of goods on the streets for anything but loading or unloading. Of course, this power was not rigorously applied. A major problem for all categories of police regulation was the requirement of the law that the offense be proved a public annoyance. This required testimony from members of the public, without which magistrates would not convict. The police thus relied upon volunteerism of Societies for the Reformation of Manners to secure convictions.

important to do so because the line between recreation and social disorder was easily crossed. This was particularly so for the lower class whose recreational activities occurred mainly in the public space. Thus, the evangelical impulse to civilize the sports and recreations of popular culture expressed the several facets of moral reform as moral improvement and social policing. This, too, is a theme of the whole period and not just from the evangelical revival in the late eighteenth century.

Animal sports were a case in point. Changing attitudes to the natural world created a consensus against cruelty to animals early in our period. Upper-class sensibilities changed first, of course. Whereas bear baiting had been a part of William III's welcome to Prince Lewis of Baden in 1694, by the 1730s this kind of spectacle was condemned by respectable opinion. Isolated campaigns were launched against various customs from the 1740s. From the 1780s a concerted national effort was initiated to address the issue of popular leisure. Yet until the development of urban police forces from the 1840s it was not possible to launch a serious offensive to rid the public space of the more obnoxious practices of lower-class recreation.[13]

Thus, the eighteenth-century project to bring a culture of sensibility to the public sphere could be realized only from the early nineteenth century. The temporary ascendancy of the centralizers within the state structure in the 1830s and 1840s allowed the implementation of longstanding proposals to redefine what was permitted within the public space. The Metropolitan Police Act of 1839 in London and the various improvement acts in the provincial towns were the "charters of this project." Until the 1830s, for example, the suppression of animal sports depended on the zeal of local magistrates who sometimes called in troops to suppress bull baiting and the like. The passing of the Cruelty to Animals Act of 1835 enabled the partnership between private initiative and public authority for moral reform to be placed on a surer footing. Manchester authorities formally prohibited cock and dog fighting and badger baiting in 1843. A wide range of other behavior became liable for regulation, from flying kites to beating carpets and making noise in public. The suppression of street games and the prohibitions against nude bathing in canals paralleled the loss of other kinds of public use rights, but would surely have reassured Hogarth that a reformed social morality was possible.[14]

[13] Davison et al., *Stilling the Grumbling Hive*, p. 109; Robert Malcolmson, *Popular Recreation in English Society 1700–1850* (Cambridge, 1973), pp. 118–26.

[14] These two paragraphs are drawn from Hugh Cunningham, *Leisure in the Industrial Revolution c. 1780–1880* (London, 1980), pp. 20–22, 42, 44, 79, 82; Malcolmson, *Popular Recreation*, chs. 6, 7; Robert Storch (ed.), *Popular Culture and Custom in Nineteenth-Century England* (London, 1982), pp. 14–15; Brian Harrison, "The Sunday Trading Riots of 1855," *Historical Journal*, 8, 2 (1965), pp. 219–45.

Evangelical reformers did not easily moralize public recreations, however. The process was fractured and uncertain. Indeed, the corruption of public space proceeded apace in the early nineteenth century even as it became the focused target of moral reformers. Popular recreation gained a new vitality from economic expansion and urban growth of the late eighteenth century. The increase in lower-class cultural forms threatened to overwhelm the ability of the elite classes to maintain watchful observation of its many applications. This was alarming because working-class leisure always threatened to become a challenge to public order. Thus, the movement to reform leisure was a moral and political matter, the purpose of which was not simply to cleanse the leisure habits of the lower classes, but also to bring popular recreation into the public spaces where it could be monitored and controlled.[15]

The reformed leisure offered to the lower classes from the 1820s, therefore, contained a package of morally wholesome recreations that would be visible rather than hidden, genteel rather than rough and crossclass rather than closed to the respectable classes. This effort to install "rational recreation" as the dominant leisure practice of the lower classes ultimately achieved some considerable success. "Traditional" forms of popular leisure certainly survived well into the middle of the nineteenth century, as James Greenwood and other social explorers found when they examined the low life of London in the 1860s and 1870s. Yet throughout the midcentury these leisure practices were progressively marginalized, driven underground and replaced by formalized and commercialized sports organization. Cricket, rugby and soccer – and more – were put on their modern footing from about the 1870s. The end result was that by 1880 eighteenth-century patterns of leisure had been replaced by those of the twentieth century.[16]

It was in the middle of the nineteenth century that leisure was moved into a rationalized and separate series of public spaces. This had both spatial and temporal elements. Public spaces were categorized and demarcated in ways that presumed and encouraged civilized forms of social behavior. Parks were constructed, for example, on the explicit assumption that they were for certain styles of "respectable" leisure, generally of a "family" variety. Parks were only one among a variety of new spaces that were opened as part of the rational recreation program of the middle of the nineteenth century. Museums and public libraries were part of the same agenda. New allocations of time encouraged the humanizing of

---

[15] Cunningham, *Leisure in the Industrial Revolution*, pp. 120–37, 140–51.
[16] See James Greenwood, *The Wilds of London* (repr., New York, 1985 [1874]), pp. 276–79, for a description of ratting; Wray Vamplew, *Pay Up and Play the Game: Professional Sport in Britain 1875–1914* (Cambridge, 1988).

leisure. Work and leisure time began to be more sharply delineated as the regularization of the workweek brought an end to the flexible time-keeping of prefactory economy. Unsurprisingly, the same decades of the 1850s and 1860s that saw the Saturday half-holiday also saw the initial development of seaside resorts for the masses. Cheap trains to Margate and Brighton began in the 1850s, and Blackpool was developed in the late 1860s for the factory workers of the industrial heartland.[17]

These developments continued to be driven by voluntarist activity. Recreational grounds initially were attached to pubs, but by the 1840s they were increasingly recognized to be a public responsibility. Parliament granted £100,000 for the purchase of Battersea Park in 1840, although these facilities were usually developed by public subscription. Only after the 1870s did libraries or parks become the responsibility of local governments. The legal framework for civic largess and morality was, of course, the point at which the state touched the process most closely. Acts were passed that facilitated the opening of museums on Sunday and made provision for cultural activities to be supported by the rates so that they could be free of charge. But in the middle of the nineteenth century, as in the eighteenth century, the state's function did not include the administration of the public sphere as the collective representative of its citizens. Civil society demanded one thing of the state: that it preserve, defend and patrol the boundaries of the public sphere. Naturally, this depended on where it was believed those boundaries should lie, and this was always a matter of debate. Sabbatarians, for example, were a constant threat to the provisions of a secular Sunday in the middle of the nineteenth century, and efforts to close museums in London on Sunday had to be beaten off in the 1850s. The rights of the lower classes to access to public spaces were asserted, sometimes by riots. There continued to be restrictions on band concerts in the public parks of London and elsewhere. Peel Park in Bradford was opened on Sunday only in 1867, yet it took still two more years to make refreshments available on that day.[18]

If the state was only marginally involved in filling the public sphere of leisure, it was even less thinkable that the state should define the content of the private sphere. The family was the quintessential unit of the private sphere. Family autonomy in the period covered by this book was in most

---

[17] David Kynaston, *King Labour: The British Working Class 1850–1914* (London, 1976), pp. 108–09; Peter Bailey, *Leisure and Class in Victorian England: Rational Recreation and the Contest for Control 1830–1885* (London, 1978), chs. 2, 5, 6; Donald Reid, "The Decline of St. Monday," *Past and Present*, 71 (1976), pp. 76–101; Royden Harrison, *Before the Socialists: Studies in Labour and Politics 1861–1881* (London, 1965), pp. 82–84.

[18] H. E. Meller, *Leisure and the Changing City, 1870–1914* (London, 1976), pp. 42–71, 96–99, 100–17; Cunningham, *Leisure in the Industrial Revolution*, pp. 105–06.

respects supreme. In normal circumstances the only institution of the state that was likely to breach the boundary of the family would be the personnel of the poor law. Intrusion on the private sphere from the public sphere would come more typically from some voluntary society activity with authority deriving only from the force of convention and opinion. The state could not remain entirely disinterested in the family sanctum of the private sphere, of course, and, ultimately, the state was the only agency that could define the character and limits of the private sphere. Yet the closer the state crept to the private sphere, the more problematic and contentious its role became. This was apparent throughout our period in the debates that surrounded such issues as the definition of marriage and the regulation of children at work.

Modern marriage was defined by Hardwicke's Marriage Act of 1753. For the first time the family received a legal definition as constituted by a marriage that was sanctified by the church. The act also gave legal backing to the authority of the parents over the marriage of their children under the age of twenty-one. Among other things, the act introduced a procedure that included an official license and public announcement of the proposed union; it also imposed the heavy penalty of transportation for any violation of the act by clergy. Precisely because the authority of the state was employed to sanction a particular structure of the private sphere, however, Hardwicke's act was a highly controversial measure. Indeed, the act occasioned one of the sharpest public debates of the eighteenth century. Opponents feared that the act would encourage the growth of caste habits among the upper class and that the expense of a license would discourage laborers from marrying at all. Some of this was prescient. The aristocracy did become more endogamous; and a century later a Royal Commission reported that common-law marriage remained disturbingly popular among the lower classes.[19]

Similar difficulties were encountered whenever the state moved to intervene in the workplace. The factory acts of the early Victorian period were a much delayed legislation precisely because it was so difficult to

---

[19] The impetus for the act was the practice of marriage outside the control of the canon law, which had increased markedly since the 1660s. A series of spectacular scandals among the upper class in the 1750s (such as Lord Tankerville who eloped with a butcher's daughter) were taken to suggest threats to the sanctity of inheritance and provided the impetus for the passage of the act. See J. A. Cannon, *Aristocratic Century: The Peerage of Eighteenth-Century England* (Cambridge, 1984), pp. 73–92; John Gillis, *For Better, For Worse: British Marriages, 1600 to the Present* (Oxford, 1985), pp. 140–41; Lawrence Stone, *Road to Divorce: England 1530–1987* (Oxford, 1989), pp. 96–128; Weekes, *Sex, Politics and Society*, p. 24; Rachel Harrison and Frank Mort, "Patriarchal Aspects of Nineteenth-Century State Formation," in Philip Corrigan, *Capitalism, State Formation and Marxist Theory* (London, 1980), pp. 81–99; Olive Anderson, "Civil Marriage in Victorian England and Wales," *Past and Present*, 69 (November 1975), pp. 55–86.

resolve the objections to violating the boundary of the family unit. The question of intervening in the sphere of economic exchange was easier to resolve than the question of family authority. Ultimately, a political consensus in support of factory legislation was attained by a new conception of the factory as a civilizing counterweight to the barbaric state of working-class culture.[20]

On the other hand, violation of the private sphere by official public bodies had long been recognized as legitimate to assist children who were without the protection of family. Even the stoutest defenders of the private sphere from collective regulation, like John Bright, were agreed on the justice of this. Thus, it was relatively easy to justify intervention to protect such groups as parish apprentices. Various acts of Parliament in 1802, 1844 and 1851 granted the poor law commissioners the power to regulate the conditions of apprentices' work and the authority to prosecute those who mistreated such children. Until the late nineteenth century, however, this was where the line was drawn. The fate of children born to "unsuitable" parents and their treatment within the family, for example, was a growing anxiety in mid-Victorian social commentary. Charles Dickens and Mary Carpenter were at the forefront of this particular issue. No sentiment existed, however, to trespass across the family boundary between the public and private spheres until the 1880s. Indeed, when the Infant Protection Act of 1871 criminalized the failure to notify registration authorities of a birth, it was met with fierce opposition from feminists like Josephine Butler for its intrusion into the privacy of women's lives. For the same reasons there was strong opposition to clauses in the Industrial Schools Act of 1880 that permitted police to enter brothels and remove children who were there with their mothers.[21]

[20] Robert Gray, "Languages of Factory Reform, c. 1830–c. 1860," in Joyce, *Historical Meanings of Work*, pp. 143–79; Andrew Ure, *The Philosophy of Manufactures* (repr., New York, 1968), pp. 309–12, 333–36, 408–10; Sonya Rose, *Limited Livelihoods: Gender and Class in Nineteenth-Century England* (London, 1992), pp. 70–74. There were differences between the various manufacturing sectors. Class and patriarchal concerns were fused in coal mining by male resistance to the exclusion of family labor from the pits. This only reinforced the need for the state to define the proper family structure and relationship to work and home. See Jane Mark-Lawson and Anne Witz, "From Family Labour to Family Wage?: The Case of Women's Labour in Nineteenth-Century Coal Mining," *Social History*, 13, 2 (May 1988), pp. 151–74.

[21] George Behlmer, *Child Abuse and Moral Reform in England 1870–1914* (Palo Alto, CA, 1982), pp. 1–12; George Macaulay Trevelyan, *The Life of John Bright* (New York, 1913), p. 154. The Industrial Schools Act of 1857 had allowed removal of children from families under certain circumstances. But this act seems to have been not much used.

Gender and the unstable boundary of the public and private spheres

The most clearly defined frontier between the public and the private spheres, then, traced the line between the family and society. Gender was a key category for marking the route of this boundary. At its simplest level the public and private spheres were a binary formation: the public sphere was male and the private sphere was female. Certainly, the gender capacities of each sector were regarded in this way. The ideology of domesticity provided the logic to this separation of the public and private spheres. The qualities of masculinity were suited for the public world and the qualities of femininity for the domestic world. Separate spheres for men and women described the ideology and sociology of gender relations during this period, although it is important to recognize that it did not necessarily describe the behavior of women (or men, for that matter) during the period. Women were not necessarily confined by separate spheres ideology; but they did have to reckon with it. Equally, it is important to recognize that domesticity and separate spheres were never stable constructions.[22] Indeed, the tensions and ambiguities within the arrangement of the separate spheres created a profound instability to the public–private division in civil society. The ultimate demise of the social constructions that constituted civil society in this period owed a lot to tensions and instabilities that ran along this gendered boundary.[23]

The ideological and cultural formation of separate spheres was not the invention of Victorian England. As G. M. Young pointed out many years ago, the idea of "Victorian" domesticity can be found as early as the late seventeenth century. Indeed, it is impossible to link many of the qualities of the domestic woman exclusively to any one period – and there is not much point in doing so, either. The category of "woman" as subordinate to men and as possessing inherently different qualities was deeply embedded in western culture at least from the beginning of organized Christianity. The instability that attaches to the idea of woman as alternately possessing a moral purity that equips her for domesticity and an unruly sexuality that *requires* domestication is not a Victorian or

[22] See Hunt, *The Middling Sort*, pp. 8–9, 138–40, 144–45, for separate spheres as a category and some interesting examples of the everyday instabilities within the system of domesticity during the eighteenth century.
[23] Martha Vicinus, *Separate Spheres* (Bloomington, 1974), is the founding text for the concept of separate spheres. Davidoff and Hall, *Family Fortunes*, is the standard statement linking the development of separate spheres to the creation of middle-class identity. For a critique of the Davidoff–Hall interpretation, see Amanda Vickery in "Golden Age to Separate Spheres?: A Review of the Categories and Chronology of English Women's History," *Historical Journal*, 36, 2 (1993), pp. 383–414.

an eighteenth-century invention. It may be found well established, for example, in the sixteenth century. What follows does rest upon a series of suppositions about gender relations in this period, however: that the dynamic of gender relations proceeded according to a common rhythm over this period; that the ideology of domesticity was successfully *generalized* in the culture in the eighteenth century to pervade the politics of gender relations; *and* that this pattern was also the pattern of the nineteenth century.[24]

We may distinguish three broad stages in the historical development of domestic ideology and the separate spheres in our period. Each one possessed its own particular mix of qualities and instabilities; each one, for example, saw opportunities for some women both open and close. In the first period, from the late seventeenth century to the late eighteenth century, the hegemony of domesticity and separate spheres was entrenched. Significantly, this was also the period when the understanding of the body was categorized into two distinct types of male and female. The second stage opened in the late eighteenth century and was marked by contention, debate and experimentation in new gender relationships. At the same time the discourse of evangelicalism displayed a forceful presentation of separate spheres ideology. In this period the instabilities of gender relations came as much from the example of the French revolution as they did from the internal contradictions themselves. The reverse is true for the third stage, the Victorian period from about the 1830s until the 1870s, when the hegemony of separate spheres domesticity is least contested, when it is projected as most natural and stable. Ironically, however, this was the moment of greatest instability to the ideology and structures of domesticity. This was the period when the contradictions in the system of domesticity could no longer be contained. Mid-Victorian women were the most subversive of all women. Using the conventional assumptions and discourses of domesticity, they undermined the foundations of separate spheres and collapsed the divide between public and private.

From c. 1680 to c. 1790

By the late seventeenth century, the rise of a reading public and the business of publishing had made it possible to promote widely the domestic virtues of women's character. As early as 1673 a fully worked-out description of Victorian domesticity was available in a handbook Richard

---

[24] Young, *Portrait of an Age*, p. 2, n. 1. Vickery, "Golden Age to Separate Spheres?," pp. 402–08; Denise Riley, *Am I That Name?: Feminism and the Category of "Women" in History* (Minneapolis, 1990).

Allstree entitled *The Ladies Calling*. This was not the first such handbook, but it is significant that it went through several editions in the eighteenth century and was republished for evangelical use in the 1780s. Each value of domesticity was treated in a separate chapter: modesty, meekness, compassion, affability, piety. The book was expository; it argued the case for the domestic definition of women and provided detailed codes of behavior and conduct.

But the fragility of the construction of domesticity is betrayed throughout the book. On the one hand, women were exhorted to use the faculties God gave them properly. On the other hand, women's accomplishments were said to contain many serious dangers. Thus, restraint was Allstree's main recommendation: restraint of tongues that can so easily become unnecessarily talkative and sharp; restraint of action, for modesty is the essential protection of chastity; restraint of character, for "meekness is so amiable, so endearing a quality"; restraint with entertainments because "they may be innocent, or otherwise, according as they are managed"; restraint for widows tempted to remarry younger men. The list of anxieties, fears and exhortations goes on and on.[25]

By the time Richard Steele extolled the women's character as a domestic one in 1712, he mouthed a commonplace. Praise for women who devoted themselves to home and family was to be found in the journals of comment throughout Europe. The rapid progress and refinement of domestic ideology were the major themes of eighteenth-century women's history. The Victorian discourse of domesticity was fully anticipated during the earlier century. By the middle of the eighteenth century, for example, a profusion of domestic advice books had appeared with instructions on how to make good mothers and wives. Rousseau's argument in *Emile* that the intellectual and emotional nature of women equipped them only for the domestic sphere received widespread notice in Britain. Yet this cannot have been because such a doctrine was novel to the 1760s. More likely it was because the case needed reinforcing, because at no point did domestic ideology remain uncontested.[26]

This was true from the beginning. Bernard Mandeville, for example, the Dutch emigrant to London, had shocked respectable opinion in the 1720s with his alternative vision of women as sexualized and economically independent beings. Just like his more famous assault on the hypocrisy of privileging virtue in commerce, Mandeville launched a frontal

[25] Richard Allstree, *The Ladies Calling* (London, 1787 edn.), pp. 11–12, 18–19, 51, 55, 178, 268–70.

[26] Bonnie Anderson and Judith P. Zinsser, *A History of Their Own: Women in Europe from Prehistory to the Present* (New York, 1988), vol. II, pp. 116–18; Amanda Vickery, "The Neglected Century: Writing the History of Eighteenth-Century Women," *Gender and History*, 3, 2 (Summer 1991), pp. 211–19.

attack on the notion of women as repositories of domestic piety, lacking in passion. Mandeville was unusual, of course. Still, it is remarkable that such views had disappeared by the middle of the eighteenth century. Women writers had never been ready to adopt them. The Victorian practice of women contending against domestic ideology within its own limits was inherent from the beginning. The most common female response to the kind of cloistered life recommended by Allstree was to assert the need for women's education. Indeed, the claims of women to an education constituted the main programmatic challenge to domestic ideology and separate spheres in the eighteenth century. It remained the centerpiece of the feminist program until the middle of the nineteenth century.[27]

It is not surprising that from about the 1670s this issue moved to the forefront. This was the moment when woman as consumer was first identified. The explosion in rates of female literacy between 1670 and 1690 created a ready market for books, and the advantages of various epistolary activities as suitable for women was being promoted. Writers such as Mary Astell and Bashua Makin from the 1670s were making the case that women could promulgate piety more effectively if they were trained to be more than mere ornaments for men. Astell's book *A Serious Proposal to the Ladies*, first published to great acclaim in 1691, established the foundational argument for education as an answer to domestic ideology. Later generations of feminists in the middle of the eighteenth century looked back to this book as a pathbreaking feminist document. It was significant, however, that Astell was a highly conservative thinker. For the next two centuries the feminist argument was conducted from within the discourse of domesticity, and it was Astell who prefigured that pattern.[28]

[27] It is important to realize that education did not just mean acquiring accomplishments. Increasingly, it came to mean what Hannah More called the "forming of habits" such as humility, meekness, sobriety, punctuality and the like – all of which amounted to the acquisition of domestic virtues and sensibilities that would enable women to properly fulfill their subordinate, if civilizing, partnership with men. See More, "Strictures on the Modern System of Female Education," in *The Works of Hannah More*, vol. I (New York, 1837), pp. 335–38.

[28] About 30 percent of British women could read in 1675, but by 1690 the figure was over 50 percent. Women as consumers were in tension with the notion of their greater sensibilities which, it was believed, made them liable to nervous disorders, resulting in an incipiently economic recklessness. See G. J. Barker-Benfield, *The Culture of Sensibility: Sex and Society in Eighteenth-Century Britain* (Chicago, 1992), pp. 28–32, 126–29, 163–69, 191–98; Ruth Perry, *The Celebrated Mary Astell: An Early English Feminist* (Chicago, 1986), pp. 99–119; Brewer, *Pleasures of the Imagination*, pp. 167–68; Mary Astell, *A Serious Proposal to the Ladies for the Advancement of Their True and Greatest Interest* (4th edn., New York, 1970 [1701]). At a time when education was monopolized by men, of course, to use it as the centerpiece for feminist argument was more subversive than it might appear.

Not all women were content to proceed from an acceptance of domesticity, however. There were periods such as the 1730s to the 1770s when sexual politics were more intense and confrontational. Challenges to the very idea of male superiority and difference came from Lady Mary Wortley Montagu and Catherine Macaulay among others. The very premises of domesticity were disputed by these intellectuals, and they came dangerously near to disrupting the boundary between the public and private spheres. Wortley, for example, suggested that domesticity was a constructed quality which provided the excuse rather than the cause of women's exclusion from politics and education. Wortley's challenge in behalf of women was unmatched in its boldness until the later nineteenth century, and perhaps not even then. A similar, though more moderated, argument was heard from Catherine Macaulay, who was a representative of the enormously talented group of women, known in the 1770s as the "nine muses." Macaulay delivered a slashing attack on Rousseau's claim that differences in sexual character determined the separate spheres of men and women, arguing that Rousseau's reasoning "for contradiction and absurdity outdoes every metaphysical riddle."[29]

Such challenges hardly disturbed the progress of the dominant ideology, however. When the first history of women was published in the 1770s, it consisted essentially of a historical justification of the domestication of women in the home sphere. By that time, a virtual stream of intellectual and other public commentary on the place of women was firmly in the Victorian mold.[30] It is conventional to see such tendencies as reflecting a progressive closure to women of eighteenth-century public spaces and it is certainly true that the masculinization of the public space proceeded apace. It took ever more ingenious efforts by women to elbow through the odd cracks that did appear in the edifice of domesticity. Yet, to borrow from the history of colonial rule, dominance does not imply hegemony. There are plenty of examples of women successfully exploiting these openings – Anna Seward of Litchfield would be a good example. Sexual politics were permanently unstable, and rife with tensions and struggles. This was especially true at moments when the veil of stability

---

[29] Bonnie Anderson and Zinsser, *A History of Their Own*, pp. 138–40; Sophia [Lady Mary Wortley Montagu?], *Women Not Inferior to Man* (London, 1739); Catherine Macaulay Graham, *Letters on Education with Observations on Religious and Metaphysical Subjects* (London, 1790), pp. 205–06.

[30] Colley, *Britons*, pp. 237–81; Langford, *A Polite and Commercial People*, pp. 109–16, 603–07. The sermons of James Fordyce, for example, in the mid-1760s reflected the argument that it was the soft and spiritual nature of women that endowed them with their special grace and place in the home. Hannah More argued in 1779 for the self-effacing, retiring woman: "girls should be taught to give up their opinions betimes, and not pertinaciously to carry on a dispute, even if they would know themselves to be in the right" (Langford, *A Polite and Commercial People*, p. 607).

and convention in the wider political culture was ripped away, the political space opened to all comers and the nature of political arrangements laid out for debate.[31]

This was to be the case in 1780, for example, when the Lord George Gordon riots subjected London to the worst civil disturbances of the century. Politically aware women of the middling classes seized that moment to force their way into the debating societies that were a popular craze of the time. As a site where "public opinion" was shaped and expressed, the debating societies were a nerve center of the public sphere in action. They were a male preserve, even if some allowed women into the gallery to observe. For a brief moment women took advantage of the collapse of the boundaries of the public space and asserted their public voice. Some exclusively female societies were established, which then debated whether or not to admit men. In others, women secured the right to speak and to participate. These were the first places where serious public discussion of women's political rights could take place in anticipation of the wider debates of the 1790s. This moment was soon gone, however. By the spring of 1781 these openings were closed and women were once again excluded from these forums.[32]

The period is full of such challenges, however. Sexual politics in the 1750s and 1770s seem to have been particularly stormy. This was the height of the debate on women's education. It was also a time of mobilization for war, and the occasion to define patriotic nationalism in both the Seven Years War and then the American war served to propel the masculinization of political discourse. Ideas of nationality began (for the first time?) to be gendered in the way that was to be quite common during the nineteenth century. The French, in particular, had long been identified as effete and effeminate. The rhetoric of patriotism in the 1760s and 1770s firmly established masculinity as a British quality and Britain's enemies as effeminate.

Yet the need to mobilize public opinion in the face of national danger also offered opportunities for women. The national interest, it was argued, demanded an educated and involved female citizenry. During the course of these wars, women expanded their tenuous spaces in the public sphere by appropriating various patriotic activities to add to their already

---

[31] I have found the following essay very useful for understanding the process described here: Ranajit Guha, "Dominance Without Hegemony and Its Historiography," in Guha (ed.), *Subaltern Studies*, vol. VI, *Writings on South Asian History and Society* (Delhi, 1989), pp. 210–310. For Anna Seward, see Brewer, *Pleasures of the Imagination*, pp. 571–91.

[32] Langford, *A Polite and Commercial People*, pp. 111–12; Mary Thale, "Women in Debating Societies in 1780," *Gender and History*, 7, 1 (April 1995), pp. 5–24; Donna Andrew, "Popular Culture and Public Debate: London 1780," *Historical Journal*, 39, 2 (1996), pp. 410–14, 420–22.

growing presence in charity and philanthropy. They were to do the same again during the national emergency of the 1790s. A similar dynamic operated with the cause of anti-slavery from the 1780s. Opposition to the slave trade provided ample scope to articulate the typically Victorian feminist strategy of using the rhetoric of domesticity to subvert its boundaries. The moral sensibility that was attached to women in domestic ideology was an admirable justification for them to contribute to the righteous cause of ending the slave trade.[33]

It is difficult to gauge levels of intensity in these matters. But it is worth considering the possibility that the struggles around the frontiers of domesticity and gender boundaries were more intense in the eighteenth century than at a later date. The blunt and incisive voice that can be heard in Lady Mary Wortley Montagu or even Catherine Macaulay, for example, was far removed from the tone of gentle ridicule that was the only register Victorian feminists felt free to use to deflate male pretension. Before the advent of the evangelical hegemony at the end of the eighteenth century, gender boundaries seem to have been transgressed in ways that are not found in the nineteenth century. We can instance the crossdressing craze of the 1760s and 1770s, for example, when Hannah More was to be found favorably reviewing transgender theater plays, or the lionizing of the transvestite French nobleperson, the Chévalier d'Eon, who carefully constructed a play around the doubts about his/her gender. By Victorian times, of course, crossdressing codes had been distanced into the fantasy realm of pantomime and music hall show business.[34]

Indeed, it is important to appreciate how Victorian feminists inverted the arguments of eighteenth-century feminists and retreated ever deeper into the discourse of domesticity to make their case. One of the main lines of argument from eighteenth-century feminists was to challenge male claims to superiority on the basis of physical prowess. Lady Mary Wortley Montagu was particularly scathing on this issue. But by the middle of the nineteenth century, men's physical strength had become the basis of women's claims for protection and special status. It was the failure of men to live up to the responsibilities and duties that fell to them precisely because of their greater power that Victorian feminists like Josephine Butler used to argue the case for fair treatment of women. This transformation followed from the phase of gender relations that opened in the 1790s.

---

[33] Colley, *Britons*, pp. 238–50. For the gendering of patriotism in this period, see Kathleen Wilson, *Sense of the People*, pp. 40–44, 185–205.

[34] Langford, *A Polite and Commercial People*, pp. 109–16, 603–07; Marjorie Gerber, *Vested Interests: Cross Dressing and Cultural Anxiety* (Cambridge, MA, 1992), pp. 259–65.

From c. 1790 to c. 1830

From the 1790s to the 1830s gender relations were conditioned by the combined influences of the French revolution and the revitalized evangelicalism that issued from the Clapham sect in the 1780s. These two influences worked in contradictory and complementary ways. On the one hand, the French revolution allowed for alternative formulations of gender relations to be attempted and new kinds of politics to be imagined for women. Proofs of these opportunities could be seen in plebeian and elite culture, from the claims of Mary Wollstonecraft to the increasing rates of premarital sex and common-law marriages. After the early 1820s, however, this phase was checked – the Queen Caroline case being a key event in this process. On the other hand, proceeding in parallel, was the spreading cloud of evangelicalism. The ambition of evangelicalism in this regard was to reinforce domestic ideology and stabilize gender relations.

For women, as for other subordinate social groups, there were both openings and closings. In certain areas women were greatly empowered during this period: the expanding realm of philanthropy would be an obvious example. Yet even this kind of public participation could occur only through the ideological rationale of domestic ideology. Women's roles as economic actors in husbands' businesses or workshops or even the considerable managerial facility demanded by running a household were suppressed and hidden beneath the veil of domesticity. And the tensions that resulted can be seen running through sexual politics during the period until the early nineteenth century. One legacy of this process was to color female behavior in the public–private spheres with even deeper shades of subtlety and euphemism to create the characteristic surface restraint of Victorian gender relations. Thus, by the middle of the nineteenth century the blunt realism of Montagu or Macaulay is replaced with the (likely) psychosomatic invalidism of a Florence Nightingale, or the amanuensis role of Harriet Taylor for John Stuart Mill or even the bearding of Marian Evans by George Eliot. But I am getting ahead of my argument here.[35]

[35] See Anna Clark, *The Struggle for the Breeches: Gender and the Making of the British Working Class* (Berkeley, 1995), pp. 42–62, for the sexual crisis of this period. The best statement of the role of evangelicalism in the making of domesticity is Davidoff and Hall, *Family Fortunes*, esp. pp. 114–18. See F. K. Brown, *Fathers of the Victorians* (Cambridge, 1961), for the conventional view of evangelicalism, but this view is not seriously contested by Davidoff and Hall, for example. Young, *Portrait of an Age*, pp. 2–4, anticipates much subsequent scholarship in a few sentences in his usual allusive style. See Briggs, *Age of Improvement*, pp. 69–74, 173–75, for a good description of the vitality of evangelical religion. See also Langford, *A Polite and Commercial People*, pp. 583–85; Catherine Hall, "The Early Formation of Victorian Domestic Ideology," in Sandra Burman (ed.), *Fit Work For Women* (London, 1979), pp. 21–22.

The 1790s saw the culmination of the instabilities that had permeated eighteenth-century domestic ideology. The lightening rod in this regard was Mary Wollstonecraft. Mary Wollstonecraft's *Vindication of the Rights of Woman* in 1794 launched a challenge to domestic ideology and gender relations. Much of Wollstonecraft's argument was conventional to the previous hundred years or so. This was particularly so in the way Wollstonecraft placed education at the center of her case against domesticity. Wollstonecraft repeated the arguments of Mary Astell and Lady Mary Wortley Montagu against defining women as purely domestic creatures. Like Catherine Macaulay, she was willing to confront directly the sentimentalism of conventional domesticity. The fierceness of the response to Wollstonecraft, far surpassing anything that had faced her predecessors, reflected the tender tenor of the times. Wollstonecraft's critique of female dependence and subordination was met with the claim – too easily substantiated through her personal life – that she was asserting a sexual licentiousness in contrast to the fulfillment that women could achieve within marriage.[36]

Hannah More offered the most celebrated response to Wollstonecraft, though hers was by no means the only one. An assertive woman who lived very much in the public sphere, both in her early life as a playwright and in her later years as a propagandist against the French revolution and class warfare, she was the most effective evangelical popularizer of separate spheres domestic ideology. More's writings also revealed, however, the deep contradictions that were to pervade Victorian domestic ideology. More is best known for her anti-Jacobin tracts to working men, but she was also concerned to teach middle-class women how to propagandize domestic virtues among the working class. To this end, many of her tracts provided an economic education to middle-class women in the service of preparing them to be good philanthropists. But this was itself ambiguous. While More preached the conventional line about domestic ideology, she was also empowering women with knowledge and addressing them as women of the world (as was she) rather than the submissive, quiescent creatures she ostensibly preferred them to be. Thus, she could write:

The chief end to be proposed in cultivating the understandings of women, is to qualify them for the practical purposes of life. Their knowledge is not often like the learning of men, to be reproduced in some literary composition, nor in any learned profession; but it is to come out in conduct. The great uses of study to a

[36] See *Mary Wollstonecraft: Political Writings*, ed. Janet Todd (Toronto, 1993), pp. xiv, xvii, 109–13, 141, 146, 174–78, for the various themes mentioned in this paragraph. See also Barker-Benfield, *Culture of Sensibility*, pp. 389–91. Wollstonecraft bears comparison with Paine on more than one count. Her *Vindication of the Rights of Men* published in 1792 was the first actual reply to Burke.

woman are to enable her to regulate her own mind, and to be instrumental to the good of others.[37]

Here was a curious inversion. Men's learning was bookish, otherworldly; women's learning was about the business of life! It would be a mistake to be too subtle about this. Eighteenth-century feminists aspired to use education explicitly to liberate women from the constraints of domestic ideology. Hannah More, like many of her contemporaries, championed education in the service of woman's role within the system of domestic ideology. The more education a woman received, the more she would learn that there can be "no happiness in any society where there is a perpetual struggle for power" and that those "petty and absurd contentions for equality which female smatterers so anxiously maintain" would be exposed as false.[38]

One of the places where the tension between ideology and reality flourished was in the daily organizational life of the nonconformist churches. The theology of nonconformity rested on the notion of individual salvation. Women were particularly prominent as consumers of religion; two-thirds of all Methodists were women. Thus, the possibilities existed for women to play leading roles in these denominations, and even to serve as preachers. For much of the eighteenth century, active participation by women seems to have been an open question. In many denominations women were not formally prohibited from leading roles. Methodism began to allow women preachers in 1761, for example, when John Wesley realized how effective they could be in converting the other women, who were his primary audience. Beginning in the 1780s and stretching through to the 1830s, however, there was a progressive closure of preaching opportunities for women across all of the denominations. The Baptists seem to have been the first to shut this door, but the most important move was the decision by Wesleyan Methodism in 1803 to end the rights of women to preach. Quakers continued to permit women preachers, although they were not allowed to exercise any organizational power.

There was a class dimension to this process that needs to be recognized. The presence of women preachers among the working-class Methodist congregations was one of the important issues of schism in the 1790s and early 1800s. Official Wesleyanism came to regard these sects as vulgar and unruly precisely because their greater democracy allowed

---

[37] *Complete Works of Hannah More*, vol. I, p. 363.
[38] Ibid., p. 364. See Deborah Valenze, *The First Industrial Woman* (New York, 1995), pp. 148–50; Catherine Hall, "The Sweet Delights of Home," in Michelle Perrot (ed.), *A History of Private Life*, vol. IV (Cambridge, MA, 1990), pp. 50–64; *Complete Works of Hannah More*, vol. I, p. 365.

women to play a prominent public role. Thus, after the first decade of the nineteenth century, women preachers were to be found only in the marginal cottage religions of lower-class sects. In these purely proletarian sects women remained in key leadership positions until the 1860s. But as these denominations in turn began to formalize their organization and move into permanent chapels, so an end was declared to women preachers. While these groups created their own public spaces in the barns, cottages and other "informal" meeting places made available by their members, they could maintain their own definition of what was possible. Once they moved into the official public space, they had to conform to its standards and methods.[39]

The issue of preaching was a relatively straightforward question of power. More problematic were issues having to do with female participation in the organizational life of the church. The basic formulation was fairly simply stated; women could participate in lay activities that related to the domestic ideal. Yet this disguised in fact a myriad of constantly changing and contentious boundaries. What role could women play in conversion, for example, given the attributes of superior spirituality that domestic ideology claimed they possessed? Again, the general answer was seemingly direct; they could convert in the private, not the public sphere. In practice this could seldom have been so straightforward. What, in this context, constituted the "private" sphere? Thus, the limits and consequences of the participation of women in church life posed a series of ever changing dilemmas that could not be resolved cleanly and simply. The question of who had the right to vote at church meetings and on what issues – the choice of the minister, for example – was subject to all sorts of complications. What was to be done about widows who could no longer claim to be virtually represented by their husbands, or about those women who contributed materially to the support of the chapel but were excluded from management decisions? These issues presented recurrent problems of authority in the chapels throughout the century. Nevertheless, from the 1740s there was a general trend for the public roles available to women in the chapels to narrow and for the scope for female autonomy, power and status to decline.[40]

On the other hand, struggles around these boundary issues also resulted in the opening of some important spaces. In the Anglican church there

[39] This class dimension is unsurprising. The gendering of the public space was a part of the process of a developing middle-class identity. See Davidoff and Hall, *Family Fortunes*, pp. 136–38; Deborah Valenze, *Prophetic Sons and Daughters* (Princeton, 1985), pp. 11, 32–38, 50, 55–60, 91–93, 277; Barker-Benfield, *Culture of Sensibility*, pp. 270–72.
[40] Davidoff and Hall, *Family Fortunes*, pp. 132–35, 141–44; Madge Dresser, "Sisters and Brethren: Power, Propriety and Gender Among the Bristol Moravians, 1746–1833," *Social History*, 21, 3 (October 1996), pp. 304–29.

was no tradition of female leadership, yet an intense altercation occurred in the early nineteenth century around the role of women in the pastoral work of the church. The practice of women auxiliaries dedicated to pastoral work began in Northampton in 1805 amid considerable controversy. Women resisted the opposition mounted by conservative churchmen; some, it was rumored, even threatened to leave their husbands rather than quit their auxiliary work. Initially, the purpose of auxiliary work was to collect money for charitable organization, but the auxiliaries soon took on a life of their own. Indeed, by 1819 over 10,000 women were employed by the Bible Society in 350 female auxiliary organizations. In this way a space was carved out in the church for a distinctly female philanthropic mission which was duplicated many times over elsewhere and by 1893 probably engaged close to a million women. It was not, of course, a radical development. The definition of charity work had been thoroughly domesticated by Hannah More, so that it was defined as a natural extension of the intimacy of the home. Philanthropy was domestic ideology writ large, and to that extent had been fully integrated into the separate spheres structure by the Victorian period proper. But the opportunities that it provided for women to claim some public space were to contribute to the destabilization of boundaries later in the century.[41]

The circumstances of the late eighteenth and early nineteenth centuries allowed a complex mix of contradictory signs to color gender relations. Closure in some areas was paralleled by openings in others. The social and political instabilities of the period permitted buried tensions to rise to the surface and move into some corner of the public space. Thus, women active in female reform societies after 1815 were frequently abused, even by the highest in the land. Viscount Castlereagh referred to such women as prostitutes. The example of Mary Tocker is an interesting illustration of the dangers that faced women who transgressed boundaries. Tocker was a member of a Devon business family who had the temerity to make public in 1818 the debts owed her by a leading landed family and to couple the complaint with charges of political corruption. Her letters to the newspapers occasioned a suit for libel in which Mary Tocker defended herself. The case became a *cause célèbre* and an occasion for a public debate about women in the public space which mobilized conservative opinion, and significantly divided radicals on the issue. Tocker herself was subjected to much ridicule precisely because of her violation of gendered codes of behavior.[42]

[41] Frank Prochaska, *Women and Philanthropy in Nineteenth-Century England* (Oxford, 1980), pp. 1–17, 23–26, 224.

[42] Jonathan Fulcher, "Gender, Politics and Class in the Early Nineteenth-Century English Reform Movement," *Historical Research*, 67, 162 (February 1994), pp. 57–74.

Two years later, of course, the Queen Caroline case in 1820 provided a similar opportunity for debate, this time around the more sensitive issue of standards of sexual and marital morality. Caroline's death and the return of economic prosperity served to put that genie back into its bottle until the agitation around Contagious Diseases Acts forty years later revived the issue of the double standard in full force. Likewise, during the 1820s, Owenite socialism was the site of an intense ideological debate over gender and sex roles. A similar, though weaker, challenge to gender exclusion in Chartism foundered on the usual problem of the absence of an alternative to domestic ideology. If Chartists were to argue for the vote, how could they prove their respectability except by demonstrating that the men could be sober and upright and the women pious and home-bound? One condition for the political radicalism of Chartism – as for all subsequent working-class radicalism – was that it endorse, rather than challenge, gender boundaries.[43]

The instability of the period from the French revolution lay precisely in the relative ease with which challenges to domestic ideology had pres-ented themselves to a series of ready audiences. Yet by the 1840s the kinds of possibilities that had been glimpsed, from Wollstonecraft to the Owenites, for alternative gender relations had been closed off. These closures were a multilayered process that included the ideological work of evangelicalism, the failures of sexual radicalism in Owenism and the practical politics of how Chartism or the factory reform movement was to build a winning political coalition. The public and the private sphere structured around a gendered ideology of domesticity was about to enter what seemed to be its period of greatest stability.

From c. 1830 to c. 1880

In fact instability was encased within the equipoise of mid-Victorian Britain. This was true at the very pinnacle of the system. Queen Victoria was emblematic not only for her representation as the model domestic figure, but also because she embodied the tensions within the system of domesticity. Although as queen she could hardly be expected to remain

---

[43] Thomas W. Laqueur, "The Queen Caroline Affair: Politics as Art in the Reign of George IV," *Journal of Modern History*, 54, 3 (September 1982), pp. 417–66. See Barbara Taylor, *Eve and the New Jerusalem: Socialism and Feminism in the Nineteenth Century* (London, 1983), for the possibilities that were lost with the demise of utopian socialism. See also Barbara Taylor, "The Men Are as Bad as the Masters . . .': Socialism, Feminism and Sexual Antagonism in the London Tailoring Trade in the 1830s," in Judith L. Newton, Mary P. Ryan and Judith Walkowitz (eds.), *Sex and Class in Women's History* (London, 1983), pp. 187–220; Anna Clark, "The Rhetoric of Chartist Domesticity: Gender, Language and Class in the 1830s and 1840s," *Journal of British Studies*, 31, 1 (January 1992), pp. 66–89; Anna Clark, *Struggle for the Breeches*, pp. 220–32.

silent in the public sphere, her enduring contribution to the practice of monarchy was the projection of monarchy as a family business. Yet Victoria's public and private lives were rent with the contradictions that reflected the ambiguities of domesticity itself. The deference to Albert and the downplaying of her political role after his death contrasted with the reality of her considerable political influence and the strength of her political opinions – revealed early on during the Bedchamber crisis of 1839. Similarly, the erotic tensions that ran through much Victorian culture were exposed in the real sexual and personal vitality involved in the queen's relationship with her ghillie John Brown. Most women in public life were less well placed to reconcile private power with public invisibility and so had to resort to different strategies of distancing.[44]

Florence Nightingale was a case in point. Although nursing, like charity work, had become a quasi-professionalized sphere for women by the middle of the nineteenth century, Nightingale's forceful excursion into the world of public policy and controversy could take place only in the special circumstances of the Crimean war. Nightingale followed this, however, by a quite literal retreat to her bed from which she conducted her very extensive "public" business as an authority and adviser on sanitary reform, nursing, army accounting and disease theory. From the privacy of her bedroom Nightingale projected her public presence through a voluminous correspondence. Communicating with virtually everyone through letters only, Nightingale used her psychoneurotic illness as a protective device which enabled her to focus entirely on work. It was a device that also endowed her with enormous influence and credibility precisely because it abjured all claims to public responsibility and attention.[45]

As these august examples suggest, the core instability within domestic ideology in the middle of the nineteenth century was the series of double standards it contained. Silence and denial were the essential conditions of maintaining a system that was inherently volatile. The model presented by Hannah More and others of reconciling domestic ideology with a role

---

[44] Dorothy Thompson, *Queen Victoria: The Woman, The Monarch and The People* (New York, 1990); Margaret Homans and Adrienne Munich, *Remaking Queen Victoria* (Cambridge, 1997), pp. 3–7; David Cannadine, "The Context, Performance and Meaning of Ritual: The British Monarchy and the Invention of Tradition', c. 1820–1977," in Eric Hobsbawm and Terence Ranger (eds.), *The Invention of Tradition* (Cambridge, 1983), pp. 101–64; Peter Gay, *The Bourgeois Experience: Victoria to Freud*, vol. I, *The Education of the Senses* (New York, 1984), for the eroticism of Victorian life. The erotic tension that could exist in Victorian life among highly driven and high-performing people is well illustrated, of course, by the contents of Gladstone's diary. For some examples, see Matthew, *Gladstone*, vol. I, *1809–1874*, pp. 92–95, 157–58, 237–42.

[45] For Nightingale, see *Ever Yours, Florence Nightingale: Selected Letters*, ed. Martha Vicinus and Bea Nergaard (Cambridge, MA, 1990), esp. pp. 1–12.

for women in selected areas of public affairs like charity for the poor was ultimately impossible to sustain. Thus, in practice domestic ideology was infused with conflict and insecurity and was frequently breached. Here I shall focus on two selective sites where this instability was revealed. Both center around the question of the double standard. The first case is how the question of property that women brought to a marriage threatened authority within the family. The second is the question of how rights over women's bodies invoked the location of the boundary between public and private spheres.

Until 1882 the law required that women's property pass to their husbands on marriage. The difficulties that this created had been recognized fairly early in the eighteenth century as the law of inheritance became increasingly relevant to expanding middling-class wealth. Thus, various legal devices had evolved which allowed wives to hold their own estates while at the same time retained the gendered separate spheres by investing control of these estates in the trust of male lawyers. A distinction was thus drawn for women between ownership and control. Although this was a practical discrimination, it suggested the difficulty of maintaining a gendered division between public and private spheres where property was concerned. If there was one category that was more important to Victorian society than either gender or class, it was surely property. Putting property and domestic ideology together in this way was a precarious conjunction which was exposed in the celebrated issue of Caroline Norton's marriage.[46]

Caroline Norton had been separated from her dissolute husband for some years before she entered the debate over divorce law and property that led to the reform of divorce law in 1857. She was an abused wife whose husband specialized in public humiliation, who had been denied access to her children, who had seen the money she brought to the marriage pillaged by her husband and who could gain no protection even when separated from him. Even the money she earned as a novelist was available for his use under the law. All of this made her case ripe for melodramatic representation. Caroline Norton was a classic example of how the existing state of the law failed to protect women when the system of domestic propriety broke down as a result of villainous male behavior. Although the Norton case was treated (by Catherine Norton and others) as an anomaly within domestic ideology and not as an inbuilt defect of the

---

[46] Rachel Harrison and Mort, "Patriarchal Aspects of Nineteenth-Century State Formation," pp. 86–87. Certain areas of the law that had allowed for independent property-holding by women were closed down in these years. In 1833, for example, the Dower Act removed the right of the widow to one-third of the real property owned by the husband. See Susan Staves, *Married Women's Separate Property in England 1660–1833* (Cambridge, MA, 1990), pp. 4–5.

system itself, it was inherently subversive of the separate spheres structure for two reasons.[47]

In the first place, Caroline Norton's behavior posed a constant challenge to the principle that the public sphere belonged to the husband. Almost from the moment of their marriage in 1826 the tension within the family spilled over to the public sphere. The granddaughter of Richard Sheridan, Caroline Norton had friends in high places. In 1838 her husband's legal denial of access to her children had dominated the discussion of the Infant Custody Act which provided some minimal remedy for women in her plight by providing mothers the right of access to children under seven years of age. Her work around this cause brought her some notoriety, but by the 1850s her novels and poetry had won her considerable acclaim. Painful though all the wrangling must have been, she challenged her husband in the courts and in the newspapers when the absurdities of the law reinforced the tyranny of her husband's behavior.

In the second place, her campaign brought together two of the most sensitive areas of separate spheres ideology – divorce and control over property. The sensitivity of the issues of divorce and separation was due to the questions that it raised about the control of property. Indeed, ultimately the connection between divorce law reform and women's property rights was too tight to be ignored, although until this point treatment and discussion of the issues had been proceeding on separate tracks. Divorce law reform had been on the political agenda since the early 1850s, but once the issue was admitted into Parliament the question of property rights could hardly be avoided. This was especially the case because mid-Victorian feminists seized on the issue and organized an extensive petitioning campaign to ensure that Parliament did not forget the connection.[48]

The Norton case thus mirrored the two issues of divorce and control of property which were legislated in the Matrimonial Causes Act of 1857. This act provided some protection for the property of women who were separated from their husbands; it secularized the divorce law and rationalized the legal procedures for divorce so that it was no longer necessary to obtain an act of Parliament. All of this was undoubtedly worthwhile, but

---

[47] The argument and material of the next few paragraphs rest entirely on the brilliant chapter 3 of Mary Poovey's *Uneven Developments: The Ideological Work of Gender in Mid-Victorian England* (Chicago, 1988), pp. 51–88; see also Caroline Norton, *Caroline Norton's Defense* (repr., Chicago, 1982), which is a reprint of *English Laws for Women in the Nineteenth Century* (1854), with an introduction by Joan Huddleston. Her other important contribution to the divorce law debate was *Letter to the Queen on Lord Chancellor Cranworth's Marriage and Divorce Bill* (1855).

[48] Philippa Levine, *Victorian Feminism, 1850–1900* (Tallahassee, 1987), pp. 135–40, has a good summary.

the measure remained very limited. The act did not make divorce any less expensive, nor did it end the double standard between men and women over the causes for divorce; nor most importantly did it remove married women's property from the control of their husbands. Yet in spite of its timidity, the act was intensely and heatedly debated in both Houses of Parliament in what resembled a kind of collective anxiety attack. Gladstone was so exercised about the act's consequences that he was reputed to have spoken 100 times in the House on the issue. Dire warnings were raised about the consequences to the social and moral fabric that would result from any measure that made divorce easier. If women were granted any degree of control over their property, it would establish an alternative center of authority within the domestic sphere. The fervid rhetoric may not have matched the ultimate result, but it did accurately reflect the instabilities and contradictions in domestic ideology that were exposed by the discussion of the issue of women's control over their own property.

The issues invoked by the debate over matrimonial causes reached into the very heart of the structure of the separate spheres and the civil division between public and private. But the awkward questions that were raised about control over property were quietly shelved – in spite of the centrality they occupied in Norton's pamphlets and the seventy petitions presented to Parliament and signed by most of the leading women of the day. The legislation of 1857 carefully limited its protections of property and earnings to deserted women only and thus preserved intact the domestic ideal of the responsible and dominant husband and the subordinate and dutiful wife. The issue of married women's property was not to be addressed by act of Parliament until 1870 when an act established protection for women's wages and savings accounts. An act of 1882 treated women for the first time as independent economic entities in their own right – an admission that thereby removed the rationale for their exclusion from the franchise.

The limited result of this debate in the 1850s, however, reflected the confinement of the critique of domestic ideology safely within the boundaries of separate spheres discourse. The convention whereby the logic of women's actions was not allowed to contradict the ideology of domesticity evolved in the eighteenth century and was honed to a fine art by Hannah More. Mid-Victorian women fully maintained this convention. Caroline Norton was entirely within this tradition. She quite explicitly rejected the idea of sexual equality, regarded women's inferiority as God-given and not socially constructed, and willingly conceded that women should submit to the authority of the husband. Only when the husband failed in *his* duty was it appropriate for the private sphere to be invaded by the state in the interests of preserving the domestic ideal. That is, she appealed to the rhetoric of domesticity itself to redress the wrongs done to her and other women.

There was nothing unique about Norton in this respect. The only strategy available to Victorian feminists after the 1830s was to seek out contradictions in domestic ideology itself and use them to lever gains. But demanding that men live up to their obligations exposed the double standard on which the system rested. By effectively protesting the double standard that lay at the heart of the separate spheres system, Norton at one and the same time both drew attention to the instabilities within the system of the public–private division and in equal measure shied away from the logic of her argument, ambiguously raising, then denying the claim for equal treatment. Thus, the rhetorical strategy of this argument reinforced the very domesticity that it also possessed the potential to undermine.[49]

The double standard of domestic ideology was therefore inherently unstable. These instabilities were revealed most sharply by the campaign for the repeal of the Contagious Diseases Acts from 1869 to 1886. The Contagious Diseases Acts were an attempt to control venereal disease in garrison towns by awarding police and magistrates wide powers to stop, search and send for medical inspection any woman they suspected of prostitution. Refusal to submit to medical examination was punishable by imprisonment. The necessity for such regulation had been a frequent topic of discussion as a public health issue since the 1830s and considerable support for regulation existed in the garrison towns and beyond. A pilot measure passed originally in 1864 was extended and made permanent in 1869. But the acts were immediately controversial because of their overt transgression of the boundaries between the public and the private. This was true on at least two counts.

In the first place, the acts violated basic civil liberties – contemplation of which should inspire a rethinking of the categories of Victorian liberalism. In effect, the acts permitted any woman to be hauled before a magistrate and inspected. Aside from the major constitutional issues this implied, it undercut the huge investment in notions of respectability among the working class. The reality was, of course, that no self-evidently middle-class woman would be the target of police attention. The act reinforced the importance of dress codes and public gesture and demeanor as signifiers of respectability for the working class. But the prospect of reputable wives of skilled craftsmen being dragged off the streets

---

[49] See her arguments in 1839 around the Infant Custody Bill for good examples of this: Pearce Stevenson [Caroline Norton], *A Plain Letter to the Lord Chancellor on the Infant Custody Bill* (London, 1839); Mary Lyndon Shanley, *Feminism, Marriage and the Law in Victorian England, 1850–1895* (Princeton, 1989), pp. 10–17, 74–76, 103.

into the courts was a major reason for working-class support of the campaign for repeal. In the second place, and most dramatically, the acts endorsed the symbolic and arbitrary rape of women by the state. The ultimate sanction of the acts was the brutal speculum penetration of the woman's vaginal cavity on mere suspicion of prostitution. By 1886 when the acts were finally repealed, over 5,000 women had been subjected to this indignity without any evidence of venereal disease.[50]

The fact that these were working-class women certainly made such transgressions easier to contemplate, and may explain why the acts occasioned very little debate by the upper- and middle-class male Parliament. Working-class bodies were conceptualized and represented as qualitatively different from those of the elite classes. They were seen as potentially diseased, degenerate carriers of viruses of social disorder. Working-class anatomy was easily regarded as available for various social experiments. This had been demonstrated earlier in the century when the Anatomy Act of 1832 had made pauper corpses freely available for medical dissection. The prostitute targets of the Contagious Diseases Acts were particularly threatening specimens of this reflex that working-class bodies were both dangerous infections and freely available. Prostitutes were free laborers who upended the dominant definition of that term. They exploited sin, and their bodies were incubators of disease and dirt. They epitomized the female sexuality that domestic ideology historically feared lurked beneath the carefully presented facade of *all* womanhood.[51]

The Contagious Diseases Acts were not simply acts of class and gender hypocrisy, however. They offended the deepest principles of voluntarist moral reform. These acts give the lie to the notion of the Victorian state as a laissez-faire formation. Their interventionism transgressed the most intimate boundaries of the public and private spheres. Paradoxically, therefore, it was the opposition to the acts that was "Victorian" in its demand for modesty and restraint. The hypocrisy and sanctification of the double standard that was reflected in the acts themselves belonged to a much older tradition. The acts' opponents resented the endorsement of sin by the state; they also believed the remedy for these kinds of social problems lay in voluntary association rescue work. In a sense, then – and I would not wish to press this point too far – the campaign against the Contagious Diseases Acts stood at the end point of this tradition of interventionism by voluntary associations that had first emerged in the late seventeenth century.

---

[50] For the social history of the acts, see Judith Walkowitz, *Prostitution and Victorian Society: Women, Class and the State* (Cambridge, 1980).

[51] See Ruth Richardson, *Death, Dissection and the Destitute* (London, 1988); Mary Poovey, *Making A Social Body: British Cultural Formation 1830–1864* (Chicago, 1995), chs. 3, 4.

There was irony, too, in the fact that, although the opposition to the acts was rooted in the politics of libertarianism, its ultimate success did not result in a triumph for the Victorian ideal of individual freedom from state intervention. The legacy of the campaign to repeal the acts was not to reaffirm the boundary between the public and the private. The result, rather, was to force the displacement of existing boundaries between the public and private and legitimate a new kind of interventionism – one of the immediate forms of which was a particularly nasty social purity movement mobilized by W. T. Stead, who was to lead the cry for increased state regulation and supervision of morality.[52]

The repeal campaign depended on exposing the contradictions and ambiguities of the double standard. To do this, however, was implicitly to raise the whole question of the boundaries between the public and private.[53] Like earlier campaigns around women's issues, the opposition to the Contagious Diseases Acts was articulated through the presumptions of domestic ideology itself. The solution to a supposedly inherent powerful need for male sexual release, Josephine Butler argued, was for men to adopt the same kind of chaste restraint demanded of women. This argument was fully within the tradition of domestic ideology that forswore challenge and confrontation – although it did mean denying dominant opinion in the medical world that men's nature demanded sexual release and was not inherently chaste. Butler was merely asking that men live up to the same standards as women; she was not denying that personalities were gendered.

Butler's objection to the laws was of the same order as Caroline Norton's protests against the law on women's property rights: that they violated the sanctity and purity of domesticity by legitimating a social evil, that they were based upon a misreading of human nature and that they violated the rights and liberties of women. Butler's complaint was against the way the laws disrupted the boundary between the public and the

[52] Josephine Butler, *Personal Reminiscences of a Great Crusade* (London, 1896), pp. 8–12; Bristow, *Vigilance and Vice*, p. 78.

[53] William Acton, the medical theorist and supporter of the acts, clearly recognized this. His matter-of-fact attitude toward prostitution was as subversive of domestic ideology as the opponents of the measures. Acton argued that prostitution should be treated like any other trade in terms of supply and demand and that women should be allowed to ply it if they wished. Acton did not believe free trade in sex was a warrant for men's licentiousness. In fact, the reverse was true. Men should be punished for behavior that interfered with the market economy in sex. He proposed that fathers be made responsible for their bastards, that facilities be provided for procuring affiliation orders and that pregnant women be assisted during their confinement. Such legislation, he believed, would diminish seduction, illegitimacy and infanticide. The possibility of *this* kind of discourse framing the issue was closed out because its open acceptance of sin offended the moral code that the repeal agitation tapped into. See William Acton, *Prostitution*, intro. and ed. Peter Fryer (2nd edn., London, 1969 [1869]), pp. 21–28.

private by sanctifying an intrusion into the private dignity of women and legitimating a code of immorality. Indeed, she wanted to reinforce the barriers these boundaries presented against the transgression of the state into the most private of private spheres.[54]

Despite these conservative aims, however, in questioning the definitions on which separate spheres rested, the campaign was bound to touch sensitive nerves. The initial reaction to the movement's manifesto was – Butler claimed – intense discomfort in the House of Commons followed by a conspiracy of silence in the newspapers. Once the campaign was taken into the public sphere and protest meetings arranged in the provinces, the response was frequently organized violence. Ribald comments were witnessed by Butler in the House of Commons' debates on motions to repeal the acts. In the manner of Castlereagh, Sir James Elphistone was apoplectically led to proclaim the leaders of the repeal agitation worse whores than the outcast women they defended. It was deeply ironic, therefore, that final repeal of the Contagious Diseases Acts in 1886 did not represent a triumph for the anti-statist politics that had motivated the campaign against them.[55]

Indeed, repeal brought to the surface existing tensions within the repeal movement. Josephine Butler's libertarian faction confronted those crusaders for social purity who were moral interventionists. The social purity wing of the movement had been increasingly in evidence since the early 1880s. It had forced a reluctant Butler into an alliance with newspaper editor W. T. Stead who was running a series of sensationalist campaigns around child prostitution and white slavery. Pressure from this wing of the movement had led to a clause in the Industrial Schools Amendment Act of 1880 giving police the right to enter premises believed to be brothels and remove children from their mothers. Butler had opposed this measure as an unconscionable intrusion on the rights of mothers. But her supporters were increasingly marginalized as the social purity zealots led by Laura Ormiston Chant moved to the fore. The formation of the National Vigilance Association in 1885 by W. T. Stead marked the real break with the tradition of feminism that looked to the private sphere for moral reform through voluntary associ-

---

[54] Butler, *Reminiscences*, pp. 18–19, 78–80. The original address of the repeal movement which Butler reproduces on pp. 18–19 reveals the way libertarian issues combined with the exposure of the contradictions of the separate spheres. At one point she remarks that the issue of the campaign was "where ought human legislation to terminate."

[55] Walkowitz, *Prostitution and Society*, pp. 81–82. Butler gave a long account of a debate she had with a French advocate of regulation, which revolved around their different conceptions of women; he regarded the increase in vice due to the greater seduction by women; she objected to the ignoring of the responsibilities of men. See Butler, *Reminiscences*, pp. 17–21, 124–30, 176.

ation activity. The new leadership eagerly embraced the use of state power to identify, categorize and eliminate moral evil. The contagious diseases campaign had exposed the contradictions and instabilities in the ideology that underlay the public and private spheres of civil society and had ended up contributing to a shift in the very ordering of those spheres.[56]

Shifting boundaries in the late nineteenth century

The consequences of the repeal of the Contagious Diseases Acts were therefore to breach the boundaries between public and private spheres that the campaign had originally intended to reassert. In this dialectic, the contagious diseases campaign was not unique. It was, in fact, but one in a string of mounting challenges to the traditional balance between the public sphere, the private sphere and the state. The end result was a disruption of the terrain and boundaries of the public and private spheres. This was a prolonged process. The recomposition of what belonged in the public sphere and what was the property of the private sphere did not assume a settled shape until the passage was forced by the First World War. I am interested in highlighting some of the means by which the old boundaries were breached. How the new structures were evolved is another story.

It is necessary to remark, however, that this was a development generally conceived of as a transition from individualism to collectivism. This understanding was a contemporary convention expressed most completely by A. V. Dicey. But collectivism as it came to be understood in the twentieth century was not implicit in the dynamic I have been describing here. Indeed, the disruptions to the balance between the private, the public and state were often inspired (as could be anticipated) more by the principles of the past than the promise of the future. More precisely, from the 1880s, the process of disruption to the old terrains opened the possibility to alternative configurations; it did not preordain how those configurations were to be shaped. That was the matter to be decided by politics. Indeed, how to define and fill the public sphere and its relationship with the private sphere and the state provided the central axis of politics from the 1880s. Within and between the political parties, the key policy debate was between various kinds of "libertarian" and "collectivist" policies and programs.

[56] Walkowitz, *Prostitution and Victorian Society*, pp. 248–52; Walkowitz, *City of Dreadful Delight* (Chicago, 1993), for the moral panic of the 1880s and Stead's role in it; M. J. D. Roberts, "Feminism and the State in Later Victorian England," *Historical Journal*, 31, 1 (March 1995), pp. 96–104.

Thus, in calling on the force of the state to enforce their definition of morality, the social purity activists had no intention of creating the social welfare bureaucracy of the twentieth century. Yet this was one of the end results of their enthusiastic pursuit of virtue. The increased interventionism of the state in the private sphere that began in the 1880s derived more from the same variety of moral panic that had spawned the Societies for the Reformation of Manners a century before. Indeed, on a superficial level the ingredients were quite similar. A series of political challenges converged with intellectual, social and cultural disruptions of landscapes. In this atmosphere of "crisis," childhood and prostitution were highlighted again in the efforts of social reformers.

Similarly, there remained plenty of scope for voluntary association initiative on the pattern of the past. The role of the state was still largely conceived of as ancillary to private efforts. The classic example, of course, noted in an earlier chapter, was the partnership of the poor law authorities and the Charity Organisation Society to address the question of poverty systematically. Social purity groups followed the same strategy in the 1890s against the supposed opportunities for immorality provided by the music halls. Temperance advocates and other watchdogs of public morality joined hands to demand that local authorities enforce higher standards of inspection against prostitutes soliciting in the music halls. The same strategy was followed by organizations such as the National Association for the Prevention of Cruelty to Children, which was formed in the 1880s. In Bradford, for example, the association employed three full-time inspectors in the 1890s to investigate cases of child abuse and neglect which they drew to the attention of the police to prosecute.[57]

As might be expected, however, it was in the world of the poor where the shifting frontiers of public, private and state spheres were most obviously in motion. In that world, surveillance was the usual herald of new boundaries between the spheres of civil society. Surveillance of the poor intensified, its techniques multiplied. The prying voluntary association continued to be important. The domestic visitor tradition continued – Mrs. Bosanquet, Mary Loane and Beatrice Webb were celebrated examples – but they were now joined by the professional social

---

[57] In London there was a strict architectural, engineering and alcohol licensing system for the Halls administered by the London County Council which also included moral surveillance. The Progressive Party was the main upholder of this system. See Susan Pennybacker, "It Was Not What She Said, But the Way in Which She Said It': The London County Council and the Music Halls," and, for similar contests in Manchester, see Chris Walters, "Manchester Morality and London Capital: The Battle over the Palace of Varieties," both in Peter Bailey, *Music Hall: The Business of Pleasure* (Milton Keynes, 1986), pp. 120–39 and pp. 141–61 respectively.

worker. These were increasingly hired by government bodies. Manchester council employed welfare visitors for the first time in the 1890s.[58]

The question of children provide us with some illuminating examples of these mobile frontiers. The 1870 Education Act established a locally based system of primary education. It also provided for the appointment of school attendance officers to enforce attendance and to administer the fee structure which remained a feature of primary education until 1891. By 1877 there were over 200 of these officers in London alone. They combined the social work of surveying all children of school age in their district with issuing summons for truancy and nonpayment of fees. Truant schools were established for persistent offenders, industrial schools utilized for the homeless and, in 1886 alone, for example, over 12,000 summons were issued for the nonpayment of fees. The knowledge these officers held of neighborhoods was deep and intimate. Charles Booth relied upon them as informants for his survey of the London poor in the 1880s.[59]

The question of child abuse was another area in which the sources of authority and responsibility were moving to a new footing. Abuse of children had been a longstanding subject for moral intervention. However, it was typically children without the protection of family – orphans – who were the subject of attention, and local rescue work had been the typical strategy. The Society for the Prevention of Cruelty to Children, formed in 1884, marked the appearance on the national stage of an aggressive new pressure group. Their alliance with the (also newly formed) Barnardo movement led to legislation for the "better prevention of cruelty to children" in 1889.

This act was a pathbreaking measure. It awarded the state powers that had previously belonged solidly in the private world of parental authority. Under its provisions justices were permitted to authorize the police to enter private homes when there was evidence of child abuse. If parents were convicted of cruelty to their children, the courts gained the right to consign the children to the care of other relatives, industrial schools or reformatories. At the same time, poor law guardians were expanding their authority over the care of indigent children, sometimes establishing their own nurseries and setting up foster care systems. The eugenically inspired interest in techniques of mothering to build (a bit belatedly) an imperial race led to the appointment in some places of female sanitary inspectors who were empowered to enter working-class homes to provide instruc-

---

[58] Ittman, *Work, Gender and Family Life*, pp. 166, 178.
[59] Ross McKibbin, *The Ideologies of Class: Social Relations in Britain 1880–1950* (Oxford, 1990), ch. 6; David Rubenstein, *School Attendance in London 1870–1904: A Social History* (Hull, 1969), pp. 46–48, 53, 105.

tion on child care and, of course, to also monitor behavior. Growing out of these local developments, the Infant Protection Act of 1897 greatly expanded the competence of Boards of Guardians to deal with cases of child neglect.[60]

The expanding scope of social interventionism in childhood reflected the redefinition of the category of the child. In large measure this was due to W. T. Stead's exposure of the market for child prostitution – a key event in the moral panic of the 1880s. Stead's staged purchase of a child virgin introduced to the public arena the question of the age of consent. After much debate and discussion, the Criminal Law Amendment Act of 1885 set the age of consent at thirteen and created a new crime of "gross defilement" which was intended to cover such practices as Stead had exposed. At about the same time, Andrew Mearns published his "Bitter Cry of Outcast London" where the question of incest was openly broached. Mearns bluntly stated what Sir John Simon and other knowledgeable mid-Victorians could only hint at: that "incest is common" in the rookeries of outcast London. This revelation was even more explosive than Stead's disclosures, for it touched, of course, one of the unspoken aspects of Victorian sexuality. Unsurprisingly, it took many years of pressure and presentation of evidence from the National Vigilance Association and the NSPCC to convince the Home Office to move legislatively to address the problem. In 1908 incest was officially recognized as a crime by the state. Legislation removed jurisdiction for the legal treatment of incest from the scope of the church courts where it had always belonged (apart from a brief moment in the 1650s) and placed it under the authority of the criminal code.[61]

Incest was not the only example of the internal reconfiguration of the private sphere of the family after 1880. Family law was beginning to qualify the patriarchal sovereignty of the father. In addition to the enhanced degree of financial autonomy provided by the Married Women's Property Act of 1882, mothers gained new and extended rights to custody over the children. Indeed the two – property and motherhood – were naturally connected. Both the 1870 and 1882 women's property acts were followed by acts that strengthened women's custody rights over

[60] Jane Lewis, "The Working-Class Wife and Mother and State Intervention," in Lewis (ed.), *Labour and Love: Women's Experience of Home and Family 1850–1914* (Oxford, 1986), pp. 99–120; Ittman, *Work, Gender and Family Life*, p. 179; Behlmer, *Child Abuse and Moral Reform*, p. 109; Shanley, *Feminism, Marriage and the Law*, pp. 151–55; Cunningham, *Children of the Poor*, pp. 190–217, for the explosion of studies of children and childhood in the period.

[61] Andrew Means, *The Bitter Cry of Outcast London*, ed. and intro. Anthony Wohl (Leicester, 1970), p. 61; Victor Bailey and Sheila Blackburn, "The Punishment of Incest Act 1908: A Case Study of Law Creation," *Criminal Law Review*, November 1979, pp. 708–18.

children. Beginning with the Infant Custody Act of 1873 and extended considerably by an act of 1886, separated women were granted equal rights over the children. In addition, parliamentary legislation in 1878 and 1895 began to address the question of wife abuse. The former gave wives the right to appeal to courts for a separation order in the case of mistreatment by the husband. The latter expanded a wife's autonomy by making it possible for her to leave an abusive marriage before securing a separation order and without surrendering her rights. The scope and effects of these changes in the law should not be exaggerated. Nevertheless, they do provide a sharp contrast to the conception of family authority that had existed but a short time before.[62]

The erosion of separate spheres ideology inevitably threw into contention definitions of gender and sexuality. New kinds of instabilities appear in gender and sexual categories. In the Salvation Army, for example, gender equity was prized more highly than in similar moral reforming organizations. Women were granted more equality; they were dressed in the same uniform as the men and were exposed to the same dangers of the slums and the pubs. By the same token, the Salvation Army projected an alternative version of masculinity to that of the cloth-capped Victorian artisan. Salvationist men were not effete, as their willingness to face the taunts, jeers and abuse of hooligans demonstrated. Nor did they shy away from the seamy sides of lower-class life. The male culture of the Salvation Army challenged the rough and exclusively male culture of the pub, the street and the racetrack, proclaiming a masculinity that was gentle and caring. This was a theme for the new man of the 1890s. Family roles even in working-class households were more flexible than before, with the husband sharing more of the housework and child care. Even if this was only a tendency and not a trend, it reflected nevertheless a significant departure from the model of gender roles that underlay the domestic ideology of the separate spheres.[63]

Other aspects of changing conceptions of gender and sexuality were somewhat more ambivalent. Since the content of domestic ideology could no longer be relied upon to provide a clear directory to gender roles and behavior, it was necessary to seek new sources of stability. The major

---

[62] Shanley, *Feminism, Marriage and the Law*, pp. 14–17, 131, 151–55; Rachel Harrison and Mort, "Patriarchal Aspects of Nineteenth-Century State Formation," p. 96.

[63] Paul Thompson, *The Edwardians: The Remaking of British Society* (London, 1975), pp. 297–307; Robert Roberts, *The Classic Slum: Salford Life in the First Quarter of the Century* (Harmondsworth, 1973), p. 54; Standish Meacham, *A Life Apart: The English Working Class 1890–1914* (Cambridge, MA, 1977), p. 117; Pamela J. Walker, "'I Live But Not Yet I for Christ Liveth in Me': Men and Masculinity in the Salvation Army 1865–1890," in Michael Roper and John Tosh (eds.), *Manful Assertions: Masculinities in Britain Since 1800* (London, 1991), pp. 92–112; Keith McClelland, "Masculinity and the Representative Artisan' in Britain, 1850–1880," in Roper and Tosh, *Manful Assertions*, pp. 74–79.

response to this instability from the 1880s was to attempt to restabilize sexual difference by formalistic differentiations that rested on legal, social and medical criteria. The lines of moral behavior were more openly drawn by the social purity legislation of the 1880s; the category of the prostitute, the homosexual or the child abuser was scientifically defined and dissected by sociological and medical science.

Changes in the law on prostitution in the 1880s, for example, changed the public significance and meaning of behavior. Conduct that previously had been vaguely defined now became formally classified in ways that changed identified meaning. The greater power given to the police to challenge suspected soliciting and the more precise definitions of the crime of prostitution that developed in the 1880s made it even more important for respectable women to dissociate themselves from any suspicion of belonging to the category of prostitute. Sexual crimes become more closely defined, and new ones such as indecency between men and gross defilement of minors were devised. All of this had the effect of drawing sharp and public lines between what was respectable and disrespectable behavior, and employing the authority of the state to certify and sanction such dividing lines. One result, ironically, was that the objective of abolishing prostitution by elevating the moral life of the society – the aim of reformers before this point – was abandoned. Prostitution now was treated as a problem for the state to manage and to regulate.[64]

A particularly keen example of these themes was afforded by the redefinition of homosexuality. A gay subculture had existed in London from the late seventeenth century which was episodically persecuted by the law. Until the end of the nineteenth century, however, neither the law nor the common culture had a clear understanding of what constituted homosexual behavior. The word "homosexual" itself did not appear until the late 1860s. Prosecutions under the law on sodomy (which went back to 1533) were extremely rare. Likewise, although male prostitution was hardly unknown, it was not a major aspect of homosexual culture until the nineteenth century. There was no distinction drawn in the law between acts of sodomy with men or women or, for that matter, animals. By the mid-1880s, however, redefinitions of sexuality were firmly on the agenda of politics. The "modern" legal and social definition of homosexuality dates from the additions sponsored by Henry Labouchere to the Criminal Law Amendment Act of 1885.

Labouchere's amendment was very much the product of the quirky Radical MP from Northampton, yet it was consonant with the growing practice of the medical world to classify certain behaviors as pathologies.

---

[64] Weekes, *Sex, Politics and Society*, pp. 90–91.

The importance of the amendment was that for the first time it attached a detailed precision to the meaning of homosexual acts. There was a certain symmetry to this, for the main intent of the act which Labouchere amended was to establish the age limits for heterosexual intercourse. The amendment defined as homosexual a whole range of acts of "gross indecency" that could not be classified as buggery. Mutual masturbation between men (previously not a crime at all), for example, qualified now as homosexual behavior, making its practitioners liable for imprisonment. A new level of intervention against homosexuality was inaugurated which had not existed before. It was now possible for the state to invade the most private of private spheres in the name of the public moral interest. Acts committed in the privacy of the home were now made liable to criminal prosecution.[65]

The license to invade the sanctuary of the private sphere in this arena signified a displacement of the boundaries that had traditionally separated the individual from the state. The categories that defined civil society were being dispersed; the boundaries that delineated its component parts were destabilized. The repercussions of this destruction were felt throughout all the institutions of civil society.[66] It was at the threshold of these boundaries that people like Josephine Butler stood in the 1880s. She had operated from premises that assumed the virtue of a wide space to the "private" sphere. It was exactly an assault on this sphere that led her to take up the campaign against the intrusions of the Contagious

---

[65] Norton Rictor, *Mother Clap's Molly House: Gay Subculture in England 1700–1830* (London, 1992), pp. 15–32, 261; Randolph Trumbach, "Gender and the Homosexual Role in Modern Western Culture: The Eighteenth and Nineteenth Centuries Compared," in Dennis Altman et al. (eds.), *Which Homosexuality?* (London, 1989), pp. 149–69; Trumbach, "London's Sodomites: Homosexual Behavior and Western Culture in the Eighteenth Century," *Journal of Social History*, 11 (Fall 1977), pp. 1–33; Richard Davenport-Hines, *Sex, Death and Punishment: Attitudes to Sex and Sexuality in Britain Since the Renaissance* (London, 1990), pp. 130–35; Weekes, *Sex, Politics and Society*, pp. 99–109; Rachel Harrison and Mort, "Patriarchal Aspects of State Formation," pp. 101–06; Walkowitz, *City of Dreadful Delight*, pp. 205–08. The definition of homosexuality in legal terms and the creation of the crime of gross indecency were followed by the Vagrancy Act of 1898 which subjected men convicted of importuning to six months' imprisonment.

[66] In the world of trade unions, the question of the limits of the collective will over the autonomy of the individual was a persistent site of contention. This was the subtext of the Taff Vale Case of 1899. It was the main text of the Osborne Case of 1909 which upheld the rights of the private individual to opt out of the collective decision of his union. The responsibility of the state to supervise the private world of these (and other) voluntary associations was an equally bright topic of dispute. For this theme generally, see N. Soldon, "Laissez-Faire as Dogma: The Liberty and Property Defence League, 1882–1914," in Kenneth D. Brown (ed.), *Essays in Anti-Labour History: Responses to the Rise of Labour in Britain* (London, 1974), pp. 208–33; Michael Klarman, "Osborne: A Judgement Gone Too Far?," *English Historical Review*, 103, 406 (January 1988), pp. 21–39.

Diseases Act. When, in the early 1880s, however, she was confronted with the prospect of joining Stead in his social purity campaign and swallowing its willingness to trample over the sanctity of home, family and motherhood in the name of moral reform, she hesitated, torn between the choice of fighting a clearly defined moral cause (childhood prostitution) and joining a crusade that violated her sense of where the frontier between the state and the individual should lie. Butler joined forces with Stead in his vigilance campaign. It proved to be a most unhappy alliance. She was deeply embarrassed by Stead's gross disrespect for the rights of the individuals he used to publicize his various causes. And she soon removed herself from this particular campaign. Butler, and those like her, had used the discourse of domestic ideology to spotlight its own contradictions and ambiguities. The immoral illogicalities of the double standards that domesticity spawned had been relentlessly exposed by these mid-Victorian feminists. Unknowingly they had launched a process that placed into contention the architecture of civil society itself. In so doing, the ground had been readied for the disruption of the boundaries of civil society between the private and public worlds and the responsibilities of the state.[67]

[67] M. J. D. Roberts, "Feminism and the State," pp. 99–103.

7 Exclusion and inclusion: the political consequences of 1688

The ambiguities of 1688

It is difficult not to be amazed at the ease with which a ruling monarch was dislodged in 1688–89. The revolution of 1688 became the admired centerpiece of the Whig interpretation of modern British history precisely because it was bloodless, gradualist and conservative. But understanding the significance of 1688 for the subsequent history of British politics must begin with recognizing the cynical audacity of the event. It was a coterie of the ruling class – there really is no other name for it – who conspired and collaborated with William of Orange's decision to invade. The gentry of England refused to fight for their constitutional monarch; his closest associates (even members of his own family) deserted him in droves. And it was the Lords and Commons combined who offered the throne to William and Mary with the understanding that they would recognize certain constitutional niceties.[1]

The central nicety, of course, was that the joint monarchs accept limited power and shared governance with Parliament. The dual monarchy of William and Mary – in itself an unheard-of constitutional innovation – was created in negotiation with Parliament. And as if to drive the point home, their reigns were dated from the moment the crown was offered and accepted and not from the date that James II had departed so unceremoniously.[2] The revolutionary quality of 1688–89 lay in the resolution of the problem that dominated and occasionally paralyzed English politics throughout the seventeenth century: how was the principle of monarchy to be reconciled with the presence of representative politics?

[1] Edmund Burke a century later recognized full well the effrontery of the event when he termed it a just civil war, the only means available when it was necessary to remove the king. See J. G. A. Pocock, "The Fourth English Civil War: Dissolution, Desertion and Alternative Histories in the Glorious Revolution," in Lois Schwoerer (ed.), *The Revolution of 1688–1689: Changing Perspectives* (Cambridge, 1992), pp. 52–53.

[2] This was a significant departure from past practice. At the Restoration in 1660 the interregnum was ignored and the reign dated the moment Charles I had lost his throne.

Naturally, it is only in retrospect that the issue of 1688 may be formulated so exactly. The intent of the "reluctant revolutionaries" of 1688 was shrouded in uncertainty and ambiguity.[3] The divergent intentions that animated the arteries of the political world in 1688 are ultimately not very significant. The objectives of the actors did not govern the subsequent course of events. When Lords and Commons declared that James had abdicated and that the throne could therefore be offered to William and Mary, a political dynamic was initiated that moved beyond the orbit intended by the seven original signatories of the letter of invitation to William in Holland.

The Revolution and its consequences should not be reduced to simple exclusionary formulations. Nevertheless, for my argument two key truths followed from 1688. In the first place the definition of liberty shifted decisively away from meaning an award that flowed *from* monarchs. Liberty was now inescapably established as a right that resided *in* the body of the people. The Declaration of Rights established the fact of monarchy as a contract between monarch and people – or at least some of the people. The notion of liberty as derived from a social covenant was not a new rendition; it lies in the tradition that produced the Magna Carta. Nor, it is important to stress, was this version held with untrammeled conviction after 1689. Neither history nor constitutional precedent provided indisputable justification for this version of civil society. Indeed, the reverse was true. Royalists and divine righters held all the trumping constitutional arguments in principle and in practice. This reality explains much of the hesitancy and uncertainty that accompanied 1688 and its aftermath. Nevertheless, we may judge this moment as the instant when the discourse of liberty was displaced from a kingly foundation to a footing that sought legitimation from a slightly wider public.

The most obvious constitutional consequence of 1688–89 was institutional. The second truth about 1688 and its wake was that Parliament was assured a crucial place in the governing processes of the country. In W. A. Speck's spare and penetrating observation, Parliament was now transformed from an event to an institution. This was not simply because of Parliament's pivotal role in the events of 1688 itself. The entanglement of Britain in William's European diplomacy after 1689 clamped Parliament to the process of governing. William's intervention in English affairs had been driven in the first place by his priorities as Stadtholder of the Netherlands and leader of the Protestant alliance and it soon became evident that Parliament was needed to finance the wars that William was obliged to fight. The unintended outcome was to provide the ultimate

---

[3] W. A. Speck, *Reluctant Revolutionaries* (Oxford, 1988).

justification for classifying 1688 as a Revolution; no future monarch could contemplate a replay of James II's attempt to bridle the key institutions of the nation.[4]

The events of 1688 choked off the possibility of absolutism. Equally, 1688 introduced new kinds of ambiguity and instability into the political world. There was greater consensus about the deposition of a legitimate monarch than there was about what should follow his removal. There was no agreement, for example, about which narrative could best explain how 1688 had happened. Almost one-half of the Lords and a good third of the Commons opposed proclaiming the throne vacant by virtue of James's abdication. Sharp differences prevailed over the intent and purpose of the foundational documents of the constitutional monarchy that followed 1688: the Declaration of Rights and the Toleration Act of 1689. It required about a century and a half before the conventions that governed the power of the monarchy in relation to Parliament were fully clarified. Similarly, the importance of the Toleration Act for recognizing the religious pluralism of society should not be dismissed. Yet it barely expanded the scope of religious freedom, and the civic freedoms of non-Anglicans continued to be surrounded by impediments.[5]

The 1690s were dominated by the tussle between monarch and Parliament as to where their respective lines of authority lay. It is amusing to record that even his Dutch experience had not prepared William for the challenges of dealing with Parliament. He was noted to have remarked that the "Stadtholder-King" was a king in Holland and a Stadtholder in England. When the Act of Settlement was passed in 1701, it had two purposes. The first was to declare the Hanoverian succession if Anne died without issue; and the second, perhaps as importantly, was to delimit further the power of the monarchy in response to the past decade of struggle with William. Even so, Anne and her successors were by no means reduced to political ciphers; they always had to be factored into the political calculus. The significance of 1688 therefore lay not only in its resolution of major issues of constitutional balance. An equally important

---

[4] The literature on 1688 is enormous, of course. I have found the following books most illuminating for my purposes: G. M. Trevelyan, *The English Revolution 1688–1689* (London, 1938), whose interpretation remains remarkably intact; Speck, *Reluctant Revolutionaries*; J. R. Jones, *The Revolution of 1688 in England* (London, 1972); John Morrill, "A Glorious Resolution?" and "The Sensible Revolution, 1688," both in his *Nature of the English Revolution* (London, 1993), pp. 392–418 and 419–54 respectively; Howard Nenner, "Liberty, Law and Property: The Constitution in Retrospect from 1689," in J. R. Jones, *Liberty Secured?: Britain Before and After 1688* (Palo Alto, CA, 1992), pp. 89–121; Lois Schwoerer, *The Declaration of Rights, 1689* (Baltimore, 1981).

[5] The last monarch to seriously entertain notions that he could determine the shape of his government was George IV. See Briggs, *Age of Improvement*, pp. 184–90; Brock, *Lord Liverpool and Liberal Toryism*, pp. 57–67.

legacy was the introduction of new kinds of instability into the political system and political culture. The next 200 years were shaped as much by this legacy of 1688 as they were by the glory of the defeat of absolutism.[6]

The deposition of a legitimate king in 1688 had been justified by an appeal to the sovereignty of popular will. Henceforth the political system rested on the concept of a political nation outside a theory of monarchy. This was the crucial nexus of ambiguity that was to constitute the pivotal issue for politics in the future. There was no given answer to the question of where the boundaries of the political nation were to be drawn. No consensus existed on how to decide who was and who was not to be considered a political citizen. The eighteenth-century obsession with constitutional and legal codification, the intense debate about the principles of constitutionalism and the felt need to establish a philosophical and moral basis for politics all reflected the way 1688 had settled one constitutional issue only to open a Pandora's box of even greater complexity.

Thus, the allure of a divine right monarchy in the political culture of the eighteenth century was not merely a reflex of decaying Jacobitism. It mirrored the genuine tension of a political system that encased democratic forms and the discourse of liberty within structures of authority that were soaked with paternalist assumptions. In the early part of the eighteenth-century common constitutional parlance reconciled divine right with representative government by insinuating a determinist providence that had miraculously provided replacement monarchs (William and Mary) for one who had fled (James). This mildly ludicrous aspect of eighteenth-century political philosophy – so different from the high-minded civic humanism usually proposed as the main current of the age – offered a belief system that was hardly compatible with the age of reason. Its presence signaled the ambiguous inheritance of 1688.[7]

The dilemma that 1688 posed for the political system permeated the theory of government presented first by John Locke and embraced by the Whigs as the justification for parliamentary initiative over the shape of the monarchy. Locke recognized that political authority was secured by a contractarian (although he used the term "trust") relationship between government and society. Furthermore, this contract was largely a voluntary relationship; it was not patriarchially preordained. The outstanding features of Locke's theory were its openness and its uneasily contained

---

[6] Morrill, "The Sensible Revolution, 1688," pp. 434–37, 444–45, 452–53; for Queen Anne's influence in politics, see Geoffrey Holmes, *British Politics in the Age of Anne* (London, 1967), pp. 194–216.

[7] On this, see J. P. Kenyon, *Revolution Principles: The Politics of Party 1689–1720* (Cambridge, 1977); J. C. D. Clark, *English Society*, pp. 119–41, 175–79.

contradictions. Locke placed property at the center of the origins and purpose of civil society. It was to protect property that men convened into civil association and it was property that bestowed men's stake and interest in civil society. Yet Locke was well aware that this begged the question of what was meant by property. Property was not essential; it was created by labor. The prior question was whether a man's labor was not also a form of property and, if so, what were its implications for the organization of political structures.

Locke spent a lot of time grappling with this issue. Yet it remained an unresolved ambiguity at the heart of his thinking which permitted Lockean theories to be used to justify a wide range of social and political arrangements. Locke can be read as providing a philosophical justification for a range of political constructions from pure individualism to some form of communitarianism. In this ambiguity Locke expressed the implicit conundrum of the revolution settlement: how to avoid the logic of a republican political order and how to refuse the lower classes membership in the political nation. Whig politics after 1689 circled around the need to brake the justifications used to oust James from sliding toward democratic republicanism. Whigs needed to draw boundaries that would allow only qualified citizens into the political arena while at the same time providing a convincing rationale for rule by a limited class. Thus, Whiggism spawned an increasingly convoluted and sophisticated set of arguments to avoid opening the door to democracy. The politics of Whiggism were colored by this quandary until they were consigned to inconsequence in the 1880s. But it was an ambiguity that suffused all liberal politics until the end of the nineteenth century. Once John Wilkes had introduced the question of political reform into the agenda of politics, Liberals and Radicals were also to confront this problem. The nature of Liberal and Radical politics from the late eighteenth century was to be largely determined by their response to the issue.[8]

Thus, the ambiguities and absences inherent to the revolution settlement shaped the course of politics for two centuries after 1688. A political world was produced that was distinctive to this epoch. The central question driving both parliamentary and popular politics was where to

[8] See Peter Laslett, "Introduction," to John Locke, *Two Treatises of Government* (New York, 1963), pp. 15–135; Kenyon, *Revolution Principles*, pp. 47–50, 128–45, 200–08. For a new interpretation of Locke that argues for the subsumption of his individualism under his communitarian side, see Matthew H. Kramer, *John Locke and the Origins of Private Property: Philosophical Explorations of Individualism, Community and Equality* (Cambridge, 1997). For the key relationship between liberty and property, see H. T. Dickinson, *Liberty and Property* (London, 1976). On the difficulties in defining "property" in relation to the liberty of black slaves, see Henry Horwitz, "Liberty, Law and Property, 1689–1776," in J. R. Jones, *Liberty Secured?*, p. 167.

draw the limits of the political nation. This was not a matter that washed with the same intensity over the whole period, nor were its ebbs and flows unchanging. Nevertheless, the dilemma of how to include the "people" in the political sphere without being swamped by *all* the people comprised a central dynamic to the political history of the period. This was true up until the very last moment, when this system of politics was about to crumble in 1867. Even then, powerful instincts within the political class struggled to evade the onset of a democratic suffrage. Britain stumbled into political democracy. It did so because the central instability bequeathed by 1688 – how to draw the boundaries of the political nation – ultimately could not be resolved in any other way.

I am therefore interested in highlighting the fundamental tension in the political system between inclusion and exclusion: whom to include and whom to exclude from the political nation. In this chapter I am concerned to explain how the content of politics in the eighteenth century was shaped by this dynamic, and further how, toward the end of the century, the instabilities it created threatened the very boundaries of the political world. The containment of this threat by political "reform" and the ultimate displacement of this terrain of politics after 1867 will be the subject of the next chapter. In making this argument, it is not my purpose to provide a comprehensive account of the political culture or history of either the eighteenth or nineteenth centuries. My central concern is to propose a framework for understanding the broad political sweep of this period, rather than to supply a complete accounting of politics. Much will be left out in the interest of brevity – and this will be particularly striking for the period between 1790 and 1815. Needless to say, my emphasis reflects a sense of where the main weight of historical explanation should lie.

Exclusion and inclusion: 1688 to the 1830s

A fundamental paradox lay at the heart of British politics from 1688 until the end of our period. On the one hand, the boundaries of the parliamentary political nation were becoming more constricted. On the other hand, the scope for political expression and participation *outside* those formal boundaries remained wide and even expanded. Thus, the qualities of exclusion and inclusion were mutually compatible. They reinforced and qualified each other. Exclusion was modified by all sorts of exceptions and evasions. Likewise, the possibility of inclusion in the political system was confined by the very fact that its methods rested upon informal customs and practices that had no standing in the formal constitution.

A variety of common measurements demonstrate how the zone of participation in the formal political system became *more* restrictive from the 1680s to the 1860s. In the twenty turbulent years before 1715 the growth of the electorate outpaced population growth, so that 4.6 percent of the nation were electors by the end of Anne's reign. This was the democratic highpoint of the period. Over the next century this pattern was reversed. Between 1715 and 1832 a declining proportion of the population was enfranchised. By 1832 the formal political nation remained at the same level it had been in 1688 – about 2.6 percent of the population. It was the accomplishment of the "great" reform act of that year to restore the size of the electorate relative to population to the level of 1715. About one in four men held the vote in 1722 and this proportion was not much changed by the middle of the nineteenth century. The elections of 1710, 1715 and 1722 had a higher percentage of adult males voting than at any election *before* 1868. The first reform act of 1832 was consistent with this trend toward greater exclusivity. Women were formally excluded from the parliamentary electorate for the first time in 1832. Likewise, the standardization of electoral qualifications and the end of local franchises almost certainly excluded artisans and lower middle-class retailers from the small borough electorates.[9]

The same tendency to narrowing was evident in other parts of the constitution. Acts of Parliament in 1696 and 1729 attempted to freeze the expansion of the franchise beyond the limits laid down in prior petitions. These acts, quaintly known as "Last Determination Acts," reflected the ongoing search for the elusive site of "finality" to the limits of the political nation. The numbers of nomination boroughs controlled by local patrons tripled over the course of the eighteenth century. There were similar tendencies in town government, although it is dangerous to generalize, and important to realize that oligarchical control in the cities was usually fiercely contested. Nevertheless, eighteenth-century urban politics moved inexorably toward diminished popular control and a kind of urban bossism. Many of the most important cities in the nation were closed corporations and others – particularly the developing ones – possessed only manorial government. London government was "reformed" in 1725 to reduce the power of the Common Council. In Norwich the powers of the elected freemen were reduced in 1730; midcentury Bath and Tiverton

[9] Borsay, "Introduction," in Borsay, *Eighteenth-Century English Town*, p. 27; John Cannon, *Parliamentary Reform 1640–1832* (Cambridge, 1973), pp. 40–43; Geoffrey Holmes, *The Electorate and the National Will in the First Age of Party* (Lancaster, 1976), p. 11; Holmes, *The Making of a Great Power: Late Stuart and Early Georgian Britain 1660–1722* (London, 1993), pp. 324–32. The restriction of the political world is the dominant theme of Vernon, *Politics and the People*, but he confines himself to the nineteenth century.

were ruled by boss-dominated machines, as was late-century Bethnal Green.[10]

Yet the steady drift toward exclusion was not predetermined. Between the Glorious Revolution and the 1720s, the system was more open to an inclusive definition of the political nation than at any time until after 1867 and 1884. At no other time was the electorate freer of the influence of oligarchy and clientage than between 1689 and 1722. The possibility of radical politics had been introduced by 1688. Independent lower-class politics were fostered by the example of revolution and also by the realities of elite politics. The events of 1688–89 had forced the political elite to take the search for political legitimacy outside the closets of St. James's Palace and into the public sphere of clubs, corporations and the like. This began at the very moment that negotiations opened over the revolutionary settlement. One of the pressures on William to accept the Declaration of Rights was the appeals to "out-of-doors" public opinion and the lively press and pamphlet debate that accompanied it. Throughout the 1690s Whigs and Tories endeavored to strengthen their political position by competing for popular support. The pattern was established whereby elite politics sought to attach some section of the popular classes in support of its particular political agenda. In London, at least, it was this competition that underlay the extensive enfranchisement of those years as Whigs and Tories handed out the vote to widening segments of the middling classes. For a brief moment the possibility was allowed for popular involvement within the boundaries of the political nation.[11]

But the tendencies to closure also had their origins during this period of openness. The struggle for power in the boroughs led to the refinement of techniques of political manipulation that were to remain in use throughout the period. In this the Whigs were the prime movers. Indeed, although the Whigs initially were the most open to wider boundaries of the political nation, by the mid-1690s the mainstream Whigs had committed to oligarchy. Thus, political stabilization meant political exclusion not only for the benighted Tories after 1715, but also for the middling and other sorts of the people. For a few decades, the Tories picked up the fallen demotic mantle of the Whigs, fused it with the

[10] Cannon, *Parliamentary Reform*, p. 34; Corfield, *Impact of English Towns*, pp. 153–54; H. T. Dickinson, *The Politics of the People in Eighteenth-Century Britain* (London, 1995), pp. 14, 100–04; Frank O'Gorman, *Voters, Patrons and Parties: The Unreformed Electorate of Hanoverian England 1734–1832* (Cambridge, 1989), pp. 18–22.

[11] Gary Stuart DeKrey, *A Fractured Society: The Politics of London in the First Age of Party 1688–1715* (Oxford, 1985); DeKrey, "Political Radicalism in London after the Glorious Revolution," *Journal of Modern History*, 55 (December 1983), pp. 585–617; Schwoerer, *Declaration of Rights*, pp. 285–86; W. A. Speck, *Tory and Whig: The Struggle in the Constituencies 1701–1715* (London, 1970).

rituals of "merrie England" and the culture of Jacobitism and thus established that peculiar attachment of the English lower classes to politically conservative elites.[12]

It was the Whigs who initiated the various measures to confine the political space. They did this at the local as well as the national level. In Norwich, for example, after 1715, the Whigs effectively captured local political institutions which they ruthlessly used to extend their political hegemony. Most famously, of course, the Whig tendency to oligarchy was revealed by the succession of parliamentary acts designed to contain the threat of expansive politics. The Last Determination Acts, the Septennial Act of 1716 (which replaced the Triennial Act of 1696, an act which marked, perhaps, the floodtide of openness), the tightening of the Toleration Acts and the unsuccessful effort to close off future entitlements by the Peerage Bill of 1719 were all Whig initiatives.[13]

The principles of inclusion in the political nation were, in theory, quite straightforward: possession of sufficient property to ensure freedom from the control and clientage of the mighty and powerful. Ever since the Putney Debates of 1647 independence had been marked as an essential qualification for political responsibility. Colonel Ireton had laid out the conservative case at Putney that only those men whose economic position guaranteed their independence of views should be allowed to qualify for the vote. This became the mainstream Whig view. Indeed, the connection between property and independence became more compelling as Parliament grew in importance and the institutions of government – improvement commissions and the like – expanded.

As a consequence, there was constant juggling between the appropriate level of property-ownership that qualified someone for a particular job. This was always the subject of much worried debate. The property qualification for a member of Parliament was different from that of a justice of the peace. The latter was set in 1732 at an estate worth £100 per year. By an act of 1710 the former was required to be in possession of a copy- or freehold estate of £600 per year. Even this was not considered enough by some and attempts were made in the 1760s and 1780s to raise the qualification. After 1832, the complications intensified. The match between the quantity of property and the level of participation in politics became more difficult to calibrate. In spite of efforts inside and outside

---

[12] See J. H. Plumb, *The Growth of Political Stability in England 1675–1725* (Harmondsworth, 1967), for the treatment that has shaped all other interpretations. Plumb's account treats instability as a problem that needed to be solved instead of a circumstance that contained political possibilities beyond a simple restoration of the Stuarts.

[13] Kenyon, *Revolution Principles*, pp. 178–93; O'Gorman, *Voters, Patrons and Parties*, pp. 11–14. For the importance of local Jacobitism as one basis of opposition politics in Norwich after 1715, see Kathleen Wilson, *Sense of the People*, pp. 378–87.

Parliament to abolish the property qualification, it remained the key dividing line for inclusion.[14]

In large part, the difficulty lay in the meaning of property itself. Property was not an unproblematic concept. During the eighteenth century, for example, there was the question of how to count nonlanded wealth. Did the rentier have the same stake in the country as the gaiter-legged squire? Many thought he did not. In the instance of land, there were sundry conditions under which the franchise could be held. Definitions of landed property were themselves conditional and contested. Depending on the circumstance, property could mean the substantial estate or the "potwallopers" who, as the name implied, were all those in possession of pots and pans who were not also receiving alms or charity. "Property" was hardly an automatic criterion for deciding who should be included and who should be excluded from membership in the political nation. The connection that was assumed between property and independence was qualified in many ways.

Freehold property was a different legal entity than copyhold property. It was the former that was generally regarded as a superior qualification for the franchise because it was assumed to bestow untrammeled ownership and thus ensure complete independence. But this was not always the case. Freehold-ownership was frequently complicated by the fact that many estates were mortgaged up to the hilt. The specter this raised of estate-owners being in thrall to holders of commercial paper was not a pretty one, given the suspicion that surrounded the monied interest in eighteenth-century politics. Thus voices were heard in the 1780s demanding a mortgage-free status as a condition for the franchise. In any case, about one-third of property-holders were copyholders, which covered a multitude of different legal tenures. Sometimes these included the franchise and sometimes they did not. Copyhold, however, was popularly believed to be surrounded by all sorts of obligations and constraints on independence. Thus, the rights and status of landed property were more complicated than might at first glance appear, and were often the site of conflict and tension.[15]

The model qualification for membership in the political nation, then, of a compact freehold estate, unencumbered by debts or obligations and recognized in law and custom, was mostly a fiction. Land was not the only kind of property, even though the principles of representation tended to assume that it was. From the 1690s there was an ongoing debate about

[14] Langford, *Public Life and the Propertied Englishman*, pp. 278–87, 420, 483–85; Stone, "Results of the English Revolutions," p. 91; Helen E. Witmer, *The Property Qualifications of Members of Parliament* (New York, 1968), pp. 41, 85, 140–44, 204.

[15] Langford, *Public Life and the Propertied Englishman*, pp. 64–68.

how or if to accommodate other kinds of property-ownership and particularly commercial wealth. This was primarily addressed to the parliamentary franchise and other key positions of state power such as the justice of the peace. The property qualification for members of Parliament was not expanded to include nonlanded wealth until 1838. This illustrated the difficulties of Lockean theory; it allowed no easy inclusion of different kinds of property even though the heart of the commercial system, the Bank of England, was fully recognized as part of the constitution. The link between representation and landed property remained strong throughout the period, although it transmuted into a ratepayer definition of property-ownership by the 1830s.[16]

Lifting our gaze from those qualified to participate in parliamentary politics to a wider horizon of the political public reveals varying boundaries of inclusion and exclusion. Bodies of little importance nationally such as improvement commissions or turnpike authorities usually had much lower property qualifications than either those for justice of the peace or the parliamentary franchise. Where to draw the line of inclusion for these bodies – where the proper boundary of gentility rested – was a difficult and contentious issue. It was agreed that the boundary would run through the middling classes; yet the precise location was seldom self-evident. For a street improvement commissioner, £1,000 of personal property was the standard qualification. In Westminster this rose to £2,000. The court of requests in Halifax had a property qualification of £50 of real property or £1,000 of personal property. By the 1780s, however, this came to be regarded as too low because it allowed the court to become dominated by small retailers; unsuccessful efforts were made to raise the level so as to exclude these middling-class types.[17]

There was usually some distance between the legal qualifications for formal participation in political power and the reality of their application. Many strategies were devised, for example, for evading the 1710 act which set the property qualifications for members of Parliament. Property could be "borrowed" until the oath of office had been taken; estates could be collusively transferred and then returned once the legal proceedings had been completed. Such evasions permeated the length and breadth of the political system, and they mitigated the formal exclusions the system contained. Although the Test and Corporation Acts imposed quite strict exclusions on the participation of dissenters in government, these rules were commonly evaded and many offices were explicitly exempted from their reach.

[16] Ibid., pp. 58–59; Witmer, *Property Qualifications*, pp. 153–55.
[17] Langford, *Public Life and the Propertied Englishman*, pp. 234–48. This is a subject that would be worth closer investigation for the nineteenth century as well.

Thus, even the principled distinctions between exclusion and inclusion in the political system were highly unstable categories. The relationship between the spheres of inclusion and exclusion was not one of binary opposites; it was an integral and complementary relationship. At every point the tendencies of the political system toward greater restriction were counterbalanced by the presence of alternate spaces for participation in the political process. Just as the possession of full rights of political citizenship was hedged around with all sorts of restrictions, so the opportunities for the middling and the lower classes to participate in some aspect of politics were increasingly manifest from 1688.

Three areas of this expanding sphere are worthy of particular note: the wide allocation of governing functions outside Parliament, the creation of a vital and lively "public sphere" of politics and the rituals of popular politics. The first two have already been introduced in relation to the structures of government and of civil society, and they will be briefly addressed here.[18] The third theme, however, is of more immediate relevance and will receive a fuller treatment.

The localist pattern of the state structures in this period meant that the functions of government were delegated throughout a wide range of social groups. To staff the expanding responsibilities of local government, recruitment had to reach deep within the social structure. The land taxes or the assessed taxes could not be collected any more than the vestry or poor law could be run without the civic involvement of large numbers of middling and lower classes. Indeed, administering the land tax was delegated to people of fairly humble status who were typically members of a local political public engaged in a variety of political and community services. The parish officers, tax assessors, churchwardens and overseers in poor law administration possessed a social standing that was not much higher than the poor law recipients themselves.[19]

We can note, for example, John Carrington, a small farmer of Tewlin in Hertfordshire, whose diary between 1798 and 1810 was fortunately preserved. Carrington left the farm in care of his son and worked virtually full time on his various civic duties, for which he received modest compensation. Carrington was a civil servant of the localist state. He occupied four offices: surveyor of highways, chief constable of a division of the Liberty of St. Albans, tax assessor and collector for Bramfield, and overseer of the poor. These tasks called upon a wide variety of expertise and talents. He needed to manage and supervise subordinates, to be a social worker in his administration of the poor law, a legal expert familiar

---

[18] See pp. 161–64, 193–96.
[19] Dickinson, *Politics of the People*, pp. 93–124; Brooks, "Public Finance and Political Stability," pp. 289–90, 296.

with the statutes for quarter sessions presentments, an inspector of licenses and bread weights, an army recruiter under the Militia Acts, and knowledgeable about the complex rules and regulations on the land and the income taxes.[20]

In the urban centers vestry government was similarly inclusive. Vestries were the one organ of government where class and gender restrictions often did not apply until the closure of the early nineteenth century. A lively political life marked many of the urban vestries until reform put an end to it. In London at the beginning of the eighteenth century, something like two-thirds of male householders had the municipal franchise. Both urban and rural civic political culture possessed significant channels of inclusion, therefore. The business of government pulled into its orbit a wide spectrum of the social scale, and, in the urban areas in particular, there were constant pressures to admit new candidates to elite circles.[21]

More than any other aspect of civil society, the exclusionary tendencies of formal politics were qualified by the dense network of regional and national civic associations, political clubs, coffee shops, newspapers and pamphlet literature that comprised the public sphere of politics. From the very beginning of the period, the public sphere was painted with a rainbow of different political activities and organizations. Until the middle of the eighteenth century, the character of the politics in the public sphere was heavily inflected with Jacobite and Tory tendencies. From the middle part of the century, new variants joined and (in the case of Jacobite politics) replaced these older forms. Loyalist political associations, for example, appeared out of the patriotic culture stimulated by the Seven Years War and the American war. These associations served as prefigurative forms of middling-class political organization in the provinces. By the 1790s the urban gentry was well practiced at creating local political networks. They were particularly adept at mobilizing lower-class support. It was well recognized by the urban patriciate that "the key to popular participation lay in orchestrating it from below, by rooting it in accepted patterns and by fitting it to the shape and nature of existing communities."[22]

---

[20] W. Branch Johnson (ed.), *"Memorandoms for . . .": The Diary Between 1798 and 1810 of John Carrington* (London and Chichester, 1973), pp. 10–18.

[21] Kathleen Wilson, "Urban Culture and Political Activism in Hanoverian England: The Example of Voluntary Hospitals," in Hellmuth, *Transformation of Political Culture*, pp. 182–84; Webb and Webb, *The Parish and the County*, pp. 79–103.

[22] John Money, "Freemasonry and the Fabric of Loyalism," and H. T. Dickinson, "Popular Loyalism in Britain in the 1790s," both in Hellmuth, *Transformation of the Political Culture*, pp. 244–50 and 519–21 respectively (quote, p. 519); Paul Monod, *Jacobitism and the English People 1689–1788* (Cambridge, 1989), pp. 28–32.

This became a more problematic exercise as the eighteenth century progressed. The opportunities of the public space also could be used by others. John Wilkes's supporters were able to mobilize so effectively against the government in the 1760s because the potential public was already organized in a network of social and political clubs. Indeed, it needs to be emphasized that *organized* structures for political mobilization in the public space developed almost from the moment that William and Mary took their seats on the throne. The first constituency association was established by Tories in the 1690s. From that point such associations proliferated. This was especially true in the towns, of course; counties seldom developed the same kind of ongoing political and electoral machinery. Throughout the 1720s and 1730s various political organizations in both London and leading provincial towns catered to the range of partisan opinion. London was the most important center of this culture. Its active newspaper press had originated in the oppositional politics of Jacobitism and defied all attempts at control by the Whig oligarchy. But London mirrored the active and contentious political world that was to be found in all provincial towns by the early part of the eighteenth century.[23]

Manipulation of the franchise was the key battleground of this public sphere of politics. It was to remain an important electoral strategy until the 1880s. The function of political organization was to shape the electorate to each party's advantage. The Tories had first organized at the constituency level in London precisely to counter Whig attempts to manipulate the franchise. During the crisis of 1714 the Whigs set up a sophisticated club to combat Jacobitism by extending the franchise to men of property who were not freemen. Such tactics became a permanent part of the electoral scenery in the larger boroughs. Blatant electoral manipulation was behind the Whig creation of 200 new freemen in Norwich just before the election of 1701. In Colchester two nights before the election of 1705, 125 freemen were sworn in. These strategies of manipulation were integral to the electoral politics of the eighteenth century and were, in turn, bequeathed to the registration associations that were set up in the constituencies after the Reform Act of 1832.[24]

---

[23] Brewer, "English Radicalism," pp. 358–60; John Money, "Birmingham and the West Midlands, 1760–1793," in Borsay, *Eighteenth-Century Urban Town*, pp. 294–314; see also Money, "Provincialism and the English Ancien Régime': Samuel Pipe-Wolferston and the Confessional State,' 1776–1820," *Albion*, 21, 3 (Fall 1989), pp. 389–425; Kathleen Wilson, *Sense of the People*, pp. 27–83.

[24] See Dickinson, *Politics of the People*, pp. 207–08; Speck, *Tory and Whig*, pp. 47–63; Holmes, *Politics in the Age of Anne*, pp. 312–21; Kathleen Wilson, *Sense of the People*, pp. 386–87, for Whig manipulation of the franchise in Norwich.

A wide range of political forms were accommodated within this public sphere. The sedate debating clubs and assembly rooms of the middling and upper classes were paralleled by networks of lower-class associations which spawned the corresponding societies and the radical underworld of the 1790s. The politics of the popular classes played a prominent role in the public sphere from the 1690s. In addition to the extensive and growing print and associational culture that historians have carefully recorded from the 1790s, there was the raucous repertoire of highly ritualized ceremonies and customs that marked the participation of the popular classes in the political system.[25] These forms developed from the 1690s and remained intact until the 1860s. They were particularly evident at election times when they served to allow the voice of the people to be heard – if nothing else. Throughout the course of the eighteenth century the practices of this culture of popular politics became more elaborate, reaching maturity around the 1780s before beginning a long, and slow, degenerative decline.

The public rituals of popular politics during this period first emerged from the party competition of the 1690s. Parliamentary politics dictated an appeal to popular loyalties as a necessary part of party rivalry . A collection of political protocols emerged designed entirely for nonelectors that both mobilized and expressed political sentiments. The customs and rituals that infused the system developed out of the practices that inhabited the ritual year of "merrie England." These religious and seasonal events were rapidly dying out by the end of the seventeenth century. The Glorious Revolution hastened the secularization of the public calendar. Monarchy and social authority after 1688 could only furtively claim any element of the sacerdotal, in spite of Anne's attempts to reinstitute the royal touch as a cure for scrofula. Indeed, the main narrative for the history of public expression of popular wills was not merely the demise of a religious communal culture, but more its replacement by a civic and political culture that was configured in the same forms.[26]

Like the customs of "merrie England," the practices of popular politics were highly ritualized and socially conservative. They were specifically tailored both to accommodate the participation of the excluded and to confirm the social hierarchy. These structures were carried over into the popular politics of Victorian England until 1867. Indeed, these patterns of popular politics were replicated in the new constituencies created after

[25] See Kevin Gilmartin, *Print Politics: The Press and Radical Opposition in Early Nineteenth-Century England* (Cambridge, 1996), and Ian McCalman, *Radical Underworld: Prophets, Revolutionaries and Pornographers in London 1795–1840* (Cambridge, 1988), for studies of the print culture of this popular politics.

[26] Ronald Hutton, *The Rise and Fall of Merry England: The Ritual Year 1400–1700* (Oxford, 1996), pp. 230–62.

1832. Throughout the mid-Victorian period, the rowdy traditions of the address, the canvass and the nomination ceremonial remained central to constituency politics. They do not last beyond 1867, however. The last recorded "chairing" of a candidate was in Dover in 1857. Only the announcement of the poll from the town hall balcony or some other public place remained from this old system after the 1860s.[27]

The vocabulary of political communication in this domain and its forms of representation were distinctive. They constituted a different language from the conventions of mobilization and organization that emerged after 1880. Prior to 1880, for example, iconography was a particularly important idiom of popular politics. Politics were mobilized and expressed through pictorial, visual and oral images, as well as through print culture. Politics were also expressed in the public space, rather than being tucked away in the private sphere. It was in the middle of the nineteenth century that political meetings began to be restricted to ticket holders only, and this signified a move toward more formal styles of political engagement. The replacement of open voting with the secret ballot in 1871 was the ultimate expression of this kind of privatized politics. Before the 1870s, however, the dominant place for politics was in the public space where its ritualized forms proclaimed both the power-lessness and the power of popular participation. The accommodation provided for the unrepresented in the public space only highlighted the exclusion of its participants from the official political nation. Lower-class political interventions were open to control and manipulation by the elite. They were also disciplined internally by the rules of custom. Yet, it remained true that popular politics were an organized intrusion of "the people" into the public space of politics in order to claim political "rights."[28]

Cultural and social inversion was a main theme to popular political culture. The category of the election itself was turned into a charivari in some places. The most famous of these pieces of political theater was the Garret mock election which was first held after 1688 to commemorate a legal victory of the village against an enclosure attempt. It then became an annual event. In its origins, the Garret mock election was entirely a plebeian festival day which supplemented the official calendar of political feast days. The symbolic power of the event was such, however, that by the 1770s it had degenerated into a place where national figures came to

---

[27] Frank O'Gorman, "Campaign Rituals and Ceremonies: The Social Meaning of Elections in England 1780–1860," *Past and Present*, 135 (May 1992), pp. 79–114; Vernon, *Politics and the People*, pp. 49, 79, 81–102.

[28] James Vernon has dealt most fully with this aspect of this culture and detailed its vitality throughout the middle of the nineteenth century; see his *Politics and the People*, pp. 109–16, 131, 152–54, 230. See also Dickinson, *Politics of the People*, pp. 42–49.

present their own version of political theater. This elite appropriation was an authentic genuflection to the power of popular ritual. It demonstrated how the patterns of popular politics were orchestrated by rhythms of reciprocity between elites and plebeians.[29]

The varieties of these reciprocal patterns were assorted and complicated. They tended to possess the common pattern of opening a space in the hierarchy of political power for the politically excluded. A case recorded in the annals of town government in Edinburgh in the 1720s contrasts the theater of Garret with the horsetrading of complementary favors. In this case the lord provost wrote to the incorporation of hammermen – an artisan guild with powers of representation in the city – asking them to admit as a member Alexander Brand who had come highly recommended by many "persons of distinction and good friends to the city." The provost clearly needed to find a place for this person as a favor to one of his superiors. He therefore reached down into his client pool to exercise the patronage and influence which oiled all politics in the eighteenth century. The benefits to the members of the incorporation were not spelled out in this particular case. They probably did not need to be. The lesson is that even the politically excluded were not without some tradable political commodities in the system.[30]

Election time customs and ceremonials best expressed the reciprocities of inclusion and exclusion. These ceremonials were designed to emphasize the limits to oligarchic power. They entered the element of consent into the process of securing and affirming political loyalty and social authority. Great care was taken to disguise the brute power of the oligarchy. Eviction of tenants for political reasons was very rare, for example. Any suggestion of domination or intimidation had to be carefully avoided. Even the most dependent voters in the most closed constituencies were assiduously courted in a mating ceremony which walked the boundary between requesting deference while respecting independence. In English political culture and in its system of social authority the two qualities of deference and independence were frequently integrated rather than in conflict. This was a curiosity to English culture which did not extend, of course, to Wales or Scotland, let alone Ireland. English political culture was clearly oligarchic. Yet the oligarchies had to negotiate and work for consent and thus in some way be accountable. This was the point of the

[29] John Brewer, *The Common People and Politics 1750–1790s* (London, 1986); Brewer, "Theater and Counter-Theater in Georgian Politics: The Mock Elections at Garret," *Radical History Review*, 22 (1979–80), pp. 7–40. The line between masquerade and politics was frequently blurred; see Terry Castle, *Masquerade and Civilization: The Carnivalesque in Eighteenth-Century English Culture and Fiction* (Stanford, 1986), p. 3.
[30] Houston, "Popular Politics in the Reign of George II," pp. 188–89.

public expression of political rituals; they bore the character of elite submission to the judgment and assent of the governed, subaltern classes. As such, they emphasized the independence of the voters and the "rights" of the nonvoters to political expression. The finely tuned rituals and ceremonies of popular politics created a space where the legitimacy of political authority was displayed to public inspection and affirmed.[31]

By the same token, however, the boundaries between deference and independence were unspecified and inherently indeterminate. The culture of popular politics was innately volatile and capricious, therefore. Precisely because these political rituals were reliant upon custom and upon the vagaries of particular situations it was quite impossible to predict how they would proceed. Election riots might or might not be sparked when a patron overstepped the bounds of independence or offended sensibilities. Deference was granted as an act of independence by free-born Englishmen; it could be withdrawn if the paternal bargain seemed to be violated. Popular politics were ritualized with their own ceremonies and habits and were internally disciplined by their own customary rules. Yet there were no procedures to gauge in advance what was permissible and what was not. No formal standards existed to evaluate and assess transgressions. Popular politics were an unstable social cocktail which could explode at any moment when the balance of reciprocity was estimated to have been disrupted. Politics in the public space stayed this way until after the second reform bill of 1867.[32]

The politics of contention

Politics were a broader affair than elections; they were also about ideology and, most fundamentally, about the constitution. Since the practice of appealing to public opinion was installed after 1688, the people were entered into politics even though there was no formal place for them in the constitution. This was the ultimate problem that occupied constitutional debate throughout the period. It was not the only force animating the course of politics, nor was the weighty matter of its content always at the forefront of public discussion. Nevertheless, the role of the people was the issue to which all matters concerning the constitution were in the end obliged to return. And it was this issue that came to lie at the core of the program of radicalism forged in the eighteenth century which dominated popular politics for most of the nineteenth century. Here, I am concerned

[31] O'Gorman, *Voters, Patrons and Parties*, pp. 225–36, 237–43; 245–51; Dickinson, *Politics of the People*, pp. 22–31.
[32] O'Gorman, *Voters, Parties and Patrons*, pp. 245–51, 259–60, 262–85.

only with the way the main elements of that tradition developed in the early part of our period.[33]

The issues of oppositional politics were writ large almost as soon as the ink was dry on the Declaration of Rights. They were rooted in the political realities of the 1690s and also in the political theory that had been developed in the seventeenth century to explain the civil wars. Two aspects of political reality were important. The first was that in order to fight William III's wars, new centers of bureaucratic power were created. The logistical and administrative structures of war and taxation constituted a state that stood at some distance from direct parliamentary control. This fiscal-military state was therefore viewed with deep suspicion because it posed an implicit threat to the proper constitutional balance of power. A second new departure in politics was the growth of patronage networks out in the public space. These networks were one of the strategies of political mobilization. By the end of the 1690s opposition politics had seized upon both of these developments and had coalesced around the notion that together they threatened to disrupt the balance of forces in the constitution and to introduce a renewed tyranny of monarchy and oligarchy. And to hand stood a body of political theory developed by James Harrington in the middle of the seventeenth century that country Whigs and Tories could call upon in order to endow this notion with historical and theoretical legitimacy.

Close to the heart of seventeenth-century political thought was the idea of England as a mixed and balanced constitution. The civil wars of the 1640s had clarified the dangers that followed from any disruption of the equilibrium between the component parts of the constitution. Like most seventeenth-century political theorists, Harrington sought to understand the civil wars in terms of a failure of equipoise between king and Parliament. Harrington's popularizers in the 1690s generalized this notion far beyond his original intent to propose an "ancient constitution" originating in the Anglo-Saxon folkmote, which was in constant danger of subversion by monarchy. According to this view of constitutional history, the scope for monarchical intervention expanded enormously after 1688. The enlarged bureaucracy of government and the increased opportunities for the court to buy and reward its supporters

---

[33] Thus, I know that eighteenth-century opposition politics encompassed a much wider spectrum of politics than is discussed here. There were strong convergences between the different political elements of opposition. I am aware of grossly oversimplifying and of giving short shrift to other roots of opposition, particularly the Jacobite tradition, and of not dealing with the nuances that existed between Whig and Tory supporters of country ideology. For a good discussion of much that is left out here, see Linda Colley, *In Defiance of Oligarchy: The Tory Party 1714–1760* (Cambridge, 1982), chs. 4, 6.

through contracts, sinecures and places were the new expressions of executive tyranny.[34]

In the early nineteenth century William Cobbett labeled this system as "the thing" and "old corruption." By then, of course, old corruption was in its corpulent maturity. As a theory of the way the state worked, however, old corruption was a commonplace notion in radical discourse from the end of the 1690s. Unlike most bad things in the politics of the eighteenth century, the origins of old corruption could not be pinned on the Whig oligarchy established by Sir Robert Walpole after 1720. Its origins lay in the heady open politics of the first three decades after 1688, when competition between the political parties for public support refined the practices of influence buying and patronage.[35]

Old corruption was a useful handle for the opposition to Whig oligarchy to grasp. It plausibly described the network of institutional interests and personal power and advantage that lay at the heart of the British state. The phrase captured, also, the threats that this posed to liberty. The core belief of old corruption was of Parliament beleaguered by executive attempts to subvert its independence and thereby disrupt the balance of the ancient constitution in pursuit of its own power. The likelihood that the forces of oligarchy would work in this way was fundamental to eighteenth-century politics and was broadcast from the beginning of our period. By the early years of the eighteenth century the program of radical reform that was to run through the period had begun to crystallize. Calls for the removal of place-men, more frequent elections, greater accountability of government and reduced taxation were all to be heard during the reign of Queen Anne. The precise ways in which these reforms were expressed and envisaged differed, of course, and all sorts of currents flowed through the strange combination of Tory and Whig radicals that composed the main opposition to the Hanoverian state in the early eighteenth century.[36]

---

[34] Harringtonian theory in the form that it was to take in eighteenth-century politics first appeared in a speech in the House of Lords by the earl of Shaftesbury in 1675. It played no part in the debate around 1688, reviving again in the mid-1690s in response to the wars. See *The Political Works of James Harrington*, ed. and intro. J. G. A. Pocock (Cambridge, 1977), pp. 129–37.

[35] For old corruption, see J. G. A. Pocock, "Machiavelli, Harrington and English Eighteenth-Century Ideology," in Pocock (ed.), *Politics, Language and Time: Essays on Political Thought and History* (London, 1971), pp. 125–45; Philip Harling, *The Waning of "Old Corruption": The Politics of Economical Reform in Britain 1779–1846* (Oxford, 1996); W. D. Rubinstein, "The End of Old Corruption' in Britain 1780–1860," *Past and Present*, 101 (1981), pp. 55–86; Dickinson, *Politics of the People*, p. 199.

[36] Geoffrey Holmes, *Politics, Religion and Society in England 1679–1742* (London, 1986), pp. 35–56.

Yet fundamentally this conception of politics as a struggle against those forces that sought to reduce independence into a servile dependency divided the political world into the qualities of vice and virtue. Politics was presented as a morality play in which "the people" were identified as the repository of virtue. Constantly thwarting the will of the people were the self-interested forces of corruption that fastened onto the state. The legacy of this worldview ran through nineteenth-century popular politics, which employed the same kind of highly developed moral categories to frame political issues. William Gladstone's success as a political leader was achieved precisely because he could tap into this language and its categories. Politics thus became a struggle to recapture a lost purity and virtue, and for this "the people" were the chosen weapon. Given this understanding of the world, however, it meant that those virtues or agencies that combated corruption and embodied virtue were accorded a great respect and importance. There were two of these that were particularly operative in the dynamic of popular politics throughout our period: the law and the idea of independence.[37]

The common law occupied a revered place in popular conceptions of the constitution. Common law was the central legacy of the ancient constitution and the most important protection against tyranny. Many of the campaigns of oppositional politics revolved around the law. The case of John Wilkes was only the most celebrated. The law was integral to the culture of opposition, both as a sphere of conflict where rights could be defined and secured and as a bulwark against overpowerful oligarchs. The treason trials of the 1790s were the moment when the law was presented with its greatest test in this respect. It came through with flying colors. Radicals saw themselves maintaining freedoms and rights through the courts and depending on the honesty of juries to prevent persecution. Defending the independence of the law was a siren call to action capable of mobilizing a wide swathe of radical sentiment. Jeremy Bentham wrote a pamphlet against the government's attempt to stack the jury in the case of Thomas Wooler, publisher of the radical periodical the *Black Dwarf*, who was prosecuted for seditious libel in 1817. The consciousness of the past was very powerful in all of this. Radicals saw themselves in the tradition of the great martyrs of the seventeenth cen-

---

[37] This feature of nineteenth-century politics tends to be treated in isolation from its eighteenth-century roots. It is to be distinguished from the evangelical moralism of official politics, of course. It is important to note that the other prominent feature of this kind of popular politics was Protestant religion. Protestantism was an important aspect of opposition politics and culture that I will not deal with here, but it is important to register its presence. On the moral character of nineteenth-century politics, see Joyce, *Democratic Subjects*, pp. 176–90; Vernon, *Politics and the People*, pp. 278–79, 317–19.

tury and seventeenth-century trial literature was a staple of radical politics at that time.[38]

For the individual in politics, however, the most important guarantor of political virtue was the preservation of independence. Political theory accorded possession of property as the essential requirement of independence. Mainstream opposition ideology combined hostility to oligarchical methods with a recognition that the limits of the political nation should stop at those without the necessary "independence" to protect them from the corrupting influences of special interests. This meant that most of "the people" were to be excluded from power as being dependent in one degree or another. Naturally, there was no clear agreement on where the particular line between socially independent and socially dependent groups ran, and this was yet another source of dynamic instability in the system. At the time of the Wilkite campaign, for example, there were disagreements between Wilkes and the Whigs over his desire to expand concepts of independence beyond those in possession of landed property to include the aspirations of urban and professional elites.

Oppositional politics in this period were not rooted in the assumption that an enlarged political franchise was a guarantee of good government. Indeed, the reverse was true. Democratic proceedings were believed to lead directly to disorderliness. The case of vestry government in the late eighteenth century was taken to illuminate the tendency of democratic systems to encourage a demagogy which denied the possibility of virtuous or good government. The experience of the Gordon riots, for example, reinforced this dark view of the people. By this time, the debate on the franchise was a century old. Yet only very gradually and with the greatest reluctance did the debate on the franchise become a discourse about an *extension* of the political nation. The original debate on the franchise after 1689 had focused around *raising* the level of qualification for the vote in order to ensure a purer kind of government. Similarly, when the secret ballot was first advocated in 1689 it was not proposed as an expression of liberal democracy but more as a way of removing the corruptions of "influence" from the electoral process. The first hesitant suggestions for franchise enlargement did not appear until the 1730s and 1740s.[39]

[38] James Epstein, *Radical Expression: Political Language, Ritual and Symbol in England 1790–1850* (Oxford, 1994), pp. 21–58; F. K. Donnelly, "Levellerism in Eighteenth and Early Nineteenth-Century Britain," *Albion*, 20, 2 (Summer 1988), pp. 261–69.

[39] Dickinson, *Politics of the People*, pp. 177–78, 201–02; Brewer, "English Radicalism," pp. 326–27; *Political Works of James Harrington* ed. Pocock, p. 145. It was the experience of the Gordon riots that soured Edmund Burke's enthusiasm for "the people" and led him to a fully developed critique of the implications of democracy before the French revolution confirmed his position: Ian McCalman, "Mad Lord George and Madam La Motte: Riot and Sexuality in the Genesis of Burke's *Reflections on the Revolution in France*," *Journal of British Studies*, 35, 3 (July 1996), pp. 343–67.

In conventional politics, independence was a counterweight to democracy. In popular political culture, independence possessed different resonances. As has been noted, property was the most important signifier of independence, but property was not an unproblematic concept, and could be extended to include skill, labor and reason. The culture of popular politics attached different qualities to the meaning of independence. Independence was an extremely important concept for English popular politics, as it was for high politics. The demarcation of a space where "independence" from control thrived was the basis of local radical politics in the eighteenth century. There was a flowering of lower-class associations in the public space during the eighteenth century. The craft societies, the trade unions, the friendly and benefit societies, the eighteenth-century purse clubs and other convivial, social and even moral reforming societies that dotted the urban landscape after about 1700 all represented a defined space of autonomy and independence that was as common among the lower classes as its more familiar representations were among the higher social groups. Certain groups possessed a particularly highly developed self-consciousness of independence. These types tended to stand in constant opposition not only to oligarchy but often to both political parties as well.[40]

Craftsmen were a core independent group. This would be especially evident at times when they were resisting threats to their craft protections. Industrial change was the most frequent agency that called independence into question, and struggles around this issue are characteristic of the period. Some groups like the Newcastle keelmen were well known for the ferocity with which they defended their autonomy in the eighteenth century. The same defense of autonomy was mounted by shoemakers, tailors and Owenite building workers in the face of industrial change in the 1820s and 1830s. The political radicalism of such groups stemmed from their resistance to the threats posed to their work autonomy. Within working-class political and social culture in the nineteenth century, independence from clientage and control was a recurring animating force. Maximizing the freedom from dependence in all its aspects of life – from work to credit – was the core value of the labor aristocracy of the middle of the nineteenth century. It was one of the sources for the enduring interest in land reform in radical politics in the nineteenth century.[41]

[40] See Hunt, *The Middling Sort*, pp. 194–96, for the kinds of ways the high political theory of independence was translated into the popular consciousness in the case of Ambrose Barnes, a late seventeenth-century worthy of Newcastle.

[41] The Newcastle keelmen were so independent that they built and maintained their own hospital. See Kathleen Wilson, *Sense of the People*, pp. 62, 315–75, for a study of independent radical politics in Newcastle; Vernon, *Politics and the People*, pp. 105–07, 312–13, 315–16; Patrick Joyce, *Visions of the People: Industrial England and the Question of Class, 1840–1914* (Cambridge, 1991), pp. 32–34, 83, 99, 107.

Independence was a core category of popular and elite politics that needs to be tracked throughout the whole period, therefore. Victorian historians have not fully appreciated the eighteenth-century genesis of the idea. During the debates on the second reform bill in 1866–67, for example, the main argument of reformers was that *some* working men had now shown themselves worthy of the vote by reason of having attained independence through self-improvement. The problem – as always – was to find the cutoff in the working class for this quality. Gladstone was the main exponent of this sophistry, and the eighteenth-century character of his language is striking: "in the present state of society, while some are dependent and some ignorant, it is right to make some distinction; and not invest all with the right to the political franchise."[42]

Independence was a highly unstable concept, however, precisely because it was inseparable from dependence. It was impossible to speak of independence without speaking also of dependence. On the one hand, popular electoral politics were capable of erupting into class violence when "traditional rights" were violated, such as the right to demonstrate at the hustings or to protest at the harsh implementation of the Riot Act. On the other hand, networks of clientage and patronage reached deep into the social structure to entangle the same sorts of people in the politics of oligarchy. Craftsmen held the value of independence in high regard; they were also especially subject to the pressures of clientage. Thus, artisans were integrated into the structures of patronage in early eighteenth-century London politics, like the carpenter who controlled fifty votes, or the humble waterman vestrymen of St. Margaret's and St. John's who were created electors in 1741 and 1749 to work in the government interest. Independence was a sensitive nexus of social relations which could have purchase only in a society where clientage and deference lubricated the social hierarchy.[43]

Ironically, for a ruling-class coup, 1688 greatly increased the potential for lower-class politics. In contrast to previous major national occurrences, the Glorious Revolution allowed the possibility for a specifically lower-class narrative of events. The turmoil of 1688 was one of the few political upheavals that did not involve the defeat of "people." The popular narrative that followed 1688 was framed in the same constitutionalist terms as the debates between Whig and Tory factions and

---

[42] Catherine Hall, "Rethinking Imperial Histories: The Reform Act of 1867," *New Left Review*, 205 (1992), pp. 17–19. There has been a tendency to emphasize the "manly" qualities of independence in the nineteenth century. But it was also capable of being held by women, too, especially in the context of maintaining the independence of the family from the effects of debt.

[43] This is a subject that could well stand further research, particularly into the nineteenth century. See Nicholas Rogers, "Popular Protest in Early Hanoverian England," *Past and Present*, 79 (May 1978), pp. 85–100; Kathleen Wilson, *Sense of the People*, pp. 61–67.

theorists. But the emphases were different. In the popular version a more inclusive political nation was imagined; the right of resistance embodied in 1688 was privileged over the Bill of Rights and the notion of religious equality was introduced into the political culture which then opened the way for a broader meaning of equality to be installed in the later eighteenth century. This was the origin of what is called "popular constitutionalism." It was a protean phenomenon. Within its tent in the first half of the eighteenth century could be encompassed the popular political customs noted earlier and (in another part of the tent) the appeal of Jacobite sentiment.[44]

The idea of 1688 as a people's revolution sank deep roots into popular radicalism. The critique of the political structures that popular constitutionalism offered formed one of the major ideological currents flowing through lower-class politics well into the nineteenth century. By the end of the eighteenth century, some of the discourses of popular radicalism, such as Jacobitism, had entirely disappeared. New frameworks had appeared, such as the less historically based appeal of Thomas Paine to the natural rights of man. Painite radicalism marked an intellectual break with popular constitutionalism, but it did not succeed in capturing the program of radicalism for itself. By the early nineteenth century, Paine's prescriptions were one set among a veritable supermarket of programmatic offerings. Popular constitutionalism unified the competing vocabularies and discourses. This was particularly true for the agenda of radicalism once the Napoleonic wars had ended. The mass platform of those years claimed that betrayal of the ancient constitution by the government justified the appeal to forcible resistance as a strategy to bring on yearly Parliaments, the ballot and universal suffrage. This political imagination derived from the popular version of 1688 and it was an inspiration that animated all early nineteenth-century radicals, and beyond. Strong echoes of popular constitutionalism may be heard in the mass movement in support of the Tichborne Claimant in the 1870s.[45]

[44] Protestantism was part of popular constitutionalism, and gave a xenophobic strain to popular politics that identified foreign otherness as Catholic and effete. Aristocratic styles that borrowed from French and Italian culture were prime targets for this culture of national identity. For national identity, Protestantism and popular politics, see Colley, *Britons*; Gerald Newman, *The Rise of English Nationalism: A Cultural History 1740–1830* (New York, 1987); Hugh Cunningham, "The Language of Patriotism," *History Workshop Journal*, 12 (Autumn 1982), pp. 8–33; Marc Baer, *Theatre and Disorder in Late Georgian London* (Oxford, 1992), pp. 33, 66, 72, 192–206, for a fascinating study of this nationalism in action against Italian opera.

[45] Kathleen Wilson, "Inventing Revolution: 1688 and Eighteenth-Century Popular Politics," *Journal of British Studies*, 28, 4 (October, 1989), pp. 350–76. The relevance of Jacobitism to popular political ideology as more than just a traditional residual has been well established by Monod, *Jacobitism and the English People*, pp. 45–49, 170–82, and Colley, *In Defiance of Oligarchy*, pp. 146–74, for popular Toryism. See John Belchem,

The convergence of popular and mainstream radicalism, the fact that they spoke the same language of constitutionalism, allowed opposition movements to seek support from those who stood outside the political nation. The excise crisis of 1733 was the moment which may conveniently mark the beginning of an organized opposition that looked to some element of the excluded public for support. It also marked the moment when Jacobitism as a main vocabulary of popular opposition began to be displaced by more purely libertarian, and autonomous, constitutionalism. Added to this was the national dimension of the out-of-doors agitation against Walpole's scheme. The excise crisis should not be romanticized. The constitutionalist discourse was expertly used by merchants opposed to a general excise for purely self-interested reasons. Still, the excise crisis is important for the way it demonstrated the possibility of an extraparliamentary constitutionalist opposition. This model was followed by the movement against the cider tax in the 1760s which combined parliamentary pressure with the careful organization of "public opinion" in the countryside. And this pattern of mobilization led directly into Wilkes and the Association Movement of the 1780s. It was John Wilkes, however, who first revealed the full potential of calling in "the people" to redress the disrupted balance of the constitution.[46]

The Wilkite movement was the first mass movement to successfully project the ideology of popular constitutionalism into a political program that challenged the frontiers of exclusion bounding the political sphere. Wilkes went beyond the well-established practice of enlisting the support of those "out-of-doors" in his cause. More than any other previous movement, the Wilkite campaign built its legitimacy on the support of those excluded from the political nation. This was a complicated matter, but the opportunities that presented themselves to Wilkes reflected a changing sociopolitical dynamic to the public space of extraparliamentary politics.

"Republicanism, Popular Constitutionalism and the Radical Platform in Early Nineteenth-Century England," *Social History*, 6, 1 (January 1981), pp. 1–32; Epstein, *Radical Expression*, pp. 9–27. For Tichborne, see pp. 286–87.

[46] Dickinson, *Politics of the People*, pp. 116–23, 177–78; Corfield, *Impact of English Towns*, p. 156; Kathleen Wilson, *Sense of the People*, pp. 124–37; Brewer, "English Radicalism," p. 328; Patrick Woodland, "Extra-Parliamentary Political Organization in the Making: Benjamin Heath and the Opposition to the 1763 Cider Excise," *Parliamentary History*, 4 (1985), pp. 115–31; Paul Kelly, "Constituents Instructions to Members of Parliament in the Eighteenth Century," in Clyve Jones (ed.), *Party and Management in Parliament 1660–1784* (Leicester, 1984), pp. 169–84. During the excise crisis the practice was revived of constituents insisting on "instructions" to representatives as to how they should vote on particular issues in Parliament, and on the practice of reporting back. The purpose was to control oligarchy now that elections were held only every seven years and were often uncontested. Instructions were used in the 1740s and again in the 1780s. It was against this practice that the theory of virtual representation was developed most famously, of course, by Edmund Burke.

Prior to Wilkes a major strategy of popular politics had been to secure political influence by levering the differences within elite politics. The opportunities for this diminished considerably after the accession of George III in 1760. For one thing, the long political exile of the Tories now drew to an end. Their integration into the political establishment proceeded apace. This undercut the alliance between the people and the Tories that went back to the 1690s. The common interest between the Tories and the people was their shared exclusion from political power. After 1760 this mutual disadvantage no longer applied. In addition, at the same moment, the sociology and politics of the aristocratic elite displayed a distinct shift toward homogenization. Tendencies toward endogamous marriage patterns were one index of these caste-like trends. One effect of these developments was to diminish the practice of elites looking to the popular classes for political support. At the same time the middling-class presence in the provinces was beginning to stake its claims for a political voice.[47]

A more self-assured assertive middling-class pose was but one of the challenges that pervaded politics and culture from the 1760s. Yet certainly a more contentious class tone began to creep into the political culture. The elite began to mobilize around symbols of patriotism and nationalism, and launched a campaign to appropriate these symbols for conservative politics. George III's assertions of monarchical influence, the loosening of restraints upon executive power and the hounding of Wilkes all revived the consciousness of political closure. Oligarchy and executive tyranny seemed to be on the march again. Wilkes's challenge to political hierarchy was matched and complemented by events in the American colonies. John Brewer has pointed out that both domestic and colonial agitations refocused the meaning of "reform" from the purification of a corrupt oligarchy to include an independent Parliament secured through changing the system of representation. The American problem of taxation and representation indirectly, but unmistakably, allowed the issue of universal male suffrage to escape from the realms of philosophical daring into the glare of the public space. It was in 1776, after all, that John Cartwright made the first call for universal suffrage.[48]

[47] This is the argument of Kathleen Wilson, "A Dissident Legacy: Eighteenth-Century Popular Politics and the Glorious Revolution," in J. R. Jones, *Liberty Secured?*, pp. 299–344. It is an argument that is consistent with the data of Cannon, *Aristocratic Century*, showing how upper-class social and political power expands particularly through the last half of the eighteenth century. The 1760s is the time when this becomes really noticeable.

[48] John Brewer, *Party, Ideology and Popular Politics at the Accession of George III* (Cambridge, 1976), pp. 174, 208–15, 250–55; Colley, *Britons*, p. 209; Colley, "Whose Nation?: Class and National Consciousness in Britain 1750–1830," *Past and Present*, 113 (November 1986), pp. 97–117; Kathleen Wilson, *Sense of the People*, pp. 277–84.

The Wilkite campaign launched a frontal attack on the operation of oligarchical politics. It marked a major turning point in the development of opposition ideology. The core issue of the Wilkite movement was the need to bring oligarchy under control. How this was to be accomplished was the subject of much debate and the Wilkite program was a mixture of the old and the new. But in the final analysis Wilkes moved popular constitutionalism beyond the traditional "country panaceas of place and pensions bills and more frequent (triennial or annual) Parliaments" to include newer demands such as the extension of the franchise that "sought to give those out-of-doors a structural, permanent role in the political process." A program of parliamentary reform was developed for the first time. It included such measures as the publication of parliamentary debates, the redistribution of seats, the removal of place-men, more frequent elections, greater accountability of members to constituents, the secret ballot, more equal representation and (most controversially) a greater degree of enfranchisement. These notions all drew directly from the complex of ideas that composed popular constitutionalism. They were now presented for the first time as a national demand. For the next century reform politics were to pursue this agenda. At the heart of this program lay a more inclusive definition of the political nation. Expanding the political nation, breaching the boundaries of 1688, was now firmly stamped on the agenda of popular politics. And it was not to be erased.[49]

Thus, it was the Wilkite movement and the American revolution rather than the French revolution that delivered the political program of nineteenth-century popular radicalism. This is not to suggest that the French revolution may be deleted from the story of how the political nation was to be defined in this period. Yet for the particular storyline that is highlighted here, there are two points that stand out as especially important: first, the role of the French revolution in forcing a challenge to the conventions of all politics, and, secondly, the way it legitimated the intrusions of the people into politics. Neither of these were in themselves new; both were raised to a level of intensity that was unknown before.

The French revolution allowed the unthinkable to be imagined in politics. It was for this reason that from the 1790s the boundaries of the politically (and socially) possible were continually tested and stretched. The corresponding societies of the 1790s, Spencean radicalism and the mass platform after 1815 are among the best known of the political challenges to convention. I have already noted the striking challenges in gender politics where Mary Wollstonecraft and Owenite women socialists

[49] Brewer, *Party, Ideology and Popular Politics*, pp. 164–65; Brewer, "English Radicalism," pp. 343–54; Kathleen Wilson, "A Dissident Legacy," pp. 328–29; Kathleen Wilson, *Sense of the People*, pp. 438–39.

were part of a widespread confrontation to male power and privilege. In spite of the repression of the 1790s and beyond, the end political result of the wars against revolutionary France included a diversification of oppositional programs and ideas. By 1815 radicalism contained many competing vocabularies and had been revitalized by the example of the French revolution.

By the same token, however political conservatism was also invigorated. Edmund Burke seized the historicism of popular constitutionalism for Conservative politics. In *Reflections on the Revolution in France*, he proclaimed that history legitimated only the morality of political gradualism. The reformulated conservative politics that came out of the French revolutionary era, however, was not without its radical consequences. Loyalist politics consciously sought to mobilize segments of the lower classes in its cause. And, as in the previous wars of the century, opportunities expanded for women to engage with the political world. The functional role of conservatism in the political world was not simply a matter of blanketing radical impulses.[50]

Nevertheless (and this is the second point), after the defeat of Napoleon, reform regained its place on the political agenda. It did so largely because the French revolution had extended the possibilities for the role of "the people" in the political nation. In that respect, the work of the Wilkite movement and the mobilizations around the American war were resumed. After 1815 it was obvious that a genuine mass politics existed whose relationship with the political elite had become extremely tenuous. This presence was by no means the only stimulant to "reform." Ideological currents like free trade that were flowing through the political world pointed to the need to dismantle the fiscal-military state that had won the Napoleonic wars. Nonetheless, the out-of-doors agitation that broke out after 1815 endowed political reform with a special urgency. For it was not merely agitation and riot that had to be confronted.

The inroads of the lower classes into the public sphere of politics were not confined to the construction of the mass platform, the insolent newspaper press or sophisticated machinery of organization. From the end of the eighteenth century, the barriers protecting political institutions against the "lesser sort" bowed under severe strain. Franchise qualifica-

---

[50] Mark Philp (ed.), *The French Revolution and British Popular Politics* (Cambridge, 1991); Philp, "Vulgar Conservatism, 1792–1793," *English Historical Review*, 110, 435 (February 1995), pp. 42–69; Peter Spence, *The Birth of Romantic Radicalism: War, Popular Politics and English Radical Reformism 1800–1815* (Aldershot, 1996); E. P. Thompson, *Making of the English Working Class*, pp. 491–514; Belchem, "Republicanism, Popular Constitutionalism and the Radical Platform"; James Epstein, "Understanding the Cap of Liberty: Symbolic Practice and Social Conflict in Early Nineteenth-Century England," *Past and Present*, 122 (February 1989), pp. 75–118.

tions had become much devalued by inflation. It proved increasingly difficult to keep the lower classes out of political institutions like vestries or improvement commissions. Lower-class political influence had increased, was increasing and needed to be diminished. This was the task of Liberal reform. The Webbs noted a heightened struggle in vestry politics at the end of the Napoleonic wars between popular forces and those who wished to push back the gains demotic politics had made at that level of government. It was, they wrote, "the surging into the Vestry meetings of ... the populous parishes of large numbers of parishioners" that led to the campaign to restrict the franchise after 1815.[51]

Thus, the nexus of politics after the Napoleonic wars was a renewed version of the quandary of the revolution settlement of 1688–89. How was the political nation to be defined in a way that would adequately represent interest without opening the door to the corruptions of democracy? The challenge of politics from 1815 through the 1830s was to restabilize the system of political authority to contain the pressures on its existing boundaries of inclusion and exclusion. Those pressures derived from a variety of sources, some of which were to be found deep inside high politics. Growing divisions within Toryism spawned an increasingly fragile political self-confidence. The Tory wing of the governing elite cracked in 1828 when it gave way on the issue of Catholic emancipation in 1828. The Tories thereby demonstrated that the Constitution was not immutable. Wellington and Peel opened the door for political reform. And through that door walked the Whigs. For the most part, the Whigs were convinced that their mission demanded the completion of Charles Fox's unfinished agenda of the 1780s to gate the road against an ever lurking oligarchy. Yet whatever variety of political tradition was used to justify political reform, the inescapable question remained: who should and who should not be included in the political nation? It was this question that 1832 was designed to answer once and for all.[52]

[51] This may be a general feature of the later eighteenth century, but it is a question that needs more research. See Langford, *Public Life and the Propertied Englishman*, p. 429, for the increased presence of middling classes in rural government. See Webb and Webb, *The Parish and the County*, pp. 79–103; Sydney Webb and Beatrice Webb, *Statutory Authorities for Special Purposes* (London, 1964), pp. 446–49 (quote, p. 446).

[52] J. C. D. Clark, *English Society*, pp. 383–408.

8 Exclusion and inclusion: defending the politics of finality 1832–1885

Political stabilization and reform

The revolution of 1688 had created a political system that rested upon the principles of inclusion and exclusion. Yet precisely because those categories required constant affirmation, negotiation and recognition, this system was never free of instability. The boundaries between exclusion and inclusion needed to be continually patrolled and policed. By the early nineteenth century a complex of political and social tensions stretched thin the credibility of those boundaries. This was a process that flowed as much from divisions within elite politics as from the challenges mounted from nonelite politics. The issue that confronted the political world by 1830, then, was how to stabilize the political system. Specifically, how were the frontiers of inclusion and exclusion to be redrawn, political democracy staved off and trust restored in the existing structures of political authority? How was it possible to conduct viable politics in the arena defined by the existing principles of inclusion and exclusion? This was not a new dilemma, but it remained the dominant, recurrent predicament within which politics was enacted from the 1830s to the 1880s. The opening gambit of the political establishment was the reform bill of 1832.

The reform bill of 1832 remains one of the landmarks of nineteenth-century British history. The narrative to explain it that was constructed at the time of its passing continues to cast a long shadow. In broad terms, the bill was trumpeted as yet another example of the sense and sensibilities of the traditional Whig aristocracy, newly returned to power in 1830. It was the first step in the democratization of politics. The worst anomalies of the old unreformed system were removed. The most egregious disparities in representation – the notorious rotten boroughs – were corrected; recognition was finally accorded to the shifts that had occurred in the social and economic geography of the nation, and towns like Manchester were awarded seats in the Commons. The balance between land and urban property began to be adjusted, even if the continuing predominance of the former remained unaltered. Most of all, of course, the expansion of the electorate from under around 400,000 to around 600,000 meant the inclusion of new middle-class types in the political nation. In short, the reform bill was seen to reflect the dramatic changes of the industrial revolution and to register the social changes that followed in its wake.[1]

Historians have long recognized the difficulties with this narrative. Most of all, they have struggled with the central paradox of 1832: that the ultimate results failed to match the noise and heat that had been generated. There was no question about a transfer of power after 1832. Indeed, there was hardly a tremor to the placid serenity of the serried ranks of the landed interest seated in the House of Commons. Outside Parliament electoral politics carried on much as they had before. It is hard to see how democratization was advanced by the reform bill, apart from the somewhat abstruse notion that it demonstrated the mutability of the constitution. It proved that the constitution could be changed from within. Yet this was true only in the same sense that historians have been wont to console the memory of the Chartists with the thought that their six points were ultimately written into law about eighty years after 1848. Such a perspective merely highlights the limitations of the measure itself, of how many things it did not change. And this perspective, too, is quite consistent with an emphasis on the limits of social and economic change in the period of "industrialization." So what has all the fuss been about?

The answer to that lies, perhaps, in the relationship between the reform bill and "the people." This relationship was fraught at the time with ambiguity; subsequent historical treatment replicated that equivocation. Historical discussion of the bill has typically revolved around three issues: the role played by popular agitation in its passing, the dangers of revolution posed by this agitation and the extent to which the bill was a middle-class reform. All of these issues were formulated at the moment of reform itself. The first point, of course, is reasonable and debatable, the second is unanswerable and the third seems to be misplaced.

It was undoubtedly the case that Lord Grey and his colleagues were acutely aware of the relationship between political reform and public order. It is far less obvious that they had in mind a determination to

[1] J. R. M. Butler, *The Passing of the Great Reform Bill* (London, 1914); Charles Seymour, *Electoral Reform in England and Wales: The Development and Operation of the Parliamentary Franchise 1832–1885* (repr., Hamden, CT, 1970 [1915]), pp. 2–5. D. C. Moore, *The Politics of Deference: A Study of the Mid-Nineteenth-Century English Political System* (Hassocks, 1976), is the major statement for 1832 as an attempt to restore old electoral communities.

enfranchise the middle class. Certainly, there is precious little evidence that this was the ultimate result. There was no decisive change in the social composition of Parliament, no evidence of new kinds of policies that could be linked to exclusively "middle-class" interests. Although the electorate got bigger, its social profile varied greatly from place to place. The standardization of the franchise may have caused some in the middling class to *lose* the vote, especially in the smaller towns. This was particularly true at the boundary where the craftsman and small retailer melted into the middling ranks. It was generally the case, however, that those capable of acquiring the franchise before 1832 were also those who were likely to be electors after 1832. The relationship between 1832 and the middle class has been particularly hard for historians to fathom. If the measure was designed to bring the middle classes into the constitution, why were its results so limited in this respect?[2]

One way of answering that question would be to reconceive the link between society and politics. Thus, if it is not the case that 1832 reflects a deep structural change in the society that produced the "middle class" out of the "middling classes" then either those changes were not taking place, or they did not translate into the political sphere. Indeed, it may be the case that a better conception of the relationship between the people and the reform bill would be to see the reform bill as one of those influences that constituted the changing idea of the middle class itself. From this view, the notion that the Reform Act of 1832 was a middle-class measure reflected a narrative that was invented at the time to explain the course of events in the early nineteenth century. This narrative was not entirely imagined, of course; there *was* a relationship between the politics of the Reform Act and "the people." Yet it was not a one-way, or dependent relationship. There was a considerable space between the structural shifts in the society and the way these shifts found expression in politics. Within that space, it has been argued, lay the rhetoric of politics which both explained events and created their meaning. Thus, in this sense, the Reform Act can be seen as a rhetorical strategy which constructed the idea of middle-classness. It is possible to say that the Reform Act was complicit in the "invention" of the notion of middle-classness itself.[3]

---

[2] G. Kitson Clark, *Making of Victorian England*, pp. 5–7, 123; Woodward, *Age of Reform*, pp. 79–93; E. P. Thompson, *Making of the English Working Class*, pp. 888–909. On the social intentions of the framers of 1832, see D. C. Moore, "Concession or Cure: The Sociological Premises of the First Reform Act," *Historical Journal*, 4, 1 (1966), pp. 39–59, and E. P. Hennock, "The Sociological Premises of the First Reform Act: A Critical Note," *Victorian Studies*, 14, 2 (March 1971), pp. 321–27.

[3] On the construction of middle-classness and 1832, see Dror Wahrman, *Imagining the Middle Class: The Political Representation of Class in Britain, c. 1780–1840* (Cambridge, 1995), pp. 1–18, and *passim*.

This is itself an extremely neat rhetorical device which reconciles the ambiguities of political reform in this period. It is not my purpose to contest this perspective, which has a power that commands attention. My focus is somewhat different. I am less concerned to resolve the paradoxes that attach to political reform than to displace them. The category of the "middle class" was both a construction and an expression of a real social stratum. In the context of 1832, however, it served the two purposes of inclusion and exclusion. Middle class was a class and gender signifier which described that category of (male) person potentially eligible for inclusion within the political nation. It was also a principle of discrimination to weed out those who were, or should be, outside the circle of political power. In these respects, 1832 *was* a middle-class reform bill more than it was a reform bill designed to restore aristocratic authority. Yet there was nothing obvious or essential about the quality of middle-classness that the bill represented. The concept was exceedingly ambiguous and its meaning was highly arbitrary. There was no clear understanding or definition of what was meant by "middle class." Yet, without some understanding of the category, the political crisis of 1830–32 could not be resolved. The central political problem was to find a logic that would express these contradictory principles.

This is one way of locating reform in the immediate context of the 1830s. It is also important to contextualize 1832 in the longer-term rhythm of politics, however. It was not simply a successful and modest readjustment of political structures. It was also a place in the longer-term continuities of inclusion and exclusion. It is conventional even in revisionist accounts to link 1832 firmly to a narrative that begins in the later eighteenth century. Yet this does not provide a sufficiently broad perspective. By my reckoning 1832 was not only a response to a particular political crisis that could be seen building since about 1780. More profoundly, the first Reform Act was an attempt to resolve the problem that 1688 had introduced: how and where to draw the lines around the political nation. The shape assumed by the ultimate act was the product of many contingent and exigent influences, but it was devised to restore stability to the old constitution.[4]

By 1830 the recognition that political change was likely if not inevitable was widely shared within the political elite. All shades of elite political opinion, however, agreed that the ultimate question of reform was how

---

[4] What is now surely the conventional view of 1832 is expressed by O'Gorman, *Voters, Parties and Patrons*, p. 217: "it is difficult to see a departure in the direction of democracy in 1832." However, 1832 did reinforce the growing tendency to partisan voting. See John A. Phillips and Charles Wetherell, "The Great Reform Act of 1832 and the Political Modernization of England," *American Historical Review*, 100, 2 (April 1995), pp. 411–36.

best it could be limited. The differences within elite politics revolved more around their historical perspectives on why reform was necessary and what it was supposed to accomplish than they did on the actual clauses themselves. Liberal Tories in the 1820s – who have good claims to be the first nineteenth-century liberals – were political Malthusians, convinced that the major tendency of the period was the pressure of population on property and that any reform must work to maintain the viability of the old constitution. Lord Liverpool, prime minister from 1812 to 1827, regarded the question of political reform as proceeding from the proposition of what kinds of persons *ought* to be *elected* rather than who should be the *electors*. This expressed a common convention. For example, it was clearly true that the removal of civil disabilities from Catholics in 1829 severed the last principled opposition to constitutional change. It is important to note, however, that Catholic emancipation was accompanied by *raising* the Irish county franchise from the 40–shilling to the £10 level in a conscious effort to deprive Catholic Association supporters of the vote.[5]

Grey and his Whigs were no less cautious. Indeed, perhaps they were more timid. Whig analysis was caught in a compelling historical narrative about an overpowerful executive. At its core, the politics of Whiggism in 1832 were animated by the mission to complete the task that Charles James Fox never managed to accomplish in the late eighteenth century. The dominant faction in Whig government in 1831–32 were the lineal descendants of the Foxite Whigs. Excluded from power since the 1780s, their politics were essentially those of eighteenth-century Whiggism burnished and elaborated by Fox and his followers. The Whig reform mentality was preoccupied by the dangers of monarchy and fear of the depredations of the mob. As in the past, independent property was the prophylactic the Whigs offered against both these perils. The clamor from out-of-doors – the Bristol riots, Captain Swing and the rest – was as distasteful to the Whigs as the incipient tyranny that was assumed to beat in the breasts of the monarchs. And they showed no mercy in dealing with its depredations.[6]

Political reform was therefore about exclusion as much as it was about inclusion. The task of reform in early nineteenth-century politics was to restore authority to the political structures. It was agreed that this was to be achieved by finding the level of property qualification that would meet the pressure of population without succumbing to the inrush of democracy. Where such a line lay was very much a matter for debate. The internal discussions that formulated the bills of 1831–32 revolved entirely

[5] Brock, *Lord Liverpool and Liberal Toryism*, pp. 34–41.
[6] L. G. Mitchell, "Foxite Politics and the Great Reform Bill," *English Historical Review*, 108 (April 1993), pp. 338–64; Mandler, *Aristocratic Government*, pp. 19, 44–73, 128–31.

around how much needed to be done to end the agitation and maintain intact the "old constitution." Discussions about the secret ballot were linked to the level of property qualification that could be trusted to use the franchise wisely under that condition. Once the decision had been made to retain open voting, and thus protect "influence," it was felt that the borough franchise could be set at the relatively "low" figure of the £10 householder.[7]

It was not simply the difficulties of tying wealth to social status that were the cause of uncertainty. The problem extended to what was meant by the "middle class" and exactly who could be enclosed within that category. Historians have tended to assume that middle-class status was obvious. Yet this is far from true. There was an intense debate around that very issue in the early 1830s. The meaning of middle-class was highly uncertain, not only where it shaded off into the upper or lower classes, but even as to its basic core. One commentator in 1830 went so far as to deny that the middle classes were involved in manufacture or commerce. Some radical vocabularies stretched the boundaries of the middle class to encompass the propertyless. In a few confused conservative minds, lawyers and other professionals lay outside its confines. Nevertheless, there were certain common beliefs.[8]

All reformers, for example, were insistent on distinguishing the middle class from the "mob." There was general agreement that Parliament should be attentive to "public opinion." Parliament, however, was conceived of as a deliberative assembly, not a representative body; it did not need to take everyone's opinion into account. Parliament did need to reflect "interests," however. Thus, the advisability of ensuring a voice for the commercial, manufacturing and professional classes. The key issue was where the lines of demarcation were to be drawn in order to achieve this virtual representation. In broad terms, 1832 settled that balancing act by redrawing the boundaries of the political nation along the line of the propertied ratepayer. This was not a particularly liberalizing measure. Indeed, it served to strengthen the barrier of property qualification for inclusion in the political nation. On the other hand, as a measure of exclusion, the ratepayer principle possessed the inestimable advantages of capturing sufficient numbers of the middling classes and resolving the residual debate about the relative virtues of different kinds of property.

[7] Patricia Hollis, "Introduction," in Hollis (ed.), *Pressure from Without* (London, 1974), p. 2; Jonathan Parry, *The Rise and Fall of Liberal Government in Victorian Britain* (New Haven, 1993), pp. 44–45; E. A. Smith, *Lord Grey 1764–1845* (Oxford, 1991), pp. 259–65. A favored Whig argument for open voting was that it ensured the continued influence of the nonvoter who could make his opinion known to the appropriate electors; see Mandler, *Aristocratic Government*, pp. 168–69.
[8] Wahrman, *Imagining the Middle Class*, pp. 298–327.

The ratepayer was not a discovery of the reformers of the 1830s, however. A trial run for framing inclusion and exclusion around this category of property had been the reforms of vestry government in 1818 and 1819 mentioned earlier in connection with the organization of the poor law. The act of 1819 was a permissive measure which allowed select vestries to be established on petition from the largest ratepayers of the district. It was eagerly seized upon. By 1823 over 2,000 parishes had availed themselves of the privileges provided by the act to "reduce the power of the masses . . . and enable the middle classes to seize control of parish meetings or open vestries from the hands of the unruly democracy." Naturally, it was the towns that offered the most tempting targets for reformers, for the most conspicuous examples of vestry democracy were to be found in urban locales. Yet the task of rolling back democracy was not only a theme of urban politics. In the rural parish of Burwash, Sussex, for example, the act of 1819 facilitated a transfer of power from the small tradesmen to the large farmers. Indeed, from the perspective of reform, it was the small tradesmen who were the most problematic candidates for enfranchisement because they were perceived as the most corruptible by dependency.[9]

The possibilities for popular participation in vestry government continued to shrink throughout the 1820s. An act of 1823 gave parishes the right to transfer vestry business into a ratepayer-elected committee. An act of 1828 closed a loophole in the Sturges Bourne Acts which had allowed the option of submitting certain decisions of select vestries to popular referenda. Hobhouse's Act of 1831 standardized the ratepayer franchise for the London vestries; it introduced the secret ballot and "produced results very unfavorable to democracy" by encouraging the spread of the select vestry movement. The Hobhouse Act was unusual in one notable respect, however. It privileged class over gender by enfranchising some women ratepayers. More commonly, however, the reach of the political nation did not extend to women. The political nation was increasingly defined in male terms.[10]

One purpose of political reform was to close off existing spaces in politics for women. The line of gender exclusion in politics was more heavily drawn in the nineteenth century than in the eighteenth century. Both the Reform Act and the Municipal Corporations Act explicitly excluded women from parliamentary and local government franchises.

[9] Prest, *Liberty and Locality*, p. 12; Roger Wells (ed.), *Victorian Village: The Diaries of the Reverend John Coker Egerton, Curate and Rector of Burwash, East Sussex 1857–1888* (Stroud, 1990), pp. 9–10.

[10] Webb and Webb, *Statutory Authorities*, pp. 446–49; Redlich and Hirst, *History of Local Government*, pp. 167–68; Vernon, *Politics and the People*, pp. 17–19, for a more benign interpretation of Hobhouse's Act.

Yet this particular principle of exclusion continued to be a contested terrain. The courts did not act decisively on the parliamentary franchise for ratepaying women until 1868, when it was denied. Until then a few women had claimed and exercised the vote as ratepayers. A year later, Jacob Bright carried an amendment in the House of Commons giving women ratepayers the local government franchise. In 1872 the courts narrowed this to unmarried women, although there was no restriction for school board elections. The local government reforms of the 1880s enforced a strict gender franchise, and this was not lifted until 1894 for parish councils and 1907 for county councils.[11]

Political reform, however, was not principally about the franchise in 1832. Enlarging the voting public was secondary to reapportioning political power through matching the redistribution of seats with the representation of interests. It was in the interests of balance that closed boroughs survived in such large numbers after 1832. They were seen as refuges for talented persons (like William Gladstone or David Ricardo) who deserved to be given a parliamentary voice, or as a way for particular groups like merchants or colonial interests to acquire some merited political influence. The fear of reform was that it would destroy such channels and substitute the rule of an uninformed public opinion open to the perversions of corrupt influences. Reform was designed to preserve against this danger and to secure "the rule of property by men of intelligence and respectability."[12]

Indeed, the question of how to distribute the share of representation between the legitimate interests remained central to all Liberal reform measures until the 1860s. Representation of interests rather than by weight of numbers was the main theme of the reform bill offered by Lord John Russell and William Gladstone in 1866. Whig notions of how the various interest groups in the country could best be represented and what adjustments were necessary to restore a good balance between the various sectors of society framed the Cabinet discussions of this proposal. And the issue remained an important part of the Liberal package of reform into the 1880s. Far from marking the end of Britain's "ancien régime," the 1832 reform bill revitalized the supremacy of a system that was driven and dominated by a Whig aristocracy and Whig political assumptions.[13]

It was not the design of the 1832 reform bill to begin the inexorable

---

[11] Vernon, *Politics and the People*, pp. 17–18. Before the age of reform there was considerable ambiguity about female franchises at the local level. A legal precedent in 1739 had confirmed female voting rights in vestry elections, for example.

[12] E. A. Smith, *Lord Grey*, p. 327; Seymour, *Electoral Reform in England and Wales*, pp. 320, 329, 345–47; Parry, *Rise and Fall of Liberal Government*, pp. 45–46; T. A. Jenkins, *Gladstone, Whiggery and the Liberal Party 1874–1886* (Oxford, 1988), pp. 1–17.

[13] Biagini, *Liberty, Retrenchment and Reform*, pp. 315–18; Seymour, *Electoral Reform in England and Wales*, pp. 333–40.

movement toward parliamentary democracy. The ambition, rather, was to undercut that prospect. It aimed to do this by revitalizing the structures of virtual representation. Thus, the structures of politics remained largely unchanged. Most features of the "unreformed" system remained in place. Over forty pocket boroughs survived. The old fancy franchises remained in the possession of their owner for life. More than sixty members of Parliament continued to sit as nominees of large landowners in England and Wales. Methods of evading the property qualifications common to the unreformed system continued to exist in the world of reformed politics. The practices of splitting freeholds and of granting artificially low rent charges to create voters were just two of the more salubrious practices that the new system carried over from the old. Bribery was endemic in the pocket boroughs. The purchase of seats remained possible even in large constituencies like Liverpool. Those places addicted to corrupt elections before 1832 failed to break the habit afterward. Corporations like Leicester and Bristol continued to use public funds and charities as part of political competition.[14]

The issue of "corrupt practices" is a fitting illustration of these continuities. Corruption was endemic to the realities of eighteenth-century local politics. Corruption, however, was a question of definition – it was an unstable category – and a matter of place. High-minded sentiment was appropriate in the chamber of the House of Commons where eloquent murmurings deploring corruption were a staple rhetoric. In the real world of electoral politics, however, bestowing various emoluments of money or goods upon nonelectors was an extension of the reciprocities of deference. Political loyalty was expected of those in the service of, or in some way connected to, the political elite. This was to be as true in the factory towns as it was in the rural estates. The landlords of South Devon marched their tenants to the poll like well-drilled soldiers in 1835. So too did the entrepreneurial shipbuilder Charles Palmer lead "his" shipyard workers to the poll in Jarrow (a new town) in 1864, as if he were a feudal lord. Even in boroughs where the dominant interest behaved with the utmost propriety toward tenants and others, it was still expected that money would be spent at those businesses where artisan or small shopkeeper votes were to be had. These same voters might then expect some special service – an extra order of meat or extra pairs of shoes – on election day. It was an arbitrary consequence of legal definition that this might constitute bribery.[15]

[14] Norman Gash, *Politics in the Age of Peel* (2nd edn., Hassocks, 1976); Seymour, *Electoral Reform in England and Wales*, pp. 123–25, 129–31, 445–47; Vernon, *Politics and the People*, pp. 112, 141.
[15] For the importance of the politics of influence, see T. J. Nossiter, *Influence, Opinion and Political Idioms in Reformed England: Case Studies from the North East 1832–1874* (Hassocks, 1975), pp. 45–104.

The first act of Parliament to plot a line between reciprocity and bribery was the Treating Act of 1696. This act declared that any candidate who gave meat, money, drink or entertainment to procure a vote was to be disqualified and the election was voided. It had little effect. Subsequent legislation was no more successful in its discriminations. Indeed, there was general agreement that bribery did not diminish after 1832. It may even have worsened. The £10 householders turned out to be quite as venal as the old electors. This was due in part to the inadequate machinery used to combat corruption. Yet more fundamental was the reality that in the constituencies corruption was not seen as corruption. Showing "regard" for constituents and "serving" one's friends were integral to the reciprocity of political relationships. This outlook was as natural in the middle of the nineteenth century as it had been a hundred years before. In 1843 it was reported that neither candidates, voters nor agents exhibited any consciousness that treating and other briberies were dishonorable. The legal penalties for such acts may have cast a shroud of silence over them, but the law did not define their morality. Some tightening of the definition of corruption was attempted in 1854 when audits of election expenses were required for the first time. Enforcement of this law was hampered by the familiar absence of an efficient system of implementation. Indeed, the election of 1865 was reported to have been awash in more corrupt expenditure. Not until after 1867 were serious efforts made to redefine electoral behavior.

In 1868 responsibility for punishing corruption was transferred from the House of Commons to the courts. This was a significant step. The treatment of corruption was removed from the self-interested realm of politics into the distanced sphere of the law. At the same time political reform undercut the social practices that allowed corruption to thrive. The secret ballot removed the scope for practical demonstrations of deference. Electoral politics became more professionalized. These measures did not entirely root out behavior that was inappropriate to the conduct of elections. But they did mean that treating and the like could no longer be justified as expressing the social relations of hierarchy. The Elimination of Corrupt Practices Act in 1883 marked the culmination of these trends. This act placed firm limits on the amount of money that could be spent in elections and laid down strict rules for the amounts of expenditure in each category. Election practices like the treating of electors to beer or other goods and services were now defined as corrupt practices equivalent to outright bribery, and they were subject to the same punishment. The most effective provision of the act, however, was to hold candidates responsible for the conduct of the election behavior of their agents. Penalties for conviction were severe. The act undoubtedly changed electoral behavior, but it also reflected changes that were already in train. By the 1880s the world of politics was no longer bounded by the practices of social reciprocity and deference.[16]

As this suggests, popular politics retained their "premodern" forms after 1832. The hustings were as rowdy and ceremonially ritualistic as before. The number of contested elections increased somewhat, but continued to follow the pattern of the past rather than presage that of the future. Although the numbers fluctuated considerably – rising as high as 63 percent in 1837 – the more usual pattern was for only about 50 percent of constituencies to be contested. With the election of 1868 this proportion rose to 70 percent, below which level it was never again to fall in peacetime. As in the past, politics responded primarily to local stimuli. Constituency politics were sharpened only on those relatively rare occasions when major national issues intruded. The regional level seems to have been the most important horizon of political perception for most elections in the middle of the nineteenth century. This gave a different pattern to electoral geography from the local imperatives of the eighteenth century or the national perspectives of the twentieth century. The first elections that could be said to be fought everywhere from a national perspective were those of 1874 and 1880.[17]

Equally, the impact of 1832 on the shape and size of the electorate remained ambiguous. It did not reverse the long-term trend of an electorate that comprised a *diminishing* proportion of the population. Indeed, the post-1832 electorate was more selective than the old, unreformed electorate. Statistically, 1832 may even have slowed down the expansion of the electorate; the pace of the increase intensified quite noticeably from the late eighteenth century. Only 18 percent of adult males held the vote after 1832, as compared to 14 percent beforehand. The wide variation in the numbers of the urban electorate that had characterized the old system continued past 1832. In Leeds only 7 percent of males held the vote; in Manchester it was 27 percent and in Oldham 14 percent. The qualitative leap in the level of enfranchisement comes only after 1867 and 1884.[18]

Historians have tended to be impressed with the way parliamentary politics in this period prefigured twentieth-century party divisions. But it

---

[16] For the previous two paragraphs, see O'Gorman, *Voters, Patrons and Parties*, pp. 48–50, 170–71; Seymour, *Electoral Reform in England and Wales*, chs. 7–8, 13–14; Patrick Joyce, *Work, Society and Politics: The Culture of the Factory in Later Victorian England* (Hassocks, 1980), ch. 6; Cornelius O'Leary, *The Elimination of Corrupt Practices in British Elections 1868–1911* (Oxford, 1962).

[17] Miles Taylor, *The Decline of British Radicalism 1847–1860* (Oxford, 1994), pp. 7–11, 19–20; Nossiter, *Influence, Opinion and Political Idioms*, pp. 2, 167, 184–91, 197–99.

[18] O'Gorman, *Voters, Patrons and Parties*, pp. 179–82, 204–22; Vernon, *Politics and the People*, pp. 32–39.

is the faint outlines of those divisions and the ease with which the lines were crossed that is the outstanding feature. Outside Parliament the overall effect of 1832 was to reinforce the preexisting predictors of political partisanship. This was particularly the case with religion, which since the 1780s had emerged as the most reliable and constant index of political affiliation. Inside Parliament, there was a renewed importance attached to the "independence" of the member of Parliament after the 1840s. Political leaders like Palmerston and Derby in the middle of the nineteenth century resembled the great captains of the last century. At election time the popularity of candidate labels such as "Conservative-Liberal" or "Supporter of Lord So and So" was an accurate mirror of the general looseness of the lines dividing the groupings in Parliament. Thus, throughout the mid-Victorian years, parliamentary politics bore "a greater resemblance to the idiom and convention of Hanoverian politics than to the two-party politics of the later nineteenth century."[19]

Indeed, the issues of Hanoverian politics remained capable of animating the agenda of early and mid-Victorian politics. The politics of the Chartist movement are both too complicated and too familiar to be extensively treated here. Chartism had many faces, and historians have tended at one time or another to treat all of them as expressing its true meaning. Chartism was both a national and a local movement; it was both a class and a "populist" movement; and it was both backward- and forward-looking. From our perspective the most important theme of Chartism is precisely how it replayed on a much extended scale many of the themes of eighteenth-century radical politics. This is not to deny that the structures of political and social authority would have been upended had the six points been enacted. It was precisely for that reason that Chartism posed a class challenge to conventional politics that ultimately had to be faced and faced down. Yet Chartism confronted the politics of stabilization using the program and the methods of eighteenth-century radicals. None of the six points of the Charter was new to radical politics; most had been commonplace from at least the 1770s. Indeed, the Chartists deliberately withdrew the one item that would have signified a departure from the past: a gender-blind universal suffrage. The strategy of using mass politics to pressure and threaten – O'Connor's "peaceably if we may, forcibly if we must" tactic – was the central strategy of the politics of contention throughout our period. Even the style of leadership

---

[19] Miles Taylor, *Decline of British Radicalism*, p. 10. For the argument that the reform act did decisively change political practice, see J. A. Phillips, *The Great Reform Bill in the Boroughs: English Electoral Behaviour 1818–1841* (Oxford, 1992); Phillips and Wetherell, "The Great Reform Act of 1832." But much of the evidence presented in these places can be contextualized (more persuasively, I think) to argue for continuity rather than change. See also O'Gorman, *Voters, Patrons and Parties*, pp. 60–61, 116–17, n. 20.

contained strong parallels with the past. Feargus O'Connor was a very different political personage from John Wilkes, and O'Connor was by no means the only contender for leadership status. Yet the element of personal charisma in Chartism followed the earlier tradition established by Wilkes and continued by "Orator" Henry Hunt.[20]

Chartist politics were reminiscent of the past in another way, too. Chartism was a response to the fear that "old corruption" was about to be restored. There was good reason for this fear in the 1830s. A main theme of Whig reform was to install statist reforms – the new poor law, the new police forces and the like – that seemed to presage a re-formed executive power. Contesting executive tyranny was not a fanciful anachronism in the 1830s or 1840s. Indeed, this was an apprehension that ran well into the mid-Victorian years and deserves more attention than historians have chosen to pay to it. In the mid-1850s it seemed that the constitutional balance between legislative and executive power had once again been disrupted in favor of the latter. The demise of the East India Company after the mutiny of 1857 was expected to occasion a fruitful new seedbed for government to exercise its patronage and power in India.[21]

The Crimean war was largely responsible for the revival of the issue of executive power as a focus of popular politics. Some, like John Bright, responded by toying with the idea of extending the franchise as a way of ensuring popular control over the ever lengthening tentacles of central power. This was a notion that had more appeal to the organized working class than it did to any other social group. Nonetheless, Chartism had entered into the political discourse the idea of working-class enfranchisement, so there was political space for this strategy to play. It was not obvious at the time, however, that risking the franchise card would turn into the trump of the century. The imbalance in the constitution would more likely be redressed by older gambits. Thus, the response of mainstream radicalism was to turn to the traditional Whig solution of institutional reform. Proposals to reform the civil service in the 1850s were less the opening moves toward a twentieth-century professionalized bureaucracy, and more an evolution in the campaign against old corruption. The demands of the Administrative Reform Association, for example, were not an attempt to introduce a rationalized Weberian structure to

---

[20] Gareth Stedman Jones, "Rethinking Chartism," in Stedman Jones, *Languages of Class: Studies in English Working-Class History 1832–1982* (Cambridge, 1983), pp. 90–178. See also Asa Briggs (ed.), *Chartist Studies* (London, 1959); James Epstein, *The Lion of Freedom: Feargus O'Connor and the Chartist Movement* (London, 1982); John Belchem, *"Orator" Hunt: Henry Hunt and English Working-Class Radicalism* (Oxford, 1985); James Epstein and Dorothy Thompson (eds.), *The Chartist Experience, 1830–1860* (London, 1982).

[21] Miles Taylor, *Decline of British Radicalism*, p. 257.

government careers. They were another version of the "old radical [demand for a] purification of the legislature and the enhancement of the Commons' power through increasing the number of independent MPs."[22]

This, too, was the main theme of popular politics as represented by David Urquhart's movement against Palmerston's conduct of foreign policy in the 1850s. The Urquhart movement mobilized working-class support in the mid-1850s around the notion that Palmerston had revived an overpowerful, secretive executive, evasive of democratic control. Urquhart propaganda treated Palmerston as a new Chatham. It replayed the familiar tunes of eighteenth-century radicalism: corrupt and secret devices were being used to disturb the constitutional balance; the power of the House of Commons needed to be restored over the executive; foreign affairs were distorting domestic politics. This agenda was not simply the mirror of the admittedly very great eccentricities of its erstwhile leader and founder, David Urquhart. It was an agenda that was commonplace to the world of political ideas in the 1850s. Popular politics continued, therefore, to contain the potential to be mobilized by an eighteenth-century discourse and worldview.[23]

The 1832 bill was not entirely without innovation, however. One of the most important was the standardization of procedures for registering the electorate. In its turn, this implied new organizational strategies. The old instruments of local political mobilization – rituals, ceremonials, influence and the rest – remained formidably powerful. They were joined now, however, by a more formal machinery of politics. Organized electoral machinery appeared and much of the day-to-day work was delegated to registration officials who replaced the electoral agents of the old system. In the large urban centers registration became the principal instrument of identifying, retaining and mobilizing electoral support. In contrast to the past, registration required a more or less continuous attention, even in nonelection years. This task tended to be overseen by firms of solicitors who specialized in the work.[24]

---

[22] Ibid., pp. 247–51, 292 (quote, p. 249); Olive Anderson, "The Administrative Reform Association," in Hollis, *Pressure from Without*, p. 286.

[23] Briggs, *Age of Improvement*, pp. 433–34. The latest piece on Urquhart is Miles Taylor, "The Old Radicalism and the New." See also Olive Anderson, *A Liberal State at War*, pp. 139–52; Richard Shannon, "David Urquhart and the Foreign Affairs Committees," in Hollis, *Pressure from Without*, pp. 239–61. On the relationship between the mid-Victorian press and politicians, see Stephen Koss, *The Rise and Fall of the Political Press in Britain* (London, 1981), pp. 121–66.

[24] Phillips, *The Great Reform Bill in the Boroughs*, p. 303; Parry, *Rise and Fall of Liberal Government*, pp. 54, 72–80, 87; Cannon, *Parliamentary Reform*, pp. 240–50, 255–57; Gash, *Politics in the Age of Peel*, p. 394; O'Gorman, *Voters, Patrons and Parties*, pp. 67–90; Fraser, *Urban Politics*, pp. 186–88.

Registration was not merely an administrative device for ensuring compliance with the franchise law, however. The key to political mobilization rested on how many supporters could be legally registered as electors and how many opponents could be prevented from registering. Registration became a routine procedure for excluding potential voters from the political nation. The law provided ample scope for this because the meaning of the qualifications for the franchise was uncertain. Like the property qualifications of the eighteenth century, the definition of the 40–shilling freeholder or £10 leasehold was hardly straightforward and lent itself to varying interpretation. Overseers and clerks to the councils were awarded great power to decide who fell within those guidelines and there was ample space in the rules for all sorts of dirty tricks. To qualify for the franchise the potential voter had to be free and clear of all taxes, for example. The practice developed therefore of manipulating tax-collection dates in order to strike people from the register. It was estimated that around 150,000 people were disenfranchised by this tactic at some time between the first and second reform bills.

Moreover, the complexities of the registration process diminished the potential electorate. Registration procedures varied greatly across constituencies and the system produced many incomplete and defective registers. At one and the same time the process of registration made it difficult to claim a vote and easy to mount a challenge. Registration required application to the overseers in the counties and the clerks in the boroughs. Anyone could object to anyone else and (initially) there was no obligation to notify the applicant of an objection. About 40 percent of all potential voters in the boroughs were disqualified by such measures. The large boroughs in particular suffered massive exclusions. Over the years, Tower Hamlets, for example, lost about 5,000 voters to objections and another 11,000 from the uncertainties of the law on compounding occupiers. In Liverpool and Coventry only around one-half of the £10 occupiers typically appeared on the register.[25]

Much of the work of restricting the size of the electorate fell to the newly formed registration societies. As early as 1834 over 650 voters had been struck from the rolls in Leeds. The manipulation of registration was developed to a fine art, however, by the Anti-Corn Law League in the 1840s. The League demonstrated that the reformed system contained plenty of room for the kind of electoral manipulation that had corrupted the old system. Thus, freeholds were secured by the League for its supporters to qualify them for the vote. Likewise, the League became

---

[25] J. A. Thomas, "The System of Registration and the Development of Party Organization 1832–1870," *History*, 35 (1952), pp. 81–98; Seymour, *Electoral Reform in England and Wales*, p. 366.

expert at mass challenges to reduce the numbers of electors. In South Cheshire, for example, in the mid-1840s the League organized a challenge to between 2,000 and 3,000 voters out of a total of 8,000.

The work of registration societies after the demise of the League is not well documented, but it undoubtedly continued. In Liverpool in 1865 the secretary of the Liberal Association himself made out 3,000 of the 9,000 objections that were issued in the city. One-third of these were thoroughly frivolous and were sent out with the sole purpose of nullifying votes. Historians have argued that lack of interest in the vote by "the people" in mid-Victorian Britain merely illustrates their happiness with the Liberal hegemony and the absence of "class" sentiment. Surely this is to miss the point. The elaborate legalities of the franchise and the active work of registration societies to disqualify people obviously biased the whole system toward limiting inclusion in the electoral nation to "the upper few who pulled the strings of party organization." This, of course, was precisely what the designers of the Reform Act had intended.[26]

Elsewhere in the political system the same exclusionary tendencies were apparent. Although there was no gender barrier in the poor law electorate, the ratepayer was even more explicitly mandated as marking the boundary of the political nation. In drawing up the poor law franchise, the commissioners of the poor law had it precisely in mind "to avoid the opportunity for excitement and mob pressure afforded by public meetings." It was for this reason that secrecy was introduced into the voting system for the first time. Balloting at public meetings and oral declarations of the poll were explicitly forbidden in the election of guardians. Such practices were a treasured ritual of parliamentary politics. They were hardly considered seemly for the more serious business of poor law elections in which the moral probity of the poor and the expenditures of the rate payers were at stake. Voting papers were delivered by hand to each ratepayer to be completed in the privacy of his or her own home. Likewise, until 1894, the qualifications to serve as guardian were higher than the parliamentary franchise – requiring occupation of a property rated at £40 per year.[27]

---

[26] The best account of the workings of the electoral system at this level remains Seymour, *Electoral Politics in England and Wales*, pp. 126–28, 135, 144–51, 161–64 (quote, p. 164). This aspect of the system does not figure very large in Vernon's *Politics and the People*, even though it provides evidence for his argument for progressive narrowing of access to politics in this period.

[27] Sydney Webb and Beatrice Webb, *English Poor Law History: Part II. The Last Hundred Years*, vol. I (London, 1929), pp. 119–20 (quote, p. 120); Brundage, "Landed Interest and the New Poor Law"; Brundage, "The Landed Interest and the New Poor Law: A Reply," *Economic History Review*, 90 (1975), pp. 347–51.

Finality abandoned: 1867 and the making of modern politics

Throughout the mid-Victorian years the commitment to political reform by the parliamentary elite remained tentative and uncertain. It took some time for even good Whigs to see what historians have claimed to see in 1832 from its beginning – that it was only the first installment of reform. It was true that the pressures of both parliamentary and popular politics ensured that reform remained a constant item on the political agenda. Reform continued to be conceived, however, within the same exclusionary limits as before 1832. Not until 1848 did Lord John Russell abandon the notion that the bill of 1832 was a final measure. Gladstone voted against a Ballot Act in 1858 and the reform bill of 1859, and he did not commit to more political reform until 1865. John Stuart Mill, believing the suffrage was a trust, not a right, argued in favor of open voting rather than allowing the "selfish partialities of the . . . voter's personal interest, or class interest, or some mean feeling in his own mind" to hide in the secrecy of the voting booth. Twentieth-century concepts of democracy did not drive even the most open-minded Liberals of the middle of the nineteenth century.[28]

There was little difference between Liberals and Conservatives on the issue of working-class enfranchisement. Liberals tended to favor some reduction in the property qualification. Conservatives favored lateral extension by various kinds of "fancy" franchises which embodied property as a test of fitness. Whichever one was preferred, the reform bills that were proposed (in 1852, 1854, 1860 and 1866) were firmly in the reform tradition of the past. They were not intended to move the political system to a more democratic openness; their purpose was merely to reduce the value of the property franchise. None of the measures proposed manhood suffrage – which was the outermost limits of Radical–Liberal political discourse in this period.

In fact, working-class enfranchisement was not the point of these putative reform bills. Their intent was to shave the impediments of the act of 1832 to further middling-class admission to the franchise. The act of 1859 explicitly rejected the idea of lowering the franchise qualification. Instead, it proposed to extend the political nation by introducing new definitions of the property qualification. Thus, possession of £60 in a

---

[28] F. E. Gillespie, *Labour and Politics 1850–1867* (repr., London, 1967), pp. 98, 104, 106, 114, 159, 166, 168–96. How to limit the franchise was the focus of debate among parliamentary Radicals; see Miles Taylor, *Decline of British Radicalism*, p. 170; see Mill, *Considerations on Representative Government*, p. 209 (quote), and *passim*, for his arguments against the secret ballot. Mill's use of the word "trust" in place of "right" reminds us that his intellectual worldview was closer to John Locke than to T. H. Marshall.

savings bank or paying £20 per year as a lodger were suggested as possible credentials for ensuring the respectability of new voters. The dangers of democracy continued to shape the debate, as they had before 1832. Democracy meant government by those who had no propertied stake in the country and therefore no independence of judgment. The problem was how to find the right level of property-ownership that would, as Disraeli put it in 1859, guarantee independence from patronage control, yet be selective enough to be convincingly respectable.[29]

These were still the concerns in 1867, when the reform act was passed that began the process of mass male enfranchisement. In the past, historians have debated the relative importance of outside agitation or changing intellectual conviction to the ultimate passage of the second reform act of 1867. This argument need not occupy our attention. The more pertinent issues are twofold: first, the limited ambitions of the Reform Act of 1867 and, secondly, how those narrow intentions of the Reform Act of 1867 were thwarted. The act of 1867 set in motion a process that unraveled the balance between exclusion and inclusion. The boundaries that had confined the political nation and defined politics since the Glorious Revolution were breached. This was the crucial rupture in the political narrative of the nineteenth century. For the first time the possibilities were opened for new kinds of politics.[30]

Yet it was all a mistake. Virtually nobody intended reform in the 1860s to introduce mass democracy. In both the world of letters and in the world of politics, the dominant sentiment was for limited measures. The dangers of democracy to civilized society were a major preoccupation. Thomas Carlyle rehearsed those dangers cholerically in *Shooting Niagara* and Matthew Arnold mounted a more measured case in *Culture and Anarchy*. Both were texts of 1867; although *Culture and Anarchy* was not published until 1869, the essays that composed it began to appear in the year of the reform bill. Five years later, in the second edition to his account of *The English Constitution*, Walter Bagehot echoed the fear that excessive deference to the *vox populi* would devalue good government.[31]

There were solid reasons for such civilized people to be concerned. The reform debate coincided with a series of rude eruptions on the placid face of mid-Victorian equipoise. Race, empire, gender and class contextualized the reform debate in the mid-1860s, although it is easy to forget this in our focus on the parliamentary course of events. Rebellion in

---

[29] Parry, *Rise and Fall of Liberal Government*, pp. 209–10; Seymour, *Electoral Reform in England and Wales*, pp. 242–46.
[30] Maurice Cowling, *Disraeli, Gladstone and the Fear of Revolution* (Cambridge, 1969); Royden Harrison, *Before the Socialists*.
[31] Bagehot, *English Constitution*, pp. 16–27.

Jamaica and the subsequent controversy over Governor Eyre's suppression of the revolt tumbled into a debate about social authority. The first stirrings of demand for women's suffrage opened the challenge to domestic ideology that was to break out in full force over the Contagious Diseases Acts. The first Fenian terrorist campaign on the mainland with the raid on Chester Castle and subsequent bombings in Manchester and London was a reminder that England itself was not immune to violence. Trade union violence in the Manchester brickmaking and the Sheffield cutlery trades suggested that not all working men had supped the elixir of "respectability." Here were a succession of "others" that defined precisely the dangers contained in democracy. They were all in their different ways variants of Carlyle's "nigger question."[32]

Although reform was a major issue in the election of 1865, neither manhood suffrage nor equal electoral districts were contemplated. Another gentle extension of the franchise in line with the moving frontier of respectability was the main expectation. From the 1840s the meaning of "working-class" had been reconstructed to allow for the qualities of "respectability" and "independence" to be extended into their male ranks. The difficulty, as always, was at which exact place in the social hierarchy the line could be drawn between the respectable and the residual classes. Russell and Gladstone in 1866 were willing to contemplate a place somewhere between the £10 and the £6 ratepayer. However, when it was discovered that even the upper limit would enfranchise large numbers of working men there was a strong move in the Cabinet to withdraw the bill. In the event this proved impossible. Nevertheless, Gladstone presented the bill as reinforcing the status quo, pointing to the complicated franchise arrangements the measure contained. Even this was not enough for the Tories, who wanted to load the bill further with a written test for the franchise which was claimed to be more difficult than the clerkship exam for the civil service.[33]

The same concern with limits guided the efforts of the minority Conservative government that took power when the Whigs collapsed. Recog-

[32] Bernard Semmel, *Democracy Versus Empire: The Jamaica Riots of 1865 and the Governor Eyre Controversy* (New York, 1969), pp. 135–48; Hall, "Rethinking Imperial Histories," pp. 14–27; John Newsinger, *Fenianism in Mid-Victorian Britain* (London, 1994); Richard Price, "The Other Face of Respectability: Violence in the Manchester Brickmaking Trades, 1859–1870," *Past and Present*, 66 (August 1975), pp. 110–32.

[33] Mid-Victorian respectability and independence for the working class are discussed in Tholfsen, *Working-Class Radicalism*, pp. 216–22, 246–57; Geoffrey Crossick, *An Artisan Elite in Victorian Society: Kentish London 1840–1880* (London, 1978), pp. 134–39, 194–98, and *passim*. See Keith McClelland. "Time to Work, Time to Live: Some Aspects of Work, and the Re-Formation of Class in Britain, 1850–1880," in Joyce, *Historical Meanings of Work*, pp. 180–209, for the cult of respectability in the workplace. See also F. B. Smith, *The Making of the Second Reform Bill* (Cambridge, 1966), pp. 51, 61, 63–69.

nizing that household suffrage was to be the basis of the franchise, it was thought desirable to hedge this with all sorts of qualifications. One of Disraeli's ideas was to adopt a version of the vestry franchise where a low property qualification combined with plural voting for multiple properties. Dudley Baxter and John Lambert, the government statisticians, were kept busy figuring out at which ratable value this franchise could be awarded to *prevent* the working class from gaining a majority. This was difficult to achieve on the basis of the household franchise, and thus fancy franchises were included in the early stages of the bill.

Disraeli's reckless acceptance of amendments from Radical MPs in order to stay in power is generally regarded as the reason for the eventual large extension of the franchise. Yet this is not quite right. There were two clauses that ultimately caused the skin of the body politic to burst – the lodger franchise and the compounding of rates clause. Neither contained the original intent to enlarge the franchise. Indeed, the lodger franchise was initially restrictive since it disenfranchised single men of all classes who were more likely to live at home or in lodgings. By 1869 this clause had only added about 12,000 new voters to the rolls. Similarly, although the compounding amendment was to provide the breakthrough to a mass electorate, this was not implicit in either the amendment or the ultimate bill.[34]

It took nearly twenty years for the full impact of 1867 to be realized. Indeed, the ultimate growth in the electorate was the result of the effort to finetune the franchise to the exact location of the line between inclusion and exclusion. Nonetheless, within the provisions of the Reform Act to restrict the franchise ticked the time bomb of electoral democracy. The problem originated in the attempt to tie the franchise to the idea of the household while at the same time restricting the definition of a household to exclude those who fell below the line of respectability. Parliament spent many hours debating exactly what defined a household in an effort to secure the necessary clarification of this criterion. The result was that possession of the franchise became a matter of squabbling over what was a dwelling and what was not a dwelling.

[34] F. B. Smith, *Making of the Second Reform Bill*, pp. 146–47, 195, 200–02. The clauses of the Bill hit various classes in different ways. The one-year lodger residency requirement, for example, benefited the working class and tended to disadvantage the single middle-class male. On the other hand, lodgers had to claim the vote and were not notified if they were challenged. This requirement would be more likely to disadvantage the working-class voter who would be less likely to have time, resources or inclination to challenge officialdom. The result of this was to continue the exclusionary practices of the earlier period, but with the very important difference that they tended to hit hardest an age rather than a class category: it tended to be single (and therefore young) men of all classes who were the main category excluded from the franchise of 1867. See Duncan Tanner, *Political Change and the Labour Party 1900–1918* (Cambridge, 1990), pp. 110–17.

The abolition of the £10 rating requirement which qualified a dwelling for franchise purposes made this issue particularly problematic. It was understood that anything below £10 would capture large numbers of working men. The original act had tried to close this window by prohibiting compounding (that is the payment of rates in a rent) for any dwelling or part of a dwelling rated separately for poor law purposes. The intention of Parliament seems to have been to draw the boundary of the political nation at the tenement occupiers: that is, those who occupied dwellings where the landlord did not reside, and who were clearly not lodgers. At the same time Parliament had abolished the distinction between compounding householders and personal ratepayers. Thus, the question of what constituted a dwelling became a particularly crucial issue. The rating authorities could consider tenement occupiers as ratable for poor law purposes and thus as qualifying for the vote. Parliament tried to protect against this possibility – that tenement occupiers would be granted the vote – by requiring that occupiers pay rates directly and not compound it in their rent. Since overseers were obliged to rate owners of apartment buildings rather than occupiers, the latter would be excluded from the vote.[35]

This solution proved to be illusory. Rating authorities continued to regard multiple occupancy dwellings as ratable for poor law purposes. Although this particular anomaly was resolved by an act of 1869, there was still enormous variation between constituencies in the application of the law. In addition the meaning of the "household" in the context of a multiple dwelling continued to be highly ambiguous. The intent of the law had been to deny the possibility of more than one household in a house. But in 1878 Dilke sponsored an act that made separate dwelling areas within a house count as a household for registration purposes. Both of these measures served to break the lock of exclusion around property that the Reform Act had tried to retain. Once the final legal challenges to Dilke's Act had been removed in 1881, large-scale registration in places like the London boroughs sundered the restrictions that 1867 had contained. The constraints of exclusion had finally been breached.[36]

At the same time registration as a strategy of franchise restriction was greatly reduced. Registration procedures after 1867 continued to vary

[35] John Davis, "Slums and the Vote 1867–1890," *Historical Research*, 64, 155 (October 1991), pp. 377–86.
[36] John Davis and Duncan Tanner, "The Borough Franchise After 1867," *Historical Research*, 69, 170 (October 1996), pp. 306–27; John Davis, "Slums and the Vote"; Seymour, *Electoral Reform in England and Wales*, pp. 354–58; Biagini, *Liberty, Retrenchment and Reform*, pp. 279–80. Between 1871 and 1881 the electorate grew by 26 percent compared to a 15 percent rate of population growth, thus breaking the pattern of the previous 200 years.

from place to place. The act had set down no national standards. Much depended on the opinion or competence of the particular revising barrister or on the discretion of overworked poor law officials. This is one reason why there was such a wide variation in enfranchisement between constituencies after 1867. Towns with few tenements presented fewer rating problems because of the absence of the complexities of the compounding law. Such towns, therefore, saw larger numbers of the male working class enfranchised. At the same time, registration remained both partisan and inefficient. Henry Broadhurst, the Labour member of Parliament, was only one celebrated victim of this system. He was elected to the House of Commons before he was able to qualify for the vote. Ultimately, these anomalies were addressed in acts of 1878 and 1885 which prohibited the indiscriminate use of objections to registrants for the purpose of party advantage. In this way, too, the structures of inclusion and exclusion were dissolved.[37]

A further result of the logic of 1867 was to displace the representation of interests from the definition of parliamentary reform. For the first time, possession of the vote became *the* central meaning to parliamentary reform. Redistribution of seats became dependent on the fact of population and not on the need to adjust to the changing prominence of particular interest groups. This changeover happened almost naturally as growing registration highlighted the contradictions that were produced by different franchise systems for the boroughs and the counties. A slight change in residence could change one's electoral status. This affected working men most particularly. A significant agitation around this issue was mounted by the miners of the North West in the 1870s. At the same time agricultural laborers who were gaining a newfound voice in other areas, too, began to chafe openly under the limitations of the county franchise. Rural popular liberalism began to press for agricultural laborers to come under the same electoral qualifications as the urban workers. Those counties that were partly industrial saw a much greater number of working-class electors registered under the £12 occupiers' franchise, which few agricultural laborers possessed. It became quite impossible to justify these arbitrary distinctions. By 1884 Gladstone was pointing out that the variations in the franchise were now greater than ever before because of the way these different standards of qualification worked.

The consequences of 1867, therefore, made the Third Reform Act of 1884 inevitable. Household suffrage was extended to the rural areas. The Third Reform Act equalized the county and borough franchises and implied an overhaul of the principles of representation by seats. It

[37] Seymour, *Electoral Reform in England and Wales*, pp. 353, 364–77.

brought together the issues of franchise and representation in a way that none of the previous bills had done. The result was that the "longstanding representative system was in tatters, and Britain had taken the essential steps on the road to democracy." Even at this late date the reflexes of exclusion around the criteria of property were not entirely dead and there were faint proposals to link votes to tax liability. Aside from the obvious continued restriction around along gender lines, 1884 did not remove all the barriers to one-man/one-vote. Ancient franchises remained and composed about 20 percent of the county vote. Such anomalies were rapidly becoming marginal to the system, however, and could hardly be regarded as formidable defenses against inclusion. The 1884 act made explicit what had been only a hope in 1867: that the removal of the barriers to a fully inclusive political nation was clearly in sight, including the incorporation of women. Between 1866 and 1886 the electorate grew from 1 million to 4.4 million; by 1915 it had grown to 6 million.[38]

Systems of political mobilization also changed quite decisively between 1867 and the mid-1880s. They did so gradually, however, and not without one last reminder that the past was not yet a distant country. The most important mass movement of the period between the second and third reform bills was the curious case of the movement in support of the Tichborne Claimant. This campaign opened in 1867; by the mid-1880s it had faded away. It has typically been accorded short shrift by historians – even more so than those other oddities of the Victorian political world who do not fit its progressive image such as David Urquhart or Joshua Toulmin Smith. It is easy to see why historians have failed to take it seriously as a representation of popular politics. The campaign rested on a clear fraud. It revolved around the claims of one Arthur Onslow, a butcher, to be the lost heir to the fortune of the Tichborne family. In spite of clear evidence that this was not so, Onslow attained a celebrity status for a while and even secured the support of some key family members. He rapidly faded to the level of fairground freak once he lost a key legal case. His lawyer, Michael Kenealy, subsequently established the Magna Charta Association which became the largest mass movement between Chartism and the Labour Party. Kenealy was a charlatan and a rogue, yet his standing was such that he managed to secure election to Parliament as the member for Stoke-on-Trent for a brief term.[39]

[38] For the preceding two paragraphs, see ibid., pp. 286, 289, 458, 468–73, 478–82; Parry, *Rise and Fall of Liberal Government*, pp. 280–82 (quote, p. 280). See Andrew Jones, *The Politics of Reform 1884* (Cambridge, 1972), for the parliamentary history of the third reform bill.

[39] This account is derived entirely from Rohan McWilliam, "Radicalism and Popular Culture: The Tichborne Case and the Politics of 'Fair Play,' 1867–1886," in Biagini and Reid, *Currents of Radicalism*, pp. 44–64.

It would be easy to dismiss this movement as a form of nineteenth-century popular theater, were it not for the fact that "theater" is not merely about plays. A movement that lasted well over a decade, was able to sustain its own apparatus of mobilization such as a series of newspapers and secured the support of such journals as *Reynolds' News* deserves more than a passing mention in the popular history of the nineteenth century. What we make of it is another matter. For our purposes, however, its political program provides a clue. The politics of Tichborne belonged entirely to the world of popular radicalism that was born out of the politics of 1688. Like all previous movements, the Magna Charta Association drew upon the image of an overpowerful executive that needed to be checked. It proposed to do this by an eclectic appeal to tradition, including restoration of the power of the crown and support for the powers of the House of Lords. At the center of its program lay many of the old chestnuts of traditional radicalism including the abolition of the income tax, triennial Parliaments and the need for a system of law and government that was free from corruption and influence. The name itself, the Magna Charta Association, invoked linkages between the resistance to tyranny, the "free-born Englishman" and the Chartists' charter. Its propaganda explicitly harked back to the radical tradition of the seventeenth-century revolution and the Bill of Rights. A particular target of the association was the secret ways of the law and the influence of lawyers on the system of government. This was partly due to Kenealy's own unfortunate experience with the legal profession; he had been disbarred for his behavior over the case. But it also reflected a vision of the law as driven by "fair play" and morality rather than by the formalistic science that was currently receiving codification in the Judicature Acts of 1873.

The Tichborne campaign possessed an internal symmetry between the past and the present. On the one hand, it embodied the last gasp of a radical program that was embedded in the politics and ideology of the seventeenth and eighteenth centuries. On the other hand the Magna Charta Association was one of the founding organizations of Henry Hyndman's Democratic Federation in 1881, the forerunner of the first avowedly Marxist political organization in the country. Then again, the referencing of the crown and the House of Lords, for example, reflected early signs of the use of these institutions as popular, conservative icons in the style of the twentieth-century media. This was the moment when the ceremonial and rituals of monarchy began to be orchestrated and marketed. The ubiquitous souvenir mugs issued on notable royal occasions were first distributed to all schoolchildren in 1887. Even as it anticipated the future, however, the Tichborne campaign and its aftermath stand as the last great mass movement of the period 1688–1880.[40]

By the 1880s, the vocabulary of political programs came to draw upon a different language than in the past; the strategies of mobilization follow different scripts. I do not need to describe the dynamics of these changes in detail; at bottom, they proceeded from the enlargement of the electorate that rendered obsolete the traditional methods of mobilizing and expressing support. The distinctive feature of political mobilization after 1880 was the creation of *formal* structures of organization, like the caucus system, to channel and represent political affiliation. In terms of the techniques of political mobilization, the Ballot Act of 1872 was a more radical measure than the second reform bill. The Ballot Act turned voting from a public act to a private act. It thereby undermined the collective ceremonials and rituals that had been characteristic of the old system. Voting was no longer an expression of crossclass communities bound together by reciprocal obligations.[41]

The Ballot Act ended the tension within the political system between dependence and independence. Balloting was now an act of individual political affirmation. It pushed another bit of politics into the private sphere. Mass support had now to be mobilized by means other than the theatrical styles of a pretended paternalism. The relationship between the spectacle of politics and the content of politics was also ruptured, therefore. Spectacle in politics had depended upon the wonder of crossclass relationships and partnerships. This was no longer necessary. Ceremonial continued to be essential to the process of politics, of course. But it was no longer integral to the content of politics. The emblematic shift in this respect was the consignment of lord lieutenants and other local gentry to an increasingly ceremonial role in the politics of the counties and boroughs. These icons of the past were suitable ornaments to trundle out for opening sessions of the county or borough councils and for presiding over the local bazaar. They were no longer owed, nor were they accorded, the sort of deferential allegiance that suggested real dependence.[42]

The machinery of electoral politics changed quite dramatically. Over the period between the second and third reform bills a new class of professional electoral agents emerged to maintain constituency organiz-

---

[40] Until c. 1870 the presentation of royal ritual was shabby and inelegant. This seems to change with the carefully orchestrated celebrations on the occasion of the Prince of Wales's recovery from typhoid in 1872. See W. Kuhn, "Ceremony and Politics: The British Monarchy, 1871–1872," *Journal of British Studies*, 26, 2 (April 1987), pp. 133–62; Cannadine, "Context, Performance and Meaning of Ritual," pp. 120–38.

[41] See Nossiter, *Influence, Opinion and Political Idioms*, p. 7.

[42] For the consignment of the aristocracy to ceremonial events, see David Cannadine, *The Decline and Fall of the British Aristocracy* (New Haven, 1990), esp. part I.

ation. They replaced the solicitors who had typically done the work of registration and electioneering. Both Liberals and Conservatives created new kinds of structures immediately after 1867 to coordinate the local constituency associations with the national leadership. The Liberals were slower to do this than the Conservatives. The caucus system and the National Liberal Federation were put in place only after the Liberal defeat at the election of 1874. In spite of this, it was generally true that the Liberal organizational structure was more effective than that of their rivals. On the other hand, the Conservatives pioneered mass mobilization of a different kind when the rebels of the Fourth Party formed the Primrose League in 1884 as a way to motivate volunteer enthusiasm for election campaigns. The League soon became a mass organization of one million members who staged new productions of political theater throughout the year to project the Conservatives as the party of imperial patriotism. Still, in spite of the Primrose League, mass politics became less ritualized and ceremonial and tended to retreat to the ongoing routine of the committee room.[43]

Election campaigns also changed. The elections of 1874 and (more clearly) 1880 rank as the first "modern" elections in which a clear choice existed between two distinct parties and programs. Similarly, Gladstone's campaigning throughout Midlothian in 1880 was the first election canvass that explicitly sought endorsement for a political program policy from the democratic masses. The assumptions about inclusion that underlay this effort were distinct from the rituals and ceremonies that had characterized popular politics before 1867. The importance of the Midlothian campaign was that Gladstone appealed to the "people" as part of the political nation and not, as Wilkes and those who followed him had done, as an outside pressure group whose noise and disturbance could force the political elite to eschew its corrupt ways. The Midlothian campaign contained none of those rowdy, threatening overtones; it was an appeal to the ultimate tribune of sovereignty of the people en masse. Gladstone's political genius – some would argue his ultimate nihilism – was to smash the sedate politics of Whiggism, perhaps before its natural course was run. By 1880 Gladstone saw that the barriers of exclusion were fast crumbling and he accepted the necessity for political accounta-

---

[43] See H. J. Hanham, *Elections and Party Management: Politics in the Time of Disraeli and Gladstone* (2nd edn., Hassocks, 1978), pp. 93–154, 233–48, 347–68, for organizational changes. The transitional nature of the period 1867–84 is the main theme of this book. For the Conservative organizational efforts, see E. J. Feuchtwanger, *Disraeli, Democracy and the Tory Party: Conservative Leadership and Organization After the Second Reform Bill* (Oxford, 1968); Fraser, *Urban Politics*, pp. 192–94; J. H. Robb, *The Primrose League 1883–1906* (New York, 1942); Martin Pugh, *The Making of Modern British Politics 1867–1939* (New York, 1982); Pugh, *The Tories and the People 1880–1935* (Oxford, 1985).

bility to the same democratic forces that he had personally viewed with considerable equivocation well into the 1860s.[44]

The end of the old forms of popular politics meant the end to a fabric of popular politics that expressed inclusion through strategies that were spontaneous and carnivalesque. Historians may easily fall into the temptation to romanticize these older structures of inclusion as more authentic than the formal structures of inclusion that replaced them.[45] It was true enough that the space of politics after the 1880s filled with formations that practiced their own kinds of exclusions. Yet the key difference between the political world that marked the period 1688–1880 and that which followed lay in the expansive potential each possessed.

The possibilities for limitless expansion were unknown to the political structures before 1880. Indeed, as I have argued here, the political world was defined by boundaries that were primarily exclusionary. The unintended effect of 1867 was to set in motion a dynamic that undermined the foundations of the balance between inclusion and exclusion. After 1884 exclusions from the political system remained, but they were increasingly seen as anachronisms. The continued exclusion of women constituted the largest remaining obstacle to an inclusive political system and suggested that class was more easily transcended than gender in this sphere. Yet the intensity of the debate on the politics of gender exclusion that opened after the mid-1880s reflected the growing weakness of opponents to women's suffrage as well as the strength of their opposition.

The bias of the definition of political nation had shifted from how people were to be excluded to how they were to be included. This change introduced a range of new political possibilities which gradually occupied the stage on which politics was played after the 1880s. The language of democracy could be now spoken as a foreseeable reality. This does not mean that democracy was uncontested. The politics of the period after the 1880s to 1914 contained plenty of anti-democratic forces. And the political programs of democracy provided a new level of contestation and debate. Still, it was now possible to contemplate opening the political system in ways that had not been plausible before. New groups like working-class men and women of all classes could more easily claim

---

[44] Whether Gladstone's position was a function of commitment on his part, or conversion, or a function of his rhetoric does not need to be entered for the sake of this argument. See Biagini, *Liberty, Retrenchment and Reform*, pp. 412–25; Parry, *Rise and Fall of Liberal Government*; Pugh, *Making of Modern British Politics*, pp. 1–3; see John Vincent, *The Formation of the Liberal Party 1857–1868* (London, 1966), pp. 211–35, for the emergence of Gladstone as a democratic symbol. Gladstone had pioneered the technique of stumping the country in the late 1860s. See Hanham, *Elections and Party Management*, pp. 202–06.

[45] This is the argument in Vernon, *Politics and the People*, pp. 158, 338.

admission to the political nation. Spaces were created in politics for new associational groups to obtain access – trade unions and employers' associations, for example. New kinds of political programs could compete for a place on the national agenda – the politics of labor and the welfare state that were to dominate the first two-thirds of the twentieth century began to emerge. Class – or perhaps it might be more accurate to say a particular construction of class – emerged as a key marker of electoral politics, replacing religion. National politics emerged in an ongoing way, instead of episodically as had been true before. These politics were not necessarily better than those of the period 1688–1885; they played out in a different arena, with different boundaries and different dynamics. Between 1867 and the mid-1880s the boundaries of the old system were ruptured and a new politics was created.

9   The stabilities and instabilities of elite authority: social relations c.1688–c.1880

Class, populism and paternalism

How may we understand the nature of social authority in the period of this book? How was elite power secured and maintained? How was consent generated? How were social relations between the classes mediated in the culture, outside the formal structures of law?[1] Merely to ask these questions introduces a series of paradoxes about British social relations during this period. The apparatus of government as it related to social authority was highly localized, deeply personal and, taking the national perspective, weakly deployed. Outside Ireland – a big exception – political and social stability was seldom in question. Yet Britain was not an orderly place. It was, in fact, quite disorderly, as foreign contemporaries frequently remarked and as historians have confirmed. Securing social authority was not blandly unproblematic. Conflict and contention were endemic. Thus, order and disorder among the populace, respect and disrespect for authority and status, strength and weakness of the forces of law and order – all describe the qualities of British social relations.[2]

The conventions and procedures which governed social relations in this period were capable of containing such contradictions. There was a specificity to those social relations that has not been fully appreciated. To the contrary, historians have been constantly tempted to regard the social relations of this period as straining to reach the embrace of the class society of the twentieth century.[3] This is a temptation that it would be

---

[1] As has been suggested, the law was a crucial arena when social relationships needed repairing, but the question addressed in this chapter is what made people obey the law.

[2] There is an extensive bibliography on this. For a sample, see, of course, Charles Tilly, *Popular Contention in Great Britain 1758–1834* (Cambridge, MA, 1995); Walter Shelton, *English Hunger and Industrial Disorders: A Study of Social Conflict During the First Decade of George III's Reign* (London, 1973); John Bohstedt, *Riots and Community Politics in England and Wales, 1790–1810* (Cambridge, MA, 1983); Mark Harrison, *Crowds and History: Mass Phenomena in English Towns 1790–1835* (Cambridge, 1988).

[3] Most famously, of course, Edward Thompson succumbed to this temptation in *The Making of the English Working Class*. The history of the eighteenth-century lower class

well to avoid, but which must be faced before the questions raised at the beginning of this chapter can be approached.

The notion of class is both a hindrance and an asset to the present project. It is a hindrance when we seek to understand social relations in this period through the prism of class consciousness. Indeed, to proceed in such a way would be to divert attention away from what was particular about social relations in this period. The kind of "consciousness" that prevailed among the lower classes does not fit any meaningful model of class derived from the twentieth century. Indeed, in this sense, talk of class impedes a proper historical contextualizing of social movements and social behavior.[4] Sightings of class in the popular consciousness of the eighteenth century are rare enough for Edward Thompson to have suggested most usefully many years ago that it was quite possible to have a class society without class consciousness among the mass of the people. Although Thompson limited that observation to the eighteenth century, my own inclination is to extend its implications well into the nineteenth.[5]

Equally, class is an asset which it would be unwise to liquidate from historical practice or, in the manner of a more recent scholarly seduction, to dissolve into the purely representational.[6] How can we fail to recognize the class stratifications in this society? How can they *not* be part of our analysis? The period of this book saw class power exercised in more

continues to be written from this perspective. See John Rule, *The Labouring Classes in Early Industrial England 1750–1850* (London, 1986); C. R. Dobson, *Masters and Journeymen: A Prehistory of Industrial Relations 1717–1800* (Beckenham, 1980).

[4] Owenism provides a good example of this. The economic and the political theory of Owenism belonged to the traditions of the seventeenth and eighteenth centuries. Politically Owenism was bounded by the tenets of eighteenth-century radicalism. It was neither "utopian," in Marx's phrase, nor modern. The central role that Owenism assigned to the state was "clearly an inheritance of seventeenth- and eighteenth-century concerns." The sociopolitical assumptions of Owenism were thoroughly paternalistic. Owenism was "a final attempt to revive classical republicanism" in Britain and his visionary *New View of Society* was "the last influential statement of a rationalist doctrine to be published in England." By the same token, Owenism always had the potential to go beyond conventional boundaries, as evidenced by the egalitarian gender relations it imagined, and by the 1850s it was moving toward the idea of the state as an agent of socialism. It was precisely its visionary elements that provides its historical interest. See Claeys, *Machinery, Money and the Millennium*, pp. 192–93 (quote, p. 193); Claeys, *Citizens and Saints: Politics and Anti-Politics in Early British Socialism* (Cambridge, 1989), pp. 7, 27–29, 329 (quote). For Owen's paternalism, see V. A. C. Gatrell, "Introduction," in Owen, *A New View of Society. And Report to the County of New Lanark*, ed. Gatrell (Harmondsworth, 1970), pp. 20–21, 44–47, 79 (quote).

[5] E. P. Thompson, "Eighteenth-Century English Society: Class Struggle Without Class?," *Social History*, 3, 2 (May 1978), pp. 133–66. Thompson could hardly argue differently, of course, given the thesis of his *Making of the English Working Class* that class consciousness had been attained by the working class by 1832.

[6] The best example of the revisionist alternative on class for the nineteenth century is Joyce, *Democratic Subjects*. For more extended remarks on revisionism of this sort, see Richard Price, "Languages of Revisionism."

blatant ways than at any other time in modern British history. The most striking attribute of the sociology of society over the period 1688–1880 was precisely the unvarying grip of the landed elite on the cultural, social, political and economic capital of society.[7] I do not intend, therefore, to dismiss class or its expressions from this period. I take it as given that society was stratified in ways that make it possible to talk about class groupings in this period. There were obviously organizations that were middling-class or lower-class in character. Accompanying these organizations were discourses that disputed the existing arrangements of class power and, to varying degrees, imagined alternative configurations of authority relationships.

Chartism, in particular, was a class movement the revolutionary implications of which have recently been too easily overlooked. Chartism was not a twentieth-century class movement, however. The challenge Chartism posed to class rule is not diminished by allowing that its programs and discourses cannot be slotted into twentieth-century frames of reference about class or politics. Chartists, like the French revolutionaries, claimed to speak for all "the people" including richer and poorer; they drew distinctions between groups as much on the moral ground of behavior as on a particular social position. This of course remained true of "class" politics after the demise of Chartism, although by the late nineteenth century it was true in a series of thoroughly different senses. The Labour Party might present its program as serving the interests of all "the people," but by this it meant that the ultimate agenda was determined by the working people.

This contrast suggests the importance of the sociocultural context in which social relations are embedded. Social relations attain meaning because of the way they are actualized in society. We know about them because of how people act and the social practices they perform. Particularly significant for our reading of social relations are the institutional, organizational and ideological environments through which they are expressed. The key difference in the sociocultural context of social relations in our period and the modern era lay in the absence of a self-conscious institutional and ideological presence that could make claims in the society on behalf of the lower classes. Class action in our period – such as

---

[7] Lawrence Stone and Jeanne C. Fawtier Stone, *An Open Elite?: England 1540–1880* (Oxford, 1986); Cannon, *Aristocratic Century*. This is not to suggest that the hegemony of the landed classes remained unchanged. The centers of power were multiplying, not diminishing, during this period. Power itself was increasingly diffused. The middling classes expanded enormously and their social stratification became more elaborate and fragmented. The same was true for the laboring classes, the sociology of which decomposed and recomposed as the shift from agriculture into various forms of manufacture proceeded.

an election riot – thus did not possess the same meaning or implication that class action in the twentieth century would have. The problem is not with the fact of class in this society; the problem is to explain how the social relations of this class society were governed by structures and conventions which cannot be appreciated through the terminology or framework of class. To put it another way: the language of class was different.

The language of class is always unstable. The question historians need to address is the particular content of its instabilities and imprecision. Throughout the eighteenth century and the first two-thirds of the nineteenth century, the meaning of class was not measured against material levels of wealth or precise sociological locations. When Gregory King calculated the population of England and Wales in 1695, he conceptualized a gently sloping pyramid with twenty or so various status and class levels. King's categories were not contingent on wealth or inheritance, and it was more important to him that his research on population size was generally confirmed by biblical prophecy. The codes available to describe social being and social hierarchy did not possess the conceptual capacities to link social being with social place in the manner of census classifications or the positivist methods of modern sociology.[8]

By the middle of the eighteenth century, the first tremors were registered of a shift in terminology from "ranks and orders" to the idea of "classes." Various attempts to link social classification with economic and social forces were made. Yet these did not establish a conceptual dominance. They competed with such alternatives as the language of ethnicity which defined all English people against all foreigners. It is entirely historically appropriate that the first mention of the "working classes" appears in Britain in 1789. Nevertheless, the notion of class at that time remained stationed in a context that lay close to the eighteenth-century enthusiasm for classifying artifacts according to their internal properties, whether they be animals, languages or persons. The early attempts to link particular social groups to particular levels of wealth have to be seen in this context rather than as precursors of the positivist social scientists of a century later. There were times when the modern meaning of class seemed about to appear, and then times when it disappeared and older meanings revived to represent social relations. The terms "working" and "middle" classes (with the emphasis on the plural in both cases) are commonly found in the early nineteenth century, yet there was no clear appreciation of how they could be tied to the sociology of society – or

[8] Charles Wilson, *England's Apprenticeship*, pp. 228–29.

even that such a linkage was desirable. Searching for modern "class" in this period is not a rewarding adventure.[9]

The uncertainty as to who was and who was not to be included in the middle classes for the purposes of political reform was noted earlier. This was not exceptional; languages of class remained open well into the middle of the nineteenth century. This was particularly true for the lower classes. There was no Marx to confer a neat and tidy economic criterion. Certainly, labor as the source of all wealth was widely accepted. Yet those, like John Wade, who theorized from this had a conception of social function that emphasized the interdependence of each group upon the other. Thus the popularity of such notions as the "industrious classes" which could encompass a wide range of wealth, status and occupation. Social hierarchy continued to be represented with a high degree of terminological imprecision well into the middle of the nineteenth century. The best kind of social investigation until the 1880s was done by Henry Mayhew, who explored the culture of the London poor in the 1850s. Mayhew was concerned to classify and to order, but not from the perspective of a socioeconomic structural explanation. Although Mayhew had a solid understanding of the political economy of the poor, his approach was essentially that of the ethnographic anthropologist. Mayhew was a social explorer, not a positivist social scientist, and it would be misleading to locate him in that context.[10]

Thus, at the end of the Chartist era, the language of class retreated and the vocabulary of ranks and orders revived. During the 1850s and 1860s influential attempts were made to democratize this language by categories that crossed the lines of wealth or status. The notion of the "gentleman" was one such order which was widely employed in liberal ideology. It had the inestimable advantage of turning attention away from groups and toward individuals. Great efforts were made to redefine the idea of the "gentleman" so that it could encompass working men who dressed cleanly, behaved courteously and practiced self-improvement. Voluntary association social programs, such as the Working Men's Club movement, were founded with this in mind. This resurgence of an epistemology of social classification that was closer to the eighteenth century than to the twentieth was not an anachronistic "survival" that needs special explana-

[9] Penelope Corfield, "Class by Name and Number in Eighteenth-Century Britain," in Corfield (ed.), *Language, Class and History* (Oxford, 1991), pp. 101–30.

[10] [John Wade], *The History of the Middle and Working Classes* (repr., New York, 1966 [London, 1833]), pp. 161–69; Henry Mayhew, *London Labour and the London Poor*, 4 vols. (London, 1861). See also Eileen Yeo, "Mayhew as Social Investigator," in *The Unknown Mayhew*, ed. Yeo and E. P. Thompson (New York, 1972), esp. pp. 69–70, 90–94.

tion. It was consonant with the way the social and economic realities of the time were perceived and ordered.[11]

Those realities allowed room for other ways of expressing social relations. The instability of class terminology in the period reflected how that particular discourse was unable to capture fully the dynamic of social relations. Thus, it is necessary to admit other lexicons into our reading of social relations in both the eighteenth and the nineteenth centuries. "Populism" and "paternalism" are the most commonly employed candidates. Frequently they are seen as alternatives to the language of class; but this is unnecessarily limiting. Populism and paternalism complement rather than replace the notion of class. And, like "class," each term has advantages and disadvantages which it is best to be clear-eyed about.

Populism is frequently used to depict nineteenth-century lower-class politics. If it is meaningful for the nineteenth century, however, it is even more descriptive of lower-class behavior and action in the eighteenth century. Populism captures, for example, the prevailing idea that social and political relations should be governed by a code that discriminated morally on the basis of individual behavior rather than on class position. There could be good capitalists and bad plutocrats, good kings and wicked princes. Populism also registers the central content of lower-class political consciousness over the period: that social relations be governed by reciprocal obligations and duties, that social and political rights should be free from clientage and that politics were embedded in notions of popular constitutionalism. As a term, "populism" captures nicely the uncertainty contained within a system of social relations that was governed by elaborate codes of reciprocity. These codes were essentially arbitrary; they were dependent upon a reflexive custom that sought legitimacy against a real or imagined past. It was for this very rational reason that social relations were volatile and unpredictably spontaneous.[12]

At the same time, populism had no mooring in the material culture and it can be taken to inform a wide range of phenomena. Many differ-

[11] Geoffrey Crossick, "From Gentlemen to the Residuum: Languages of Social Description in Victorian Britain," in Corfield, *Language, Class and History*, pp. 150–78; Asa Briggs, "The Language of Class in Early Nineteenth-Century England," in Briggs and John Saville (eds.), *Essays in Labour History* (London, 1967), pp. 43–73; Wahrman, *Imagining the Middle Class*, pp. 59–60.

[12] The most complete expression of populism as a way of describing lower-class consciousness is to be found in Joyce, *Visions of the People*, pp. 115–16, 174–80, 246–52. In premodern societies, the past is the basis of reflexivity, tradition the "mode of integrating the reflexive monitoring of action with the time–space organization of the community. It is a means of handling time and space, which inserts any particular activity or experience within the continuity of past, present and future, these in turn being structured by recurrent social practices": Anthony Giddens, *The Consequences of Modernity* (Palo Alto, CA, 1990), pp. 36–37.

ent meanings may be lumped under one title. These are serious weaknesses. Demonstrations in favor of the good old cause of popular constitutionalism may be termed populist, as may the loyalist riots of the 1790s, or the anti-Semitic riots around the Jew Bill of 1753, or the Murphy riots in the 1860s, even though we know these were often contrived by conservative elites. It is relevant to note that nobody actually called themselves "populists" in either eighteenth- or nineteenth-century Britain, nor was there anything one could call a populist social or political program.

A further difficulty lies in the tendency to employ populism to privilege the idea of crossclass collaboration and cooperation and to deny the significance of class. The result of this usage of populism is to propagate a new version of Peter Laslett's "one-class society," and to extend it well into the nineteenth century. In this iteration it is the role of conflict, and particularly of class conflict, in the dynamics of elite authority that is diminished. The underlying historical premise to the notion of populism is a harmonious social system. Yet it seems unwise to drop notions of conflict and tension from our accounting of the dynamics of social relations. The trick surely is to find a way of locating conflict and cooperation as interdependent, as working for both harmony and disruption.

The second term used to describe social relations in place of class, paternalism, is most commonly engaged to frame the forces of balance in this society. Like populism, paternalism is an expression that possesses a breadth of meaning that is both useful and problematic. It conjures a warm and cozy set of social relationships, of bluff, honest squires and hearty, loyal subjects – a latter-day feudalism embedded in a polite and commercial society. Such a formulation would clearly be a mistake. A strict sociological definition of "paternalism" (what Max Weber would call patrimonialism) implies an authority system that allowed untrammeled power to the elite. Yet this would not describe social authority in this period. The elite of our period had a closed recruitment pattern, the rule of which was bounded by fairly well-defined restraints – for example, notions of legality. So, if we use the term "paternalism," we must understand that it describes a style and a field of force (to use one of Thompson's phrases) as much as a set of structures.[13]

---

[13] Anthony Giddens, *The Class Structure of Advanced Societies* (London, 1973), p. 123; E. P. Thompson, *Customs in Common: Studies in Traditional Popular Culture* (New York, 1993), pp. 18–26. I deliberately avoid the term "patriarchalism" to describe this society, even though the term could be made to fit much of the dominant sociological themes of the period, because class rule applied to men as well as to women. Obviously, just as the system of authority was paternal and encompassed capitalism, so it contained powerful patriarchal aspects. Max Weber used the term "patrimonial" to include the kinds of social

This field-of-force convention would help avoid a further difficulty with the category of "paternalism": that it disguises the base forces that infused this society. The culture of both the eighteenth and nineteenth centuries paraded its various sensibilities, and much has been made of them by historians. Yet sensibility seldom qualified the primacy of market valuations or the iron fist of authority and power. Edward Thompson has aptly described the (early) eighteenth century as the site of a rapacious commercial imperialism, a predatory phase of agrarian and commercial capitalism where the state itself was among the package of spoils available for plunder. Somewhat later, an "enlightened" man like Jeremy Bentham raised not a finger to save his manservant from the gallows for stealing a watch; and, later still, religious men who were also trade unionists were transported to the ends of the earth. The boughs of the public hanging tree continued to bend under the weight of executions until 1868, although the load was greatly lightened after a pruning of the capital statutes in 1838. There is little to be gained, however, by drawing balance sheets of, on the one side, the paternal elements of this society and, on the other side, the commercial elements, as if these elements were in competition to define the society. In fact, these different aspects were symbiotic and not contradictory.[14]

One final disadvantage to describing social relations as paternalist is that it implies an unproblematic hierarchy. Such an idea must be decisively rejected. It is undeniably true that the map of class relations was dotted with spaces for crossclass alliances and cooperation. Yet this hardly meant that the exercise of elite authority was unproblematic. The absence of theories or systems that allowed for systematic social and political inclusion in the governing processes meant that the enterprise of social authority required constant maintenance. If, as has been argued, eighteenth-century society was indeed an "ancien régime," it was a constructed entity rather than a naturally evolving formation. Patrician rule occurred within the context of a constant awareness of its instability. The point at which deference tipped over to defiance could never be anticipated in advance. Social authority in this period was rent with uncertainty. The threat was not of a world turned upside down. The threat lay in the proximity of a rough, rowdy and disrespectable

relations that I allude to as "paternal." He instanced the justices of the peace as examples of the way patrimonial power was qualified by the need to rely upon administration by notables. But "patrimonial" implies a system based on fidelity and loyalty, rather than contract, as was more the case in Britain in this period. See Max Weber, *Economy and Society: An Outline of Interpretive Sociology*, ed. Guenther Roth and Claus Wittich (New York, 1968), vol. III, pp. 1006–15, 1028–31, 1059–64.

[14] Langford, *Public Life and the Propertied Englishman*, pp. 484–92; V. A. C. Gatrell, *The Hanging Tree: Execution and the English People 1770–1868* (Oxford, 1996), pp. 7–11.

world that could suddenly disrupt the august stillness of polite society.[15]

Does this somewhat elaborate schedule of qualifications mean that "paternalism" does not enhance our understanding of the authority relations of this period? Many would reply that it surely does. I would disagree. The salient disposition of paternalism in this period is that it was at one and the same time a code, a mask and a style. It was a code in the sense that the culture of authority operated through the conduits of deference, patrician responsibility and the reciprocities of obligation and duty. It was a mask in the sense that, to be effective, leadership and social standing had to be projected as patrician, patriarchal and paternal. Everybody knew that beneath this mask lurked many unpaternal propensities. And it was a style that could characterize a wide range of social groups, and not just the patrician elite. Paternalism was therefore the only real currency of authority that could be cashed.

Paternalism was a manner of authority that was infinitely adaptable. It allowed those whose roots lay in trade, manufacturing or letters to engage in authority relations, as well as those whose lineages reached back to the Conquest. The paternal style was the common theme to all aspects of social authority in this period. Paternalism could be deployed to assert the authority of the landlord on his estate and the farmer in his freeholding. Equally, the paternal style was perfectly compatible with the most modern forms of capitalist exchange. Manufacturers used paternal strategies to confirm and assert authority over their labor forces. This was as true of the manufacturers of Lancashire in the middle of the nineteenth century as it had been of the proto-industrialists of a century and a half before. The strongest link between capitalist discipline and the paternal style was routed through patriarchy and the family. The family unit was the unit of subcontracted labor in the early factories and coal mines precisely because it allowed patriarchy to substitute for managerial control. Various forms of this relationship ran throughout nineteenth-century factory society. Industrial discipline and family discipline, both different elements of paternal discipline, were in constant combination throughout the period.[16]

[15] The treatment of social relations as basically unproblematic is a constant theme of conservative revisionist scholarship. For the eighteenth century, the best statements of this position are J. C. D. Clark's *English Society* and *Revolution and Rebellion*. In the scholarship of the nineteenth century, this perspective is to be found, of course, in the work on high politics and, most significantly, in revisionist labor history; see Parry, *Rise and Fall of Liberal Government*; Biagini, *Liberty, Retrenchment and Reform*; and the various works by Patrick Joyce. For an alternative view, see Jeremy Black and Jeremy Gregory, *Culture, Politics and Society in Britain 1660–1800* (Manchester, 1991), pp. 3–4.

[16] Langford, *Public Life and the Propertied Englishman*, pp. 448–92; J. C. D. Clark, *English Society*, pp. 42–63, 121–41; Joyce, *Work, Society and Politics*. This style, I should briefly

Since all three categories of class, populism and paternalism address some aspect of social relations in this period, I am going to use them all, singly and together, to illuminate the dynamics of elite authority. The central problem I am concerned to address is how it was that social relations could be expressed through the paternal style in the context of a society that encompassed a dynamic middling class and a rowdy lower class. In order to do that we need to understand both the roots of stability and the inherent instabilities that accompanied the exercise of elite power. And, finally, we need to understand the demise of the particular system of elite authority that was described by this dynamic and the birth of a society where social relations were organized primarily through notions of class.

The roots of stability

The habit of authority in social relations was anchored in the persistent presence of the landed elite. From the ducal pinnacles to the base of the squirearchy and the tenant farmers, the power and position of the landed classes was the fundamental social fact of the period. Until the end of the nineteenth century, the strands of political, economic and social power all returned at some point to the authority of the landed interest. It is tempting to treat landed power in this period as somehow contrary to the movement of the history of the age and to set it in opposition to the other loci of influence and power, such as the urban elites. This would be erroneous. Tension and conflict often crackled between these diverse power centers. Still, gentry power was in no way incompatible with the major sectors of economic and social change in the period.

Landed wealth and position were deeply implicated in the generation of newer sources of capital. The landed classes in this period were never left behind by the movement of history. The history of the British aristocracy (just to take the titled segment of the landed classes for the moment) was a history of fortunes made and fortunes lost, of demographic crisis that threatened patrimonial lines of inheritance, of estates that were often encumbered to the hilt. Yet the aristocratic presence survived because its history was also one of economic innovation, of profit maximization, of funding economic development, at home and abroad. The landed interest conjoined the capitalist spirit with patrician social and cultural forms

note, was consistent with the patriarchalism of high political theory in the eighteenth century – the attempt to invent a providential divine right of monarchy that would reconcile kingly authority with the violation of hereditary monarchy committed by the revolutionaries of 1688.

of authority. This was the genius of the British aristocracy, which they imparted to the culture as a whole.[17]

After the Restoration in 1660, however, the landed classes did more than survive. They soared to the acme of power and position. From the final third of the seventeenth century to the great agricultural depression of the later nineteenth century (which shattered the economy of the landed estate), landownership became more concentrated and landed power more consolidated than at any other time. This was, of course, an uneven process. The decline of the small landowner has been much exaggerated by nineteenth-century commentators and others. At some times and in some places there was rapid turnover of the lesser proprietors. Yet the proportion of those owning less than 300 acres actually did not change much over the period and country as a whole. Considerable regional variations existed, of course. Strict settlement did not always operate to benefit consolidation. Nevertheless, after all the necessary qualifications, taken as a whole, there was a decided trend toward the concentration of land into the hands of the large aristocratic landowner. Aristocratic power thickened during the period and even accelerated during the nineteenth century. Over 90 percent of the richest owners listed by John Bateman's survey in 1870 had owned their land since before 1700.[18]

At the top of the social pyramid the titled peers progressively closed their ranks to newcomers. Only 7 of the 117 new peers of the eighteenth century were drawn from outside the gentry ranks. Over the whole period 1660–1880, only 7 percent of Lawrence and Jeanne Stone's elite landowners were businessmen. The process of closure was most marked during the eighteenth century when this elite extended its hold on the offices of state while at the same time restricting access to its ranks through marriage or education. The notion of movement into the landed classes has been somewhat exaggerated in the past. Access to the ranks of the great landowning class was extremely difficult and rare.[19]

Fortunately, the peerage was not the only element of the landed classes, and the lower down the landed gentry scale one went, the more movement into the ranks of the landed groups there was. So the old generaliz-

[17] For the frequent fragility of aristocratic existence, see Lawrence Stone, *The Crisis of the Aristocracy 1558–1641* (Oxford, 1967); J. V. Beckett, *The Aristocracy in England 1660–1914* (Oxford, 1986), pp. 288–316; David Cannadine, "The Landowner as Millionaire: The Finances of the Dukes of Devonshire," in his *Aspects of Aristocracy: Grandeur and Decline in Modern Britain* (London, 1995), pp. 165–83.

[18] J. V. Beckett, "The Pattern of Land Ownership in England and Wales, 1660–1880," *Economic History Review*, 37 (February 1984), pp. 1–22; Beckett, *Aristocracy in England*, pp. 87–90.

[19] Cannon, *Aristocratic Century*, pp. 33, 112–22; Stone and Stone, *An Open Elite?*, p. 280.

ation about middling-class types getting the chance to own their piece of patrician heritage does retain more than a slight truth. The important point, however, is that, when they secured land, middling-class estate owners also inherited the obligations and authority of gentry paternalism. Thus, in 1863 Francis Crossley, the carpet manufacturer, bought a country estate the title of which included various manorial rights and the obligation to appoint the incumbent of the local church. In this way paternal authority was exchanged between the classes.[20]

The same was true elsewhere in the groves of social authority. In local government the larger country gentlemen progressively absented themselves from the quarter sessions – that centerpiece of county authority – throughout the eighteenth century. As a class they were taken up with national politics. Thus, their places on the bench were taken by lesser gentry who became fervent keepers of the flame of paternal ideology. Until the 1880s these types continued to compose over 60 percent of the local magistrates in the counties – although in the urban areas the Municipal Corporations Act rapidly displaced county gentry from the bench, and by 1886 they constituted only 11 percent of urban justices.[21]

In the final analysis, the persistence of landed power rested on the ability of the gentry as a class to ride the shifting currents and opportunities of economic growth and development. The landed classes of Britain were a bourgeois gentry, profit- and risk-takers and entrepreneurs. Their economic interests spread across the full range of sectors available for investment. As landholders they were astutely motivated to maximize the benefits of their holdings. The highly active land market in the eighteenth century, for example, was driven in part by the desire to consolidate scattered holdings into units that would better enable them to meet their family demands and other exigencies. In the nineteenth century, the evidence mainly suggests a successful exploitation of nonagricultural resources and an ability to adjust their financial circumstances to the changing opportunities of the time. This included urban development and the empire.[22]

Urban investments were a traditional outlet for aristocratic wealth; their importance in this period was the convergence they allowed between landed and urban elites. One result was that landed elite involvement in

[20] Jonathan Powis, *Aristocracy* (Oxford, 1984), p. 43.

[21] Pocock, "Introduction," in Pocock, *Three British Revolutions*, p. 10; Webb and Webb, *The Parish and the County*, pp. 377–79; Carl Zangerl, "The Social Composition of the County Magistracy in England and Wales, 1831–1887," *Journal of British Studies*, 11, 1 (November 1971), pp. 113–25.

[22] Beckett, *Aristocracy in England*, pp. 134–229; C. Clay, "Property Settlements, Financial Provision for the Family, and the Sale of Land by the Greater Landowners," *Journal of British Studies*, 21, 1 (Fall 1981), pp. 18–38; Cannadine, "Landowner as Millionaire."

the manufacturing sector of the economy was deepened. In industrial towns like Cardiff, for example, this connection meant that the landed elite played a preeminent role in local politics well into the nineteenth century. This may have been something of an extreme case, and in the great provincial towns conflict between the traditional landowning elite and the newly emergent urban groups rose and fell throughout the period. Only in the resort towns – first the spas and then, from the 1860s, the high-class seaside towns – was the aristocratic presence more fully integrated.[23]

I have already touched on the relationship between the landed elites and financial and commercial capital. As with other sectors of economic development, the aristocratic elite were present at the creation of England's commercial imperial exploits. Sir Walter Raleigh's various adventures in the later Elizabethan era were funded by aristocratic venture capitalists. The commercial imperialism of the eighteenth century provided ample opportunities for the connection to be extended and deepened. And, as has been suggested, the strong connections between the financial sector of the City and the state structures aided this enterprise. It is not surprising, therefore, that by the end of the nineteenth century the landed elite were major shareholders in the empire. The notion of "gentlemanly capitalism" is a perfectly sensible way of expressing the political and cultural connections between finance capitalism and the landed gentry.[24] The problem with the idea of "gentlemanly capitalism" is not that it is sociologically or culturally inaccurate or inappropriate – although it is here that historical debate on the issue has settled. The greater danger to the idea is that it reinforces a view of English elite formation as "traditional" and therefore static and somewhat anachronistic. Nothing could be farther from the truth.[25]

The paternal style of the English landed elite was not merely a flexible

[23] David Cannadine, "Introduction," in Cannadine (ed.), *Patricians, Power and Politics in Nineteenth-Century Towns* (New York, 1987), pp. 2–9; Cannadine, *Lords and Landlords: The Aristocracy and the Towns 1774–1967* (Leicester, 1980), esp. pp. 21–77; R. W. Sturgess, *Aristocrat in Business* (Durham, 1975).

[24] Lance Davis and Huttenback, *Mammon and the Pursuit of Empire*, pp. 173–82. Cain and Hopkin, *British Imperialism*, pp. 23–67, give the main argument, of course, for "gentlemanly capitalism." See also Ingham, *Capitalism Divided?*, pp. 136, 226.

[25] For the debate on gentlemanly capitalism, see M. J. Daunton, "Gentlemanly Capitalism and British Industry 1820–1914," *Past and Present*, 122 (February 1989), pp. 119–58; Daunton, "Reply to Rubenstein," *Past and Present*, 132 (August 1991), pp. 170–87; W. D. Rubinstein, "Gentlemanly Capitalism and British Industry," *Past and Present*, 132 (August 1991), pp. 151–70; Rubinstein, *Capitalism, Culture and Decline*; Michael Barrett Brown, "Away with All the Great Arches: Anderson's History of British Capitalism," *New Left Review*, 167 (January–February 1988), pp. 22–51; Geoffrey Ingham, "Commercial Capital and British Development: A Reply to Michael Barrett Brown," *New Left Review*, 172 (November–December 1988), pp. 45–65.

construct, able to adapt to a changing society. It was integral to the particular phase of economic expansion and growth that I have described in this period. Economic and social change were a condition of the persistence and the expansion of the styles and structures of paternalism. Paternalist structures were not a function of an "old" social system, remnants of feudalism that had somehow been left behind and successfully adjusted to new conditions. They were not a remnant at all; they were a highly serviceable authority system that was adaptable to many social circumstances and usable by social groups beyond the landed elite. The paternal style was a functional system of social authority for a structure of economic change which manifested itself mainly in fragmented, small-scale and localized forms. The dynamic of economic and social change in the period 1680–1880 *created* and *reinforced* the paternal style of social authority. Gentrification was integral to the progress of manufacturing. The manufacturing sector was *gentrified* by the market forces of commercial capitalism.

The expansion of the coal industry in the county of Durham in the later seventeenth century provides us with a clear demonstration of this. I have already referred to the economic process of this expansion: how it created a regional industrial revolution in the pattern of economic change in this period. Naturally, this also had identifiable social consequences. New groups were created, new social alliances were forged. The social morphology was transformed in a way that was characteristic of the relationship between social and economic change in this period. The progression was not from a dynamic "middle class" that then became an anti-aristocratic bourgeoisie. The social consequence of economic revolution in the parishes of the North East was to expand the web of paternal relationships and to create new ones. Relationships of economic dependence and clientage were conceived that replicated the social habits and patterns of the past. A new gentry was created. Older, previously minor, gentry families stepped on an escalator of upward mobility to become less minor. New entrants to the region like the Bowes family seized the opportunity to win gentry status. The latter, in particular, immediately began to act as if they had been squires of the manor since 1066.[26]

The commercialization of the coal economy reinforced this tendency to duplicate paternal social relations. The North East coalfield was increasingly linked to markets outside the region, and particularly to London. Thus, the merchants of Newcastle (who controlled access to the London markets) and those of London (who controlled the markets themselves)

---

[26] Levine and Wrightson, *Making of an Industrial Society*, pp. 356–67, 394–98.

played a significant role in the determination of the North East coal industry's economic fortunes. As they did so, the chains of connection between the owners and the pitmen in the pit villages tightened. The common interests of the gentry owners and the pit laborers against urban merchants were emphasized. This was not simply an expression of benign paternal social relations between gentry and workers. It was a strategy propagated by pit-owners as a way of ensuring their authority over the production process, the better to allow them to maintain profit margins by controlling labor costs.

In the case of Durham, the centerpiece of this paternal strategy was the notorious miners' bond. The bond was the yearly hiring agreement between workers and employers; it specified the conditions and price of labor, although it also left room for bargaining. Most importantly it guaranteed a stable labor force at a known price for a year. The bond was projected as a manifestation of the reciprocity between labor and capital, and of the mutual duties and obligations between the two. It was an expression of the paternal style adapted to the particular circumstances of the North East coalfield. The bond was not merely a paternal gift, however, even though it held certain advantages for the miners. Since the bond tied labor to a particular mine under a specific set of conditions, it was actually an early eighteenth-century managerial device designed to secure a more precise control over labor.[27]

At about the same time in the same area, the ironworks owned by Ambrose Crowley was being organized to replicate the organic society of the paternal imagination. Using much the same design as Robert Owen a century later at New Lanark, life at Crowley's was regulated down to the slightest detail. This was not an embryonic precursor of modern management in early modern guise. To the contrary, it was the patriarchal model of social relations writ large and adapted to this particular phase of capitalism. It was the only management theory available to manufacturing capitalists and to their successors in the nineteenth century. The coal companies, the factory owners and railway companies of the Northern industrial towns were the inheritors of this theory of management. They were led naturally to paternal strategies of labor management, using the imagery of the family, for example, to create a sense of community between the workforce and the employer. Capitalism is capable of supporting many different forms of social relations. In

[27] Nef, *Rise of the British Coal Industry*, vol. II, pp. 164–65; Michael W. Flinn, *The History of the British Coal Industry*, vol. II, *1700–1830: The Industrial Revolution* (Oxford, 1984), pp. 352–61. Such a strategy was not peculiar to Durham, nor to this period, nor to the coal industry. In Scotland, colliers had been subject to a legal state of quasi-bondage until 1799.

this case surplus value could be quite adequately extracted by paternal grace.[28]

The supreme advantage of this style of elite authority was that it possessed a tried and proven historical track record of success at securing consent. A patrician and patriarchal conception of social relations provided a persuasive and coherent discourse which continued to be viable well into the nineteenth century. The fierce industrial struggles and political contestation of the 1830s and 1840s, for example, were followed by a widespread revitalization of paternal strategies – even if they were not always named as such. These strategies assumed many manifestations. In the 1840s and 1850s an extensive literature was churned out, the central theme of which was the paternal reciprocities of duty between worker and employer. This literature broadcast in a different tone from that of the Benthamite centralizers. In place of the harsh condemnations of working-class culture and the need for intervention to root out uncivilized practices, the qualities of responsibility and duty of the upper classes were trumpeted. Thus, employers were "the successors of the feudal barons, they it is . . . upon whom, in great measure, depends the happiness of large masses of mankind."[29]

Such worthy sentiments were part of a distinct softening in the social attitudes of radical liberalism. A new Christian paternalism was added to the range of social attitudes held by the urban and provincial, middle-class elites. These groups began to shed the class-warfare language of the 1830s, and their laissez-faire utilitarianism began to mellow. As a result a more nuanced and diverse discourse on social problems and class relations began to be heard from the middle-class liberals of the industrial towns. Appeals were issued for a kinder sort of Christianity than that dispatched by a providential, judgmental, atonement-demanding God. The use of the paternal model in charity interventions – a traditional model, after all – fitted in well with this. In class relations, the need for

[28] It has been a cause of mild surprise in the scholarship that the British industrial revolution did not spawn modern management theory. Yet such an invention was not necessary while the paternal style remained credible. See Sidney Pollard, *The Genesis of Modern Management: A Study of the Industrial Revolution in Great Britain* (Harmondsworth, 1968), pp. 71–76; Robert Colls, " 'Oh Happy Children': Coal, Class and Education in the North East," *Past and Present*, 73 (November 1976), pp. 92–99; P. W. Kingsford, "Labour Relations on the Railways, 1835–1875," *Journal of Transport History*, 1, 2 (1953), pp. 71–74. But see P. Tyson, "Cost Accounting in the Industrial Revolution," *Economic History Review*, 46, 4 (1993), pp. 503–17, for a contrary view.

[29] Arthur Helps, *The Claims of Labour: An Essay on the Duties of the Employers to the Employed and an Essay on the Means of Improving the Health and Increasing the Comfort of the Labouring Classes* (London, 1844), pp. 33–34. The general literature on the paternal style is enormous and has never been properly recognized. See, for example, Henry Booth, *Masters and Men* (London, 1853); A Preston Manufacturer, *Strikes Prevented* (London, 1854).

"good feeling" and "kindness" by the upper classes toward the lower classes was emphasized. Most significantly, employers were conceptualized as friend, father and protector who "are awakening to a sense of the important duty owing to their workpeople."[30]

The revitalization of paternal strategies of social authority from the 1840s was remarkably widespread. It was found even in the most recalcitrant quarters of the employing class. After some bruising strikes in his coalfields in the 1830s and 1840s, for example, Lord Londonderry shifted to a more proactive paternalism. He assisted in the establishment of schools in order to "cement those old ties of attachment" between workers and employers that had eroded somewhat. The same departures were found in those parts of the Scottish coalfield where large companies dominated the scene. Unlike most colliery owners, the Peases of Barnard Castle, County Durham, tolerated trade unions – partly a function of their Quaker faith. Still, this did not stop them acting out their role as patrician supervisors of the wellbeing of their employees. Flower shows were patronized, neatly kept gardens received their social approval, housing was provided.[31]

Like all paternal bargains, this one had its price. Temperance was the employer-approved culture of the pits owned by the Pease family. Miners could be evicted from company housing if their sons accepted employment at other mines. The strong Methodist presence in this area complemented this culture of the paternal style. Methodism was not only a religion of consolation and self-activity. Its emphasis on submission and duty made it perfectly compatible with paternal social relations. Indeed, its chapels were often heavily subsidized by the local employers. Most owners were less benevolent than the Peases. Discipline in the pits was generally harsh and authority was arbitrary and unrestrained. Payment in kind or by chit, rather than in coins of the realm, remained common in some places well into the 1870s, especially in modern, heavy industry like ironworks. As in the eighteenth century, owners assumed a paternal power which they delegated to managers or viewers who used the model of the father-dominated family to rule their charges. "Managers exercised the owners' patronage and themselves patronized the many village activities with their active participation or financial donations."[32]

[30] Tholfsen, *Working-Class Radicalism*, pp. 125–54. The quote is from William Felkin, the Nottingham manufacturer in 1851 (p. 139).

[31] Colls, "'Oh Happy Children,'" p. 99; James A. Jaffe, *The Struggle for Market Power: Industrial Relations in the British Coal Industry 1800–1850* (Cambridge, 1991), pp. 92, 172–74; Alan Campbell, *The Lanarkshire Miners 1775–1874* ((Edinburgh, 1979), pp. 214–31; Robert Moore, *Pit-Men, Politics and Preachers: The Effects of Methodism on a Durham Mining Community* (Cambridge, 1974), pp. 82–85.

[32] Moore, *Pit-Men, Politics and Preachers*, pp. 80–82, 85 (quote).

If we focus for the moment on the benign face of paternalism, we find a bundle of these kinds of strategies available for common use in industry until the 1880s. Exploiting a common religious bond was a favorite tactic; special feast days were invented; the birthdays, homecomings and marriages of employers' children were celebrated; 'Owd Jacob Bright maintained the personal touch with his laborers by poking his head around their door to make sure their homes were clean, their children disciplined and that no wife beating was going on. More useful, perhaps, were the houses that some Clyde shipbuilders provided for their workers in the 1860s, complete with mortgages and building societies. None of this contradicted the existence of class. Nor were such strategies the only ones available to factory owners. Their significance lay in the way they provided another sphere for the exercise of elite authority through a style of social relations that derived from the tradition of the landed patriciate. Seeking discipline and order through the paternalist style was the predominant method of assuring elite authority until the end of the nineteenth century.[33]

The case of Samuel Courtauld's silk-weaving factory in Essex is worth noting as an example. In response to the incursion of Chartist activity in the area, an offensive was launched in the 1840s that was designed both to reinforce male authority at work and in the family, and to instill domestic values within working-class women. On the one hand were the usual panoply of paternal provisions such as community festivals, coal allowances and company housing. Since the workforce was largely female, however, elaborate structures were created to ensure the inculcation of the virtues of domesticity. Modest and neat dress was required among the women, and a two-month natal leave policy enforced so that newborn babies could be nursed rather than bottle-fed – as was more common among working-class women. Facilities were created to propagate the virtues of the middle-class home. Housework skills were taught in maternal meetings; a nursery was established where middle-class standards of child rearing ruled. This was not a success. These efforts reached their peak in the 1870s, after which they began to crumble. The female labor

[33] Joyce, *Work, Society and Politics*, pp. 92, 139, 141–49, 176–78, 181–83, 205–10, 218–20; Reinhard Bendix, *Work and Authority in Industry: Ideologies of Management in the Course of Industrialization* (paperback edn., Berkeley, 1974), pp. 48–49; Joseph Melling, "Employers, Industrial Housing and the Evolution of Company Welfare Policies in Britain's Heavy Industry in West Scotland, 1870–1920," *International Review of Social History*, 26, 2 (1981), pp. 255–301. For a case study, see Jack Reynolds, *The Great Paternalist: Titus Salt and the Growth of Nineteenth-Century Bradford* (London, 1983). But for a critique of the extent and viability of paternal strategies, see Ted Koditschek, *Class Formation and Urban Industrial Society: Bradford 1750–1850* (Cambridge, 1990), pp. 424–34.

market began to change and new models of arbitrating social relations gained acceptance. In the 1880s, women began to resist these kinds of paternal interventions more effectively. When women weavers went on strike in 1860 against a rate reduction, Courtauld responded like a hurt and disappointed father. By the mid-1880s, trade union representation had appeared among the women workers and the whole structure of authority relations was in the process of change.[34]

The paternal style of social authority could be applied in other sectors of social relations, too. Voluntary association social reform and charity activity was one huge public space which offered opportunities for the urban middling classes to learn the culture and practice of paternal largess. This was not a template for all social reforming activity; it does not fit the temperance movement, for example. Nevertheless, middle-class philanthropy was deeply colored by the ethos of patrician intervention. Even when the idea behind the social institution was to teach bourgeois values – as in the Mechanics' Institutes or the Working Men's Clubs – the style of organization and leadership was heavily tempered with paternal assumptions and methods. These were the spaces where the paternal style was implanted in the practice and consciousness of middle-class culture as the model to follow in the construction of social relationships with their subalterns.[35]

The adoption of paternal styles of social relations by the middling classes suggests the ambiguities of their relationship with the landed patriciate. This relationship was more tangled, perhaps, than any other aspect of social relations. The first complication, of course, is that it was a relationship within an elite. On the one hand, there were a growing number of locations in the eighteenth century where middling-class and landed elites could collaborate in generally patrician-style enterprises. Urban culture in particular was honeycombed with such institutions. This served to foster the tendency of emulation. On the other hand, it would obviously be mistaken to assume that middling-class–patrician relations moved along the axis of emulation alone. Such activities also served to carve out a sphere of autonomy and political presence for the middling classes. Urban culture was also the site of demands for access to power from middling-class groups. Middle-class consciousness was

---

[34] Lown, *Women and Industrialization*, pp. 96–99, 108–12, 118, 126–27, 160–64, 193–94.

[35] Kathleen Wilson, "Urban Culture and Political Activism," pp. 182–84. On the paternal style in nineteenth-century middle-class philanthropy and other class initiatives, see John Seed, "Theologies of Power: Unitarianism and the Social Relations of Religious Discourse," in R. J. Morris (ed.), *Class, Power and Social Structure in British Nineteenth-Century Towns* (Leicester, 1986), pp. 137–38, 144–45; Morris, *Class, Sect and Party*, pp. 320–21; Richard Price, "The Working Men's Club Movement and Victorian Social Reform Ideology," *Victorian Studies*, 15, 2 (Autumn 1971), pp. 117–48.

forged in constant contrast to the upper-class ideal, in collaboration with and in opposition to patrician behavior and images.[36]

Competition and convergence describe the relationship between the middling classes and the patriciate. It is helpful, I think, to imagine middle-class consciousness as a spectrum bounded at one end by emulation of the landed elite and at the other end by competition with its styles and politics. The question of patriotic identity provides an illustration of this. The wars of the eighteenth century were especially important in affording the upper classes the opportunity to secure patriotism as an upper-class quality. A major cultural offensive was launched by the aristocracy to appropriate for itself the virtues of patriotism and service and to shed the suspicion that their cosmopolitan loyalties were stronger than their national ties. A large part of this effort aimed at differentiations. A new attention was paid, for example, to badges of distinction within the aristocratic elite; uniforms and medals became important icons of distinction. Domestically, too, elite identity was reshaped to validate their claim to embodying national values. A carefully constructed classicism was projected in their landscape gardens and architecture; the arts were attended to and the notion of monarchy was transformed from an instrument of tyranny to a defender of liberty. The French revolution put the seal on this turnabout. George III pioneered the kind of monarchy that Victoria was to epitomize: a pious family concerned to do its duty. George III morphed from potential despot to good old "Farmer" George.[37]

National mobilization required by war also created a zone of opportunity for the middling class to demonstrate *their* patriotic sensibility, however. Beginning with the war of Jenkins' ear, 1738–42, and continuing through the wars of the midcentury, the middling classes too learnt to dress up, to be warrior heroes and to pin medals on their breasts. Festooned with honors and bejeweled with the elite qualities of bravery, service and the like, middling-class figures could assert their status as a patriotic elite. On the home front, patriotic associations, militia companies and various societies for women's war charity activities offered the chance for the middle classes to assert their claims to parity with the elite

---

[36] For tensions between the middling classes and the patriciate from the middle of the eighteenth century in Halifax, see the useful study by John Smail, *The Origins of Middle-Class Culture: Halifax, Yorkshire, 1660–1780* (Ithaca, 1994), pp. 121–63.

[37] Newman, *Rise of English Nationalism*, pp. 25–47. "God Save the King" became a permanent fixture in the theaters during his reign. The transformation of the image of monarchy achieved by George III was nearly undone, of course, by his son. Although there were fears of monarchical power as late as the 1830s, these were quickly removed by the accession of the young and domesticated Victoria. A similar apotheosis of monarchy occurred toward the end of the nineteenth century. But this hardly mattered, for the essential connection between the paternal landed elite, patriotism and national identity had already been established.

guardians of the nation. The end result was a remarkable turnaround in the political character of patriotism. From being a property of radicalism that was hostile to conservative forces, patriotism was commandeered as something that could be claimed by the middling classes as well as the elite. Indeed, the middling classes developed their own capacity to generate a sense of specifically *British* national identity. These means were especially evident after about 1750 in England's internal colonies of Wales and Scotland. Ireland was a much harder nut to crack. On the Celtic fringe the process of national integration was measured both by the invention of Gaelic and Welsh traditions (such as the kilt and the eisteddfod) and the dramatic decline in speaking native languages. The properties that came to be associated with Scottishness and Welshness at this time were in reality inventions of middle-class exiles in London.[38]

Possession of elite status by the middling classes was, however, variable and uncertain. It was this that injected a strong dose of instability into middle-class–elite social relations. Tension between the middle and upper classes is a constant feature of middle-class consciousness throughout the period. At different moments, in different places and within different spheres of experience a particular arrangement of values is revealed. There were vast differences within the middling classes – far greater in scale, we may judge, than within the other two classes. As late as the 1860s in Glasgow, for example, nearly one-half of middle-class households were associated with small businesses: only one-quarter were big businessmen, and most of those in manufacturing (a mere 14 percent) were in artisan production. The larger the urban area, the more the middling-class presence took on the character of an assertive independence. By the later seventeenth century, London aldermen had severed entirely their ties of origin with the landed gentry and had become distinctively and self-consciously middling class. They did not rush to buy landed estates. Yet by the same token, in the middle of the eighteenth century, some 50 percent of the sons of these aldermen were sent to acquire a gentry style of education, and about 40 percent married into gentry families.[39]

[38] See Kathleen Wilson, "Empire, Trade and Popular Politics in Mid-Hanoverian Britain: The Case of Admiral Vernon," *Past and Present*, 121 (1992), pp. 74–109; Colley, *Britons*; Colley, "Whose Nation?"; Cunningham, "Language of Patriotism"; Black and Gregory, *Culture, Politics and Society*, pp. 82–100.

[39] Stana Nenadic, "Businessmen, the Urban Middle Class, and the 'Dominance' of Manufacturers in Nineteenth-Century Britain," *Economic History Review*, 44, 1 (1991), pp. 66–85. See Rogers, "Money, Land and Lineage," where it is remarked that "the esteem of the peerage did not contradict the fact that the dominant ethos of society was bourgeois and plutocratic" (p. 454). See also Dror Wahrman, "National Society, Communal Culture: An Argument about the Recent Historiography of Eighteenth-Century Britain," *Social History*, 17, 1 (January 1992), pp. 56–61.

This illustrates quite nicely the content of ambiguity and complexity that colored middle-class social relations. The dynamics of elite–middling-class relations were interdependent and intensely contradictory. Patronage and clientage were as integral to the system of middling-class–elite social relations as was civic independence. Even in the urban areas where the middle classes were most strongly represented, the strategies of social relations they adopted were essentially ambiguous. Collaboration with the landed elite blended with the desire for access by the middling class. The possibilities of a specifically bourgeois consciousness were greatly limited by this dynamic. And it is unsurprising that eighteenth-century class tensions were often sharper between the middling classes and the elites than they were between the lower and upper classes. Like social relations generally, those between the middling classes and the landed elite were inherently unstable. It is to the general question of instability that we must now turn.

Instabilities of elite authority

The paradox of elite authority during the two centuries covered by this book was that those qualities that secured consent were precisely those that delivered instability to the system. The reciprocities of deference, duty and obligation were the main agencies that sustained social authority; they were also the wellsprings of volatility in the social system. The problem lay in the complexion of the qualities themselves. The claims and expectation of reciprocity, deference, duty and obligation were essentially arbitrary. It was quite impossible to compile a list of specific propositions that would embody qualities that were intrinsically cultural and psychological. No formal institutional arrangements existed to formulate rules and procedures or to arbitrate and govern relationships between and within social groups. This meant that securing assent to authority had to rest upon informal conventions such as respect for personal authority. If these failed, intervention from the law was about the only alternative. This did not imply the absence of rituals and procedures; it implied rather the absence of a systematized repertoire to provide a reliable program to the theater of social interaction.

The result was that social relations were inseparable from popular culture; popular culture provided the conduits through which social relations were mediated. This was true in many senses. It was in popular culture that the lower classes most often made contact with the upper classes. This might occur on the occasion of a public ritual, or when something was being asked of one of the parties – such as the reminder through a bread riot, perhaps, that the patriciate owed certain obligations to the plebeians. Popular culture was the arena where the exercise of elite authority could be greeted or challenged. Indeed, for the lower classes, popular culture was the only such arena. The story of popular culture during this period, therefore, is more than just the story of the rights and rituals of a customary culture: it is integral to understanding the fragilities and contradictions within paternal social relations.

But, of course, this popular culture was not a static formation. Indeed, the particular form of popular culture was historically specific to this period. It both blossomed and faded during these two centuries. And this was also an important component to the dynamics of elite authority. The rise and decline of this popular culture is one way of telling the story of how the social relations of elite authority were displaced by the formalized social relations of class at the end of the nineteenth century.

The most proximate origins of the popular culture of our period were as recent as the Restoration. The Restoration of the Stuarts in 1660 immediately created the space for the revival of practices suppressed under Commonwealth puritanism. These were welcomed by the authorities because they were believed to serve as a guarantor of traditional hierarchy. Indeed, some popular customs were revived with official encouragement in the hope that they would effectively inoculate the lower classes against the republicanism that was known to lurk in the puritan spirit. This was the moment when Merrie England was inaugurated. From the beginning, therefore, popular culture was entangled with paternal collaboration.[40]

The vital characteristic of popular culture was its informality. It was this which differentiated the popular culture of our period from both preceding and succeeding historical periods. From earlier forms, the popular culture of this period was distinguished by its central role in the system of social relationships and by its occasional ability to resonate at a national level either in politics or in ritual or in disorder. But the absence of formal structures to channel its actions separated this popular culture from what was to follow. Even without formal structures, however, it was a culture with a considerable capacity to mobilize and a significant potential to destabilize social peace. At the same time, the resources of this popular culture were quickly exhausted. Chartism notwithstanding, the ability of popular culture to project into a formal, political, organized presence – or series of presences – was limited. It was a dynamic force, the energies of which were always bounded and contained.

The capacity of the popular culture of our period to activate the food riot, for example, reflected a coherent and rational mental framework of

---

[40] Hutton, *Rise and Fall of Merry England*, esp. chs. 4 and 7.

social relations on behalf of the participants in the action. The disruptive potential of such acts was substantial; yet its disruption was enclosed within the reciprocities of the paternal system. Once the magistrates had been called to their duty to order lower prices, or the riot had been dissipated, the whole affair was over. No traces remained. By contrast, the socialist cycling club or political party, or the Conservative working men's political clubs of Lancashire, generated and reflected an ongoing, permanent politics expressing very different social relations. Nevertheless, the key quality of the popular culture of our period was precisely its unruly potential. The popular culture of this period was a permanent qualification to the poise of elite authority.

Popular culture posed a standing challenge to elite authority because it was a *rough* culture – a culture of contention. Its internal conventions and procedures derived their legitimacy from the highly uncertain category of "custom." It was no requirement of "custom" that it be anchored in a firm conception of a historical or political universe. At one end of the spectrum of "custom" stood a genuinely well-established usage which often possessed a quasi-legal status. These practices were often associated with property usage, and eighteenth-century jurists worked hard to make them accountable to statute law – a process that continued until the end of the nineteenth century. At the opposite pole, custom could be legitimated as an activity that had "always" been done, even though the "always" often fell a long way short of time immemorial.

The absence of foundational rules and formal understanding of what constituted custom was one reason why popular culture was highly regionalized. Different areas produced diverse forms of skimmingtons or rough music, for example. The most enduring and elaborate forms of this popular culture were found in areas where a mixed proto-industrial and agrarian economy dominated the community. In the large towns, of course, the force and presence of popular culture was weaker. In the small towns, however, popular culture tended to retain its traditional hues throughout our period. Wherever it was employed, however, an appeal to custom implied the force of an informal law that emanated from the "rights of the people." Custom was not necessarily truly traditional, but it could form an arena of conflict because it involved the assertion of rights. These rights could be as trivial as the privilege to bait a bull on a certain day in the year, or as fundamental as property usages.[41]

"Rough music" provides an example of the roughness of popular culture. As a statement about moral conduct, rough music operated according to variable community standards which placed justice in the

[41] Bob Bushaway, *By Rite: Custom, Ceremony and Community in England 1700–1880* (London, 1982), pp. 5–27; E. P. Thompson, *Customs in Common*, pp. 4–12.

hands of the community rather than in the hands of a judicial bureaucracy. Rough music also involved unrefined behavior – banging of pots outside windows and the rest – which characterized popular culture as a whole. Wife selling as a form of popular divorce was another example of a "rough" practice that was emblematic of this popular culture. This practice had never received any official sanction, and by the later eighteenth century evangelicals began to attack the practice fiercely. Yet, until the early nineteenth century, little action against it was taken by lay or clerical authorities. The issue entered the magistrates' yearbooks only in the 1830s, and wife selling retained a popular legitimacy until the 1880s. Similarly, *contra* Keith Thomas, the belief in magic was widely held among rural people especially into the 1860s and even beyond. The Primitive Methodists still held to a belief in witches into the early nineteenth century, although they were the only nonconformist sect that did.[42]

Offensives to purge popular culture of those elements that were not in accord with elite sensibilities were ineffective. Indeed, this cultural formation expanded and strengthened over the two centuries from the Restoration. Its practices remained vigorous well into the final two-thirds of the nineteenth century. After that moment they disappeared quite suddenly. Indeed, from the early part of the nineteenth century the matrix of practices and customs that composed this culture began to crumble under the pressure of a variety of influences. And from the 1850s popular culture's least respectable practices, like wife selling, were driven from open public view. Not all of these corrosive agents were cultural or political, although the purposeful evangelical offensive from the 1780s always tends to occupy scholars' main attention.

There was nothing particularly new about a beleaguered popular culture. Calendar customs had been episodically targeted by elites since the middle ages. Perhaps the most notable campaign before our period was that beginning with the puritans of the late sixteenth century. Still, while it is true that the evangelical offensive from the 1780s took its toll, especially in the towns, it was a gentler process from the 1840s or so that was the more powerful dissolvent. Ironically, it was a campaign of appropriation undertaken less out of religious zeal and more out of a sense that popular customs were unworthy that turned out to be most successful in eroding this rough culture.

Popular culture succumbed in the first instance to the fatal embrace of the revitalized paternalism of the midcentury that has already been noted.

---

[42] E. P. Thompson, *Customs in Common*, pp. 467–531; David Vincent, *Literacy and Popular Culture 1750–1914* (Cambridge, 1989), pp. 159–60, 171–72, 180; James Obelkevich, *Religion and Rural Society: South Lindsey 1825–1875* (Oxford, 1976), pp. 283–87.

In addition to the alternative programs offered to the working classes by the rational recreation movement, local elites began to appropriate customs and ceremonies and drain them of popular content and potential contention. Appropriation aimed to make safe for elite authority those aspects of popular culture that had become associated most closely with lower-class action. Thus the rough character of the rural Whitsuntide holiday was gradually tamed throughout the middle of the nineteenth century. Rowdy festivities of social inversion that included extortion of gifts from social betters in the public space were formalized into the anodyne custom of friendly society club day. At a slightly later date, the harvest home was transformed from a raucous feast day which usually ended at the local pub into an orderly dinner provided by farmers, presided over by the vicar and accompanied by a religious service. Similarly, from the 1870s local elites in the Southern towns began to patronize and control Guy Fawkes night, converting it from a self-organized expression of lower-class community to a safe celebration of national redemption.[43]

In addition, a process of cultural nationalization was in train by the 1880s. Apart from some attention to the newspaper press, this has been very little studied. This new configuration of popular culture was formal and commercial. Formalized sporting events, national networks of print and visual entertainment media – most obviously the music hall and the new journalism – rapidly made obsolete the older forms of popular culture and activity. Cultural regionalism, which had been a central characteristic of the popular culture of our period, was modified by such developments as the replacement of local time zones by Greenwich mean time. The linking of the regions by the rail network also served to expand horizons beyond the local focus that had been the seedbed of the older popular cultures and customs. It is often forgotten that this happened fairly late; even places as close to London as the Weald of Kent and Sussex were penetrated by rail only in the 1870s.[44]

[43] E. P. Thompson, *Customs in Common*, pp. 442, 453, 456, 476–77, 505–08, 515–18, 520–22, 528–29; Bushaway, *By Rite*, pp. 240–60, 265–73. See Flora Thompson, *Lark Rise to Candleford* (Oxford, 1945), p. 131, for an account of rough music last experienced in this Oxford village in the 1860s; Alun Howkins, *Whitsun in Nineteenth-Century Oxfordshire*, History Workshop Pamphlet No. 8 (Oxford, 1972); Obelkevich, *Religion and Rural Society*, pp. 58–60; Robert Storch, "'Please to Remember the Fifth of November': Conflict, Solidarity and Public Order in Southern England, 1815–1900," in Storch, *Popular Culture and Custom*, pp. 71–99.

[44] Vincent, *Literacy and Popular Culture*, p. 182. One of the fundamental changes in popular culture that deserves to be noted is the way it becomes dominated, after about 1870, largely by sporting activity that was organized through rules that were themselves the product of bureaucratic, national processes. On the professionalization of sports with particular attention to its related commercialization, see Vamplew, *Pay Up and Play the Game*; Meller, *Leisure and the Changing City*, pp. 225–36.

As regions were tied into the metropolitan-driven culture, their local cultures became redundant artifacts of an older world. The case of dialect is an obvious example. By 1900 it was a quaint badge of peculiarity to be exploited by popular entertainers like Gus Elen or Harry Lauder. The growing weight of a national culture in the last decades of the nineteenth century hastened the dissolution of the links with a genuinely more distant past. In Flora Thompson's rural Oxfordshire, the last of the ballad storytellers who entertained in local pubs with saga-length tales handed down by oral culture disappeared in the 1880s. Such customs and ceremonies became candidates for heritage status. Morris dancing in the older popular culture was a specifically lower-class activity which could be associated with charivari and lords of misrule. In the modernist culture of the twentieth century, morris dancing was transmuted into a national tradition, taught to primary-school children in the new elementary schools. Thus transformed, popular culture ceased to be a source of instability to social relations and more a subject for antiquarian study and delight.[45]

The end of a popular culture of raucous rowdiness presumed the end of paternal social relations. Rough popular culture and paternal social relations were locked in a doomed liaison. One could not survive without the other. Popular culture furnished the resources, the capacities, for opposition to paternal authority. Yet it needed the practices of paternal social relations to legitimate its presence. Likewise, paternal social relations stood in a similar relationship to popular culture: the practices of popular culture were its chance to patronize and connect with the common people. Once social relations could no longer be expressed through the paternal style, popular culture ceased to have a function in the system of elite authority.

The demise of paternal social relations followed from the ultimate inability of the system to accommodate the contradictions that were inherent in its exercise of authority. If the culture of paternalism was integral to economic and social change during this period, it was also true that its boundaries and its codes were continually breached and tested by the necessity to accommodate change. Serious challenges to the viability of the paternal style flowed from a variety of economic, social and political sources, and eventually it proved impossible to accommodate the changes

---

[45] See Flora Thompson, *Lark Rise to Candleford*, pp. 62–64, for the last of the storytellers in Lark Rise. The process of expansion of horizons is also caught in this book by the main character's move from Lark Rise to suburban Candleford Green to work in the Post Office. For morris dancing, see Howkins, *Whitsun in Nineteenth-Century Oxfordshire*, pp. 10–14. On the music hall, see Bailey, *Music Hall: The Business of Pleasures*, passim. For a general discussion of the social construction of popular history, see Raphael Samuel, *Theaters of Memory*, vol. I, *The Past and Present in Contemporary Culture* (London, 1994).

demanded within the boundaries of paternalism. The main storyline that narrates the coming of class-based social relations is the erosion of the paternally based system.

The game laws of 1671 confining the right to hunt to the landed gentry provide a particularly apt illustration of the instabilities within paternal social relations. These laws first defined poaching as a crime. Until the game laws were promulgated, only the crown's animals had been protected. Poaching was thus created as the characteristic rural crime of the period. The game laws dispensed a harsh justice in the defense of the landed gentry's claim to property rights in the beasts of nature. Assaults on game keepers were treated more seriously and punished more firmly than assaults on police constables. The law on poaching was progressively refined so that by 1816 poachers were liable for transportation. Merely to threaten keepers with a gun was a hanging offense from 1803. Even the possession of hunting dogs by those not qualified to own them was subject to legal sanction.

Yet, as if in tandem, the rough cultural practice of poaching seems to have increased over the period in which the game laws operated. Nor did repeal of the laws in the 1830s diminish its persistence. This was not surprising, because repeal did not permit the propertyless to claim game. Thus, after the 1830s, poaching remained a common feature of rural life. Highly organized gangs remained active in East Anglia until well into the 1850s – in one case even possessing a bank account and a treasurer. In the 1860s and 1870s there were determined outbreaks of Rebecca outrages (a traditional Welsh protest where men dressed as women and painted their faces black) which asserted popular access to the closure of certain fishing rights on the River Wye in South Wales. These incidents proved as impermeable to police penetration as the earlier outbreaks of Rebecca violence had been in the late eighteenth and early nineteenth centuries.[46]

The game laws were a flashpoint for social relations. They denoted the unacceptable face of paternalism. They pushed the claims of paternal authority closer toward the endgame of untrammeled privilege. The game laws represented as audacious a claim as the act of elite rebellion in 1688. Under this law only several hundred men in each county possessed the right to hunt. Yet the restraints of the law were felt not merely by the subaltern classes. Farmers too felt their force. Indeed, by the middle of

[46] Archer, *"By a Flash and a Scare"*, pp. 222–40; P. B. Munsche, *Gentleman and Poachers: The English Game Laws 1671–1831* (Cambridge, 1981), pp. 25–27, 102–104; David Jones, "The Second Rebecca Riots: A Study of Poaching on the Upper Wye," *Llafur*, 2, 1 (Spring 1976), pp. 32–56; David Williams, *The Rebecca Riots: A Study in Agrarian Discontent* (Cardiff, 1954); David Jones, *Before Rebecca: Popular Protests in Wales 1793–1835* (London, 1973). There was a final revival of this style of popular protest on the river Wye in the 1880s.

the eighteenth century, the laws were being applied without discrimination to farmers as well as to the poor. On occasion they could even be applied against other gentry.

Once the laws became a source of elite tension, a contradiction within the heart of the system, they were doomed. It was an absurdity that impoverished squires could shoot at will whereas wealthy monied merchants were excluded. Even more inconsistent was the exclusion of other landed classes. The laws were useful as an opportunity for landowners to exercise reciprocal generosity by granting the right to others to hunt, or by asking permission to cross property that was not their own. Still, farmers began to claim that game was the property of those whose land it happened to be on, and that rights of hunting access needed to be secured rather than assumed. Blackstone lent his authority to this position. Even so, repeal of the game laws was delayed by the sense that they were integral to the maintenance of social hierarchy. Only when they were seen to be so divisive as to diminish elite authority could repeal be secured.[47]

The game laws were emblematic of the contradictions within paternal social relations because they involved conflict over land usage. Competing claims to land usage were endemic to the structure of elite authority. Enclosure was the most consistently disruptive force to the established patterns of social relations. Enclosure was a process in which the reality of paternal social relations inherently contradicted its rhetoric. On the one hand it was a manifestation of the growing economic and social power of the gentry. Large landowners were unquestionably the major beneficiaries of the movement. The smallest land-users were unquestionably the biggest losers. In this respect, the indignant historiography of the Hammonds and others has been fully vindicated. On the other hand, enclosure also expanded the opportunities for smaller landholdings to be established or to increase.

Enclosure was not unidimensional in its social effects, and its impact varied from area to area.[48] Changes in ownership at the bottom end of the landholding scale were as important a result of enclosure as dispossession. Thus, common land enclosed at Dunkirk near Canterbury in Kent during the land shortage of the Napoleonic wars was let in small plots at cheap rents. By the 1820s a small group of owner-occupiers had been created, holding properties up to nine or ten acres. This peasantry

---

[47] Munsche, *Gentleman and Poachers*, pp. 109–15, 129, 166–67; Douglas Hay, "Poaching and the Game Laws on Cannock Chase," in Hay, Peter Linebaugh, et al. (eds.), *Albion's Fatal Tree: Crime and Society in Eighteenth-Century England* (London, 1975), pp. 189–253.

[48] The turnover of land-ownership was probably greater in the arable heartland of the Midlands where most of the research has concentrated. See Neeson, *Commoners*, pp. 223, 240–48.

had disappeared by the 1860s, yet it illustrates how the social disruption of enclosure came not only from an end to access to the land. It could also come from those (sometimes unconnected with the community) who seized the opportunities offered by the opening of the land market to become landowners. Enclosure encouraged an expansion of the rural middling classes. In much the same way as manufacturing capitalism expanded the small industrial workshop, so it has often been forgotten that a progressively capitalist agrarian economy spawned a large land-owning class of small proprietors.[49]

Within this social structure the key contest was between different conceptions of property usage. On the one side stood the claims of customary usage – and there were many forms that this could take. On the other side were the priorities of a market economy that denied the right of custom to arbitrate access. In this contest, the market had the law increasingly on its side. As early as 1607 the landmark Gateward case tied the exercise of user rights to the actual ownership of a piece of property and not simply to its occupiership. Legal changes seldom proceed in a simple linear fashion. Yet this issue seems more straightforward than most. The trend of the legal cases was to curtail the rights of common ownership while extending those of personal property in land.[50]

At the same time, however, it has been well established that a thick network of common rights and usages mapped the countryside of eighteenth-century society. These rights were embedded in a dense maze of law and regulation which shaded into the functions of local government. The use of common land was subject to close supervision so that its resources could be fairly distributed. Local officers were appointed to administer these rules which open another window onto England's "much-governed" status in this period. Management of these usages was tied closely to the people of the community. The pasture of the commons, for example, was overseen by pindars who in their turn were directed by the fieldsmen. The use of common land was governed by customary law from which none was exempt. Squires, farmers and rectors were frequently hauled before the courts for some infraction or other of the rules.[51]

Pastoral placidity concealed an easily triggered turbulent potential in rural society. Between the 1740s and 1770s there were thousands of

---

[49] Michael Turner, "Enclosures in Britain," pp. 270–78; Reay, *Microhistories*, pp. 140–41; Neeson, *Commoners*, pp. 289–92. Some would argue that this small proprietor class in agriculture was, in fact, a peasantry. See Mick Reed and Roger Wells, "Introduction," in Reed and Wells (eds.), *Class, Conflict and Protest in the English Countryside 1700–1880* (London, 1990), pp. 4–24.

[50] E. P. Thompson, *Customs in Common*, pp. 103–09, 130–35; Neeson, *Commoners*, pp. 254–55, 289–92.

[51] Neeson, *Commoners*, pp. 138–52.

collisions between keepers and poachers on Cannock Chase over game and fish. East Anglia was the scene of the bread-or-blood riots of 1816. The Weald of Kent and Sussex was dangerous enough in the 1830s and 1840s that commercial travelers went armed and farmers kept loaded weapons beside their beds. Captain Swing, of course, roamed here in the early 1830s, burning barns, smashing machines and threatening farmers engaged in progressive land use. This particular eruption of social conflict was unusual, although even in more normal times tensions simmered continually. A local study of East Anglia for the first two-thirds of the nineteenth century linked the incidence of economic depression to the violent crimes of arson, animal maiming and machine breaking in a pattern that persisted with impressive regularity until the 1870s. Indeed, as late as 1870 a wave of rioting and arson was associated with an enclosure movement in Falkenham Heath. It is a simple but revealing fact that in this corner of England – which was, admittedly, prone to violence – the rural police were issued with cutlasses until the mid-1860s.[52]

The tensions that ran through paternal structures of social relations were particularly evident in agriculture. It was in the rural sector of society that the reciprocities of paternalism first began to falter, and by the 1830s the fabric of paternalism was badly rent. The story of eighteenth- and early nineteenth-century social relations in agriculture is the tale of how economic and social change progressively gutted the content from the paternal system.[53]

This was a process that began with changes in agricultural labor economics in the midcentury; the practice of yearly hirings declined and settlements that granted poor law benefits became more difficult to acquire. The large-scale enclosures from the 1760s closed access to common lands and diminished the possibilities of security and independence. Enclosure implied a political economy that responded to market pressures, increased dependence on wage labor and a heightened insecurity. Within this general story, there were a wide number of variables that qualified its particulars. Thus, the shift from a yearly hiring labor market to a weekly wage labor market occupied a long period of transition. Regional variations were important. In Scotland and the Northern coun-

[52] On the statistical patterns of crime, especially against property, see J. M. Beattie, *Crime and the Courts in England 1660–1800* (Cambridge, 1986), pp. 199–237, for a good summary of the historiography and results of local study of Surrey and Sussex. See also Douglas Hay, "War, Dearth and Theft in Eighteenth Century: The Record of the English Courts," *Past and Present*, 95 (1982), pp. 117–60; Hay, "Poaching and the Game Laws on Cannock Chase," p. 193; A. J. Peacock, *Bread or Blood: The Agrarian Riots in East Anglia: 1816* (London, 1965); Wells, *Victorian Village*, p. 8; Archer, *"By a Flash and a Scare"*, pp. 83–84, 107, 117, 122–25, 134, 141, 155.

[53] A study of this process at the local level, which focuses on the nineteenth century, is to be found in Obelkevich, *Religion and Rural Society*, pp. 23–102.

ties, for example, yearly hirings remained common until the end of the nineteenth century. Even in Kent there continued to be a statute hiring fair held every year in Canterbury until the 1880s.[54]

The protracted and uneven progress of the short-term labor market in agriculture is worth noting for a moment. It provides a case study of the material reasons why "continuity" is such a persistent quality over the period. In rural society in particular, the restraints of continuity were powerful enough to contain decisive change until the 1870s. The false start of the threshing machine in the 1830s is an example of that. Furthermore, it was precisely this balance between change and continuity in the society as a whole that allowed the paternal style to remain a convincing representation of social relations so late into the nineteenth century.

Changes in the labor market of agriculture were the economic context for the imperative to modify poor law policies. The poor law was the key nexus of the paternal system. Since its inception, the poor law had been the arena where the reciprocities of paternal social relations were displayed to most social and political effect. A critical shift seems to have occurred in the middle of the eighteenth century, both in the terms of the discussion about the poor law, to which I have already alluded, and also in the very structure of the labor market. This was the moment when the balance tipped from a labor market that paid some homage to paternal relationships toward a labor market that was entirely and increasingly subject to the judgment of market forces. Naturally the advantages of articulating social relations through a paternal ideology remained strong. Throughout the period there was a constant play between admitting the reality of market relations and asserting an imagined community tied together by paternal concerns.

Thus, we see the familiar oscillation in the poor law between the principles of coercion and compassion. This was not only a moral debate; it was also a contention about labor market structures. At times of labor shortage, compassion tended to prevail; at times of labor surplus, a harsher tone was adopted. The Speenhamland policy of 1798 which reasserted the tie between poor law relief and the cost of living embodied that tension. Similarly, the varied responses of the magistracy to the frequent food riots that punctuated the landscape of eighteenth-century England illustrated the competing demands of a political economy of market forces and one of communitarian collectivism. The enforcement of the statute laws designed to regulate market processes weakened greatly over the century. Nevertheless, these laws embodied the vision of

[54] Snell, *Annals of the Labouring Poor*, pp. 45–46, 72–93, 166–69, 336–37; Neeson, *Commoners*, pp. 46–47; G. E. Mingay, *The Victorian Countryside* (London, 1981), vol. I, pp. 305–06, vol. II, pp. 508–11.

a society that qualified and controlled market forces. Such values were available to meet the subsistence crises of the 1790s. Even the assize of bread – as blatant a piece of economic regulation as one could wish to find – was revived in the 1790s after languishing unused for many years. This was to be the last time such laws were enforced.[55]

The demise of paternal social relations was a matter much debated by contemporaries. It has been an underlying theme of much of the traditional scholarship from the Hammonds onward. In truth the picture presents a more complicated syncopation than a straight-line decline. The enclosure movement, the erosion of common rights and the expanding reach of the market all gave credence to the idea of an environment that was practically unsympathetic toward paternal reciprocities. Similarly, economic pressures were forcing a growing disjuncture between the ideal and the actual role of the rural elite as guardians of paternal values. There were persistent complaints in the first two-thirds of the eighteenth century about the failure of the rural ruling class to attend properly to their governing duties. Only a small core of the same people were typically willing to perform the traditional volunteer duties of local government. And too often these were the lesser gentry, not the large magnates.[56]

This situation began to turn around from about the middle of the eighteenth century. Paternalism was reinvigorated in the countryside; the rural gentry renewed their interest in the duties of paternal governance. Prominent gentry families became more active in county government. But the big change was the increasing engagement of the clergy who were appointed to the bench in large numbers from the middle of the eighteenth century. The clergy now began to assume a major burden of the duties of the magistracy, and it was under their auspices that paternal authority revived in the later eighteenth century. This is not to suggest that this revival was free of strain. Food riots in the North West during those years contained plenty of evidence of hostility toward the clerical class and magistracy. Nonetheless, there was a heightened articulation of paternal social relations, and this was particularly the case where the poor laws were concerned.[57]

Magistrates were the stoutest defenders of a paternal implementation of the poor law. It would be a mistake to romanticize or exaggerate the

[55] We must remember that when we speak of rural areas we are also speaking of areas of manufacturing. The subsistence riots in 1740, 1756, 1766, 1795 and 1800 were not affairs of agricultural laborers, but of tinners, colliers, weavers etc. On the assize of bread, see Sydney Webb and Beatrice Webb, "The Assize of Bread," *Economic Journal*, 14 (June 1904), pp. 213–18; E. P. Thompson, *Customs in Common*, pp. 199–207.
[56] Langford, *Public Life and the Propertied Englishman*, pp. 371–78, 384, 390–92, 401–02.
[57] Ibid., pp. 405–07, 414–16; A. Booth, "Food Riots in the North-West of England 1790–1801," *Past and Present*, 78 (1977), pp. 84–107.

paternal interest of the magistracy. Yet they were more open to generous social policies than the ratepaying farmers and tenants. The magistracy tended to support the notion of a paternalistic poor law in the interest of social peace and the imagined community of paternal social relations. Justices from across the country made strong protests before the Royal Commission on the Poor Laws in 1832 against the "injustice" and "oppression" that the ratepayer-dominated vestries tended to dole out to the poor. Larger landowners, too, tended toward this position. Proposals to mitigate the harshness of new poor law policies and to redress rural poverty by granting allotments to laborers found support among this group, for example. Unsurprisingly, the farmers opposed such moves, precisely because they would reduce the laborers' dependence on the market economy, enhance their independence and encourage an ill-disciplined labor force.

More than anything else, therefore, the poor law debate that led to 1834 was an ideological struggle around these two approaches to social policy. The new poor law of 1834 was not designed to restore paternal social relations; it was designed to restabilize social relations. Formally, the new poor law was a triumph for the social policy of the free labor market that farmers had been moving toward since the 1750s. In reality, it failed to achieve this model and at the local level was sufficiently modified to retain the faint insinuations of its paternal past. This remained true until the 1860s and 1870s when the state and the Charity Organisation Society joined forces to execute the agenda of 1834. Still, the intent of the new poor law was fully recognized at the start by those it affected as well as by its administrators. Opposition to the implementation of the new poor law was not confined to the urban centers of the North of England. Serious riots and a wave of incendiarism were associated with its arrival in East Anglia. Full-scale riots occurred in some places, accompanied by attacks on farmers and local strikes broken by army and coast guard forces. And for the first five years or so the new policies were inseparable from eruptions of unrest and arson.[58]

The viability of the system of paternal authority was severely tested by the events of the 1830s and 1840s. It is not surprising, therefore, that concerted efforts were made to reconstruct paternal social relations through intensive voluntary association work. I have referred to these efforts elsewhere. They were a holding operation; they could not cement the fractures endemic to paternal social relations which had been exacerbated by such moves as the new poor law. The fragilities of paternal social

[58] Dunkley, "Paternalism, the Magistracy and Poor Relief"; Dunkley, "The Landed Interest and the New Poor Law: A Critical Note"; Brundage, "Landed Interest and the New Poor Law"; Archer, *"By a Flash and a Scare"*, pp. 98, 103.

relations were particularly exposed during the mid-Victorian years, even as a social equipoise fell on class relations at the national level. Equipoise was a scarcer quality at the local level where schizophrenia may better describe the morphology of social relations. In industrial relations, for example, paternal collaboration in factory industry, or in the artisan trades like building would suddenly be shattered by fierce and bitter quarrels.[59] The social placidity of these decades disguised a fine balance which historians have had a hard time accounting for. I shall not attempt to remedy that failure here, except insofar as it touches on my explorations of the dynamics of elite authority.

In the first place, it is important to insist that mid-Victorian social relations were a construction that had to be secured and gained; they were not inherent in the natural quiescence of the working class or the hegemony of the upper or middle classes. The defeat of Chartism in 1848 was enormously important in inducing a soaring confidence amongst the political elite, which allowed them to contemplate the possibility of equipoise. Equally, strategies that adopted the paternal style as a means of securing elite authority and inducing consent in industry, for example, like the miners' bond or the patriarchalism of the Oldham factories, were never unproblematic. They were always very brittle, and the bonds of attachment that they represented could be fractured in a moment. I shall return to this shortly.

In the second place, the structures of social authority in the mid-Victorian period were extensions of those of the eighteenth century. This does not mean that the formations of social relations were the same; they clearly were not. Yet the competing exigencies of paternalism and deference, independence and negotiation, cooperation and conflict, animated class relations. It is for this reason that, as has been noted, the language of class as a system of ranks and orders experiences a revival into the 1850s. The propensities of paternal social relations were also present in most quarters of quotidian life. The ubiquity of domestic service, for example, served to replicate and to validate the hierarchies of the paternal style. All sections of the middle classes and large numbers of the working classes employed domestics in large numbers.[60] As an instance of the continued relevance of the paternal style in social relations, and of the kinds of circumstances that accompanied its demise, we can return to the case of the miners' bond.

The bond established regimes of work and social relations in the

---

[59] See Richard Price, *Masters, Unions and Men*, chs. 2–4, for examples of this pattern in the building industry.

[60] Domestic service became the largest occupation for women in this period; it also came to be a defining quality of middle-class life in the culture. See Edward Higgs, *Domestic Servants and Households in Rochdale 1851–1871* (New York, 1986).

Durham coalfield in the eighteenth and nineteenth centuries. It also incited industrial struggle. The big strikes of 1731, 1765, 1831 and 1844 – and many of the smaller ones, too – were disputes about the limits of authority and subordination that were expressed in the bond. The bond was an archetypal instrument of paternal discipline applied to industrial class relations. It ran a fine course between being an instrument of employer discipline and a zone of negotiation. The bond was also a mechanism of reciprocity. On the one hand, binding became more elaborate as the eighteenth century wore on, and penalties were specified more precisely for a wide range of offenses. On the other hand, the bond could never be imposed unilaterally; some degree of negotiation was always involved. It was precisely the attempt to renegotiate the conditions of the bond by the short-lived "Tommy Hepburn" union in the early 1830s that exposed the cavity at the heart of paternal social authority. Challenged by the collectivity of their employees, the mine-owners of the North East launched a violent and thorough counterattack. Just as they had in 1765 and at other times, the owners brought to bear the full force of their control of the local state. The magistracy and the military force of the gentry yeomanry were arrayed against the miners.[61]

These conflicts remained bounded by the limits of the paternal structures of authority, however. They laid bare the contradictions and fragilities that were inherent in such a system. They did not produce redefined social relations. Restriction of production by the miners and the enforcement of the bond through the weapon of the law composed the main themes of the social relations of production. The final abolition of the bond in 1869 announced that its usefulness as an instrument of social authority had expired. By the time the bond ended, it was decrepit. A strike at the Thornley Pit was the occasion of the fatal blow. This was as it should have been. Thornley had been a center of struggle against the bond in the eighteenth century and a locus of support for the union of 1831. Out of this strike in 1869, exactly on cue, the first permanent trade union was born. Three years later the first modern collective bargaining agreement was negotiated in 1872. Class relations had finally arrived in this industry. Authority and consent were now secured by the trade union, collective bargaining and the method of collective regulation.[62]

[61] Levine and Wrightson, *Making of an Industrial Society*, pp. 394–95, 404–27; Jaffe, *Struggle for Market Power*, pp. 100–05, 152–55; J. L. Hammond and Barbara Hammond, *The Skilled Labourer 1760–1832* (New York, 1970), pp. 15–30.
[62] Dave Douglass, "The Durham Pitman," in Raphael Samuel (ed.), *Miners, Quarrymen and Saltworkers* (London, 1977), pp. 247–48, 254–56, 270–75; Raymond Challinor and Brian Ripley, *The Miners' Association: A Trade Union in the Age of the Chartists* (London, 1968), pp. 94–110; E. M. Welbourne, *The Miners' Unions of Northumberland and Durham* (Cambridge, 1923), pp. 144–45.

The styles and modes of paternalism were becoming dilapidated elsewhere in the manufacturing sector in the middle of the nineteenth century. The factory-owners of the urban North West expended considerable energy donning the mantle of squire and manorial lord. There were some impressive testaments to their efforts in the systems of community loyalty that were constructed around their factories. Neighborhood cultures were often shaped by the cultural predilections of the particular factory-owner. These owners were following the only script of social authority they knew, the script of paternal control that Crowley and Richard Arkwright had also followed in their factories. There was no long-term future in this. The difficulty was that the paternal bargain was becoming an impossible contract to deliver. Employers always had to reserve the right to ask their workers to share the burden of market downturns, for example. As markets became more nationally integrated and more linked into international fluctuations, such requests were bound to increase. In such circumstances, the precise frontier between subaltern obedience and the repudiation of elite authority was disturbingly unclear.

Paternal social relations in industry in the middle of the nineteenth century presented the edifice of a Potemkin village. The short distance between deference and defiance in this social system can be seen in many examples of social conflict. The Preston spinners' strike of 1853 provides some nice examples. Parties of factory workers had just embarked on employer-sponsored trips to the seaside as the celebrated strike erupted. In one case a group stopped before the master's house to sing "A Fine Old English Gentleman." Yet only a short time before another mill-owner had been hooted in his own mill. And at the very moment that the seaside excursions were departing, the police were in the process of arresting those who were collecting funds in support of the small strikes already occurring. When the strike proper broke out, it soon turned nasty and violent. This was quite typical of industrial conflict in a paternal system of social relations.[63]

The dualities of the system of paternal social relations informed modes of behavior. If paternalism extended the amiable face of community, it could also deliver the iron fist of arbitrary discipline and punitive punishment. Likewise, in such a system, the only real alternative to worker

---

[63] Joyce, in *Work, Society and Politics*, pp. 93–96, notes the fragility of deference and the ease with which reciprocities collapsed when they were unfulfilled. The key to understanding the social dynamics of paternal authority is precisely to understand its instabilities and limits. See also H. I. Dutton and J. E. King, "The Limits of Paternalism: The Cotton Tyrants of North Lancashire, 1836–1854," *Social History*, 7, 1 (January 1982), pp. 59–74; Dutton and King, *"Ten Per Cent and No Surrender": The Preston Strike 1853–1854* (Cambridge, 1981), pp. 37, 79–82.

deference was anarchic violence. What existed in between? It is for this reason that the rejection of employer authority in the middle of the nineteenth century often assumed charivari forms, just as it had a century before. In the case of the Preston strike mentioned above, disapproval of one employer was expressed by a band playing outside the factory as groups of men and women danced and played rudely. There were few other "languages" available to express a divorce between employers and their workers. No arenas existed where the two parties could meet on equal terms; neither the law nor social convention in reality provided that space until the advent of collective bargaining. Thus, there was little that was "modern" about class relations in industry until the coming of collective organization after the 1880s. Rough music and other forms of ritualistic ridicule were common; humiliation, ridicule and physical assault on recalcitrant workmen were common tactics of industrial action. Even violence against employers or overseers was not unknown. The lack of discipline that frequently accompanied the conduct of strikes was the obverse of a system of authority that rested on paternal authority rather than formalized systems of negotiation and bargaining.[64]

The coming of class relations

Paternal social relations were not finally displaced by class-based social relations until the end of the nineteenth century. It bears repeating that the decay of this system of securing social authority was a long-term process. Since stability and instability were inherent to the system itself, it was necessary to launch occasional efforts at renewal that would restore or repair the mainsprings of paternal social relations. Social relations in the middle of the nineteenth century were dotted with such efforts. From the early nineteenth century, however, it was increasingly difficult to rejuvenate the model in a convincing way, and the curious quality of mid-Victorian class relations was the result. Naturally, the impending doom of the paternal system is evident only in retrospect. Nevertheless, by the 1890s, it had been replaced by formalized and organized class relations as the dominant mode of arranging and expressing social relations.

It will be obvious to the specialist reader that the logic of my argument leads to a different perspective on class formation than is presented in Edward Thompson's *Making of the English Working Class*. Class formation is obviously not a once and for all, one-time only thing; nor is it an

---

[64] The ritual and iconography of industrial conflict in the middle of the nineteenth century has been little studied in Britain, in contrast to France. For "premodern" strike tactics in the eighteenth century, see Rule, *Experience of Labour*, pp. 185–88.

exclusive process of identity formation. Still, in spite of the extensive discussion that Thompson's book continues to evoke, in spite of the effective detailing of the absences that it contains (gender, ethnicity, the middle classes and the like) and, finally, in spite of postmodern efforts to revise our very thinking about class itself, the location and understanding of the process that Thompson was describing have generally been left undisturbed. Even as revisionist historiography rejected framing the social consciousness of the nineteenth century in the context of class, it continued to operate as if the central argument of the book that the working class was formed in the early nineteenth century were true. I am not much inclined to get involved in these scholastic debates here. I wish to locate this particular moment of class experience in a different context.[65]

It is best to start by reformulating the problem that Thompson was addressing: the process of political and social radicalism in the early nineteenth century. As will already be clear, explaining oppositional politics of that period as moving along an axis of class development wrenches them out of their essentially eighteenth-century context. It makes more sense to interpret these politics – as in the case of Chartism – as operating within the boundaries of the preceding period, rather than as prefiguring class relations of the twentieth century. The same is true of the structures of trade unions. Labor historians have deployed all manner of special arguments to find the necessary links between trade unions of the early and middle nineteenth century and their future progeny to avoid placing them firmly in the tradition of the local craft societies that first appeared in the early eighteenth century.

Nevertheless, the early nineteenth century did mark a significant stage in the process I have been discussing in this book. From the standpoint of economic relations, the process charted by Thompson is more accurately described as a decisive stage in the decay of a particular model (and image) of artisan production. The process advanced along a wider front than simply the artisan sector alone, but cultures and livelihoods of the skilled craftsmen, or those with a claim to a skill, were the most sensitive to the changes that were imminent. Such groups possessed the capacity to raise protest in print, person and politics against those changes. Artisans

---

[65] See Harvey J. Kaye and Keith McClelland (eds.), *E. P. Thompson: Critical Perspectives* (Philadelphia, 1990), for a good selection of the direction that criticism of Thompson has taken. For a critique of Thompson's view of eighteenth-century class, particularly around his tendency to discount the middling classes, see Peter King, "Edward Thompson's Contribution to Eighteenth-Century Studies: The Patrician–Plebeian Model Re-Examined," *Social History* 21, 2 (May 1996), pp. 215–28. See Eric Hobsbawm's essay "The Making of the Working Class 1870–1914," in his *Workers: Worlds of Labour* (New York, 1984), pp. 195–213, for an argument similar to that which follows.

were to be found, therefore, at the center of all responses to the challenge to traditional standards and conditions of work that directed the production changes of the period.

This did not result in the "making" of a factory working class, however. Labor process change in this period resulted in a bastardized style of artisan production which I discussed earlier in this book. The plight of the handloom weavers was only the most dramatic and best publicized manifestation of a process of economic and social change that affected wide swathes of artisan groups. The same process could be seen at work with the expansion of the "dishonorable" sector of production in most skilled crafts in the 1820s through the 1840s. There was nothing new in this process; it was the characteristic form of deskilling that accompanied labor market expansion. What was peculiar to the early nineteenth century were the scale and concentration of the process.[66]

The political context of the late eighteenth and early nineteenth century was also unique. A significant stage was reached in the explicit rejection by the state of the paternal bargain. This followed from a long history of tension around the role of regulation in production, either of a corporate sort such as apprenticeship rules, or of a state-supported variety such as wage regulation. Issues like these were a constant source of social contention. They were additional examples of how the limits and reality of the paternal bargain were constantly being tested. Apprenticeship regulation, for example, was a persistent cause of conflict both before and during the eighteenth century. From the 1790s, however, a concerted campaign was launched from the London engineering shops against apprenticeship as a tyrannical restraint on masters' freedoms. This effort fed directly into the bonfire of legal controls over production that began in 1809 when Parliament repealed statutory regulations in the woolen trade. This was followed by the repeal of the Statute of Artificers, and it was completed in 1814 with the end of magistrates' power to set minimum wages.[67]

[66] Similar processes also marked European artisan histories. See Friedrich Lenger, "Beyond Exceptionalism, or Towards the Comparative Study of Working-Class Formation: Notes on the Artisanal Phase of the Labour Movement in France, England, Germany and the United States," paper presented at conference, "The Formation of Labour Movements: Comparative Perspectives," Alkmaar, The Netherlands, 31 May–2 June 1990; Christine Eisenberg, "The Comparative View in Labour History: Old and New Interpretations of the English and German Labour Movements Before 1914," *International Review of Social History*, 34, 3 (1989), pp. 403–32; Joyce, *Visions of the People*, ch. 4.

[67] Keith Burgess, *The Origins of British Industrial Relations: The Nineteenth-Century Experience* (London, 1975), pp. 5–24; George, *London Life in the Eighteenth Century*, pp. 200–01, 233–34; Rule, *Experience of Labour*, pp. 95–119; E. P. Thompson, *Making of the English Working Class*, pp. 272, 565, 595–96; T. K. Derry, "The Repeal of the Apprenticeship Clauses of the Statute of Apprentices," *Economic History Review*, 3 (1931–32), pp. 68–86.

Even this was not enough to displace the paternal model of social relations as I have described it above. As I have endeavored to demonstrate, the system of social relations that sought consent through a paternal style of social authority remained viable until the final two-thirds of the nineteenth century. After c. 1880 its practices and its discourses rapidly diminished as the defining pattern of social relations.[68] One key signifier was organizational. By the late nineteenth century, classes, groups and individuals related to each other increasingly as citizens through collective organization. The political subject was now regarded as a free-standing individual, not as a member of a community. The possibilities of paternal (though not patriarchal) hierarchy were denied. Equally the possibilities opened for the working classes to secure the institutional power to project their normative values onto the structures of social relations. How are we to understand this shift? What broad forces were at work to erode a system of elite authority that as late as the 1860s seemed to be a viable framework within which social relations could be both realized and conceived?

If the coming of class relations was not as dramatic as it is usually portrayed, it was, however, relatively sudden. The structures of paternalism collapsed under the weight of their own contradictions; they crumbled in the face of competing systems from the middle or working classes. And they were overthrown by acts of political will. The process was almost invisible, and was not apparent until it had happened. It resembled the growing decay of a piece of clothing used too much and for too long. No short explanation is available to understand this process. Nevertheless, I would suggest five major themes that can provide the main lines of explanation for the decay of the system of social relations as it has been described in this chapter and its replacement by formalized class relations.

First, a new way of understanding social stratification emerged out of the positivist social science of the late nineteenth century. We do not need to consider whether this framework "created" the notion of class as a description of consciousness or whether it "reflected" it. My own view is that it did both. Yet its key role was to offer new vocabularies for self- and collective representation that convincingly replaced the prevailing medley of terminologies that had marked our period. This new sense of class was tied to certain material criteria arranged in an economic hierarchy. It was now believed that society could be understood as a sociological construct

---

[68] This is not to say that it disappeared completely. But there is a fundamental difference between the welfare capitalism that some railway companies like the North East Railway began to practice after the 1880s and the claims of paternal authority they exercised before.

with certain attributes applied to certain groupings. Thus, it was now possible to say what "working-class" meant by referring to specific conditions. Most importantly for present purposes, this new way of thinking about social relations lent itself to new kinds of social representation around organizations that altered social and political relations in new and challenging ways. It was now possible to contemplate systems of social relations that were not dependent on notions of paternal reciprocity and obligation. The combined presence of new kinds of narratives and new organizations allow us to conceptualize social relations around the notion of class only from the later nineteenth century.[69]

Secondly, one reason why this new conception of hierarchy could catch on was because it made sense of what was happening elsewhere in the society. Politics provided an apt illustration of this theme. It is unnecessary to enter again into the political process of democratization of the franchise after 1867. Yet in declaring an end to an exclusive political nation and in opening the spaces for new programs and new organizations, patrician politics were no longer viable. It was an example that was to be followed wherever patrician social relations dominated. Thus, in the Working Men's Club movement in the mid-1880s, there was a sudden revolt against patron control and influence and a democratization of the national association. The gentlemen were driven out of this important cultural and social organization and the working-class members claimed it as their own. This replicated what was happening elsewhere in politics. The patrician role was increasingly a ceremonial one. It retained a symbolic power; but that was a very different kind of power from the kind which had secured political consent for the past 150 years.[70]

As the case cited above suggests, a third theme is the local focus of the decay of paternal systems of elite authority. Indeed, outside England it was a process that to one degree or another was joined with or displaced by the politics of ethnic identity. This was most obviously the case in Ireland. Still, at the local level, the old vocabularies and styles of social relations were inadequate to meet the needs of the time. In those industries where unions had been present in the early and middle years of the nineteenth century, for example, the mainly local and informal habits of organization and negotiation were increasingly replaced by the formal and the national. In some instances, the collapse of viable paternal

---

[69] Joyce (ed.), *Class: A Reader* (Oxford, 1995), pp. 3–20; Rosemary Crompton, *Class and Stratification: An Introduction to Current Debates* (Cambridge, 1993), pp. 4–5; Joanna Burke, *Working-Class Cultures in Britain 1890–1960* (London, 1994), pp. 1–26. For an interesting reflection of this shift in Germany which parallels the British experience exactly, see Dennis Sweeney, "Work, Race and the Transformation of Industrial Culture in Wilhelmine Germany," *Social History*, 23, 1 (January 1998), pp. 31–62.

[70] See Richard Price, "Working Men's Club Movement," pp. 133–39.

authority was revealed in stark and shocking detail. The Manningham Mills strike in Bradford in 1891, which destroyed the paternal factory regime of Samuel Lister, was one such well-known example.[71]

Fourthly, local processes were embedded within global environments that were both national and international in dimension. To take the former first, a process of cultural integration rose to the surface after about 1870. Culture was nationalized and identified as primarily a *national* phenomenon. This did not mean that regionalism disappeared. Indeed, this was the very period when certain regionalisms like "the cockney" were created; it did mean that the relationship of the regional to the whole changed. Soccer teams were united into national leagues; music hall stars were stars in Arbroath as well as London. National integration diversified the processes of representation, communication and consent building. It also complicated the ways in which social authority was mediated. When the Education Act of 1870 establishing primary schools was implemented in the rural areas, for example, one effect was to put in place a school teacher who could become an alternative center of authority to the squire and vicar. Paternal styles of social relations were made obsolete by these means, too.[72]

But, fifthly and finally, such national initiatives were also part of a wider international context which it is important to register here, even if it is impossible to treat fully. The great depression of 1876–96 marked the end of Britain's very short period of manufacturing dominance in world markets and introduced an increasing challenge to productive capacities across all sectors of the economy from shoes to coal. The economic intersections between the national and international were a topic of growing preoccupation and anxiety throughout the late nineteenth century. Land usage changed dramatically and suddenly as the economics of the large landed estate were undermined by food imports from the new world. Changes in the world political economy could impact directly on the way social relations were conducted. The strike at Manningham Mills in 1891, for example, was sparked by the company's need to reduce costs

---

[71] Richard Price, *Masters, Unions and Men*, esp. chs. 5 and 6; Richard Price, *Labour in British Society: An Interpretive History 1780–1980* (London, 1986), pp. 149–51, 120–27. The railways provide other examples from the 1880s in which the displacement of paternal social relations is clearly revealed. The Manningham Mills strike led directly to the formation of the Independent Labour Party: ibid., pp. 149–50.

[72] This was the moment when the idea of an archetypal working-class culture begins to be invented – or rather *reinvented* – using the data collected by the new social observers of the period. Thus, it is only after c. 1880 that the cockney as he and she were represented in twentieth-century culture were invented as a "traditional" working class of London. For the cockney, see Gareth Stedman Jones, "The 'Cockney' and the Nation, 1780–1988," in David Feldman and Gareth Stedman Jones (eds.), *Metropolis London: Histories and Representations Since 1800* (London, 1989), pp. 278–79, 294–312.

if its products were to leap the newly imposed McKinley tariff in the United States.

More usually, such connections between the world and local economies were less immediate. Still, the changed world political economy did make redundant social relationships that rested on acceptance of a paternal hierarchy. In order to meet the kinds of competitive pressures of the new world order, all aspects of social relations had to change, from styles of industrial management to hierarchies of technical training, to notions of how social welfare policies related to questions of national efficiency.[73] Authority in industry or in the world of politics, or social authority, could no longer be secured simply by the assertions of place within a status hierarchy. The structures of elite authority that I have described in this chapter had fulfilled their historical purpose. This did not imply that "traditional" symbols, rhetoric or personnel were to be of no account in the future. It meant that their relevance and role changed. Stability and instability in society were no longer a function of the dynamics and contradictions of the paternal style; they now responded to different stimuli. Social authority and consent had been modernized.

[73] See, for example, Bernard Elbaum and William Lazonick, *The Decline of the British Economy* (Oxford, 1986); Lazonick, "Production Relations, Labor Productivity, and Choice of Technique: British and United States Cotton Spinning," *Journal of Economic History*, 41 (September 1981), pp. 492–515; Richard Price, *Labour in British Society*, pp. 93–130.

Afterword

The central argument that has gone before may be easily restated. The two centuries from the late 1700s to the late 1900s formed a distinct period in the history of modern Britain. The historical configurations of this period were provided by the particular balance that obtained between containment and change. This balance was not a tension between the contradictory forces of progress and the forces of tradition, although historians are constantly tempted to view it in this way. The relationship between the influences that compelled change and the restraints that contained those energies was reciprocal and integrated. Naturally, in each domain of historical experience examined here the dynamic interaction between the processes of change and of containment assumed different forms.

For example, the economy of manufacturing was capable of enormous expansion within the methods and systems that had traditionally provided its capacities. Yet, it was constrained by, among other things, the predominance of small-scale organization and the commercial orientation of the political economy. The historical significance of the cotton-spinning industry is that it signaled an early example of how the constraints of the manufacturing system could be transcended. Those constraints were not, however, dysfunctional to the relationships between the various economic sectors in this period. Whatever was true in the twentieth century, the political economy of manufacturing does not seem to have sacrificed the interests of one sector to the priorities of another.

The dynamic in the sphere of the state structures was shaped by the forces of localism and by their ability to contain pressure from the center. Indeed, there is little evidence of concerted efforts from the center to disrupt this arrangement. The attempt in the 1830s to shift the bias in state structures toward the initiative of the center was a failure, and found little enthusiasm beyond a small group of Benthamite ideologues and Whig politicians. A similar and related process characterized the balance between the private and the public spheres which was protected and defined by boundaries of gender and of class. The process was gendered in the sense that it was reinforced by and replicated in domestic ideology and it was classed in that the dynamic element came from the assertive energies of the middling classes. Shifting these boundaries was inhibited primarily by the gender politics of domesticity.

Within the political world, the abiding legacy of 1688 was a major constraint. This inheritance was not only a heritage of liberty. It was more the ambiguous patrimony of political inclusion and political exclusion. How monopoly rights in the political world should be defined was an enduring dilemma. This quandary was essential to the profiles of all politics in the period – high or low, Tory or Whig, radical or conservative. Popular politics were contentious and open – another inheritance of 1688. Yet their heat and noise were ultimately enclosed by limits that followed from the settlement of 1688. These limits were not merely the perimeters formed by law and property; they included also the political discourse of the popular constitution. While the idea of the popular constitution framed the history of politics, the possibilities of the political imagination were encased within politics that were toned with populist moralism and cloaked in the style of paternalism.

Similar configurations allowed social relations to be realized within the practices of paternalism, even though these were usually hollow reeds of mere convention. The rough culture that dominated our period possessed its own distinctive capacities. Indeed, in the arena of local practice, social relations posed challenges to paternal assumptions and acted in confrontational, even "class," ways. But this did not qualify the social relations of this period as prefiguratively class relations. This was not a question of consciousness, however we categorize it. There was clearly plenty of consciousness among the lower classes in our period. The absence was more mundane; it was the organizational capacities of class relations that were lacking. The ultimate resort of social relations was to call upon the reciprocities of social authority. In this way the various practices and cultures that composed social relations were expressed. By this means, too, the status of social authority was also confirmed.

By the late nineteenth century, endings were in sight for these formations. All of the terrains I have mapped in this book were being redrawn. Boundaries were being relocated; new institutions and relationships were moving to different zones of engagement within society. Naturally, as they did so, different qualities came to the fore to condition and describe social and institutional relationships. This was a process that occurred at multiple levels of experience and it was a process, too, in which the legacies of the past retained an enduring persistence. Yet a cluster of changes during the late nineteenth century shifted the morphologies of the social, cultural, economic, ideological and political spheres into patterns that were to mark the contours of the twentieth century.[1] The remaking of society after c. 1880 is a conventional observation. The important question here is: how is that process of remaking to be understood in the context of the argument of this book?

A starting point would be to look at the internal dynamics of the particular historical domain. A recurrent motif to my argument has been how the historical formations of the period ultimately outgrew the capacity of their historical space. By the final quarter of the nineteenth century the possibilities of the old system suffered from terminal exhaustion. The procedures, structures and institutions which managed a particular set of relationships became inadequate to meet the demands of the present. The containment of change could no longer be achieved through methods that had protected the boundaries of the old system. This has been shown to be the case across a wide range of experience in society, from economic through political to social relations.

After 1880 it was increasingly impossible, for example, to conceive of social relations through the constructs of paternal authority, even though this hardly implied the end of any sociopolitical role for the gentry. The politics of exclusion finally stumbled over their own contortions and contradictions, as did domestic ideology, which was undermined by the well-intentioned subversions of mid-Victorian women. Once this had happened, it was possible to imagine new divisions of responsibility between the public and the private, and the floodgates were opened to the rising tide of demands from diverse political quarters – liberal, socialist, reactionary and conservative – for new procedures and programs of intervention in the lives of individuals.

There is a nice irony to the fact that it was the expanding forces of localism that ultimately breached the traditional boundary between the local and the center. The need to move this boundary derived from the impetus of localism as it struggled to meet new social responsibilities from the 1870s. The first sign of a serious challenge to the established structures of economic relationships was the Great Depression of 1876–96. This immediately revealed the inadequacies of the Victorian version of free trade. Yet, as the case of free trade vividly illustrates, the energies of particular discourses or formations were exhausted at varying rates. Free trade was to retain a secure place in the policy-making circles of the nation long after it had ceased to describe the political economy of the period

---

[1] "In so far as there have ever been great chasms rather than mere subterranean murmurings in the deep structures of British social history, it seems to me that they occurred in the 1870s and 1880s, and then again in the 1960s and 1970s, rather than in the apparently more dramatic and cataclysmic happenings of either of the two world wars": Harris, *Private Lives, Public Spirit*, pp. 252–53.

covered by this book. Victorian free trade was not finally interred until capitalism itself was threatened by the financial crisis of 1931.

By the 1880s the changing configuration of world relationships demanded a new economic regime in Britain. Free trade was able to retreat to its final strongholds of the City of London and the treasury establishment. Manufacturers had no such recourse; they had to face the reality of American or German competition in the very heart of the empire. By 1914 the shoe industry had already experienced an American invasion of the domestic market and a subsequent recovery of its position. Likewise, the machine tool industry had lost its preeminence in the 1890s, only to regain some ground in the early 1900s. The pressure of international competition provided an essential impetus to the advancement of the production methods of industrialism in the British economy. Even where that was less true – in engineering, for example – the lessons of American-style methods of efficient organization of the labor processes were not lost on British employers, however partial their success in utilizing best practices. The economy of manufacture was outgrowing its limits; changing world realities were dragging it into the universe of modern industry.[2]

It is a commonplace for historians to note the rapid change that was wrought in Britain's place in the world in the course of the late nineteenth century. Yet it is worth attending to this change once again because the imperial factor was integral to the decay of the domestic formations of the era covered by this book. The imperial factor in British history assumed a radically new dimension during this period and it intruded upon domestic society in significantly different ways.

In the period covered by this book, the character of British imperialism was inherently expansionist, even if it did not always need to manifest itself in territorial acquisitions. Commercial imperialism knew no boundaries. Its purpose was trade and exchange. In the early part of the period, it used the weapons of protectionism – the trade company and the navigation acts – to gather the fruits of trade. Yet its impetus was not to accept the restriction of formal empires. Thus, commercial imperialism transmutes in the middle of the nineteenth century to free trade once the instruments of protection and force had done their work. Formal empire, on the other hand, was autarchic and never had much use for the exchange and movement of capital around the world. Thus, in the era of free trade, formal empire was looked upon with distaste.

The "new" imperialism that opened c. 1880, however, demanded formal empire. For Britain this meant a *retreat* into empire. Britain was

[2] Roy Church, "The Effect of the American Export Invasion on the British Boot and Shoe Industry 1885–1914," *Journal of Economic History*, 28, 2 (1968), pp. 223–54; Roderick Floud, *The British Machine-Tool Industry 1850–1914* (Cambridge, 1976), pp. 71–80.

likely to attain the lion's share in any open imperial struggle. Yet it was not a struggle that Britain could win, as it had been able to contemplate victory in earlier times. The difference between the imperial competition of the late nineteenth century and similar struggles in the past was that for much of our period Britain had faced one competing power at a time. By contrast, the late nineteenth-century world was a multilateral world. Britain faced several potentially imperial powers, all of roughly equal strength. Other candidates stood waiting in the wings to join the ranks of the imperial nations. The strategic and diplomatic realities of this multi-lateral world were hard lessons for Britain to absorb, as the struggles over whether to continue to seek naval superiority in the 1890s and early 1900s suggest.[3]

The impact of this new world political economy on British culture and politics was deep and profound. It produced a different kind of imperial culture, one that was more defensive and inward-looking, and which sought to consolidate its authority both in the metropole and in the colonies.[4] The interpenetration of imperial and domestic themes began to be configured differently from the past. The empire became integral to national identity, for example. This was true in terms of culture and it was true in terms of international and domestic politics. It was increasingly difficult to draw distinctions between what was relevant to the home society and what mattered to Britain as an imperial nation. Imperial tasks powered political and social agendas. This mandated different kinds of resource mobilization than it had in the past. In the two centuries from 1680, Britain had acquired plenty of experience in mobilizing its re-sources to defend and enlarge its imperial project. Yet it did so at specific moments to face specific crises, usually of war. After 1880 the changed world political economy required a more constant attention to mobilizing

[3] G. W. Monger, *The End of Isolation: British Foreign Policy 1900–1907* (London, 1963), pp. 10–11, 163, 313.

[4] In the empire, changing distinctions divided colonizers and colonized. One example is provided by sexual attitudes. Throughout much of the nineteenth century, the conduct of colonizers – both official and civilian – was not much regulated. Only occasionally did the transgressive behavior of settlers, officials and even missionaries break into the public view. There were some spectacular examples of violations of racial barriers in frontier societies like South Africa well into the nineteenth century. The general veil of silence drawn over these matters began to be lifted by the 1880s as the lines around race and culture were more sharply drawn to buttress imperial rule. In India, for example, an insistence on the qualities of manly British masculinity in contrast to effeminate Bengali masculinity attained a new precision and focus as a direct response to the rise of Indian nationalism among the Hindu middle class. See Edward Said, *Culture and Imperialism* (New York, 1993), pp. 188–90; Ronald Hyam, *Empire and Sexuality: The British Experience* (Manchester, 1990), pp. 157–79, 200–01; Noel Mostert, *Frontier: The Epic of South Africa's Creation and the Tragedy of the Xhosa People* (London, 1992), pp. 238–40, 346–47, 439–41, 452–55, 624–25; Mrinilani Sinha, *Colonial Masculinity: The "Manly Englishman" and the "Effeminate Bengali" in the Late Nineteenth Century* (Manchester, 1995), pp. 14–18.

the resources of the country in the service of imperial competition, and this resonated with growing volume throughout domestic politics.

Efficiency was therefore a key concept of the late nineteenth century, precisely because the organization of domestic society suddenly became essential to the imperial venture. Efficiency was not an important virtue during our period. As the history of industrial organization amply demonstrates, efficiency was sought by the addition of new units to a given task. By the late nineteenth century, a more complicated notion of efficiency takes hold, illuminated in economics by ideas of marginal utility. Efficiency now began to be sought through maximizing the use value of individual units. How to best mobilize the resources of the nation – educational and human as well as economic and material – was one of the faultlines dividing the different policy positions in the political world itself. As a domestic issue, national efficiency cut across party lines because it was an indispensable imperial need.[5]

The intersection of imperial and domestic issues decisively changed the role and dynamic of the imperial factor in British politics and society. From about 1880 all the major political and social issues were shaped by the convergence of their relevance for both empire and home. Concerted efforts were made to convert a basically insular working-class culture into a culture fit for an imperial race, for example. In this effort, the category of "race" is employed to associate the working class with the imperial project. Race separated the working class from the subaltern classes of empire and linked it to the other classes in society.[6] General William Booth of the Salvation Army erected a program of social intervention to transport the slum dwellers of "darkest England" into the wholesome spaces of work colonies in the empire – a kind of imperial venture within the imperial venture.

The health and education of the young, as always in social reform initiatives, were a favorite target of these efforts. Youth movements like the Boy Scouts or the Boys' Brigade combined the twin purposes of inculcating an imperial patriotism with the domestic benefits that would come from a healthy, purposeful and efficient lower class at home.[7] So it

---

[5] For this theme, see Bernard Semmel, *Imperialism and Social Reform: British Social–Imperial Thought 1895–1914* (New York, 1968).

[6] Thus, the category of race was separated from the category of class. In the early nineteenth century, race and class overlapped and were almost interchangeable. By the end of the nineteenth century, race was being used as a category that transcended class and united the working class with the national imperial project. That, at least, was the intention; its success is a matter for debate. See Susan Thorne, *Congregational Missions and the Making of An Imperial Culture in Nineteenth-Century England* (forthcoming, Palo Alto, CA).

[7] General Booth, *In Darkest England and the Way Out* (London, 1890). For youth movements, see John Springhall, most particularly *Youth, Empire and Society: British Youth Movements 1880–1940* (London, 1977). See also J. A. Mangan, "The Grit of Our

was also with that prime Victorian value, motherhood. Previously motherhood had been a nexus for domestic virtue, important because of its civilizing potential of inherently dangerous classes. It now became important also because of its relevance to the reproduction of a sturdy imperial race. Some were even prepared to argue that motherhood was too important to be left to mothers and required the attention of the state. By their very creed, imperialists were also social reforming collectivists.[8]

The end of the era covered by this book, then, was declared by a process of historical change that moved along two axes. The first was internal to the formations themselves. By 1880, the systems that had governed the shape of British society 1680–1880 were meeting their own limits and threatening to overrun the constraints of their boundaries. The second axis of historical change, however, intruded from outside as the changing external world forced a reconfiguration of Britain's imperial role. The outcome of these forces was to proclaim an end to the world I have described above. Yet it would be a mistake to close by insisting that a thoroughly new world was born. The ending I have declared is not an ending which sees "change" establish a predominance over "continuity." It would take no great effort of imagination to demonstrate themes of continuity throughout the late Victorian and Edwardian decades. Continuity and change are threads that weave through all societies at all historical times. They do so, however, in different patterns and in different shades. And so it was in the late nineteenth century: distinct terrains, demarcated and confined by differently placed boundaries, distinguished this world from that of the previous two centuries.

Forefathers': Invented Traditions, Propaganda and Imperialism," in John Mackenzie (ed.), *Imperialism and Popular Culture* (Manchester, 1986), pp. 120–21, for the role of education in the imperial mission. Consistent with the ethos of gentlemanly capitalism this role was to produce efficient governors rather than efficient technicians.

[8] Anna Davin, "Imperialism and Motherhood," *History Workshop Journal*, 5 (Spring 1978), pp. 9–66.

Index

Printed in the United Kingdom
by Lightning Source UK Ltd.
113812UKS00001B/232-240

9 780521 657013